Expert SQL Server 2005 Development

Adam Machanic
with Hugo Kornelis and Lara Rubbelke

Expert SQL Server 2005 Development

Copyright © 2007 by Adam Machanic, Hugo Kornelis, Lara Rubbelke

ISBN-13 (pbk): 978-1-59059-729-3

ISBN-10 (pbk): 1-59059-729-X

Printed and bound in the United States of America 9 8 7 6 5 4 3 2 1

Trademarked names may appear in this book. Rather than use a trademark symbol with every occurrence of a trademarked name, we use the names only in an editorial fashion and to the benefit of the trademark owner, with no intention of infringement of the trademark.

Lead Editor: James Huddleston
Technical Reviewer: Greg Low
Editorial Board: Steve Anglin, Ewan Buckingham, Gary Cornell, Jason Gilmore, Jonathan Gennick,
    Jonathan Hassell, James Huddleston, Chris Mills, Matthew Moodie, Jeffrey Pepper, Dominic Shakeshaft,
    Matt Wade
Senior Project Manager: Tracy Brown Collins
Copy Edit Manager: Nicole Flores
Copy Editor: Ami Knox
Assistant Production Director: Kari Brooks-Copony
Senior Production Editor: Laura Cheu
Compositor and Artist: Kinetic Publishing Services, LLC
Proofreader: Elizabeth Berry
Indexer: Beth Palmer
Cover Designer: Kurt Krames
Manufacturing Director: Tom Debolski

Distributed to the book trade worldwide by Springer-Verlag New York, Inc., 233 Spring Street, 6th Floor, New York, NY 10013. Phone 1-800-SPRINGER, fax 201-348-4505, e-mail orders-ny@springer-sbm.com, or visit http://www.springeronline.com.

For information on translations, please contact Apress directly at 2560 Ninth Street, Suite 219, Berkeley, CA 94710. Phone 510-549-5930, fax 510-549-5939, e-mail info@apress.com, or visit http://www.apress.com.

The information in this book is distributed on an "as is" basis, without warranty. Although every precaution has been taken in the preparation of this work, neither the author(s) nor Apress shall have any liability to any person or entity with respect to any loss or damage caused or alleged to be caused directly or indirectly by the information contained in this work.

The source code for this book is available to readers at http://www.apress.com in the Source Code/Download section. A companion web site for this book, containing updates and additional material, can be accessed at http://www.expertsqlserver2005.com.

To Kate: Thanks for letting me disappear into the world of my laptop and my thoughts for so many hours over the last several months. Without your support I never would have been able to finish this book. And now you have me back . . . until I write the next one.
—Adam Machanic

Contents at a Glance

Contents

Foreword

Databases are software. I've based the second half of a software development career that began in 1978 on this simple idea.

If you've found this book, chances are you're willing to at least entertain the possibility that databases and their attendant programmability are worthy of the same rigor and process as the rest of an application. Good for you! It's a great pleasure for me to join you on this journey, however briefly, via this foreword.

There is a good possibility that you've grown as skeptical as I have of the conventional wisdom that treats the "back end" as an afterthought in the design and budgeting process. You're now seeking actionable insights into building or improving a SQL Server 2005 design and development process.

The book you're holding is chock-full of such insights. And before turning you over to Adam, Hugo, and Lara, I'd like to offer one of my own.

I suggest that we stop calling the database the "back end." There is a dismissive and vaguely derogatory tone to the phrase. It sounds like something we don't want to pay much attention to, doesn't it? The "front end," on the other hand, sounds like the place with all the fun and glory. After all, it's what everybody can *see*. The back end sounds like something you can safely ignore. So when resources must be trimmed, it might be easier and safer to start where people can't see ... right?

Wrong. Such an approach ignores the fact that databases are software—important, intricate software. How would our outlook change if we instead referred to this component as the "foundational layer"? This term certainly sounds much weightier. For instance, when I consider the foundational layer of my family's house, I fervently hope that the people who designed and built it knew what they were doing, especially when it comes to the runoff from the hill in our backyard. If they didn't, all of the more obvious, fancy stuff that relies on the proper architecture and construction of our home's foundational layer—everything from the roof to the cable modem to my guitars—is at risk. Similarly, if the *foundational layer* of our application isn't conceived and crafted to meet the unique, carefully considered needs of our customers, the beauty of its user interface won't matter. Even the most nimble user interface known to mankind will fail to satisfy its users if its underlying foundational layer fails to meet any of the logical or performance requirements.

I'll say it again: Databases are software. Stored procedures, user-defined functions, and triggers are obviously software. But schema is software, too. Primary and foreign keys are software. So are indexes and statistics. The *entire* database is software. If you've read this far, chances are that you know these things to your core. You're seeking a framework, a mindset with which to approach SQL Server 2005 development in an orderly fashion. When you've completed this incredibly readable book, you'll have just such a context.

My work at Microsoft since 1999 has led me to become an advocate for the application of rigorous quality standards to all phases of database design and construction. I've met several kindred spirits since I went public with this phase of my work in 2005, including Adam and Hugo. If you apply the advice that the authors offer in the pages that follow, you'll produce more scalable, maintainable databases that perform better. This will then lead to applications that perform better and are more maintainable, which will make your customers happier. This state of affairs, in turn, will be good for business.

And as a bonus, you'll be both a practitioner and a proponent of an expert-level tenet in the software and IT industries: Databases are software!

Ward Pond
Technology Architect, Microsoft SQL Server Center of Excellence
http://blogs.technet.com/wardpond
sqlwriter@comcast.net

About the Authors

**ADAM MACHANIC** is an independent database software consultant, writer, and speaker based in Boston, Massachusetts. He has implemented SQL Server solutions for a variety of high-availability OLTP and large-scale data warehouse applications, and also specializes in .NET data access layer performance optimization. Adam has written for *SQL Server Professional* and *TechNet* magazines, serves as the SQL Server 2005 Expert for SearchSQLServer.com, and has contributed to several books on SQL Server, including *Pro SQL Server 2005* (Apress, 2005). He regularly speaks at user groups, community events, and conferences on a variety of SQL Server and .NET-related topics. He is a Microsoft Most Valuable Professional (MVP) for SQL Server and a Microsoft Certified IT Professional (MCITP).

When not sitting at the keyboard pounding out code or code-related prose, Adam tries to spend a bit of time with his wife, Kate, and daughter, Aura, both of whom seem to believe that there is more to life than SQL.

Adam blogs at `http://www.sqlblog.com`, and can be contacted directly at `amachanic@ datamanipulation.net`.

HUGO KORNELIS has a strong interest in information analysis and process analysis. He is convinced that many errors in the process of producing software can be avoided by using better procedures during the analysis phase, and deploying code generators to avoid errors in the process of translating the analysis results to databases and programs. Hugo is cofounder of the Dutch software company perFact BV, where he is responsible for improving analysis methods and writing a code generator to generate complete working SQL Server code from the analysis results.

When not working, Hugo enjoys spending time with his wife, two children, and four cats. He also enjoys helping out people in SQL Server–related newsgroups, speaking at conferences, or playing the occasional game.

In recognition of his efforts in the SQL Server community, Hugo was given the Most Valuable Professional (MVP) award by Microsoft in January 2006 and January 2007. He is also a Microsoft Certified Professional.

Hugo contributed Chapter 9, "Working with Spatial Data."

LARA RUBBELKE is a service line leader with Digineer in Minneapolis, Minnesota, where she consults on architecting, implementing, and improving SQL Server solutions. Her expertise involves both OLTP and OLAP systems, ETL, and the Business Intelligence lifecycle. She is an active leader of the local PASS chapter and brings her passion for SQL Server to the community through technical presentations at local, regional, and national conferences and user groups. Lara's two beautiful and active boys, Jack and Tom, and incredibly understanding husband, Bill, are a constant source of joy and inspiration.

Lara contributed Chapter 5, "Encryption."

About the Technical Reviewer

 **GREG LOW** is an internationally recognized consultant, developer, author, and trainer. He has been working in development since 1978, holds a PhD in computer science and MC*.* from Microsoft. Greg is the lead SQL Server consultant with Readify, a SQL Server MVP, and one of only three Microsoft regional directors for Australia. He is a regular speaker at conferences such as TechEd and PASS. Greg also hosts the SQL Down Under podcast (http://www.sqldownunder.com), organizes the SQL Down Under Code Camp, and co-organizes CodeCampOz.

Acknowledgments

Imagine, if you will, the romanticized popular notion of an author at work. Gaunt, pale, bent over the typewriter late at night (perhaps working by candlelight), feverishly hitting the keys, taking breaks only to rip out one sheet and replace it with a blank one, or maybe to take a sip of a very strong drink. All of this, done alone. Writing, after all, is a solo sport, is it not?

While I may have spent more than my fair share of time bent over the keyboard late at night, illuminated only by the glow of the monitor, and while I did require the assistance of a glass of Scotch from time to time, I would like to go ahead and banish any notion that the book you hold in your hands was the accomplishment of just one person. On the contrary, numerous people were involved, and I hope that I have kept good enough notes over the last year of writing to thank them all. So without further ado, here are the people behind this book.

Thank you first to Tony Davis, who helped me craft the initial proposal for the book. Even after leaving Apress, Tony continued to give me valuable input into the writing process, not to mention publishing an excerpt or two on `http://www.Simple-Talk.com`. Tony has been a great friend and someone I can always count on to give me an honest evaluation of any situation I might encounter.

Aaron Bertrand, Andrew Clarke, Hilary Cotter, Zach Nichter, Andy Novick, Karen Watterson, and Kris Zaragoza were kind enough to provide me with comments on the initial outline and help direct what the book would eventually become. Special thanks go to Kris, who told me that the overall organization I presented to him made no sense, then went on to suggest numerous changes, all of which I ended up using.

James Huddleston carried me through most of the writing process as the book's editor. Sadly, he passed away just before the book was finished. Thank you, James, for your patience as I missed deadline after deadline, and for your help in driving up the quality of this book. I am truly saddened that you will not be able to see the final product that you helped forge.

Tracy Brown Collins, the book's project manager, worked hard to keep the book on track, and I felt like I let her down every time I delivered my material late. Thanks, Tracy, for putting up with schedule change after schedule change, multiple chapter and personnel reorganizations, and all of the other hectic interplay that occurred during the writing of this book.

Throughout the writing process, I reached out to various people to answer my questions and help me get over the various stumbling blocks I faced. I'd like to thank the following people whom I pestered again and again, and who patiently took the time out of their busy schedules to help me: Bob Beauchemin, Itzik Ben-Gan, Louis Davidson, Peter DeBetta, Kalen Delaney, Steven Hemingray, Tibor Karaszi, Steve Kass, Andy Kelly, Tony Rogerson, Linchi Shea, Erland Sommarskog, Roji Thomas, and Roger Wolter. Without your assistance, I would have been hopelessly stuck at several points along the way.

Dr. Greg Low, the book's technical reviewer, should be granted an honorary PhD in SQL Server. Greg's keen observations and sharp insight into what I needed to add to the content were very much appreciated. Thank you, Greg, for putting in the time to help out with this project!

To my coauthors, Hugo Kornelis and Lara Rubbelke, thank you for jumping into book writing and producing some truly awesome material! I owe you both many rounds of drinks for helping me to bear some of the weight of getting this book out on time and at a high level of quality.

An indirect thanks goes out to Ken Henderson and Joe Celko, whose books inspired me to get started down the writing path to begin with. When I first picked up Ken's *Guru's Guide* books and Joe's *SQL for Smarties*, I hoped that some day I'd be cool enough to pull off a writing project. And while I can't claim to have achieved the same level of greatness those two managed, I hope that this book inspires a new writer or two, just as theirs did me. Thanks, guys!

Last, but certainly not least, I'd like to thank my wife, Kate, and my daughter, Aura. Thank you for understanding as I spent night after night and weekend after weekend holed up in the office researching and writing. Projects like these are hard on interpersonal relationships, especially when you have to live with someone who spends countless hours sitting in front of a computer with headphones on. I really appreciate your help and support throughout the process. I couldn't have done it without you!

Aura, some day I will try to teach you the art and science of computer programming, and you'll probably hate me for it. But if you're anything like me, you'll find some bizarre pleasure in making the machine do your bidding. That's a feeling I never seem to tire of, and I look forward to sharing it with you.

Adam Machanic

I'd like to thank my wife, José, and my kids, Judith and Timon, for stimulating me to accept the offer and take the deep dive into authoring, and for putting up with me sitting behind a laptop for even longer than usual.

Hugo Kornelis

I would like to acknowledge Stan Sajous for helping develop the material for the encryption chapter.

Lara Rubbelke

Introduction

Working with SQL Server on project after project, I find myself solving the same types of problems again and again. The solutions differ slightly from case to case, but they often share something in common—code patterns, logical processes, or general techniques. Every time I work on a customer's software, I feel like I'm building on what I've done before, creating a greater set of tools that I can apply to the next project and the next after that. Whenever I start feeling like I've gained mastery in some area, I'll suddenly learn a new trick and realize that I really don't know anything at all—and that's part of the fun of working with such a large, flexible product as SQL Server.

This book, at its core, is all about building your own set of tools from which you can draw inspiration as you work with SQL Server. I try to explain not only the *hows* of each concept described herein, but also the *whys*. And in many examples throughout the book, I attempt to delve into the process I took for finding what I feel is the optimal solution. My goal is to share with you how I think through problems. Whether or not you find my approach to be directly usable, my hope is that you can harness it as a means by which to tune your own development methodology.

This book is arranged into three logical sections. The first four chapters deal with software development methodologies as they apply to SQL Server. The next three chapters get into advanced features specific to SQL Server. And the final four chapters are more architecturally focused, delving into specific design and implementation issues around some of the more difficult topics I've encountered in past projects.

Chapters 1 and 2 aim to provide a framework for software development in SQL Server. By now, SQL Server has become a lot more than just a DBMS, yet I feel that much of the time it's not given the respect it deserves as a foundation for application building. Rather, it's often treated as a "dumb" object store, which is a shame, considering how much it can do for the applications that use it. In these chapters, I discuss software architecture and development methodologies, and how to treat your database software just as you'd treat any other software—including testing it.

Software development is all about translating business problems into technical solutions, but along the way you can run into a lot of obstacles. Bugs in your software or other components and intruders who are interested in destroying or stealing your data are two of the main hurdles that come to mind. So Chapters 3 and 4 deal with exception handling and security, respectively. By properly anticipating error conditions and guarding against security threats, you'll be able to sleep easier at night, knowing that your software won't break quite as easily under pressure.

Encryption, SQLCLR, and proper use of dynamic SQL are covered in Chapters 5, 6, and 7. These chapters are not intended to be complete guides to each of these features—especially true of the SQLCLR chapter—but are rather intended as reviews of some of the most important things you'll want to consider as you use these features to solve your own business problems.

Chapters 8 through 11 deal with application concurrency, spatial data, temporal data, and graphs. These are the biggest and most complex chapters of the book, but also my favorite.

Data architecture is an area where a bit of creativity often pays off—a good place to sink your teeth into new problems. These chapters show how to solve common problems using a variety of patterns, each of which should be easy to modify and adapt to situations you might face in your day-to-day work as a database developer.

Finally, I'd like to remind readers that database development, while a serious pursuit and vitally important to business, should be *fun*! Solving difficult problems cleverly and efficiently is an incredibly satisfying pursuit. I hope that this book helps readers get as excited about database development as I am.

CHAPTER 1

■ ■ ■

Software Development Methodologies for the Database World

Database application development is a form of software development and should be treated as such. Yet all too often the database is thought of as a secondary entity when development teams discuss architecture and test plans—many database developers do not seem to believe that standard software development best practices apply to database applications.

Virtually every application imaginable requires some form of data store. And many in the development community go beyond simply persisting application data, creating applications that are **data driven**. A data-driven application is one that is designed to dynamically change its behavior based on data—a better term might, in fact, be **data dependent**.

Given this dependency upon data and databases, the developers who specialize in this field have no choice but to become not only competent software developers, but also absolute experts at accessing and managing data. Data is the central, controlling factor that dictates the value any application can bring to its users. Without the data, there is no need for the application.

The primary purpose of this book is to bring Microsoft SQL Server developers back into the software development fold. These pages stress rigorous testing, well-thought-out architectures, and careful attention to interdependencies. Proper consideration of these areas is the hallmark of an expert software developer—and database professionals, as the core members of any software development team, simply cannot afford to lack this expertise.

This first chapter presents an overview of software development and architectural matters as they apply to the world of database applications. Some of the topics covered are hotly debated in the development community, and I will try to cover both sides, even when presenting what I believe to be the authoritative answer. Still, I encourage you to think carefully about these issues rather than taking my—or anyone else's—word as the absolute truth. I believe that software architecture is an ever-changing field. Only through careful reflection on a case-by-case basis can we ever hope to come close to understanding what the "best" possible solutions are.

Architecture Revisited

Software architecture is a large, complex topic, due mainly to the fact that software architects often like to make things as complex as possible. The truth is that writing superior software doesn't involve nearly as much complexity as many architects would lead you to believe. Extremely high-quality designs are possible merely by understanding and applying a few basic principles.

Coupling, Cohesion, and Encapsulation

There are three terms that I believe every software developer must know in order to succeed:

- **Coupling** refers to the amount of dependency of one module in a system upon another module in the system. It can also refer to the amount of dependency that exists between systems. Modules, or systems, are said to be **tightly coupled** when they depend on each other to such an extent that a change in one necessitates a change to the other. Software developers should strive instead to produce the opposite: **loosely coupled** modules and systems.

- **Cohesion** refers to the degree that a particular module or subsystem provides a single functionality to the application as a whole. **Strongly cohesive** modules, which have only one function, are said to be more desirable than **weakly cohesive** modules that do many operations and therefore may be less maintainable and reusable.

- **Encapsulation** refers to how well the underlying implementation is hidden by a module in a system. As you will see, this concept is essentially the juxtaposition of loose coupling and strong cohesion. Logic is said to be **encapsulated** within a module if the module's methods or properties do not expose design decisions about its internal behaviors.

Unfortunately, these definitions are somewhat ambiguous, and even in real systems there is a definite amount of subjectivity that goes into determining whether a given module is or is not tightly coupled to some other module, whether a routine is cohesive, or whether logic is properly encapsulated. There is no objective method of measuring these concepts within an application. Generally, developers will discuss these ideas using comparative terms—for instance, a module may be said to be *less* tightly coupled to another module than it was before its interfaces were **refactored**. But it might be difficult to say whether or not a given module *is* tightly coupled to another, without some means of comparing the nature of its coupling. Let's take a look at a couple of examples to clarify things.

WHAT IS REFACTORING?

Refactoring is the practice of going back through existing code to clean up problems, while not adding any enhancements or changing functionality. Essentially, cleaning up what's there to make it work better. This is one of those areas that management teams really tend to despise, because it adds no tangible value to the application from a sales point of view.

First, we'll look at an example that illustrates basic coupling. The following class might be defined to model a car dealership's stock (note that I'm using a simplified and scaled-down C#-like syntax):

```
class Dealership
{
    //Name of the dealership
    string Name;

    //Owner of the dealership
    string Owner;

    //Cars that the dealership has
    Car[] Cars;

    //Defining the Car subclass
    class Car
    {
        //Make of the car
        string Make;

        //Model of the car
        string Model;
    }
}
```

This class has three fields. (I haven't included code access modifiers; in order to keep things simple, we'll assume that they're public.) The name of the dealership and owner are both strings, but the collection of the dealership's cars is typed based on a subclass, Car. In a world without people who are buying cars, this class works fine—but unfortunately, as it is modeled we are forced to tightly couple any class that has a car instance to the dealer:

```
class CarOwner
{
    //Name of the car owner
    string name;

    //The owner's cars
    Dealership.Car[] Cars
}
```

Notice that the CarOwner's cars are actually instances of Dealership.Car; in order to own a car, it seems to be presupposed that there must have been a dealership involved. This doesn't leave any room for cars sold directly by their owner—or stolen cars, for that matter! There are a variety of ways of fixing this kind of coupling, the simplest of which would be to not define Car as a subclass, but rather as its own stand-alone class. Doing so would mean that a CarOwner would be coupled to a Car, as would a Dealership—but a CarOwner and a Dealership would not be coupled at all. This makes sense and more accurately models the real world.

To better understand cohesion, consider the following method that might be defined in a banking application:

```
bool TransferFunds(
    Account AccountFrom,
    Account AccountTo,
    decimal Amount)
{
    if (AccountFrom.Balance >= Amount)
        AccountFrom.Balance -= Amount;
    else
        return(false);

    AccountTo.Balance += Amount;
    return(true);
}
```

Keeping in mind that this code is highly simplified and lacks basic error handling and other traits that would be necessary in a real banking application, ponder the fact that what this method basically does is withdraw funds from the AccountFrom account and deposit them into the AccountTo account. That's not much of a problem in and of itself, but now think of how much infrastructure (e.g., error-handling code) is missing from this method. It can probably be assumed that somewhere in this same banking application there are also methods called Withdraw and Deposit, which do the exact same things. By recoding those functions in the TransferFunds method, it was made to be weakly cohesive. Its code does more than just transfer funds—it also withdraws and deposits funds.

A more strongly cohesive version of the same method might be something along the lines of the following:

```
bool TransferFunds(
    Account AccountFrom,
    Account AccountTo,
    decimal Amount)
{
    bool success = false;
    success = Withdraw(AccountFrom, Amount);

    if (!success)
        return(false);

    success = Deposit(AccountTo, Amount);

    if (!success)
        return(false);
    else
        return(true);
}
```

Although I've noted the lack of basic exception handling and other constructs that would exist in a production version of this kind of code, it's important to stress that the main missing piece is some form of a transaction. Should the withdrawal succeed, followed by an unsuccessful deposit, this code as-is would result in the funds effectively vanishing into thin air. Always make sure to carefully test whether your mission-critical code is atomic; either everything should succeed, or nothing should. There is no room for in-between—especially when you're messing with peoples' funds!

Finally, we will take a brief look at encapsulation, which is probably the most important of these concepts for a database developer to understand. Look back at the more cohesive version of the `TransferFunds` method, and think about what the `Withdraw` method might look like. Something like this, perhaps (based on the `TransferFunds` method shown before):

```
bool Withdraw(Account AccountFrom, decimal Amount)
{
    if (AccountFrom.Balance >= Amount)
    {
        AccountFrom.Balance -= Amount;
        return(true);
    }
    else
        return(false);
}
```

In this case, the `Account` class exposes a property called `Balance`, which the `Withdraw` method can manipulate. But what if an error existed in `Withdraw`, and some code path allowed `Balance` to be manipulated without first being checked to make sure the funds existed? To avoid this, `Balance` should never have been made settable to begin with. Instead, the `Account` class should define its *own* `Withdraw` method. By doing so, the class would control its own data and rules internally—and not have to rely on any consumer to properly do so. The idea here is to implement the logic exactly once and reuse it as many times as necessary, instead of implementing the logic wherever it needs to be used.

Interfaces

The only purpose of a module in an application is to do something at the request of a consumer (i.e., another module or system). For instance, a database system would be worthless if there were no way to store or retrieve data. Therefore, a system must expose **interfaces**, well-known methods and properties that other modules can use to make requests. A module's interfaces are the gateway to its functionality, and these are the arbiters of what goes into, or comes out of, the module.

Interface design is where the concepts of coupling and encapsulation really take on meaning. If an interface fails to encapsulate enough of the module's internal design, consumers may rely upon some knowledge of the module, thereby tightly coupling the consumer to the module. Any change to the module's internal implementation may require a modification to the implementation of the consumer. An interface can be said to be a **contract** expressed between the module and its consumers. The contract states that if the consumer specifies a certain set of parameters to the interface, a certain set of values will be returned. Simplicity is usually the key here; avoid defining interfaces that modify return-value types based on inputs. For instance, a stored procedure that returns additional columns if a user passes in a certain argument may be an example of a poorly designed interface.

Many programming languages allow routines to define **explicit contracts**. This means that the input parameters are well defined, and the outputs are known at compile time. Unfortunately, T-SQL stored procedures only define inputs, and the procedure itself can dynamically change its defined outputs. It is up to the developer to ensure that the expected outputs are well documented and that unit tests exist to validate them (see the next chapter for information on unit testing). I refer to a contract enforced via documentation and testing as an **implied contract**.

Interface Design

A difficult question is how to measure successful interface design. Generally speaking, you should try to look at it from a maintenance point of view. If, in six months, you completely rewrite the module for performance or other reasons, can you ensure that all inputs and outputs will remain the same?

For example, consider the following stored procedure signature:

```
CREATE PROCEDURE GetAllEmployeeData
    --Columns to order by, comma-delimited
    @OrderBy VARCHAR(400) = NULL
```

Assume that this stored procedure does exactly what its name implies—it returns all data from the Employees table, for every employee in the database. This stored procedure takes the @OrderBy parameter, which is defined (according to the comment) as "columns to order by," with the additional prescription that the columns be comma delimited.

The interface issues here are fairly significant. First of all, an interface should not only hide internal behavior, but also leave no question as to how a valid set of input arguments will alter the routine's output. In this case, a consumer of this stored procedure might expect that internally the comma-delimited list will simply be appended to a dynamic SQL statement. Does that mean that changing the order of the column names within the list will change the outputs? And, are the ASC or DESC keywords acceptable? The interface does not define a specific-enough contract to make that clear.

Second, the consumer of this stored procedure must have a list of columns in the Employees table, in order to pass in a valid comma-delimited list. Should the list of columns be hard-coded in the application, or retrieved in some other way? And, it is not clear if all of the columns of the table are valid inputs. What about the Photo column, defined as VARBINARY(MAX), which contains a JPEG image of the employee's photo? Does it make sense to allow a consumer to specify that column for sorting?

These kinds of interface issues can cause real problems from a maintenance point of view. Consider the amount of effort that would be required to simply change the name of a column in the Employees table, if three different applications were all using this stored procedure and had hard-coded lists of sortable column names. And what should happen if the query is initially implemented as dynamic SQL, but needs to be changed later to use static SQL in order to avoid recompilation costs? Will it be possible to detect which applications assumed that the ASC and DESC keywords could be used, before they throw exceptions at run time?

The central message I hope to have conveyed here is that extreme flexibility and solid, maintainable interfaces may not go hand in hand in many situations. If your goal is to develop truly robust software, you will often find that flexibility must be cut back. But remember that in most cases there are perfectly sound workarounds that do not sacrifice any of the real flexibility intended by the original interface. For instance, in this case the interface could be rewritten any number of ways to maintain all of the possible functionality. One such version follows:

```
CREATE PROCEDURE GetAllEmployeeData
    @OrderByName INT = 0,
    @OrderByNameASC BIT = 1,
    @OrderBySalary INT = 0,
    @OrderBySalaryASC BIT = 1,
    -- Other columns ...
```

In this modified version of the interface, each column that a consumer can select for ordering has two parameters: a parameter specifying the order in which to sort the columns, and a parameter that specifies whether to order ascending or descending. So if a consumer passes a value of 2 for the @OrderByName parameter and a value of 1 for the @OrderBySalary parameter, the result will be sorted first by salary, then by name. A consumer can further modify the sort by manipulating the ASC parameters.

This version of the interface exposes nothing about the internal implementation of the stored procedure. The developer is free to use any technique he or she chooses in order to most effectively return the correct results. In addition, the consumer has no need for knowledge of the actual column names of the Employees table. The column containing an employee's name may be called Name or may be called EmpName. Or, there may be two columns, one containing a first name and one a last name. Since the consumer requires no knowledge of these names, they can be modified as necessary as the data changes, and since the consumer is not coupled to the routine-based knowledge of the column name, no change to the consumer will be necessary.

Note that this example only discussed inputs to the interface. Keep in mind that outputs (e.g., result sets) are just as important. I recommend always using the AS keyword to create column aliases as necessary in order to hide changes to the underlying tables. As mentioned before, I also recommend that developers avoid returning extra data, such as additional columns or result sets, based on input arguments. Doing so can create stored procedures that are difficult to test and maintain.

EXCEPTIONS ARE A VITAL PART OF ANY INTERFACE

One type of output not often considered when thinking about implied contracts is the exceptions that a given method can throw should things go awry. Many methods throw well-defined exceptions in certain situations, yet these exceptions fail to show up in the documentation—which renders the well-defined exceptions not so well defined. By making sure to properly document exceptions, you give clients of your method the ability to catch and handle the exceptions you've foreseen, in addition to helping developers working with your interfaces understand what can go wrong and code defensively against possible issues. It is almost always better to follow a code path around a potential problem than to have to deal with an exception.

The Central Problem: Integrating Databases and Object-Oriented Systems

A major issue that seems to make database development a lot more difficult than it should be isn't development related at all, but rather a question of architecture. Object-oriented frameworks and database systems generally do not play well together—primarily because they have a different set of core goals. Object-oriented systems are designed to model business entities from an action standpoint. What can the business entity do, and what can other entities do to or with it? Databases, on the other hand, are more concerned with relationships between entities, and much less concerned with activities in which they are involved.

It's clear that we have two incompatible paradigms for modeling business entities. Yet both are necessary components of any application and must be leveraged together towards the common goal: serving the user. To that end, it's important that database developers know what belongs where, and when to pass the buck back up to their application developer brethren. Unfortunately, the question of how to appropriately model the parts of any given business process can quickly drive one into a gray area. How should you decide between implementation in the database versus implementation in the application?

Where Should the Logic Go?

The central argument on many a database forum since time immemorial (or at least, the dawn of the Internet) has been what to do with that ever-present required logic. Sadly, try as we might, developers have still not figured out how to develop an application without the need to implement business requirements. And so the debate rages on. Does "business logic" belong in the database? In the application tier? What about the user interface? And what impact do newer application architectures have on this age-old question?

The Evolution of Logic Placement

Once upon a time, computers were simply called "computers." They spent their days and nights serving up little bits of data to "dumb" terminals. Back then there wasn't much of a difference between an application and its data, so there were few questions to ask, and fewer answers to give, about the architectural issues we debate today.

But over time the winds of change blew through the air-conditioned data centers of the world, and what had been previously called "computers" were now known as "mainframes"— the new computer on the rack in the mid-1960s was the "minicomputer." Smaller and cheaper than the mainframes, the "minis" quickly grew in popularity. Their relative lack of expense compared to the mainframes meant that it was now fiscally possible to scale out applications by running them on multiple machines. Plus, these machines were inexpensive enough that they could even be used directly by end users as an alternative to the previously ubiquitous dumb terminals. During this same period we also saw the first commercially available database systems, such as the Adabas database management system (DBMS).[1]

---

1. Wikipedia, "Adabas," http://en.wikipedia.org/wiki/Adabas, March 2006.

The advent of the minis signaled multiple changes in the application architecture landscape. In addition to the multiserver scale-out alternatives, the fact that end users were beginning to run machines more powerful than terminals meant that some of an application's work could be offloaded to the user-interface (UI) tier in certain cases. Instead of harnessing only the power of one server, workloads could now be distributed in order to create more scalable applications.

As time went on, the "microcomputers" (ancestors of today's Intel- and AMD-based systems) started getting more and more powerful, and eventually the minis disappeared. However, the client/server-based architecture that had its genesis during the minicomputer era did not die; application developers found that it could be much cheaper to offload work to clients than to purchase bigger servers.

The late 1990s saw yet another paradigm shift in architectural trends—strangely, back toward the world of mainframes and dumb terminals. Web servers replaced the mainframe systems as centralized data and user-interface systems, and browsers took on the role previously filled by the terminals. Essentially, this brought application architecture full circle, but with one key difference: the modern web-based data center is characterized by "farms" of *commodity servers*, rather than a single monolithic mainframe.

ARE SERVERS REALLY A COMMODITY?

The term **commodity hardware** refers to cheap, easily replaceable hardware based on standard components that are easily procured from a variety of manufacturers or distributors. This is in stark contrast to the kind of specialty hardware lock-in typical of large mainframe installations.

From a maintenance and deployment point of view, this architecture has turned out to be a lot cheaper than client/server. Rather than deploying an application (not to mention its corresponding DLLs) to every machine in an enterprise, only a single deployment is necessary, to each of one or more web servers. Compatibility is not much of an issue since web clients are fairly standardized, and the biggest worry of all—updating and patching the applications on all of the deployed machines—is handled by the user merely hitting the refresh button.

Today's architectural challenges deal more with sharing data and balancing workloads than with offloading work to clients. The most important issue to note is that a database may be shared by multiple applications, and a properly architected application may lend itself to multiple user interfaces, as illustrated in Figure 1-1. The key to ensuring success in these endeavors is a solid understanding of the principles discussed in the "Architecture Revisited" section earlier.

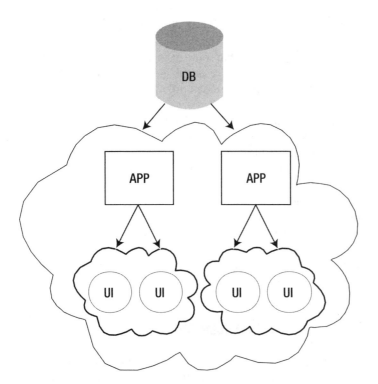

Figure 1-1. *The database application hierarchy*

Database developers must strive to ensure that data is encapsulated enough to allow it to be shared amongst multiple applications while ensuring that the logic of disparate applications does not collide and put the entire database into an inconsistent state. Encapsulating to this level requires careful partitioning of logic, especially data validation rules.

Rules and logic can be segmented into three basic groups: data logic, business logic, and application logic. When designing an application, it's important to understand these divisions and where in the application hierarchy to place any given piece of logic in order to ensure reusability.

Data Logic

Data rules are the subset of logic dictating the conditions that must be true for the data in the database to be in a consistent, noncorrupt state. Database developers are no doubt familiar with implementing these rules in the form of primary and foreign key constraints, check constraints, triggers, and the like. Data rules do not dictate how the data can be manipulated or when it should be manipulated; rather, data rules dictate the state that the data must end up in once any process is finished.

It's important to remember that data is not "just data" in most applications—rather, the data in the database models the actual business. Therefore, data rules must mirror all rules that drive the business itself. For example, if you were designing a database to support a banking application, you might be presented with a business rule that states that certain types of accounts are not allowed to be overdrawn. In order to properly enforce this rule for both the current application and all possible future applications, it must be implemented centrally, at the level of the data itself. If the data is guaranteed to be consistent, applications must only worry about what to *do* with the data.

As a general guideline, you should try to implement as many data rules as necessary in order to avoid the possibility of data quality problems. The database is the holder of the data, and as such should act as the final arbiter of the question of what data does or does not qualify to be persisted. Any validation rule that is central to the business is central to the data, and vice versa. In the course of my work with numerous database-backed applications, I've never seen one with too many data rules; but I've very often seen databases in which the lack of enough rules caused data integrity issues.

WHERE DO THE DATA RULES REALLY BELONG?

Many object-oriented zealots would argue that the correct solution is not a database at all, but rather an interface bus, which acts as a façade over the database and takes control of all communications to and from the database. While this approach would work in theory, there are a few issues. First of all, this approach completely ignores the idea of database-enforced data integrity, and turns the database layer into a mere storage container. While that may be the goal of the object-oriented zealots, it goes against the whole reason we use databases to begin with. Furthermore, such an interface layer will still have to communicate with the database, and therefore database code will have to be written at some level anyway. Writing such an interface layer may eliminate some database code, but it only defers the necessity of working with the database. Finally, in my admittedly subjective view, application layers are not as stable or long-lasting as databases in many cases. While applications and application architectures come and go, databases seem to have an extremely long life in the enterprise. The same rules would apply to a do-it-all interface bus. All of these issues are probably one big reason that although I've heard architects argue this issue for years, I've never seen such a system implemented.

Business Logic

The term **business logic** is generally used in software development circles as a vague catch-all for anything an application does that isn't UI related and which involves at least one conditional branch. In other words, this term is overused and has no real meaning.

Luckily, software development is an ever-changing field, and we don't have to stick with the accepted lack of definition. Business logic, for the purpose of this text, is defined as any rule or process that dictates how or when to manipulate data in order to change the state of the data, but which does not dictate how to persist or validate the data. An example of this would be the logic required to render raw data into a report suitable for end users. The raw data, which we might assume has already been subjected to data logic rules, can be passed through business logic in order to determine appropriate aggregations and analyses appropriate for answering the questions that the end user might pose. Should this data need to be persisted in its new form within a database, it must once again be subjected to data rules; remember that the database should always make the final decision on whether any given piece of data is allowed.

So does business logic belong in the database? The answer is a definite "maybe." As a database developer, your main concerns tend to gravitate toward data integrity and performance. Other factors (such as overall application architecture) notwithstanding, this means that in general practice you should try to put the business logic in the tier in which it can deliver the best performance, or in which it can be reused with the most ease. For instance, if many applications share the same data and each have similar reporting needs, it might make more sense to design stored procedures that render the data into the correct format for the reports, rather than implementing similar reports in each application.

PERFORMANCE VS. DESIGN VS. REALITY

Architecture purists might argue that performance should have no bearing on application design; it's an implementation detail, and can be solved at the code level. Those of us who've been in the trenches and had to deal with the reality of poorly designed architectures know the difference. Performance is, in fact, inexorably tied to design in virtually every application. Consider chatty interfaces that send too much data or require too many client requests to fill the user's screen with the requested information, or applications that must go back to a central server for key functionality, with every user request. Such issues are performance flaws that can—and should—be fixed during the design phase, and not left in the vague realm of "implementation details."

Application Logic

Whereas data logic obviously belongs in the database and business logic may have a place in the database, application logic is the set of rules that should be kept as far from the central data as possible. The rules that make up application logic include such things as user interface behaviors, string and number formatting rules, localization, and other related issues that are generally tied to user interfaces. Given the application hierarchy discussed previously (one database which might be shared by many applications, which in turn might be shared by many user interfaces), it's clear that mingling user interface data with application or central business data can raise severe coupling issues and ultimately reduce the possibility for sharing of data.

Note that I'm not implying that you shouldn't try to persist UI-related entities in a database. Doing so certainly makes sense for many applications. What I am warning against instead is not drawing a distinct enough line between user interface elements and the rest of the application's data. Whenever possible, make sure to create different tables, preferably in different schemas or even entirely different databases, in order to store purely application-related data. This will enable you to keep the application decoupled from the data as much as possible.

The Object-Relational Impedance Mismatch

The primary stumbling block that makes it difficult to move information between object-oriented systems and relational databases is that the two types of systems are incompatible from a basic design point of view. Relational databases are designed using the rules of normalization, which helps to ensure data integrity by splitting information into tables inter-related by keys. Object-oriented systems, on the other hand, tend to be much more lax in this area. It is quite common for objects to contain data that, while related, might not be modeled in a database in a single table.

For example, consider the following class, for a product in a retail system:

```
class Product
{
    string UPC;
    string Name;
    string Description;
    decimal Price;
```

```
    Datetime UpdatedDate;
}
```

At first glance, the fields defined in this class seem to relate to one another quite readily, and one might expect that they would always belong in a single table in a database. However, it's possible that this product class represents only a point-in-time view of any given product, as of its last-updated date. In the database, the data could be modeled as follows:

```
CREATE TABLE Products
(
    UPC VARCHAR(20) PRIMARY KEY,
    Name VARCHAR(50)
)

CREATE TABLE ProductHistory
(
    UPC VARCHAR(20) FOREIGN KEY Products (UPC),
    Description VARCHAR(100),
    Price DECIMAL,
    UpdatedDate DATETIME,
    PRIMARY KEY (UPC, UpdatedDate)
)
```

The important thing to note here is that the object representation of data may not have any bearing on how the data happens to be modeled in the database, and vice versa. The object-oriented and relational worlds each have their own goals and means to attain those goals, and developers should not attempt to wedge them together, lest functionality is reduced.

Are Tables Really Classes in Disguise?

It is sometimes stated in introductory database textbooks that tables can be compared to classes, and rows to instances of a class (i.e., objects). This makes a lot of sense at first; tables, like classes, define a set of attributes (known as columns) for an entity. They can also define (loosely) a set of methods for an entity, in the form of triggers.

However, that is where the similarities end. The key foundations of an object-oriented system are inheritance and polymorphism, both of which are difficult if not impossible to represent in SQL databases. Furthermore, the access path to related information in databases and object-oriented systems is quite different. An entity in an object-oriented system can "have" a child entity, which is generally accessed using a "dot" notation. For instance, a bookstore object might have a collection of books:

```
Books = BookStore.Books;
```

In this object-oriented example, the bookstore "has" the books. But in SQL databases this kind of relationship between entities is maintained via keys, which means that the child entity points to its parent. Rather than the bookstore having the books, the books maintain a key that points back to the bookstore:

```
CREATE TABLE BookStores
(
```

```
    BookStoreId INT PRIMARY KEY
)

CREATE TABLE Books
(
    BookStoreId INT REFERENCES BookStores (BookStoreId),
    BookName VARCHAR(50)
    Quantity INT,
    PRIMARY KEY (BookStoreId, BookName)
)
```

While the object-oriented and SQL representations can store the same information, they do so differently enough that it does not make sense to say that a table represents a class, at least in current SQL databases.

RELATIONAL DATABASES AND SQL DATABASES

Throughout this book, I use the term "SQL database," rather than "relational database." Database products based on the SQL standard, including SQL Server, are not truly faithful to the Relational Model, and tend to have functionality shortcomings that would not be an issue in a truly relational database. Any time I use "SQL database" in a context where you might expect to see "relational database," understand that I'm highlighting an area in which SQL implementations are deficient compared to what the Relational Model provides.

Modeling Inheritance

In object-oriented design, there are two basic relationships that can exist between objects: "has-a" relationships, where an object "has" an instance of another object (for instance, a bookstore has books), and "is-a" relationships, where an object's type is a subtype (or *subclass*) of another object (for instance, a bookstore is a type of store). In an SQL database, "has-a" relationships are quite common, whereas "is-a" relationships can be difficult to achieve.

Consider a table called "Products," which might represent the entity class of all products available for sale by a company. This table should have columns (attributes) that belong to a product, such as "price," "weight," and "UPC." But these attributes might only be the attributes that are applicable to *all* products the company sells. There might exist within the products that the company sells entire subclasses of products, each with their own specific sets of additional attributes. For instance, if the company sells both books and DVDs, the books might have a "page count," whereas the DVDs would probably have "length" and "format" attributes.

Subclassing in the object-oriented world is done via inheritance models that are implemented in languages such as C#. In these models, a given entity can be a member of a subclass, and still generally treated as a member of the *superclass* in code that works at that level. This makes it possible to seamlessly deal with both books and DVDs in the checkout part of a point-of-sale application, while keeping separate attributes about each subclass for use in other parts of the application where they are needed.

In SQL databases, modeling inheritance can be tricky. The following DDL shows one way that it can be approached:

```
CREATE TABLE Products
(
    UPC INT NOT NULL PRIMARY KEY,
    Weight DECIMAL NOT NULL,
    Price DECIMAL NOT NULL
)

CREATE TABLE Books
(
    UPC INT NOT NULL PRIMARY KEY
        REFERENCES Products (UPC),
    PageCount INT NOT NULL
)

CREATE TABLE DVDs
(
    UPC INT NOT NULL PRIMARY KEY
        REFERENCES Products (UPC),
    LengthInMinutes DECIMAL NOT NULL,
    Format VARCHAR(4) NOT NULL
        CHECK (Format IN ('NTSC', 'PAL'))
)
```

Although this model successfully establishes books and DVDs as subtypes for products, it has a couple of serious problems. First of all, there is no way of enforcing uniqueness of subtypes in this model. A single UPC can belong to both the Books and DVDs subtypes, simultaneously. That makes little sense in the real world in most cases—although it might be possible that a certain book ships with a DVD, in which case this model could make sense.

Another issue is access to attributes. In an object-oriented system, a subclass automatically inherits all of the attributes of its superclass; a book entity would contain all of the attributes of both books and general products. However, that is not the case in the model presented here. Getting general product attributes when looking at data for books or DVDs requires a join back to the Products table. This really breaks down the overall sense of working with a subtype.

Solving these problems is possible, but it takes some work. One method of guaranteeing uniqueness amongst subtypes was proposed by Tom Moreau, and involves populating the supertype with an additional attribute identifying the subtype of each instance.[2] The following tables show how this solution could be implemented:

```
CREATE TABLE Products
(
    UPC INT NOT NULL PRIMARY KEY,
    Weight DECIMAL NOT NULL,
    Price DECIMAL NOT NULL,
    ProductType CHAR(1) NOT NULL
        CHECK (ProductType IN ('B', 'D')),
    UNIQUE (UPC, ProductType)
)
```

---

2. Tom Moreau, "Dr. Tom's Workshop: Managing Exclusive Subtypes," *SQL Server Professional* (June 2005).

```
CREATE TABLE Books
(
    UPC INT NOT NULL PRIMARY KEY,
    ProductType CHAR(1) NOT NULL
        CHECK (ProductType = 'B'),
    PageCount INT NOT NULL,
    FOREIGN KEY (UPC, ProductType) REFERENCES Products (UPC, ProductType)
)

CREATE TABLE DVDs
(
    UPC INT NOT NULL PRIMARY KEY,
    ProductType CHAR(1) NOT NULL
        CHECK (ProductType = 'D'),
    LengthInMinutes DECIMAL NOT NULL,
    Format VARCHAR(4) NOT NULL
        CHECK (Format IN ('NTSC', 'PAL')),
    FOREIGN KEY (UPC, ProductType) REFERENCES Products (UPC, ProductType)
)
```

By defining the subtype as part of the supertype, creation of a UNIQUE constraint is possible, allowing SQL Server to enforce that only one subtype for each instance of a supertype is allowed. The relationship is further enforced in each subtype table by a CHECK constraint on the ProductType column, ensuring that only the correct product types are allowed to be inserted.

Moreau takes the method even further using indexed views and INSTEAD OF triggers. A view is created for each subtype, which encapsulates the join necessary to retrieve the supertype's attributes. By creating views to hide the joins, a consumer does not have to be cognizant of the subtype/supertype relationship, thereby fixing the attribute access problem. The indexing helps with performance, and the triggers allow the views to be updateable.

It is possible in SQL databases to represent almost any relationship that can be embodied in an object-oriented system, but it's important that database developers understand the intricacies of doing so. Mapping object-oriented data into a database (properly) is often not at all straightforward and for complex object graphs can be quite a challenge.

THE "LOTS OF NULL COLUMNS" INHERITANCE MODEL

An all-too-common design for modeling inheritance in the database is to create a table with all of the columns for the supertype in addition to all of the columns for each subtype, the latter nullable. This design is fraught with issues and should be avoided. The basic problem is that the attributes that constitute a subtype become mixed, and therefore confused. For example, it is impossible to look at the table and find out what attributes belong to a book instead of a DVD. The only way to make the determination is to look it up in the documentation (if it exists) or evaluate the code. Furthermore, data integrity is all but lost. It becomes difficult to enforce that only certain attributes should be non-NULL for certain subtypes, and even more difficult to figure out what to do in the event that an attribute that should be NULL isn't—what does NTSC format mean for a book? Was it populated due to a bug in the code, or does this book really have a playback format? In a properly modeled system, this question would be impossible to ask.

ORM: A Solution That Creates Many Problems

A recent trend is for software developers to "fix" the impedance problems that exist between relational and object-oriented systems by turning to solutions that attempt to automatically map objects to databases. These tools are called **Object-Relational Mappers** (ORM), and they have seen quite a bit of press in trade magazines, although it's difficult to know what percentage of database software projects are actually using them.

Many of these tools exist, each with its own features and functions, but the basic idea is the same in most cases: the developer "plugs" the ORM tool into an existing object-oriented system and tells the tool which columns in the database map to each field of each class. The ORM tool interrogates the object system as well as the database to figure out how to write SQL to retrieve the data into object form and persist it back to the database if it changes. This is all done automatically and somewhat seamlessly.

Some tools go one step further, creating a database for the preexisting objects, if one does not already exist. These tools work based on the assumption that classes and tables can be mapped in one-to-one correspondence in most cases. As mentioned in the section "Are Tables Really Classes in Disguise?" this is generally *not* true, and therefore these tools often end up producing incredibly flawed database designs.

One company I did some work for had used a popular Java-based ORM tool for its e-commerce application. The tool mapped "has-a" relationships from an object-centric rather than table-centric point of view, and as a result the database had a `Products` table with a foreign key to an `Orders` table. The Java developers working for the company were forced to insert fake orders into the system in order to allow the firm to sell new products.

While ORM is an interesting idea and one that may have merit, I do not believe that the current set of available tools work well enough to make them viable for enterprise software development. Aside from the issues with the tools that create database tables based on classes, the two primary issues that concern me are both performance related.

First of all, ORM tools tend to think in terms of objects rather than collections of related data (i.e., tables). Each class has its own data access methods produced by the ORM tool, and each time data is needed these methods query the database on a granular level for just the rows necessary. This means that a lot of database connections are opened and closed on a regular basis, and the overall interface to retrieve the data is quite "chatty." SQL database management systems tend to be much more efficient at returning data in bulk than a row at a time; it's generally better to query for a product and all of its related data at once than to ask for the product, then request related data in a separate query.

Second, query tuning may be difficult if ORM tools are relied upon too heavily. In SQL databases, there are often many logically equivalent ways of writing any given query, each of which may have distinct performance characteristics. The current crop of ORM tools does not intelligently monitor for and automatically fix possible issues with poorly written queries, and developers using these tools are often taken by surprise when the system fails to scale because of improperly written queries.

ORM is still in a relative state of infancy at the time of this writing, and the tools will undoubtedly improve over time. For now, however, I recommend a wait-and-see approach. I feel that a better return on investment can be made by carefully designing object-database interfaces by hand.

Introducing the Database-as-API Mindset

By far the most important issue to be wary of when writing data interchange interfaces between object systems and database systems is coupling. Object systems and the databases they use as back-ends should be carefully partitioned in order to ensure that in most cases changes to one layer do not necessitate changes to the other layer. This is important in both worlds; if a change to the database requires an application change, it can often be expensive to recompile and redeploy the application. Likewise, if application logic changes necessitate database changes, it can be difficult to know how changing the data structures or constraints will affect other applications that may need the same data.

To combat these issues, database developers must resolve to rigidly adhere to creating a solid set of encapsulated interfaces between the database system and the objects. I call this the **Database-as-API** mindset.

An **application programming interface** (API) is a set of interfaces that allows a system to interact with another system. An API is intended to be a complete access methodology for the system it exposes. In database terms, this means that an API would expose public interfaces for retrieving data from, inserting data into, and updating data in the database.

A set of database interfaces should comply with the same basic design rule as other interfaces: well-known, standardized sets of inputs that result in well-known, standardized sets of outputs. This set of interfaces should completely encapsulate all implementation details, including table and column names, keys, indexes, and queries. An application that uses the data from a database should not require knowledge of internal information—the application should only need to know that data can be retrieved and persisted using certain methods.

In order to define such an interface, the first step is to define stored procedures for all external database access. Table-direct access to data is clearly a violation of proper encapsulation and interface design, and views may or may not suffice. Stored procedures are the only construct available in SQL Server that can provide the type of interfaces necessary for a comprehensive data API.

WEB SERVICES AS A STANDARD API LAYER

It's worth noting that the Database-as-API mindset that I'm proposing requires the use of stored procedures as an interface to the data, but does not get into the detail of what protocol you use to access the stored procedures. Many software shops have discovered that web services are a good way to provide a standard, cross-platform interface layer. SQL Server 2005's HTTP Endpoints feature allows you to expose stored procedures as web services directly from SQL Server—meaning that you are no longer restricted to using data protocols to communicate with the database. Whether or not using web services is superior to using other protocols is something that must be decided on a per-case basis; like any other technology, they can certainly be used in the wrong way or in the wrong scenario. Keep in mind that web services require a lot more network bandwidth and follow different authentication rules than other protocols that SQL Server supports—their use may end up causing more problems than they will fix.

By using stored procedures with correctly defined interfaces and full encapsulation of information, coupling between the application and the database will be greatly reduced, resulting in a database system that is much easier to maintain and evolve over time.

It is difficult to express the importance that stored procedures play in a well-designed SQL Server database system in only a few paragraphs. In order to reinforce the idea that the database must be thought of as an API rather than a persistence layer, this topic will be revisited throughout the book with examples that deal with interfaces to outside systems.

The Great Balancing Act

When it comes down to it, the real goal of software development is to sell software to customers. But this means producing working software that customers will want to use, in addition to software that can be easily fixed or extended as time and needs progress. When developing a piece of software, there are hard limits on how much can actually be done. No project has a limitless quantity of time or money, so sacrifices must often be made in one area in order to allow for a higher-priority requirement in another.

The database is, in most cases, the center of the applications it drives. The data controls the applications, to a great extent, and without the data the applications would not be worth much. Likewise, the database is often where applications face real challenges in terms of performance, maintainability, and the like. It is quite common for application developers to push these issues as far down into the data tier as possible, leaving the database developer as the person responsible for balancing the needs of the entire application.

Balancing performance, testability, maintainability, and security are not always easy tasks. What follows are some initial thoughts on these issues; examples throughout the remainder of the book will serve to illustrate them in more detail.

Testability

It is inadvisable, to say the least, to ship any product without thoroughly testing it. However, it is common to see developers exploit **anti-patterns** that make proper testing difficult or impossible. Many of these problems result from attempts to produce "flexible" modules or interfaces—instead of properly partitioning functionality and paying close attention to cohesion, it is sometimes tempting to create monolithic routines that can do it all (thanks to the joy of optional parameters!).

Development of these kinds of routines produces software that can never be fully tested. The combinatorial explosion of possible use cases for a single routine can be immense—and in most cases the number of actual combinations that users or the application itself will exploit is far more limited.

Think very carefully before implementing a flexible solution merely for the sake of flexibility. Does it really need to be that flexible? Will the functionality really be exploited in full right away, or can it be slowly extended later as required?

Maintainability

As an application ages and goes through revisions, modules and routines will require maintenance in the form of enhancements and bug fixes. The issues that make routines more or less maintainable are similar to those that influence testability, with a few twists.

When determining how testable a given routine is, we are generally only concerned with whether the interface is stable enough to allow the authoring of test cases. For determining the level of maintainability, we are also concerned with exposed interfaces, but for slightly different reasons. From a maintainability point of view, the most important interface issue is coupling. Tightly coupled routines tend to carry a higher maintenance cost, as any changes have to be propagated to multiple routines instead of being made in a single place.

The issue of maintainability also goes beyond the interface into the actual implementation. A routine may have a stable, simple interface, yet have a convoluted, undocumented implementation that is difficult to work with. Generally speaking, the more lines of code in a routine, the more difficult maintenance becomes; but since large routines may also be a sign of a cohesion problem, such an issue should be caught early in the design process if developers are paying attention.

As with testability, maintainability is somewhat influenced by attempts to create "flexible" interfaces. On one hand, flexibility of an interface can increase coupling between routines by requiring the caller to have too much knowledge of parameter combinations, overrideable options, and the like. On the other hand, routines with flexible interfaces can sometimes be more easily maintained, at least at the beginning of a project. In some cases, making routines as generic as possible can result in less total routines needed by a system, and therefore less code to maintain. However, as features are added, the ease with which these generic routines can be modified tends to break down due to the increased complexity that each new option or parameter brings. Oftentimes, therefore, it may be advantageous early in a project to aim for some flexibility, then refactor later when maintainability begins to suffer.

Maintainability is also tied in with testability in one other key way: the better a routine can be tested, the easier it will be to modify. Breaking changes are not as much of an issue when tests exist that can quickly validate new approaches to implementation.

Security

In an age in which identity theft makes the news almost nightly and a computer left open on the Internet will be compromised within 30 seconds, it is little wonder that security is considered one of the most important areas when developing software applications. Security is, however, also one of the most complex areas, and complexity can hide flaws that a trained attacker can easily exploit.

Complex security schemes can also have a huge impact on whether a given piece of software is testable and maintainable. From a testing standpoint, a developer needs to consider whether a given security scheme will create too many variables to make testing feasible. For instance, if users are divided into groups and each group has distinct security privileges, should each set of tests be run for each group of users? How many test combinations are necessary to exercise before the application can be considered "fully" tested?

From a maintenance point of view, complexity from a security standpoint is equally as dangerous as complexity of any other type of implementation. The more complex a given routine is, the more difficult (and, therefore, more expensive) it will be to maintain.

In a data-dependent application, much of the security responsibility will generally get pushed into the data tier. The security responsibilities of the data tier or database will generally include areas such as authentication to the application, authorization to view data, and availability of data. Encapsulating these security responsibilities in database routines can be a win from an overall application maintainability perspective, but care must be taken to ensure that the database routines do not become so bogged down that their maintainability, testability, or performance suffer.

Performance

We are a society addicted to fast. Fast food, fast cars, and instant gratification of all types are well engrained into our overall mindset. And that need for speed certainly applies to the world of database development. Users seem to continuously feel that applications just aren't performing *quite* as well as they should, even when those applications are doing a tremendous amount of work. It sometimes feels as though users would rather have *any data* as fast as possible, than the *correct data* a bit slower.

The problem, of course, is that performance isn't easy, and can throw the entire balance off. Building a truly high-performance application often involves sacrifice. Functionality might have to be trimmed (less work for the application to do means it will be faster), security might have to be reduced (less authorization cycles means less work), or inefficient code might have to be rewritten in arcane, unmaintainable ways in order to squeeze every last CPU cycle out of the server.

So how do we balance this need for extreme performance—which many seem to care about to the exclusion of all else—with the need for development best practices? Unfortunately, the answer is that sometimes, we can only do as well as we can do. Most of the time if we find ourselves in a position in which a user is complaining about performance and we're going to lose money or a job if it's not remedied, the user doesn't want to hear about why fixing the performance problem will increase coupling and decrease maintainability. The user just wants the software to work fast—and we have no choice but to deliver.

A lucky fact about sticking with best practices is that they're often considered to be the best way to do things for several reasons. Keeping a close watch on issues of coupling, cohesion, and proper encapsulation throughout the development cycle can not only reduce the incidence of performance problems, but will also make fixing most of them a whole lot easier. And on those few occasions where you need to break some "perfect" code to get it working as fast as necessary, know that it's not your fault—society put you in this position!

Creeping Featurism

Although not exactly part of the balance, the tendency to overthink about tomorrow's feature goals instead of today's bugs can often be an issue. Looking through many technical specifications and data dictionaries, it's common to see the phrase "reserved for future use." Developers want to believe that adding complexity upfront will work to their advantage by allowing less work to be done later in the development process. But this approach generally backfires, producing software full of maintenance baggage. These pieces of code must be carried around by the development team and kept up to date in order to compile the application, but often go totally unused for years at a time.

In one 15-year-old application I worked on, the initial development team had been especially active in prepopulating the code base with features reserved for the future. Alas, several years, a few rounds of layoffs, and lots of staff turnovers later and no members of the original team were left. The developers who worked on the two million–line application were afraid of removing anything lest it would break some long-forgotten feature that some user still counted on. It was a dismal scene, to say the least, and it's difficult to imagine just how much time was wasted over the years keeping all of that dead code up to date.

Although that example is extreme (certainly by far the worst I've come across), it teaches us to adhere to the Golden Rule of software development: the **KISS Principle**.[3] Keep your software projects as straightforward as they can possibly be. Adding new features tomorrow should always be a secondary concern to delivering a robust, working product today.

Summary

Applications depend upon databases for much more than mere data persistence, and database developers must have an understanding of the entire application development process in order to create truly effective database systems.

By understanding architectural concepts such as coupling, cohesion, and encapsulation, database developers can define modular data interfaces that allow for great gains in ongoing maintenance and testing. Database developers must also understand how best to map data from object-oriented systems into database structures, in order to effectively be able to both persist and manipulate the data.

This chapter is merely an introduction to these ideas. The concepts presented here will be revisited in various examples throughout the remainder of the book.

---

3. "Keep it simple, stupid!" Or alternatively, "Keep it simple, sweetie," if you happen to be teaching your beloved the art of software development and don't wish to start a fight.

◼◼◼

CHAPTER 2

Testing Database Routines

What defines a great developer? Is it the ability to quickly code complex routines? The ability to implement business requirements correctly, within budget, and on schedule? Or perhaps it can be defined by how quickly the developer can track down and fix bugs in the application—or the inverse, the lack of bugs in the developer's code?

All of these are certainly attributes of a great developer, but in most cases they don't manifest themselves merely due to raw skill. The hallmark of a truly great developer, and what allows these qualities to shine through, is a thorough understanding of the importance of testing.

By creating unit tests early on in the development process, developers can continuously validate interfaces and test for exceptions and regressions. Carefully designed functional tests ensure compliance with business requirements. And performance testing—the kind of testing that always seems to get the most attention—can be used to find out whether the application can actually handle the anticipated amount of traffic.

Unfortunately, like various other development practices that are better established in the object-oriented community, testing hasn't yet caught on much on the database side. Although some shops performance test stored procedures and other database code, it's rare to see database developers writing data-specific unit tests.

There is no good reason that database developers should not write just as many—or more—tests than their application developer counterparts. It makes little sense to test a data-dependent application without validating the data pieces that drive the application components!

This chapter serves as a brief introduction to the world of software testing and how testing techniques can be applied in database development scenarios. Software testing is a huge field, complete with much of its own lingo, so the stress here is on those areas I've found to be most important for database developers. Keep in mind that some of this material may not apply to more broadly focused testing scenarios.

Introduction to Black Box and White Box Testing

A number of testing methodologies are defined within the world of quality assurance, but by and large the types of tests that can be done can be split into two groups. **Black box testing** refers to tests that make assumptions only about inputs and outputs, and as such do not validate intermediate conditions. **White box testing**, on the other hand, includes any test in which the internal implementation of the routine or function being tested is known and validated by the tester.

Although these terms break up all types of testing into two camps, the majority of what we as software developers think of as "tests" are actually black box tests. The black box variety includes unit tests, most types of functional and security tests, and basic performance testing. As testing progresses once issues are identified, testing get more pinpointed, and the tests tend to shift from black box to white box.

From a database development perspective, if data access is properly encapsulated, virtually all tests necessary to thoroughly analyze a database will be black box tests. The only exceptions to this will be times when data validation is necessary, or when performance tuning requires thorough knowledge of the access methods. For instance, retrieving (and reviewing) query plans during a performance test is an example of white box testing against a stored procedure.

Unit and Functional Testing

Developing software with a specific concentration on the data tier can have a benefit when it comes to testing: there aren't too many types of tests that you need to be familiar with. The most important type of test, and the kind you'll find yourself writing constantly, is the **unit test**.

Unit tests are black box tests that verify the contracts exposed by interfaces. For instance, a unit test of a stored procedure should validate that given a certain set of inputs, the stored procedure returns the *correct set of output results, as defined by the interface of the stored procedure being tested.* The term "correct" as used here is important to carefully define. It means correct only insofar as what is defined as the contract for the stored procedure; the actual data returned is not important. So as long as the results are in the correct format and of the correct data types given the interface's contract, a unit test should pass. Phrased another way, unit tests test the ability of interfaces to communicate with the outside world exactly as their contracts say they will.

On the other hand, just as its name implies, a **functional test** verifies the functionality of whatever is being tested. In testing nomenclature, the term "functional test" has a much vaguer meaning than "unit test." It can mean any kind of test, at any level of an application, which tests whether that piece of the application works properly. But at the database layer, this can mean only one thing: is the stored procedure returning the *correct data*? Again, I will carefully define the term "correct." This time, correct means both the kind of validation done for a unit test (data must be in the correct format), as well as a deeper validation of the accuracy of the actual values returned. The logic required for this kind of validation means that a functional test is a white box test in the database world, compared to the black box of unit testing.

Let's take a look at an example to make these ideas a bit clearer. Consider the following stored procedure, which might be used for a banking application:

```
CREATE PROCEDURE GetAggregateTransactionHistory
    @CustomerId INT
AS
BEGIN
    SET NOCOUNT ON

    SELECT
        SUM
        (
            CASE TransactionType
                WHEN 'Deposit' THEN Amount
```

```
            ELSE 0
        END
    ) AS TotalDeposits,
    SUM
    (
        CASE TransactionType
            WHEN 'Withdrawal' THEN Amount
            ELSE 0
        END
    ) AS TotalWithdrawals
FROM TransactionHistory
WHERE
    CustomerId = @CustomerId
END
```

This stored procedure's implied contract states that given the input of a customer ID into the @CustomerId parameter, a result set of two columns and zero or one rows will be output (the contract does not imply anything about invalid customer IDs or customers who've made no transactions). The column names in the output result set will be TotalDeposits and TotalWithdrawals, and the data types of the columns will be whatever the data type of the Amount column is (we'll assume it's DECIMAL).

WHAT IF THE CUSTOMER DOESN'T EXIST?

The output of the GetAggregateTransactionHistory stored procedure will be the same whether you pass in a valid customer ID for a customer that happens to have had no transactions, or an invalid customer ID. Either way, the procedure will return no rows. Depending on the requirements of a particular situation, it might make sense to make the interface richer by changing the rules a bit, only returning no rows if an invalid customer ID is passed in. That way, the caller will be able to identify invalid data and give the user an appropriate error message rather than implying that the nonexistent customer made no transactions. To fix the interface, use an outer join to the Customers table, as the following modified version of the procedure does:

```
CREATE PROCEDURE GetAggregateTransactionHistory
    @CustomerId INT
AS
BEGIN
    SET NOCOUNT ON

    SELECT
        SUM
        (
            CASE TH.TransactionType
                WHEN 'Deposit' THEN TH.Amount
                ELSE 0
            END
        ) AS TotalDeposits,
```

```
      SUM
      (
          CASE TH.TransactionType
              WHEN 'Withdrawal' THEN TH.Amount
              ELSE 0
          END
      ) AS TotalWithdrawals
    FROM Customers AS C
    LEFT JOIN TransactionHistory AS TH ON C.CustomerId = TH.CustomerId
    WHERE
          C.CustomerId = @CustomerId
END
```

A unit test against this stored procedure should do nothing more than validate the interface. A customer ID should be passed in, and the unit test should interrogate the output result set (or lack thereof) and ensure that there are two columns of the correct name and data type and zero or one rows. No verification of data is necessary; it would be out of scope, for instance, to find out whether the aggregate information was valid or not—that would be the job of a functional test.

The reason that we draw such a distinction between unit tests and functional tests is that when testing pure interface compliance, we want to put ourselves in the position of someone programming against the interface from a higher layer. Is the interface working as documented, providing the appropriate level of encapsulation and returning data in the correct format?

Each interface in the system will need one or more of these tests (see the section "How Many Tests Are Needed?"), so they need to be kept focused and lightweight. Programming full white box tests against every interface may not be feasible, and it might be simpler to test the validity of data at a higher layer, such as via the user interface itself. In the case of the GetAggregateTransactionHistory stored procedure, writing a functional test would essentially entail rewriting the entire stored procedure again—hardly a good use of developer time.

Unit Testing Frameworks

Unit testing is made easier through the use of unit testing frameworks, which provide structured programming interfaces designed to assist with quickly testing software. These frameworks generally make use of **debug assertions**, which allow the developer to specify what conditions make a test true or false.

A debug assertion is a special kind of macro that is turned on only when a piece of software is compiled in debug mode. It accepts an expression as input and throws an exception if the expression is false; otherwise, it returns true (or void, in some languages). For instance, the following assertion would always throw an exception:

```
Assert(1 == 0);
```

Assertions allow a developer to self-document **assumptions** made by the code of a routine. If a routine expects that a variable is in a certain state at a certain time, an assertion can be used in order to help make sure that assumption is enforced as the code matures. If, at any time in the future, a change in the code invalidates that assumption, an exception will be thrown should the developer making the change hit the assertion during testing or debugging.

In unit testing, assertions serve much the same purpose. They allow the tester to control what conditions make the unit test return `true` or `false`. If any assertion throws an exception in a unit test, the entire test is considered to have failed.

Unit testing frameworks exist for virtually every language and platform, including T-SQL. A project called TSQLUnit is available on the SourceForge open source project web site. Personally, I find unit testing in T-SQL to be cumbersome compared to other languages, and prefer to write my tests in a .NET language using the .NET unit testing framework, NUnit.

■Note Coding against the unit testing frameworks is out of scope for this book. For a great introduction to NUnit, I recommend *Pragmatic Unit Testing in C# with NUnit* by Andy Hunt and Dave Thomas (Pragmatic Bookshelf, 2006).

Given that unit testing stored procedures is still somewhat of a mystery to many developers, I will provide a few hints. When writing stored procedure unit tests in NUnit, the following basic steps can be followed:

1. First, determine what assumptions should be made about the stored procedure's interface. What are the result sets that will be returned? What are the data types of the columns, and how many columns will there be? Does the contract make any guarantees about a certain number of rows?

2. Next, write code using ADO.NET to execute the stored procedure. I find that using the stored procedure to fill a `DataSet` is generally the easiest way of exposing its output for interrogation. Be careful at this stage; you want to test the stored procedure, not your ADO.NET data access framework. You might be tempted at this point to call the stored procedure using the same method that the application uses to call it. However, this would be a mistake, as you would end up testing both the stored procedure and that method. Given that you only need to fill a `DataSet`, recoding the data access in the unit test should not be a major burden, and will keep you from testing parts of the code that you don't intend to.

3. Finally, use one assertion for each assumption you're making about the stored procedure. That means one assertion per column name, one per column data type, one for the row count if necessary, etc. Err on the side of using too many assertions—it's better to have to remove an assumption later because it turns out to be incorrect, than to not have had an assumption there to begin with and had your unit test pass when the interface was actually not working correctly.

Following is an example of what an NUnit test of the `GetAggregateTransactionHistory` stored procedure might look like:

```
[TestMethod]
public void TestAggregateTransactionHistory()
{
    //Set up a command object
    SqlCommand comm = new SqlCommand();
```

```
//Set up the connection
comm.Connection = new SqlConnection(
    @"server=serverName; trusted_connection=true;");

//Define the procedure call
comm.CommandText = "GetAggregateTransactionHistory";
comm.CommandType = CommandType.StoredProcedure;

comm.Parameters.AddWithValue("@CustomerId", 123);

//Create a DataSet for the results
DataSet ds = new DataSet();

//Define a DataAdapter to fill a DataSet
SqlDataAdapter adapter = new SqlDataAdapter();
adapter.SelectCommand = comm;

try
{
    //Fill the dataset
    adapter.Fill(ds);
}
catch
{
    Assert.Fail("Exception occurred!");
}

//Now we have the results -- validate them...

//There must be exactly one returned result set
Assert.IsTrue(
    ds.Tables.Count == 1,
    "Result set count != 1");

DataTable dt = ds.Tables[0];

//There must be exactly two columns returned
Assert.IsTrue(
    dt.Columns.Count == 2,
    "Column count != 2");

//There must be columns called TotalDeposits and TotalWithdrawals
Assert.IsTrue(
    dt.Columns.IndexOf("TotalDeposits") > -1,
    "Column TotalDeposits does not exist");
```

```
Assert.IsTrue(
    dt.Columns.IndexOf("TotalWithdrawals") > -1,
    "Column TotalWithdrawals does not exist");

//Both columns must be decimal
Assert.IsTrue(
    dt.Columns["TotalDeposits"].DataType == typeof(decimal),
    "TotalDeposits data type is incorrect");

Assert.IsTrue(
    dt.Columns["TotalWithdrawals"].DataType == typeof(decimal),
    "TotalWithdrawals data type is incorrect");

//There must be zero or one rows returned
Assert.IsTrue(
    dt.Rows.Count <= 1,
    "Too many rows returned");
}
```

Although it might be disturbing to note that the unit test is over twice as long as the stored procedure it is testing, keep in mind that most of this code can be easily turned into a template for quick reuse. As noted before, you might be tempted to refactor common unit test code into a data access library, but be careful lest you end up testing your test framework instead of the actual routine you're attempting to test. Many hours can be wasted debugging working code trying to figure out why the unit test is failing, when it's actually the fault of some code the unit test is relying on to do its job.

Unit tests allow for quick, automated verification of interfaces. In essence, they help you as a developer to guarantee that in making changes to a system you didn't break anything obvious. In that way, they are invaluable. Developing against a system with a well-established set of unit tests is a joy, as each developer no longer needs to worry about breaking some other component due to an interface change. The unit tests will complain if anything needs to be fixed.

The Importance of Regression Testing

As you build up a set of unit tests for a particular application, the tests will eventually come to serve as a **regression suite**, which will help to guard against **regression bugs**—bugs that occur when a developer breaks functionality that used to work. Any change to an interface—intentional or not—will cause unit tests to fail. For the intentional changes, the solution is to rewrite the unit test accordingly. But it is these unintentional changes for which we create unit tests, and which regression testing targets.

Experience has shown that fixing bugs in an application often introduces other bugs. It can be difficult to substantiate how often this happens in real development scenarios, but figures as high as 50% are likely in some cases.[1] By building a regression suite, the cost of fixing these "side-effect" bugs is greatly reduced. They can be discovered and mended during the development phase, instead of being reported by end users once the application has already been deployed.

---

1. Frederick P. Brooks, *The Mythical Man-Month* (Boston, MA: Addison-Wesley, 1995), pp. 122.

Regression testing is also the key to newer software development methodologies, such as Agile Development and eXtreme Programming. As these methodologies increase in popularity, it can be expected that database developers will begin to adopt some of these techniques more readily.

Guidelines for Implementing Database Testing Processes and Procedures

Of all the possible elements that make up a testing strategy, there is really only one key to success: consistency. Tests must be repeatable, and must be run the same way every time, with only well-known (i.e., understood and documented) variables changed. Inconsistency and not knowing what might have changed between tests can mean that problems the tests identify will be difficult to trace.

Development teams should strive to build a suite of tests that are run at least once for every release of the application, if not more often. These tests should be automated and easy to run. Preferably, the suite of tests should be modular enough that if a developer is working on one part of the application, the subset of tests that apply to only that section can be easily exercised in order to validate any changes.

CONTINUOUSLY TESTING

Once you've built a set of automated tests, you're one step away from a fully automatic testing environment. Such an environment should retrieve the latest code from the source control repository, run appropriate build scripts to compile a working version of the application, and run through the entire test suite. Many software development shops use this technique to run their tests several times a day, throwing alerts almost instantly if problem code is checked in. This kind of rigorous automated testing is called **continuous integration**, and it's a great way to take some of the testing burden out of the hands of developers while still making sure that all of the tests get run as often (or even more often) than necessary. A great free tool to help set up continuous integration in .NET environments is CriuseControl.NET, available at `http://sourceforge.net/projects/ccnet`.

Testers must also consider the data backing the tests. It can often be beneficial to generate test data sets that include every possible case the application is likely to see. Such a set of data can guarantee consistency between test runs, as it can be restored to its original state. It can also guarantee that rare edge cases are tested that might otherwise not be seen.

It's also recommended that a copy of actual production data (if available) be used for testing near the end of any given test period. Oftentimes, generated sets can lack the realism needed to bring to light obscure issues that only real users can manage to bring out of an application.

Why Is Testing Important?

There are only two reasons that software gets tested at all. First, testing is done to find problems that need to be fixed. Second, testing is done to ensure that no problems need to be fixed. It can be argued that the only purpose of software is to be used by end users, and therefore, the only purpose of testing is to make sure that end users don't encounter issues.

Eventually, all software must be tested. If developers or a quality assurance team fail to fully test an application, it will be tested by the end users trying to use the software. Unfortunately, this is a great way to lose business; users are generally not pleased with buggy software.

Testing by development and quality assurance teams validates the software. Each kind of testing that is done validates a specific piece of the puzzle, and if a complete test suite is used (and the tests are passed), the team can be fairly certain that the software has a minimal number of bugs, performance defects, and other issues. Since the database is an increasingly important component in most applications, testing the database makes sense; if the database has problems, they will propagate to the rest of the application.

What Kind of Testing Is Important?

From the perspective of a database developer, only a few types of tests are really necessary most of the time. Databases should be tested for the following issues:

- **Interface consistency** should be validated, in order to guarantee that applications have a stable structure for data access.

- **Data availability** and **authorization test**s are similar to interface consistency tests, but more focused on who can get data from the database than how the data should be retrieved.

- **Authentication tests** verify whether valid users can log in, and whether invalid users are refused access. These kinds of tests are only important if the database is being used for authenticating users.

- **Performance tests** are important for verifying that the user experience will be positive, and that users will not have to wait longer than necessary for data.

- **Regression testing** covers every other type of test, but generally focuses on uncovering issues that were previously fixed. A regression test is a test that validates that a fix still works.

How Many Tests Are Needed?

Although most development teams lack a sufficient number of tests to test the application thoroughly, in some cases the opposite is true. Too many tests can be just as much of a problem as not enough tests; writing tests can be time consuming, and tests must be maintained along with the rest of the software whenever functionality changes. It's important to balance the need for thorough testing with the realities of time and monetary constraints.

A good starting point for database testing is to create one unit test per interface parameter "class," or group of inputs. For example, consider the following stored procedure interface:

```
CREATE PROCEDURE SearchProducts
    SearchText VARCHAR(100) = NULL,
    PriceLessThan DECIMAL = NULL,
    ProductCategory INT = NULL
```

This stored procedure returns data about products based on three parameters, each of which is optional, based on the following (documented) criteria:

- A user can search for text in the product's description.

- A user can search for products where the price is less than a given input price.

- A user can combine a text search or price search with an additional filter on a certain product category, so that only results from that category are returned.

- A user cannot search on both text and price simultaneously. This condition should return an error.

- Any other combination of inputs should result in an error.

In order to validate the stored procedure's interface, one unit test is necessary for each of these conditions. The unit tests that pass in valid input arguments should verify that the stored procedure returns a valid output result set per its implied contract. The unit tests for the invalid combinations of arguments should verify that an error occurs when these combinations are used. Known errors are part of an interface's implied contract (see Chapter 3 for more information on this topic).

In addition to these unit tests, an additional regression test should be produced for each known issue that has been fixed within the stored procedure, in order to ensure that the procedure's functionality does not degenerate over time.

Although this seems like a massive number of tests, keep in mind that these tests can—and should—share the same base code. The individual tests will have to do nothing more than pass the correct parameters to a parameterized base test.

Will Management Buy In?

It's unfortunate that many management teams believe that testing is either an unnecessary waste of time or not something that should be a well-integrated part of the software development process at all. Many software shops, especially smaller ones, have no quality assurance staff at all and such compressed development schedules that little testing gets done, and full functionality testing is nearly impossible.

Several companies I've done work for have been in this situation, and it never results in the time or money savings that management thinks it will. On the contrary, time and money is actually *wasted* by lack of testing.

A test process that is well integrated into development finds most bugs upfront, when they are created, rather than later on. A developer who is currently working on enhancing a given module has an in-depth understanding of the code at that moment. As soon as he or she moves on to another module, that knowledge will start to wane as focus goes to other parts of the application. If defects are discovered and reported while the developer is still in the trenches, the developer will not need to relearn the code enough to fix the problem, thereby saving a lot of time. These time savings translate directly into increased productivity, as developers end up spending more time working on new features, and less on fixing defects.

If management teams refuse to listen to reason and allocate additional development time for proper testing, try doing it anyway. Methodologies such as test-driven development, in which you write tests against the routines before writing the actual routines, then work until the tests pass, can greatly enhance overall developer productivity. Adopting a testing strategy—with or without management approval—can mean better, faster output, which in the end will help to ensure success.

Performance Testing and Profiling Database Systems

Verification using unit, functional, and regression tests is extremely important for thoroughly testing an application, but it is performance testing that really gets the attention of most developers. Performance testing is imperative for ensuring a positive user experience. Users don't want to wait any longer than absolutely necessary for data.

Developing high-performance database applications is getting more difficult. As applications grow larger, and especially as disk space continues to get cheaper, the amount of data that must be processed by the typical application has grown to be enormous. Whereas 5 years ago applications with hundreds of gigabytes of data seemed large, today that figure is in the terabytes—and that number will only continue to grow. Jim Gray of Microsoft Research estimates that the cost for a petabyte (that's 1000 terabytes) of storage will be down to $1000 within 15 to 20 years.[2]

The key to dealing with large amounts of data in a timely manner is to reduce bottlenecks. Unfortunately, problem areas can often be subtle, manifesting themselves only under load— almost always, it seems, when a key user is trying to get some extremely important piece of data. The only way to ensure that this doesn't happen is to exercise the application to the highest level of expected load and determine which areas need improvement.

This section discusses methodologies for conducting database performance tests, but does not deal with how to fix those problems. Throughout the remainder of the book, various examples will discuss how to look at code from a performance-minded point of view and how to solve some problems, but keep in mind that this book is not intended as a thorough guide to query performance tuning. I highly recommend that readers invest in a focused performance book such as *SQL Server Query Performance Tuning Distilled, Second Edition* by Sajal Dam (Apress, 2004).

Capturing Baseline Metrics

Just as with unit and functional testing, having an overall process in place is extremely important when it comes to performance evaluation. Performance tests should be repeatable and should be done in an environment that can be rolled back to duplicate the same conditions for multiple test runs.

Keep in mind that any component in the application may be contributing in some way to performance, so starting from the same point each time is imperative. I recommend using a test database that can be restored to its original state each time, as well as rebooting all servers involved in the test just before beginning a run, in order to make sure that the test starts with the same initial conditions each time. Another option that might be easier than backing up and restoring a test database is using SQL Server 2005's database snapshot feature. Try each technique in your environment to determine which fits better into your testing system.

In addition to making sure the servers are in the same state, you should also collect exactly the same performance counters, query trace data, and other metrics in precisely the same way for each test run. Consistency is the key to not only validating that changes are effective, but also measuring how effective they are.

---

2. Jim Gray, "The Personal Petabyte, the Enterprise Exabyte," `http://research.microsoft.com/~Gray/talks/Gray%20IIST%20Personal%20Petabyte%20Enterprise%20Exabyte.ppt` (accessed April 12, 2006).

During a testing process, the first test that is run should be used as a **baseline**. The metrics captured during the baseline test will be used to compare results for later runs. As problems are solved, or if test conditions change (for instance, if you need to collect more performance counters in a certain area), you should establish a new baseline from which to go forward. Keep in mind that fixing issues in one area of an application might have an impact on performance of another area. For instance, a given query may be I/O-bound, whereas another is CPU-bound. By fixing the I/O problems for the first query, you may introduce greater CPU utilization, which in turn will cause the other query to degrade in performance if they are run simultaneously.

Baselining metrics in a database environment is generally a fairly straightforward process. Server-side traces should be used to capture performance data, including query duration and resources used. This data can then be aggregated in order to determine minimum, maximum, and average statistics for queries. In order to determine which resources are starved, performance counters can be used to track server utilization. As changes are made to fix performance issues, the baseline data can be analyzed against other test data in order to establish performance trends.

Profiling Using Traces and SQL Server Profiler

SQL Server 2005's tracing capabilities allow DBAs and developers to store or view real-time information about activity taking place on the server. With almost 200 events available for monitoring, there is a wealth of information about the state of the server available through traces. However, for most performance monitoring work, there are only a few key events that you'll need to worry about.

When initially baselining an application, I'll generally start by looking at only the `SQL:BatchCompleted` and `RPC:Completed` events. Each of these events fires on completion of queries; the only difference between them is that `RPC:Completed` fires on completion of a remote procedure call (RPC), whereas `SQL:BatchCompleted` fires on completion of a SQL batch. Different access methods, same end result.

The most valuable columns available for both of these events are `Duration`, `CPU`, `Reads`, and `Writes`.

- The `Duration` column reports the total time elapsed for the call, in microseconds (note, the Profiler tool shows this column in milliseconds by default). The duration of a query is a direct reflection on the user experience, so this is generally the one to start with. If the application is performing slowly, find the worst offenders using this column.

- The `CPU` column reports the amount of CPU time, in milliseconds, spent parsing, compiling, and executing the query. Due to the fact that this column reports compilation time, it is common to see the reported amount of time drop on consecutive queries thanks to plan caching.

- The `Reads` column reports the number of **logical** reads performed by the query. A logical I/O occurs any time SQL Server's query engine requests data, whether from the physical disk or from the buffer cache. If you see high numbers in this column, it may not necessarily indicate a performance problem, because the majority of data may be read from cache. However, even reading data from memory does cost the server in terms of CPU time, so it is a good idea to try to keep any kind of reads to a minimum.

- The `Writes` column reports the number of **physical** writes performed by the query. This means that only writes that were actually persisted to disk during the course of the query will be reported.

By using these basic columns, you can isolate potential candidates for further investigation. First, think about limits that need to be set for any given query in the system. What is the maximum amount of time that a query can be allowed to run? What should the average amount of run time be? By aggregating the Duration column, you can determine whether these times have been exceeded.

Once you've isolated possible problem areas (see the "Granular Analysis" section), you can delve deeper in with more in-depth sets of events. For instance, the Scan:Started event can be used to identify possible queries that are making inefficient use of indexes and therefore may be causing I/O problems. The SP:Recompile event, on the other hand, indicates queries that are getting recompiled by the query optimizer, and may therefore be consuming larger than necessary amounts of CPU time.

Server-Side Traces

It is important to choose your tool wisely when tracing SQL Server during performance tests. The Profiler tool that ships with SQL Server 2005 is extremely useful, and the ease with which it can be used to set up and monitor traces cannot be beat. However, in order to facilitate real-time data collection and display, SQL Server needs to continually stream the data back to the tool—and there is definitely overhead associated with doing so.

In an extremely high-transaction performance test, you should strive to minimize the impact of monitoring on results of the test by using **server-side traces** instead of the Profiler tool. A server-side trace runs in the background on the SQL Server, saving its results to a local file instead of streaming them to Profiler.

To create a server-side trace, first use Profiler to define the events, columns, and filters needed, and then click the Run button. Immediately stop the trace, click the File menu, expand the Export option, and then expand the Script Trace Definition option. Choose For SQL Server 2005 and select a filename to save the script.

Once the script has been saved, open it for editing in SQL Server Management Studio. The following line of the script must be edited, and a valid path must be specified, including a filename:

```
exec @rc = sp_trace_create @TraceID output, 0, N'InsertFileNameHere',
    @maxfilesize, NULL
```

The specified filename should *not* include an extension of any kind. One will automatically be added by the trace. You might also wish to modify the default maximum file size set at the top of the script, which is 5MB. This will help to minimize the number of rollover files created during the trace. I generally set this to 200MB as a starting point.

Once you have finished editing, the script can be run, and the trace will begin collecting data in the background. The generated script will also select back a trace identifier, which you should make note of so that you can easily control the trace later.

When you are done tracing, use the trace identifier to stop and close the trace, using the following T-SQL (in this case the trace identifier is listed as 99):

```
EXEC sp_trace_setstatus @traceid=99, @status=0
EXEC sp_trace_setstatus @traceid=99, @status=2
```

Once the trace is stopped and closed, the fn_trace_gettable function can be used to read the data from the trace file. This function takes two arguments: a full path to the trace file name—including the .trc extension automatically added by SQL Server—and the maximum number of rollover files to read. The following T-SQL would be used to read the trace file from the path C:\Traces\myTrace.trc. The number of rollover files is set high enough that all of the data will be read back, even if the trace rolled over to new files several times:

```
SELECT *
FROM ::fn_trace_gettable('C:\Traces\myTrace.trc', 999)
```

Once selected in this way, the trace data can be used just like any other data in SQL Server. It can be inserted into a table, queried, or aggregated in any number of ways in order to evaluate which queries are potentially causing problems.

Evaluating Performance Counters

For a bigger-picture view of the overall performance of a server, performance counters are an invaluable resource. Similar to SQL Server trace events, there are hundreds of counters from which to choose—but only a handful generally need to be monitored when doing an initial performance evaluation of a SQL Server installation.

The following counters are a good starting point for determining what kinds of performance issues to look for (note, the MSSQL$ counter categories include the name of the SQL Server instance, denoted here by <instance_name>):

- **Processor:% Processor Time** reports the total processor time with respect to the available capacity of the server. If this counter is above 70% during peak load periods, it may be worthwhile to begin investigating which routines are making heavy use of CPU time.

- **PhysicalDisk:Avg. Disk Queue Length** indicates whether processes have to wait to use disk resources. As a disk is fulfilling requests (i.e., reading and writing data), requests that cannot be immediately filled are queued. Too many simultaneous requests results in wait times, which can mean query performance problems. It's a good idea to make sure that queue lengths stay below 1 (meaning, effectively, that there is no queue) whenever possible.

- **PhysicalDisk:Disk Read Bytes/sec** and **PhysicalDisk:Disk Write Bytes/sec** report the number of bytes read from and written to the disk, respectively. These figures are not especially interesting on their own, but coupled with Avg. Disk Queue Length can help to explain problems. Slow SELECT queries coupled with high physical reads and low queue lengths can indicate that the buffer cache is not being effectively utilized. Slow DML queries coupled with high physical writes and high queue lengths are a typical indication of disk contention, and a good sign that you might want to evaluate how to reduce index fragmentation in order to decrease insert and update times.

- **MSSQL$<instance_name>:Locks:Average Wait Time (ms)** reports the average amount of time that queries are waiting on locks. Decreasing lock contention can be quite a challenge, but many shops have discovered that it can be solved in many cases by using either dirty reads (the READ UNCOMMITTED isolation level) or row versioning (the SNAPSHOT isolation level). See Chapter 8 for a discussion of these and other options.

- **MSSQL$<instance_name>:Buffer Manager:Page life expectancy** is the average amount of time, in seconds, that pages remain in buffer cache memory after they are read off of the disk. This counter, coupled with Disk Read Bytes/sec, can help to indicate where disk bottlenecks are occurring—or, it might simply indicate that your server needs more RAM! Either way, values below 300 (i.e., five minutes) may indicate that you have a problem in this area.

- **MSSQL$<instance_name>:Plan Cache:Cache Hit Ratio** and **MSSQL$<instance_name>: Plan Cache:Cached Pages** are counters that deal with the query plan cache. The Cache Hit Ratio counter is the ratio of cache hits to lookups—in other words, what percentage of issued queries are already in the cache. During a performance run, this number should generally start out low (assuming you've rebooted the SQL Server before starting in order to put it into a consistent state) and go up during the course of the run. Toward the end, you should see this number fairly near to 100, indicating that almost all queries are cached. The Cached Pages counter indicates how many 8KB pages of memory are being used for the procedure cache. A low Cache Hit Ratio combined with a high Cached Pages value means that you need to consider fixing the dynamic SQL being used by the system. See Chapter 7 for information on techniques for solving dynamic SQL problems.

These counters can be read using the **System Monitor console** (a.k.a. **performance monitor** or **perfmon**), although many load testing tools have built-in counter collection and reporting mechanisms. SQL Server Profiler also has the ability to import performance counter logs in order to correlate them with traces. This can be useful for helping to pinpoint the cause of especially large spikes in areas such as CPU time and disk utilization.

Big-Picture Analysis

Once you have set up performance counters and traces, you are ready to begin actual performance testing. But this raises the question, "Where to begin?" Especially in a large legacy application, running an end-to-end performance test can be a daunting task.

A first step is to determine what kinds of unit and functional tests exist, and evaluate whether they can be used as starting points for performance tests. Some load testing tools, such as Microsoft's Visual Studio 2005 Team System, have the ability to directly load test prebuilt unit tests. However, most commercial load tools are designed to exercise applications or web code directly. Try to collect as many tests as possible to cover the most-used parts of the application. Absolute coverage is nice, but is unrealistic in many cases.

The next step is to implement a load testing suite using the prebuilt unit and functional tests. Depending on which load tool you are using, this can take some time. The key is to make sure that the load tool passes random or semirandom inputs into any function that goes back to the database, in order to simulate real traffic and make sure that caching does not play too big a part in skewing numbers. Nonrandom inputs can mask disk I/O issues caused by buffer cache recycling.

Set goals for the test to determine what level of load you need to test at. If you are testing on a system that mirrors the application's production environment, try to test at a load equal to what the application encounters during peak periods. If the test servers are less powerful than the production systems, scale back appropriately. Note that it can be difficult to test against servers that aren't scaled the same as production systems. For instance, if the production database system has eight processors and is attached to a dedicated SAN, and the test database system has four processors and internal drives, there may be an I/O mismatch. In this situation it might be advisable to modify SQL Server's processor affinity on the test system such that less processor power is available, which will make the available processor to available disk I/O ratio fall into line with the actual environment in which code needs to run.

In addition to making sure that the test and production systems are scaled similarly, make sure that the SQL Server configurations in both systems are similar. For example, ensure that the maximum degree of parallelism is set similarly so that processors will be used the same way in queries on both the test and production systems. Likewise, you should monitor the RAM options to ensure that they are configured to equivalent percentages on both systems—so if your production system has 16GB of RAM but SQL Server's maximum server memory setting is 12GB, you'll want to set your test system to use 75 percent of the available RAM as well.

Once user goals are set, load tests should generally be configured to step up load slowly, rather than immediately hit the server with the peak number of users. Stepping up load more closely matches most production environments, in which the server may get rebooted or reset during a maintenance period, then slowly accept user requests and warm up its caches before encountering a larger number of requests during more active times of the day. Note that step testing may not be an accurate figure if you're testing a situation such as a cluster failover, in which a server may be subjected to a full load immediately upon starting up.

The goal of a big-picture test is to see how the system scales overall. Try to look at general trends in the performance counters to determine whether the system can handle load spikes, or generally sustained load over long periods of time (again, depending on actual application usage patterns, if possible). SQL Server traces should be run during these tests in order to capture data that can be used later for more granular analysis of specific components.

Granular Analysis

If the results of a big-picture test show that certain areas need work, a more granular investigation into specific routines will generally be necessary. Using aggregated trace data collected from a full-system test, it's important to evaluate both queries and *groups* of queries that are long running or resource intensive.

While it is often tempting to look only at the worst offending queries—for instance, those with the maximum duration—this may not tell the complete story. For instance, you may notice that certain stored procedures are taking longer than others to run during peak load. This may translate into longer user interface wait times, but may not indicate the longest user interface wait times due to stored procedures. This is due to the fact many applications call more than one stored procedure every time the interface needs to be updated with additional data. In these cases it is important to group procedures that are called together and aggregate their total resource utilization.

If stored procedures are called sequentially, duration should be totaled in order to determine the total user wait time for that group, and maximum resource utilization should be noted. If, on the other hand, they are called simultaneously (for instance, on different connections), resource utilization should be totaled in order to determine the group's overall impact on the system, and the maximum duration for the group should be noted.

For example, assume that in a given system, whenever a user logs in, three different stored procedures are called to get data for the first screen. Table 2-1 shows the average data collected for these stored procedures.

Table 2-1. *Stored Procedures Called After Login, with Averaged Data*

Stored Procedure	Duration (ms)	CPU	Reads	Writes
LogSessionStart	422	10	140	1
GetSessionData	224	210	3384	0
GetUserInfo	305	166	6408	0

If the system calls these stored procedures sequentially, the total duration that should be recorded for this group is 951 ms. Since each is called individually, total system impact at any given time will only be as much as the maximum values for each of the given columns. So we record 210 for CPU, 6408 for Reads, and 1 for Writes.

On the other hand, if these stored procedures are called simultaneously, the impact will be much different. Total duration will only be as much as the longest running of the three—422 (assuming, of course, that the system has enough resources available to handle all three requests at the same time). However, CPU time during the run should be recorded as 386, Reads as 9932, and Writes as 1.

By grouping stored procedures in this way, the total impact for a given feature can be assessed. It may be the case that individually long-running stored procedures are not the primary performance culprits, and are actually being overshadowed by groups of seemingly less resource-intensive stored procedures. This can also be an issue with cursors that are doing a large number of very small fetch operations. Each individual fetch may fall under the radar, but taken as a whole, it may become clear that the cursor is using a lot of resources.

Another benefit of this kind of grouping is that further aggregation is possible. For instance, given these figures, it is possible to determine how much impact a certain number of users logging in simultaneously would have on the system. That information can be useful when trying to reach specific scalability goals.

Fixing Problems: Is Focusing on the Obvious Issues Enough?

When evaluating the performance of a system and trying to determine where to look to fix problems, it can be tempting to focus on the obvious worst offenders first. However, some care should be taken to make effective use of your time; in many cases what appear to be the obvious problems are actually side effects of other, more subtle issues.

Looking at duration alone is often the easiest mistake to make when analyzing performance issues. Duration tells a major part of the story, but it does not necessarily indicate a performance problem with that stored procedure. It may indicate that the query had to wait for some other query—or queries—to complete, or that the query was competing with other queries for resources. When performance tuning, it is best to be suspicious of long-running queries with very low reported resource utilization. These are often not the real culprits at all.

By using the granular analysis technique and aggregating, it is often possible to find the real offenders more easily. For instance, in one fairly high-transaction system a procedure was getting called from time to time that was writing 10MB of data to the disk. This procedure reported a high duration, which was interpreted as a possible performance problem. Unfortunately, there wasn't much to tune in that stored procedure, but further aggregate analysis revealed another stored procedure in the system that was getting called over 1000 times a minute and writing as much as 50KB to the disk each time it was called. Each call to the second stored procedure reported a small enough duration that it did not appear to be causing performance problems, yet as it turned out it was causing issues in other areas. By tuning it and reducing the amount of data it was writing on each call, the average duration of the first stored procedure was reduced dramatically.

Introducing the SQLQueryStress Performance Testing Tool

Many of the performance testing techniques discussed in this chapter focus on full-system testing using commercial tools. But sometimes it's important to be able to run a quick performance test against a single query, in order to test ideas or validate changes.

SQLQueryStress is a simple, lightweight performance testing tool, designed to load test individual queries. It includes support for randomization of input parameters in order to test cache repeatability, and includes basic capabilities for reporting on consumed server resources.

This tool can be downloaded along with the source code for this book from the Apress web site (http://www.apress.com) or the book's companion web site (http://www.expertsqlserver2005.com). It will be used throughout the rest of the book to test the performance of various techniques and explain why certain methods exhibit better performance characteristics than others.

In order to get comfortable with the tool, let's take a quick tour of its capabilities. Figure 2-1 shows the main screen.

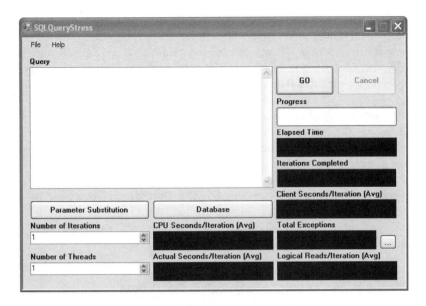

Figure 2-1. *SQLQueryStress main screen*

The main features here are as follows:

The Query area is where you can enter the query that you'd like to load test. This can be either a T-SQL query or a call to a stored procedure. You can also include variable names, which can be used for dynamic parameter substitution.

The Number of Iterations box is where you can define how many times the query should be executed by each virtual user as defined in the Number of Threads box. You can specify up to 200 threads, which will run the query simultaneously in order to simulate load.

The GO button starts the load test. During the test the Progress bar indicates the number of tests completed as compared to the number of tests to be run. The Iterations Completed box displays how many tests have actually been run, and the Total Exceptions box displays the number of exceptions that have occurred during the run. Clicking the ... button next to the Total Exceptions box pops up a window where you can view the details of the exceptions.

There are three types of time statistics collected and displayed by the tool. The Client Seconds/Iteration (Avg) box displays the average runtime over all iterations, as recorded on the client. The CPU Seconds/Iteration (Avg) and Actual Seconds/Iteration (Avg) boxes both display time statistics reported by SQL Server. The former is the average reported CPU time, and the latter is the average reported total query time. Another statistic collected and shown by the tool is the number of logical reads (which is an amalgamation of buffer cache and disk reads), in the Logical Reads/Iteration (Avg) box.

During a run, the load test can be stopped before it is complete using the Cancel button. Keep in mind that a lot of tear-down needs to take place in order to cleanly cancel a run. Especially if you're running a lot of simultaneous threads, you may see cancellations take several seconds.

Before a load test can be run, a database connection must be set up. This is done by clicking the Database button, which launches a connection settings dialog box.

The final button on the main screen is Parameter Substitution. This feature allows you to supply SQLQueryStress with a set of input values that will be dynamically applied to parameters of your query for each run, such that data caching does not incorrectly skew the results of the test.

For an example of where this might be used, consider the uspGetEmployeeManagers stored procedure in the SQL Server 2005 AdventureWorks sample database. This stored procedure has a single parameter, @EmployeeID. If this procedure were load tested in a loop and the same value were used for the parameter for every call, every run after the first would be faster thanks to data caching. This would defeat the accuracy of the test, because we would not know how the procedure would behave if uncached data was requested. To fix this problem, it's important to pass in many different values during the course of the load test.

To set this up, the query should be entered into the Query text box with a variable in the place of any parameters that need to be substituted, as shown in Figure 2-2.

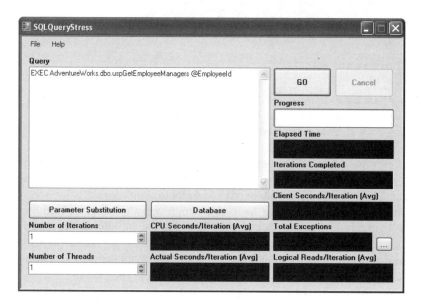

Figure 2-2. *SQLQueryStress main screen with parameterized query*

Once the query is entered in the text box, click the Parameter Substitution button, which brings up the screen shown in Figure 2-3.

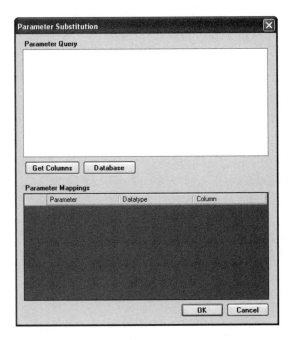

Figure 2-3. *SQLQueryStress parameter substitution screen*

The most important feature of this screen is the Parameter Query text box. This is where you define the query that pulls back the parameter values you'd like to dynamically substitute for the main query. In this case, we might want to pass in every employee ID in the Adventure-Works HumanResources.Employee table, so the following query might be used:

```
SELECT EmployeeId
FROM AdventureWorks.HumanResources.Employee
```

Once the parameter query is entered, the Get Columns button is used to set up the Parameter Mappings grid to allow the user to map the columns from the parameter query to the parameters defined in the main query. Each column in the parameter query can be mapped to one or more variables found in the main query. The completed mapping screen for this query is shown in Figure 2-4.

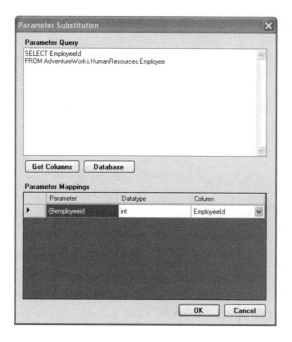

Figure 2-4. *SQLQueryStress parameter substitution screen with mapping*

After clicking OK, the load test can be run, and for each iteration a new value will be substituted in for the @EmployeeID parameter. If the tool runs out of values, it will loop around and reuse previous values in the set, until it has completed the requested number of iterations.

From the File menu on the main screen, you can enter the Options dialog box, shown in Figure 2-5. These options allow you to control some of the parameters for the test, in order to simulate various settings.

- Changing the **Connection Timeout** option makes the tool wait longer before reporting an exception if the target server does not respond.

- **Connection Pooling** can be disabled to show the affect of creating and destroying a new connection on each test iteration.

- Modification of the **Command Timeout** option will make the tool report an exception if the query does not complete in time.

- Changing the **Collect I/O Statistics** and **Collect Time Statistics** options will make the tool not collect the server time (CPU and Actual) and Reads statistics. This will make the run somewhat lighter-weight from a resource utilization point of view.

- Finally, the **Force Client Retrieval of Data** option forces the tool to loop over all data returned by the query, thereby ensuring that it is sent over the network by SQL Server. By not setting this option, there is a chance—especially with larger queries—that the majority of the data may stay buffered in SQL Server, thereby not creating a realistic amount of network stress.

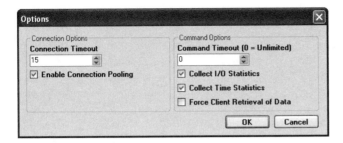

Figure 2-5. *SQLQueryStress test options configuration*

As a final note, it's important to mention that inside of the File menu is an option to save the settings for a particular query, including database connection information and parameter settings. It can take a bit of time to set up a full SQLQueryStress test, and there is no reason to lose the work if you need to rerun the same test more than once.

Summary

Software testing is a complex field, but it is necessary that developers understand enough of it to make the development process more effective. By implementing testing processes during development, more robust software can be delivered with less expense.

Database developers, like application developers, must learn to exploit unit tests in order to increase software project success rates. Database routines will definitely benefit from unit testing, although performance testing is extremely important as well—and much more popular with management teams.

During performance testing, make sure to carefully analyze the data. By recombining the numbers in various ways based on application usage patterns, it is often possible to discover performance issues that are not obvious from the raw numbers.

Testing is one of the important factors that helps differentiate good developers from truly great ones. If you're not already testing your software during the development process, the methodologies presented here can help you to implement a set of procedures that will get you closer to the next level.

■ ■ ■

CHAPTER 3

Errors and Exceptions

As software developers, we often daydream of a perfect world of bug-free software—developed on a remote island while sitting under a palm tree sipping a fruity beverage. But alas, back in the cubicle farm sipping on acrid coffee sit hoards of real developers, fighting real-world bugs that are not always our fault or under our control in any way.

Exceptions can occur in even the most stringently tested software, simply because not every condition can be checked for in advance. For instance, do you know what will happen if a janitor, while cleaning the data-center floor, accidentally slops some mop water into the fan enclosure of the database server? It might crash, or it might not; it might just cause some component to fail somewhere deep in the app, sending up a strange error message.

Although most exceptions won't be so far out of the realm of testability, it is certainly important to understand how to deal with them when and if they occur. It is also imperative that SQL Server developers understand how to work with errors—both those thrown by the server itself and custom errors built specifically for when problems occur during the run time of an application.

Exceptions vs. Errors

The terms **exception** and **error**, while often used interchangeably by developers, actually refer to slightly different conditions. An error can occur if something goes wrong during the course of a program, or it can be purely informational in nature. For instance, a program telling a user that a question mark is an invalid character for a filename is considered to be an error message. However, this may or may not mean that the program itself is in an invalid state.

An exception, on the other hand, is an error that is the result of an **exceptional circumstance**. For example, if a network library is being used to send packets and the network connection is suddenly dropped due to someone unplugging a cable, the library might throw an exception. An exception tells a caller that something went wrong and the routine aborted unexpectedly. If the caller does not **handle** the exception (i.e., capture it), its execution will also abort. This process will keep repeating until the exception is handled, or until it reaches the highest level of the call stack, at which point the entire program will fail.

Another way to think about exceptions and errors is to think of general errors as *expected* by the program. The error message that occurs when a filename contains an invalid character is informational in nature because the developer of the program predicted that such an occurrence would be common and created a code path to specifically deal with it. A dropped network connection, on the other hand, could be caused by any number of circumstances and therefore is much more difficult to handle specifically. Instead, the solution is to raise an exception and fail. The exception can then be handled by a routine higher in the call stack, which can decide what course of action to take in order to solve the problem.

Note There is some debate in the software community on whether exceptions should really be used for only exceptional circumstances. In my opinion, due to the fact that exceptions can cause abort conditions, they should be used sparingly. However, this is not always the pattern seen in commercial libraries. For example, Microsoft's .NET Framework 2.0 uses an `InvalidOperationException` to tell the caller that an instance of `Queue<T>` is empty if the caller tries to use the `Dequeue` method. Personally, I find this to be a blatant misuse of exceptions. That said, there is certainly an upside to using exceptions over errors, which is that it's more difficult for the caller to ignore an exception, since it will cause code to abort if not properly handled. If you're designing an interface that needs to absolutely ensure that the caller sees a certain condition when and if it occurs, it might make sense to use an exception rather than an error.

How Exceptions Work in SQL Server

The first step in understanding how to handle errors and exceptions in SQL Server is to take a look at how the server itself deals with error conditions. Unlike many other programming languages, SQL Server has an exception model that involves different behaviors for different types of exceptions. This can cause unexpected behavior when error conditions do occur, so careful programming is essential when dealing with T-SQL exceptions.

To begin with, think about connecting to a SQL Server and issuing some T-SQL. First, you must establish a **connection** to the server by issuing login credentials. The connection also determines what database will be used as the default for scope resolution (i.e., finding objects— more on this in a bit). Once connected, you can issue a **batch** of T-SQL. A batch consists of one or more T-SQL **statements**, which will be compiled together to form an execution plan.

The behavior of the exceptions thrown by SQL Server mostly follows this same pattern. Depending on the exception, a statement, a batch, or an entire connection may be aborted. Let's take a look at some examples to clarify what this means.

Statement-Level Exceptions

A statement-level exception aborts only the current statement that is running within a batch of T-SQL, allowing the subsequent statements within the batch to run. To see this behavior, use SQL Server Management Studio to execute a batch that includes an exception, followed by a PRINT statement. For instance:

```
SELECT POWER(2, 32)
PRINT 'This will print!'
GO
```

Running this batch results in the following output:

```
Msg 232, Level 16, State 3, Line 1
Arithmetic overflow error for type int, value = 4294967296.000000.
This will print!
```

When this batch was run, the POWER(2, 32) caused an integer overflow, which threw the exception. However, only the SELECT statement was aborted. The rest of the batch continued to run, which in this case means that the PRINT statement printed its message.

Batch-Level Exceptions

Unlike a statement-level exception, a batch-level exception does not allow the rest of the batch to continue running. The statement that throws the exception will be aborted, and any remaining statements in the batch will not be run. An example of a batch-aborting exception is an invalid conversion, such as the following:

```
SELECT CONVERT(INT, 'abc')
PRINT 'This will NOT print!'
GO
```

The output of this batch is as follows:

```
Msg 245, Level 16, State 1, Line 1
Conversion failed when converting the varchar value 'abc' to data type int.
```

In this case, the conversion exception occurred in the SELECT statement, which aborted the entire batch. The PRINT statement was not allowed to run.

Batch-level exceptions might be easily confused with connection-level exceptions (which drop the connection to the server), but after a batch-level exception, the connection is still free to send other batches. For instance:

```
SELECT CONVERT(INT, 'abc')
GO
PRINT 'This will print!'
GO
```

In this case there are two batches sent to SQL Server, separated by the batch separator, GO. The first batch throws a conversion exception, but the second batch is still run. This results in the following output:

```
Msg 245, Level 16, State 1, Line 2
Conversion failed when converting the varchar value 'abc' to data type int.
This will print!
```

Batch-level exceptions do not affect only the scope in which the exception occurs. The exception will **bubble up** to the next level of execution, aborting every call in the stack. This can be illustrated by creating the following stored procedure:

```
CREATE PROCEDURE ConversionException
AS
BEGIN
    SELECT CONVERT(INT, 'abc')
END
GO
```

Running this stored procedure with a PRINT shows that even though the exception occurred in an inner scope (within the stored procedure), the outer batch is still aborted:

```
EXEC ConversionException
PRINT 'This will NOT print!'
GO
```

The result of this batch is the same as if no stored procedure was used:

```
Msg 245, Level 16, State 1, Line 1
Conversion failed when converting the varchar value 'abc' to data type int.
```

Parsing and Scope-Resolution Exceptions

Exceptions that occur both during parsing and during the scope-resolution phase of compilation appear at first to behave just like batch-level exceptions. However, they actually have a slightly different behavior. If the exception occurs in the same scope as the rest of the batch, these exceptions will behave just like a batch-level exception. If, on the other hand, an exception occurs in a lower level of scope, these exceptions will behave just like statement-level exceptions—at least, as far as the outer batch is concerned.

As an example, consider the following batch, which includes a malformed SELECT statement (this is a parse exception):

```
SELECTxzy FROM SomeTable
PRINT 'This will NOT print!'
GO
```

In this case, the PRINT statement is not run because the whole batch is discarded during the parse phase. The output is the following exception:

```
Msg 156, Level 15, State 1, Line 1
Incorrect syntax near the keyword 'FROM'.
```

To see the difference in behavior, the SELECT statement can be executed as dynamic SQL using the EXEC function. This causes the SELECT statement to execute in a different scope, showing the change in behavior from batch-like to statement-like. The following T-SQL can be run to observe the change:

```
EXEC('SELECTxzy FROM SomeTable')
PRINT 'This will print!'
GO
```

The PRINT statement is now executed, even though the exception occurred:

```
Msg 156, Level 15, State 1, Line 1
Incorrect syntax near the keyword 'FROM'.
This will print!
```

This type of exception also occurs during **scope resolution**. Essentially, SQL Server processes queries in two phases. The first phase parses and validates the query and ensures that the T-SQL is well formed. The second phase is the compilation phase, during which an execution plan is built and objects referenced in the query are resolved. If a query is submitted to SQL Server via ad hoc SQL from an application or dynamic SQL within a stored procedure, these two phases happen together. However, within the context of stored procedures, SQL Server exploits **late binding**. This means that the parse phase happens when the stored procedure is created, and the compile phase (and therefore scope resolution) occurs only when the stored procedure is executed.

To see what this means, create the following stored procedure (assuming that a table called SomeTable does not exist in the current database):

```
CREATE PROCEDURE NonExistantTable
AS
BEGIN
    SELECT xyz
    FROM SomeTable
END
GO
```

Although SomeTable does not exist, the stored procedure is created—the T-SQL parses without any errors. However, upon running the stored procedure, an exception is thrown:

```
Msg 208, Level 16, State 1, Procedure NonExistantTable, Line 4
Invalid object name 'SomeTable'.
```

Like the parse exception, scope-resolution exceptions behave similarly to batch-level exceptions within the same scope, and similarly to statement-level exceptions in the outer scope. Since the stored procedure creates a new scope, hitting this exception within the procedure aborts the rest of the procedure, but any T-SQL encountered in the same batch after execution of the procedure will still run. For instance:

```
EXEC NonExistantTable
PRINT 'This will print!'
GO
```

Connection and Server-Level Exceptions

The remaining types of exceptions that can be thrown by SQL Server are those that abort the entire connection and those that cause the server itself to crash. These types of exceptions are generally caused by internal SQL Server bugs and are, thankfully, quite rare. At the time of this writing, I cannot provide any examples of these types of exceptions, as I am not aware of any conditions in SQL Server 2005 that cause them.

The XACT_ABORT Setting

Although users do not have much control over the behavior of exceptions thrown by SQL Server, there is one setting that can be modified on a per-connection basis. Turning on the XACT_ABORT setting makes all statement-level, parsing, and scope-resolution exceptions behave like batch-level exceptions. This means that control will always be immediately returned to the client any time an exception is thrown by SQL Server.[1]

To enable XACT_ABORT for a connection, the following T-SQL is used:

```
SET XACT_ABORT ON
```

This setting will remain enabled for the connection—even if it was set in a lower level of scope, such as in a stored procedure or dynamic SQL—until it is disabled using the following T-SQL:

```
SET XACT_ABORT OFF
```

To illustrate the effect of this setting on the behavior of exceptions, let's review a couple of the exceptions already covered. Recall that the following integer overflow exception operates at the statement level:

```
SELECT POWER(2, 32)
PRINT 'This will print!'
GO
```

Enabling the XACT_ABORT setting before running this T-SQL changes the output, resulting in the PRINT statement not getting executed:

```
SET XACT_ABORT ON
SELECT POWER(2, 32)
PRINT 'This will NOT print!'
GO
```

The output from running this batch is as follows:

```
Msg 232, Level 16, State 3, Line 2
Arithmetic overflow error for type int, value = 4294967296.000000.
```

---

1. This assumes that the exception is not handled. For more information, refer to the section "SQL Server's TRY/CATCH Syntax" later in this chapter.

Another example is a parsing exception in a lower scope. Recall that by default, the following exception does not abort the outer batch, but only the EXEC function:

```
EXEC('SELECTxzy FROM SomeTable')
PRINT 'This will print!'
GO
```

Just like the overflow exception, with XACT_ABORT set, the outer batch will be aborted in addition to the EXEC function, resulting in the PRINT statement not being evaluated.

In addition to controlling exception behavior, XACT_ABORT also modifies how transactions behave when exceptions occur. See the section "Transactions and Exceptions" later in this chapter for more information.

Dissecting an Error Message

A SQL Server exception has a few different component parts, each of which are represented within the text of the error message. Each exception has an associated error number, error level, and state. Error messages can also contain additional diagnostic information including line numbers and the name of the procedure in which the exception occurred.

Error Number

The error number of an exception is represented by the text "Msg" within the error text. For example, the error number of the following exception is 156:

```
Msg 156, Level 15, State 1, Line 1
Incorrect syntax near the keyword 'FROM'.
```

SQL Server generally returns the error message with the exception, so having the error number usually doesn't assist from a problem-solving point of view. However, there are times when knowing the error number can be of use. Examples include use of the @@ERROR function, or when doing specialized error handling using the TRY/CATCH syntax (see the sections "Exception 'Handling' Using @@ERROR" and "SQL Server's TRY/CATCH Syntax" later in the chapter for details on these topics).

The error number can also be used to look up the templatized, localized text of the error in the sys.messages catalog view. The message_id column contains the error number, and the language_id column can be used to get the message in the correct language. The following T-SQL returns the English text for error 208:

```
SELECT text
FROM sys.messages
WHERE
    message_id = 208
    AND language_id = 1033
```

The output of this query is as shown here:

```
Invalid object name '%.*ls'.
```

See the section "SQL Server's RAISERROR Function" for more information about error message templates.

Error Level

The Level tag within an error message indicates a number between 1 and 25. This number can sometimes be used to either classify an exception or determine its severity. Unfortunately, the key word is "sometimes": the error levels as generated by SQL Server are highly inconsistent and should generally not be used in order to make decisions about exceptions.

The following exception, based on its error message, is of error level 15:

```
Msg 156, Level 15, State 1, Line 1
Incorrect syntax near the keyword 'FROM'.
```

The error levels for each exception can be queried from the sys.messages view, using the severity column. A severity of less than 11 indicates that a message is a **warning**. If severity is 11 or greater, the message is considered to be an **error** and can be broken down into the following documented categories:

- **Error levels 11 through 16** are documented as "errors that can be corrected by the user."[2] The majority of exceptions thrown by SQL Server are in this range, including constraint violations, parsing and compilation errors, and most other run time exceptions.

- **Error levels 17 through 19** are more serious exceptions. These include out-of-memory exceptions, disk space exceptions, internal SQL Server errors, and other similar violations. Many of these are automatically logged to the SQL Server error log when they are thrown. Those that are logged have a value of 1 for the is_event_logged column of sys.messages.

- **Error levels 20 through 25** are fatal connection and server-level exceptions. These include various types of data corruption, network, logging, and other critical errors. Virtually all of the exceptions at this level are automatically logged.

Although the error levels that make up each range are individually documented in Books Online, the documentation is inconsistent or incorrect in many cases. For instance, level 11 is documented as indicating that "the given object or entity does not exist."[3] However, error 208, "Invalid object name," is a level-16 exception. Many other errors have equally unpredictable levels, and it is recommended that client software not be programmed to rely on the error levels for handling logic.

In addition to the levels themselves, there is for the most part no discernable pattern regarding error severities and whether the error will behave on the statement or batch level. For instance, both errors 245 ("Conversion failed") and 515 ("Cannot insert the value NULL ... column does not allow nulls") are level-16 exceptions. However, 245 is a batch-level exception, whereas 515 acts at the statement level.

---

2. SQL Server 2005 Books Online, "Database Engine Error Severities," http://msdn2.microsoft.com/en-us/library/ms164086.aspx, December 2005.

3. Ibid.

Error State

Each exception has a State tag, which contains information about the exception that is used internally by SQL Server. The values that SQL Server uses for this tag are not documented, so this tag is generally not helpful. The following exception has a state of 1:

```
Msg 156, Level 15, State 1, Line 1
Incorrect syntax near the keyword 'FROM'.
```

Additional Information

In addition to the error number, level, and state, many errors also carry additional information about the line number on which the exception occurred and the procedure in which it occurred, if relevant. The following error message indicates that an invalid object name was referenced on line 4 of the procedure NonExistantTable:

```
Msg 208, Level 16, State 1, Procedure NonExistantTable, Line 4
Invalid object name 'SomeTable'.
```

If an exception does not occur within a procedure, the line number refers to the line in the batch in which the statement that caused the exception was sent.

Be careful not to confuse batches separated with GO with a single batch. Consider the following T-SQL:

```
SELECT 1
GO
SELECT 2
GO
SELECT 1/0
GO
```

In this case, although a divide-by-zero exception occurs on line 5 of the T-SQL itself, the exception will actually report line 1:

```
-----------
1

(1 row(s) affected)


-----------
2

(1 row(s) affected)


-----------
Msg 8134, Level 16, State 1, Line 1
Divide by zero error encountered.
```

The reason for the reset of the line number is that GO is not actually a T-SQL command. It's an arbitrary identifier recognized by the SQL Server client tools (e.g., SQL Server Management Studio and SQLCMD). GO tells the client to separate the batches, sending each to SQL Server serially. So in the preceding example, SQL Server sees three individual batches of T-SQL, and does not know how many lines of code are displayed on the client side.

This seemingly erroneous line number is reported as such because each batch is sent separately to the query engine. SQL Server does not know that on the client (e.g., in SQL Server Management Studio) these batches are all joined together on the screen. As far as SQL Server is concerned, these are three completely separate units of T-SQL that happen to be sent on the same connection.

SQL Server's RAISERROR Function

In addition to the exceptions that SQL Server itself throws, users can raise exceptions within T-SQL by using a function called RAISERROR. The general form for this function is as follows:

```
RAISERROR ( { msg_id | msg_str | @local_variable }
    { ,severity ,state }
    [ ,argument [ ,...n ] ] )
    [ WITH option [ ,...n ] ]
```

The first argument can be an ad hoc message in the form of a string or variable, or a valid error number from the message_id column of sys.messages. If a string is specified, it can include format designators that can then be filled using the optional arguments specified at the end of the function call.

The second argument, severity, can be used to enforce some level of control over the behavior of the exception, similar to what SQL Server uses error levels for. For the most part, the same exception ranges apply: exception levels between 1 and 10 result in a warning, levels between 11 and 18 are considered normal user errors, and those above 18 are considered serious and can only be raised by members of the sysadmin fixed server role. User exceptions raised over level 20, just like those raised by SQL Server, cause the connection to break. Beyond these ranges, there is no real control afforded to user-raised exceptions, and all are considered to be statement level—this is even true with XACT_ABORT set.

The state argument can be any value between 1 and 127, and has no effect on the behavior of the exception. It can be used to add additional coded information to be carried by the exception—but it's probably just as easy to add that data to the error message itself in most cases. I generally use a value of 1 for state when raising custom exceptions.

The simplest way to use RAISERROR is to pass in a string containing an error message, and set the appropriate error level. For general exceptions, I usually use 16:

```
RAISERROR('General exception', 16, 1)
```

This results in the following output:

```
Msg 50000, Level 16, State 1, Line 1
General exception
```

Note that the error number used in this case is 50000, which is the generic user-defined error number that will be used whenever passing in a string for the first argument to RAISERROR.

Formatting Error Messages

When defining error messages, it is generally useful to format the text in some way. For example, think about how you might write code to work with a number of product IDs, dynamically retrieved, in a loop. You might have a local variable called @ProductId, which contains the current ID that the code is working with. You might wish to define a custom exception that should be thrown when a problem occurs—and it would probably be a good idea to return the current value of @ProductId along with the error message.

In this case, there are a couple of ways of sending back the data with the exception. The first is to dynamically build an error message string:

```
DECLARE @ProductId INT
SET @ProductId = 100

/* ... problem occurs ... */

DECLARE @ErrorMessage VARCHAR(200)
SET @ErrorMessage =
    'Problem with ProductId ' + CONVERT(VARCHAR, @ProductId)

RAISERROR(@ErrorMessage, 16, 1)
```

Executing this batch results in the following output:

```
Msg 50000, Level 16, State 1, Line 10
Problem with ProductId 100
```

While this works for this case, dynamically building up error messages is not the most elegant development practice. A step in a better direction is to make use of a format designator and to pass @ProductId as an optional parameter:

```
DECLARE @ProductId INT
SET @ProductId = 100

/* ... problem occurs ... */

RAISERROR('Problem with ProductId %i', 16, 1, @ProductId)
```

Executing this batch results in the same output as before, but requires quite a bit less code, and you don't have to worry about defining extra variables or building up messy conversion code. The %i embedded in the error message is a format designator that means "integer." The other most commonly used format designator is %s, for "string."

You can embed as many designators as necessary in an error message, and they will be substituted in the order in which optional arguments are appended:

```
DECLARE @ProductId1 INT
SET @ProductId1 = 100

DECLARE @ProductId2 INT
SET @ProductId2 = 200
```

```
DECLARE @ProductId3 INT
SET @ProductId3 = 300

/* ... problem occurs ... */

RAISERROR('Problem with ProductIds %i, %i, %i',
    16, 1, @ProductId1, @ProductId2, @ProductId3)
```

This results in the following output:

```
Msg 50000, Level 16, State 1, Line 12
Problem with ProductIds 100, 200, 300
```

■**Note** Readers familiar with C programming will notice that the format designators used by RAISERROR are the same as those used by the C language's printf function. For a complete list of the supported designators, see the "RAISERROR (Transact-SQL)" topic in SQL Server 2005 Books Online.

Creating Persistent Custom Error Messages

Formatting messages using format designators instead of building up strings dynamically is a step in the right direction, but it does not solve one final problem: what if you need to use the same error message in multiple places? You could simply use the same exact arguments to RAISERROR in each routine in which the exception is needed, but that might cause a maintenance headache if you ever needed to change the error message. In addition, each of the exceptions would only be able to use the default user-defined error number, 50000, making programming against these custom exceptions much more difficult.

Luckily, SQL Server takes care of these problems quite nicely, by providing a mechanism by which custom error messages can be added to sys.messages. Exceptions using these error messages can then be raised by using RAISERROR and passing in the error number as the first parameter.

To create a persistent custom error message, use the sp_addmessage stored procedure. This stored procedure allows the user to specify custom messages for message numbers over 50000. In addition to an error message, users can specify a default severity. Messages added using sp_addmessage are scoped at the server level, so if you have multiple applications hosted on the same server, be aware of whether they define custom messages and whether there is any overlap—you may need to set up a new instance of SQL Server for one or more of the applications in order to allow them to create their exceptions. When developing new applications that use custom messages, try to choose a random range in which to create your messages, in order to avoid overlaps with other applications in shared environments. Remember that you can use any number between 50000 and 2147483647, and you don't need to stay in the 50000 range.

Adding a custom message is as easy as calling sp_addmessage and defining a message number and the message text. The following T-SQL defines the message from the previous section as error message number 50005:

```
EXEC sp_addmessage
    @msgnum = 50005,
    @severity = 16,
    @msgtext = 'Problem with ProductIds %i, %i, %i'
```

Once this T-SQL is executed, an exception can be raised using this error message, by calling RAISERROR with the correct error number:

```
RAISERROR(50005, 15, 1, 100, 200, 300)
```

This causes the following output to be sent back to the client:

```
Msg 50005, Level 15, State 1, Line 1
Problem with ProductIds 100, 200, 300
```

Note that when calling RAISERROR in this case, severity 15 was specified, even though the error was defined with severity 16. This brings up an important point about severities of custom errors: whatever severity is specified in the call to RAISERROR will override the severity that was defined for the error. However, the default severity will be used if you pass a negative value for that argument to RAISERROR:

```
RAISERROR(50005, -1, 1, 100, 200, 300)
```

This produces the following output (notice that Level is now 16, as defined):

```
Msg 50005, Level 16, State 1, Line 1
Problem with ProductIds 100, 200, 300
```

It is recommended that, unless you are overriding the severity for a specific reason, you always use -1 for the severity argument when raising a custom exception.

Changing the text of an exception once defined is also easy using sp_addmessage. To do so, pass the optional @Replace argument, setting its value to 'Replace', as in the following T-SQL:

```
EXEC sp_addmessage
    @msgnum = 50005,
    @severity = 16,
    @msgtext = 'Problem with ProductId numbers %i, %i, %i',
    @Replace = 'Replace'
```

■**Note** In addition to being able to add a message and set a severity, sp_addmessage supports localization of messages for different languages. The examples here do not show localization; instead, messages will be created for the user's default language. For details on localized messages, refer to SQL Server 2005 Books Online.

Logging User-Thrown Exceptions

Another useful feature of RAISERROR is the ability to log messages to SQL Server's error log. This can come in handy especially when working with automated code, such as T-SQL running in SQL Server Agent jobs. In order to log any exception, use the WITH LOG option of the RAISERROR function, as in the following T-SQL:

```
RAISERROR('This will be logged.', 16, 1) WITH LOG
```

Note that specific access rights are required to log an error. The user executing the RAISERROR function must either be a member of the sysadmin fixed server role or have ALTER TRACE permissions.

Monitoring Exception Events with Traces

Some application developers go too far in handling exceptions, and end up creating applications that hide problems by catching every exception that occurs and not reporting it. In such cases it can be extremely difficult to debug issues without knowing whether an exception is being thrown. Should you find yourself in this situation, you can use a Profiler trace to monitor for exceptions occurring in SQL Server.

In order to monitor for exceptions, start a trace and select the Exception and User Error Message events. For most exceptions with a severity greater than 10, both events will fire. The Exception event will contain all of the data associated with the exception except for the actual message. This includes the error number, severity, state, and line number. The User Error Message event will contain the formatted error message as it was sent to the client.

For warnings (messages with a severity of less than 11), only the User Error Message event will fire. You may also notice error 208 exceptions ("Object not found") without corresponding error message events. These exceptions are used internally by the SQL Server query optimizer during the scope-resolution phase of compilation and can be safely ignored.

Exception Handling

Understanding when, why, and how SQL Server throws exceptions is great, but the real goal is to actually *do something* when an exception occurs. **Exception handling** refers to the ability to **catch** an exception when it occurs, rather than simply letting it bubble up to the next level of scope. This is a capability that has not been possible in T-SQL until SQL Server 2005, and its addition to the language adds some interesting development possibilities.

Why Handle Exceptions in T-SQL?

Exception handling in T-SQL should be thought of as no different from exception handling in any other language. A generally accepted programming practice is to handle exceptions at the *lowest possible scope*, in order to keep them from interacting with higher levels of the application. If an exception can be caught at a lower level and dealt with there, higher-level modules will not require special code to handle the exception and therefore can concentrate on whatever their purpose is. This means that every routine in the application becomes simpler, more maintainable, and therefore quite possibly more robust.

Put another way, exceptions should be *encapsulated* as much as possible—knowledge of the internal exceptions of other modules is yet another form of coupling, not much different than some of the types discussed in the first chapter of this book.

Keep in mind that encapsulation of exceptions is really something that must be handled on a case-by-case basis. But the basic rule is, if you can "fix" the exception one way or another without letting the caller ever know it even occurred, that is probably a good place to encapsulate.

Exception "Handling" Using @@ERROR

Versions of SQL Server prior to SQL Server 2005 did not have true exception-handling capabilities. Any exception that occurred would be passed back to the caller, regardless of any action taken by the code of the stored procedure or query in which it was thrown. The general method used to "handle" errors in those versions of SQL Server is still useful in some cases—and a lot of legacy code will be around for quite a while—so a quick review is definitely warranted.

The @@ERROR function is quite simple: it returns 0 if the last statement in the batch did not throw an error of severity 11 or greater. If the last statement did throw an error, it returns the error number. For example, consider the following T-SQL:

```
SELECT 1/0 AS DivideByZero
SELECT @@ERROR AS ErrorNumber
```

This returns the following output:

```
DivideByZero
-----------
Msg 8134, Level 16, State 1, Line 1
Divide by zero error encountered.

ErrorNumber
-----------
8134

(1 row(s) affected)
```

By checking to see whether the value of @@ERROR is nonzero, it is possible to do some very primitive error handling. Unfortunately, this is also quite error prone due to the nature of @@ERROR and the fact that it only operates on the *last statement* executed in the batch. Many developers new to T-SQL are quite surprised by the output of the following batch:

```
SELECT 1/0 AS DivideByZero
IF @@ERROR <> 0
    SELECT @@ERROR AS ErrorNumber
```

The output result is as follows:

```
DivideByZero
------------
Msg 8134, Level 16, State 1, Line 1
Divide by zero error encountered.

ErrorNumber
-----------
0

(1 row(s) affected)
```

The solution to this problem is to set a variable to the value of @@ERROR after every statement in a batch that requires error handling. Of course, if even a single statement is missed,
holes may be left in the strategy, and some errors may escape notice.

Even with these problems, @@ERROR still has a place in SQL Server 2005. It is a simple, lightweight alternative to the full-blown exception-handling capabilities that have been added to
the language, and it has the additional benefit of *not* catching the exception. In some cases,
full encapsulation is not the best option, and using @@ERROR will allow the developer to take
some action—for instance, logging of the exception—while still passing it back to the caller.

SQL Server's TRY/CATCH Syntax

The standard error handling construct in many programming languages—now including T-SQL—
is known as *try/catch*. The idea behind this construct is to set up two sections (a.k.a. **blocks**) of
code. The first section, the **try block**, contains exception-prone code to be "tried." The second
section contains code that should be executed in the event that the code in the try block fails,
and an exception occurs. This is called the **catch block**. As soon as any exception occurs within
the try block, code execution immediately jumps into the catch block. This is also known as
catching an exception.

In T-SQL, try/catch is implemented using the following basic form:

```
BEGIN TRY
    --Code to try here
END TRY
BEGIN CATCH
    --Catch the exception here
END CATCH
```

Any type of exception—except for connection or server-level exceptions—that occurs
between BEGIN TRY and END TRY will cause the code between BEGIN CATCH and END CATCH to be
immediately executed, bypassing any other code left in the try block.

As a first example, consider the following T-SQL:

```
BEGIN TRY
    SELECT 1/0 AS DivideByZero
END TRY
BEGIN CATCH
    SELECT 'Exception Caught!' AS CatchMessage
END CATCH
```

Running this batch produces the following output:

```
DivideByZero
------------

(0 row(s) affected)

CatchMessage
-----------------
Exception Caught!

(1 row(s) affected)
```

The interesting things to note here are that, first and foremost, there is no reported exception. We can see that an exception occurred because code execution jumped to the CATCH block, but the exception was successfully handled, and the client is not aware that an exception occurred. Second, notice that an empty result set is returned for the SELECT statement that caused the exception. Had the exception not been handled, no result set would have been returned. By sending back an empty result set, the implied contract of the SELECT statement is honored (more or less, depending on what the client was actually expecting).

Although already mentioned, it needs to be stressed that when using TRY/CATCH, all exceptions within the TRY block will immediately abort execution of the remainder of the TRY block. Therefore, the following T-SQL has the exact same output as the last example:

```
BEGIN TRY
    SELECT 1/0 AS DivideByZero
    SELECT 1 AS NoError
END TRY
BEGIN CATCH
    SELECT 'Exception Caught!' AS CatchMessage
END CATCH
```

Finally, it is worth noting that parsing and compilation exceptions will not be caught using TRY/CATCH, nor will they ever have a chance to be caught—an exception will be thrown by SQL Server before any of the code is ever actually executed.

Getting Extended Error Information in the Catch Block

In addition to the ability to catch an exception, SQL Server 2005 offers a series of new functions that are available within the CATCH block. These functions, a list of which follows, enable the developer to write code that retrieves information about the exception that occurred in the TRY block.

- ERROR_MESSAGE

- ERROR_NUMBER

- ERROR_SEVERITY

- ERROR_STATE

- ERROR_LINE

- ERROR_PROCEDURE

These functions take no input arguments and are fairly self-explanatory based on their names. However, it is important to point out that unlike @@ERROR, the values returned by these functions are not reset after every statement. They are persistent for the entire CATCH block. Therefore, logic such as that used in the following T-SQL works:

```
BEGIN TRY
    SELECT CONVERT(int, 'ABC') AS ConvertException
END TRY
BEGIN CATCH
    IF ERROR_NUMBER() = 123
        SELECT 'Error 123'
    ELSE
        SELECT ERROR_NUMBER() AS ErrorNumber
END CATCH
```

As expected, in this case the error number is correctly reported:

```
ConvertException
----------------


(0 row(s) affected)


ErrorNumber
-----------
245


(1 row(s) affected)
```

These functions, especially ERROR_NUMBER, allow for coding of specific paths for certain exceptions. For example, if a developer knows that a certain piece of code is likely to cause an exception that can be programmatically fixed, that exception number can be checked for in the CATCH block.

Rethrowing Exceptions

A common feature in most languages that have try/catch capabilities is the ability to **rethrow** exceptions from the catch block. This means that the exception that originally occurred in the try block will be raised again, as if it was not handled at all. This is useful when you need to do some handling of the exception but also let the caller know that something went wrong in the routine.

T-SQL does not include any kind of built-in rethrow functionality. However, it is fairly easy behavior to mock up based on the CATCH block error functions, in conjunction with RAISERROR. The following example shows a basic implementation of rethrow in T-SQL:

```
BEGIN TRY
    SELECT CONVERT(int, 'ABC') AS ConvertException
END TRY
BEGIN CATCH
    DECLARE
        @ERROR_SEVERITY INT,
        @ERROR_STATE INT,
        @ERROR_NUMBER INT,
        @ERROR_LINE INT,
        @ERROR_MESSAGE VARCHAR(245)

    SELECT
        @ERROR_SEVERITY = ERROR_SEVERITY(),
        @ERROR_STATE = ERROR_STATE(),
        @ERROR_NUMBER = ERROR_NUMBER(),
        @ERROR_LINE = ERROR_LINE(),
        @ERROR_MESSAGE = ERROR_MESSAGE()

    RAISERROR('Msg %d, Line %d: %s',
        @ERROR_SEVERITY,
        @ERROR_STATE,
        @ERROR_NUMBER,
        @ERROR_LINE,
        @ERROR_MESSAGE)
END CATCH
```

Due to the fact that RAISERROR cannot be used to throw exceptions below 13000, in this case "rethrowing" the exception requires raising a user-defined exception and sending back the data in a specially formed error message. As functions are not allowed within calls to RAISERROR, it is necessary to define variables and assign the values of the error functions before calling RAISERROR to rethrow the exception. Following is the output of this T-SQL:

```
ConvertException
----------------

(0 row(s) affected)

Msg 50000, Level 16, State 1, Line 19
Msg 245, Line 2: Conversion failed when converting the varchar value 'ABC'
to data type int.
```

Keep in mind that based on your interface requirements, you may not always want to rethrow the same exception that was caught to begin with. It might make more sense, in many cases, to catch the initial exception, and then throw a new exception that makes more sense (or is more helpful) to the caller. For example, if you're working with a linked server and the server is not responding for some reason, your code will throw a timeout exception. It might make more sense to pass back a generic "data not available" exception than to expose the actual cause of the problem to the caller. This is something that should be decided on a case-by-case basis, as you work out optimal designs for your stored procedure interfaces.

When Should TRY/CATCH Be Used?

As mentioned previously, the general use case for handling exceptions in T-SQL routines (such as within stored procedures) is to encapsulate as much as possible at as low a level as possible, in order to simplify the overall code of the application. A primary example of this is logging of database exceptions. Instead of sending an exception that cannot be properly handled back to the application tier where it will be logged back to the database, it probably makes more sense to log it while already in the scope of a database routine.

Another use case is temporary fixes for problems stemming from application code. For instance, the application—due to a bug—might occasionally pass invalid keys to a stored procedure that is supposed to insert them into a table. It might be simple to *temporarily* "fix" the problem by simply catching the exception in the database rather than throwing it back to the application where the user will receive an error message. Putting quick fixes of this type into place is often much cheaper than rebuilding and redeploying the entire application.

It is also important to consider when *not* to encapsulate exceptions. Make sure not to overhandle security problems, severe data errors, and other exceptions that the application—and ultimately, the user—should probably be informed of. There is definitely such a thing as too much exception handling, and falling into that trap can mean that problems will be hidden until they cause enough of a commotion to make themselves impossible to ignore.

Long-term issues hidden behind exception handlers usually pop into the open in the form of irreparable data corruption. These situations are usually highlighted by a lack of viable backups because the situation has been going on for so long, and inevitably end in lost business and developers getting their resumes updated for a job search. Luckily, avoiding this issue is fairly easy. Just use a little bit of common sense, and don't go off the deep end in a quest to stifle any and all exceptions.

Using TRY/CATCH to Build Retry Logic

An interesting example of where TRY/CATCH can be used to fully encapsulate an exception is when dealing with deadlocks. Although it's better to try to find and solve the source of a deadlock than to code around it, this is often a difficult and time-consuming task. Therefore, it's common to deal with deadlocks—at least temporarily—by having the application reissue the request that caused the deadlock. Eventually the deadlock condition will resolve itself (i.e., when the other transaction finishes), and the DML operation will go through as expected.

By using T-SQL's TRY/CATCH syntax, the application no longer needs to reissue a request or even know that a problem occurred. A retry loop can be set up, within which the deadlock-prone code can be tried in a TRY block and the deadlock caught in a CATCH block in order to try again. A basic implementation of a retry loop follows:

```
DECLARE @Retries INT
SET @Retries = 3

WHILE @Retries > 0
BEGIN
    BEGIN TRY
        /*
        Put deadlock-prone code here
        */

        --If execution gets here, success
        BREAK
    END TRY
    BEGIN CATCH
        IF ERROR_NUMBER = 1205
        BEGIN
            SET @Retries = @Retries - 1

            IF @Retries = 0
                RAISERROR('Could not complete transaction!', 16, 1)
        END
        ELSE
            RAISERROR('Non-deadlock condition encountered', 16, 1)
    END CATCH
END
```

In this example, the deadlock-prone code is retried as many times as the value of @Retries. Each time through the loop, the code is tried. If it succeeds without an exception being thrown, the code gets to the BREAK and the loop ends. Otherwise, execution jumps to the CATCH block, where a check is made to ensure that the error number is 1205 (deadlock victim). If so, the counter is decremented so that the loop can be tried again. If the exception is not a deadlock, another exception is thrown so that the caller knows that something went wrong. It's important to make sure that the wrong exception does not trigger a retry.

A Final Note: Defensive Programming

Exception handling is extremely useful, and its addition to T-SQL is absolutely invaluable. However, I hope that all readers keep in mind that exception handling is no substitute for proper checking of error conditions *before* they occur. Whenever possible, code *defensively*. Proactively look for problems, and if they can be both detected and handled, code around them.

Remember that it's generally a better idea to handle *exceptions* rather than *errors*. If you can predict a condition and write a code path to handle it during development, that will usually provide a much more robust solution than trying to trap the exception once it occurs and handle it then.

Transactions and Exceptions

No discussion of exceptions in SQL Server can be complete without mentioning the interplay between transactions and exceptions. This is a fairly simple area, but one that often confuses developers who don't quite understand the role that transactions play.

SQL Server is a database management system, and as such one of the main goals is management and manipulation of data. Therefore, at the heart of every exception-handling scheme within SQL Server must live the idea that these are not mere exceptions—they're also data issues.

The Myths of Transaction Abortion

The biggest mistake that some developers make is the assumption that if an exception occurs during a transaction, that transaction will be aborted. By default, that is almost *never* the case. Most transactions will live on even in the face of exceptions, as running the following T-SQL will show:

```
BEGIN TRANSACTION
GO
SELECT 1/0 AS DivideByZero
GO
SELECT @@TRANCOUNT AS ActiveTransactionCount
GO
```

The output from this T-SQL is as follows:

```
DivideByZero
------------
Msg 8134, Level 16, State 1, Line 1
Divide by zero error encountered.

ActiveTransactionCount
----------------------
1

(1 row(s) affected)
```

Another mistake is the belief that stored procedures represent some sort of atomic unit of work, complete with their own implicit transaction that will get rolled back in case of an exception. Alas, this is also not the case, as the following T-SQL proves:

```
--Create a table for some data
CREATE TABLE SomeData
(
    SomeColumn INT
)
GO
```

```
--This procedure will insert one row, then throw a divide by zero exception
CREATE PROCEDURE NoRollback
AS
BEGIN
    INSERT SomeData VALUES (1)

    INSERT SomeData VALUES (1/0)
END
GO

--Execute the procedure
EXEC NoRollback
GO

--Select the rows from the table
SELECT *
FROM SomeData
GO
```

The result is that even though there is an error, the row that didn't throw an exception is still in the table; there is no implicit transaction thanks to the stored procedure:

```
(1 row(s) affected)
Msg 8134, Level 16, State 1, Procedure NoRollback, Line 7
Divide by zero error encountered.
The statement has been terminated.
SomeColumn
-----------
1

(1 row(s) affected)
```

Even if an *explicit* transaction is begun in the stored procedure before the inserts and committed after the exception occurs, this example will still return the same output. By default, unless a rollback is explicitly issued, in most cases an exception will not roll anything back. It will simply serve as a message that something went wrong.

XACT_ABORT: Turning Myth into (Semi-)Reality

As mentioned in the section on XACT_ABORT and its effect on exceptions, the setting also has an impact on transactions, as its name might indicate (it is pronounced "transact abort"). In addition to making exceptions act like batch-level exceptions, the setting also causes any active transactions to immediately roll back in the event of an exception. This means that the following T-SQL results in an active transaction count of 0:

```
SET XACT_ABORT ON
BEGIN TRANSACTION
GO
```

```
SELECT 1/0 AS DivideByZero
GO
SELECT @@TRANCOUNT AS ActiveTransactionCount
GO
```

The output is now

```
DivideByZero
------------
Msg 8134, Level 16, State 1, Line 1
Divide by zero error encountered.

ActiveTransactionCount
----------------------
0

(1 row(s) affected)
```

XACT_ABORT does not create an implicit transaction within a stored procedure, but it *does* cause any exceptions that occur within an explicit transaction within a stored procedure to cause a rollback. The following T-SQL shows a much more atomic stored procedure behavior than the previous example:

```
--Create a table for some data
CREATE TABLE SomeData
(
    SomeColumn INT
)
GO


--This procedure will insert one row, then throw a divide-by-zero exception
CREATE PROCEDURE NoRollback
AS
BEGIN
    SET XACT_ABORT ON

    BEGIN TRANSACTION
        INSERT SomeData VALUES (1)

        INSERT SomeData VALUES (1/0)
    COMMIT TRANSACTION
END
GO


--Execute the procedure
EXEC NoRollback
GO
```

```
--Select the rows from the table
SELECT *
FROM SomeData
GO
```

This T-SQL results in the following output, which shows that no rows were inserted:

```
(1 row(s) affected)
Msg 8134, Level 16, State 1, Procedure NoRollback, Line 11
Divide by zero error encountered.
SomeColumn
-----------

(0 row(s) affected)
```

XACT_ABORT is a very simple, yet extremely effective means of ensuring that an exception does not result in a transaction committing with only part of its work done. I recommend turning this setting on in any stored procedure that uses an explicit transaction, in order to guarantee that it will get rolled back in case of an exception.

TRY/CATCH and Doomed Transactions

The introduction of TRY/CATCH syntax to SQL Server brings with it a strange new concept: transactions can now enter a state in which they can only be rolled back. In this case the transaction is not automatically rolled back, as it is with XACT_ABORT; instead, SQL Server throws an exception letting the caller know that the transaction cannot be committed, and must be rolled back. This condition is known as a **doomed transaction**, and the following T-SQL shows one way of producing it:

```
--Create a table for some data
CREATE TABLE SomeData
(
    SomeColumn INT
)
GO

BEGIN TRANSACTION

BEGIN TRY
    --Throw an exception on insert
    INSERT SomeData VALUES (CONVERT(INT, 'abc'))
END TRY
BEGIN CATCH
    --Try to commit...
    COMMIT TRANSACTION
END CATCH
GO
```

This results in the following output:

```
Msg 3930, Level 16, State 1, Line 10
The current transaction cannot be committed and cannot support
operations that write to the log file. Roll back the transaction.
```

Should a transaction enter this state, any attempt to either commit the transaction or roll forward (do more work) will result in the same exception. This exception will keep getting thrown until the transaction is rolled back.

In order to determine whether an active transaction can be committed or rolled forward, check the value of the XACT_STATE function. This function returns 0 if there are no active transactions, 1 if the transaction is in a state in which more work can be done, and -1 if the transaction is doomed. It is a good idea to always check XACT_STATE in any CATCH block that involves an explicit transaction.

Summary

It's a fact of life for every developer: sometimes, things just go wrong.

A solid understanding of how exceptions behave within SQL Server makes working with them much easier. Especially important is the difference between statement-level and batch-level exceptions, and the implications of exceptions that are thrown within transactions.

SQL Server's TRY/CATCH syntax makes dealing with exceptions much easier, but it's important to use the feature wisely. Overuse can make detection and debugging of problems exceedingly difficult. And whenever dealing with transactions in CATCH blocks, make sure to check the value of XACT_STATE.

Errors and exceptions will always occur, but by thinking carefully about how to handle them, they can be dealt with easily and effectively.

CHAPTER 4

■■■

Privilege and Authorization

SQL Server security is a broad subject area, with enough potential avenues of exploration that entire books have been written on the topic. This chapter's goal is not to cover the whole spectrum of security knowledge necessary to create a product that is secure from end to end, but rather to focus in on those areas that are most important during the software design and development process.

By and large, data security can be broken into two areas: **authentication** is the act of verifying the identity of a user to a system that controls resources, and **authorization** is the act of giving the user access to those resources. These two realms can be delegated separately in many cases; as long as the authentication piece works properly, the user can be handed off to authorization mechanisms for the remainder of a session.

SQL Server authentication is a big topic, with a diverse range of subtopics including network security, operating system security, and so-called surface area control over the server. This is an area that production DBAs must be especially concerned with but that developers can mostly ignore. Developers need to be much more concerned with what happens after authentication: that is, how the user is authorized for data access and how data is protected from unauthorized users.

This chapter introduces some of the issues of data privilege and authorization in SQL Server, from a development point of view. Included here is an initial discussion on privileges and general guidelines and practices for securing data using SQL Server permissions. For more information on security, readers should refer to Chapter 5, which discusses encryption.

Note that although authentication issues are generally ignored in these pages, you should try to not completely disregard them in your day-to-day development work. Development environments tend to be set up with very lax security in order to keep things simple, but a solid development process should include a testing phase during which full authentication restrictions are applied. This helps to ensure that rollout to a production system does not end in spectacular failure when users aren't even able to log in—although that is probably a sign the security of the system is working very well, it is generally not good for developers' job security.

The Principle of Least Privilege

The key to locking down resources in any kind of system—database or otherwise—is quite simple in essence: any given user should have access to only the bare minimum set of resources required, and for only as much time as access to those resources is needed. Unfortunately, in practice this is more of an ideal goal than an actual prescription for data security; many systems do not allow privilege to be easily escalated dynamically, and Windows-based solutions have not historically been engineered to use escalation of privilege as a means by which to gain additional access at run time.

In many non-Windows operating systems that were originally designed for multiuser access, it has long been possible to *impersonate* other users when access to a resource owned by that user is required. It is important to note that impersonation is slightly different than reauthentication; instead of logging out and resending credentials, thereby stopping whatever is running, impersonation allows a process to temporarily *escalate* its privileges, taking on the rights held by the impersonated principal. The most common example of this at an operating system level is UNIX's su command, which allows a user to temporarily take on the identity of another user, easily reverting back when done. Windows systems can handle some degree of impersonation as well, but Microsoft has only recently provided APIs—such as the .NET WindowsIdentity class—which make doing so as convenient as in UNIX systems.

Permissions in Windows systems are typically provided using **Access Control Lists** (ACLs). Granting permission to a resource means adding a user to the list, after which the user can access the resource again and again, even after logging in and out of the system. This kind of access control provides no additional security if, for instance, an attacker takes over an account in the system. By taking control of an account, the attacker automatically has full access to every resource that the account has permission to access.

By controlling access with impersonation, the user is required to effectively request access to the resource dynamically, *each time access is required*. In addition, rights to the resource will only be maintained during the course of impersonation. Once the user **reverts** (i.e., turns off impersonation), the additional access rights are no longer granted. In effect, this means that if an account is compromised, the attacker will have to also compromise the impersonation context in order to gain access to more secure resources.

The idea of security through **least privilege** involves creating users with few or no permissions, and allowing them to briefly escalate their privileges when greater access is required. This is generally implemented using **proxies**, users (or other security principals) that have access to a resource but cannot be authenticated externally. Use of low-privileged external users complemented by higher-privileged proxy users provides a buffer against attack due to the fact that the only accounts that an attacker can directly compromise from the outside have no permissions. Accessing more valuable resources requires additional work on the part of the attacker, giving you that much more of a chance to detect problems before they occur.

Creating Proxies in SQL Server

SQL Server 2005 allows creation of both server-level principals (**logins**) that cannot log in, and database-level principals (**users**) that are not associated with a login. It is only possible to switch into the execution context of one of these users or logins via impersonation, making them ideal for privilege escalation scenarios.

In order to create a proxy login (which can be used to delegate server-level permissions such as BULK INSERT or ALTER DATABASE), you must first create a certificate in the master database. Certificates are covered in depth in Chapter 5, but for now think of a certificate as a trusted way to verify the identity of a principal without a password. The following syntax can be used to create a certificate in master. (Note that before a certificate can be created in any database, a master key must be created. Again, see Chapter 5.)

```
USE master
GO

CREATE CERTIFICATE Dinesh_Certificate
ENCRYPTION BY PASSWORD = 'stROn_G paSSWoRdS, pLE@sE!'
WITH SUBJECT = 'Certificate for Dinesh'
GO
```

Once the certificate has been created, a proxy login can be created using SQL Server 2005's CREATE LOGIN FROM CERTIFICATE syntax:

```
CREATE LOGIN Dinesh
FROM CERTIFICATE Dinesh_Certificate
```

This login can be granted permissions, just like any other login. However, to use the permissions, it must be mapped to a database user. This is done by creating a user using the same certificate that was used to create the login, using the CREATE USER FOR CERTIFICATE syntax. See the section "Stored Procedure Signing Using Certificates" later in this chapter for more information on how to use a proxy login for server-level permissions.

Another type of proxy principal that can be created is a database user not associated with a server login. This is done using CREATE USER WITHOUT LOGIN:

```
CREATE USER Bob
WITHOUT LOGIN
```

This user, like any database user, can be assigned ownership and other permissions. However, it is impossible to log in to the server and authenticate as Bob. Instead, you must log in using a valid server-level login and authenticate to the database with whatever database user is associated with your login. Only then can you impersonate Bob, taking on whatever permissions the user is assigned. This is discussed in detail in the section "Basic Impersonation Using EXECUTE AS" later in this chapter.

Data Security in Layers: The Onion Model

Generally speaking, the more levels an attacker must penetrate in order to access a valuable resource, the better the chance is that an attack will not be successful. Developers should strive to carefully construct multiple layers of protection for any sensitive data, in order to ensure that if one security measure is breached, other obstacles will keep an attacker at bay.

The first layer of defense is everything outside of the database server, all of which falls into the realm of authentication. Once a user is authenticated, SQL Server's declarative permissions system kicks in, and a login is authorized to access one or more databases, based on user mappings.

From there, each user is authorized to access specific resources in the database. Another layer that can be added for additional security here is use of stored procedures. By assigning permissions only via stored procedures, it is possible to maintain greater control over when and why escalation should take place—but more on that will be covered later in this chapter.

Of course, the stored procedure itself must have access to whatever tables and columns are required, and these resources can be further locked down if necessary, using encryption or row-level security schemes.

Figure 4-1 shows some of the layers that should be considered when defining a SQL Server security scheme, in order to secure the sensitive data as well as possible. The remainder of this chapter deals primarily with how best to control access to resources using stored procedures as the primary access layer into the data once a user is authenticated.

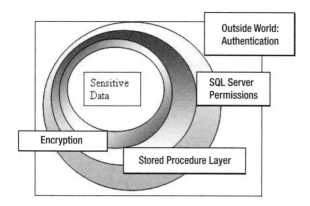

Figure 4-1. *Layering security provides multiple levels of protection against attack.*

A stored procedure layer provides an ideal layer of indirection between the data and the data access, allowing for additional security to be programmed in via parameters or other inline logic. For instance, it is trivial to log every access to sensitive data via a stored procedure, by including logging code in the procedure. Likewise, a stored procedure might be used to force users to access data on a granular basis, by requiring parameters that are used as predicates to filter data. These security checks are difficult or impossible to force on callers without using stored procedures to encapsulate the data access logic.

Data Organization Using Schemas

In versions of SQL Server prior to 2005, all database objects were both owned by database users and referenced by owner name. So to select from a table that was not owned by dbo, the table name would have to be prefixed with the name of the database user that owned it (unless you were logged in as that user). In addition to owner name prefixing, other difficult security scenarios were also created. For instance, there was no easy way to assign permissions to all of the tables owned by a certain user, meaning that ownership did not work as a method by which to easily logically segment tables into groups.

The situation changes with SQL Server 2005, thanks to support for ANSI standard schemas. Schemas are essentially containers into which any database object can be placed, and security rules applied en masse. By dividing your database into schemas, you can easily group related objects and control permissions, without having to worry about what objects might be added or removed over time. As new objects are added to a schema, existing permissions propagate, thereby allowing you to set up access rights for a given schema once, and not have to manipulate them again as the database changes.

To create a schema, use the CREATE SCHEMA command. The following T-SQL creates a schema called Sales:

```
CREATE SCHEMA Sales
```

Optionally, you can specify a schema owner by using the AUTHORIZATION clause. If an owner is not specified, the user that creates the schema will be automatically used by SQL Server.

Once a schema is created, you can begin creating database objects within the schema, using two-part naming, similar to creating objects by owner in previous versions of SQL Server:

```
CREATE TABLE Sales.SalesData
(
    SaleNumber INT,
    SaleDate DATETIME,
    ...
)
```

Once an object is created, it can be referenced by schema name; so to select from the SalesData table, the following SQL is used:

```
SELECT *
FROM Sales.SalesData
```

This same SQL is used no matter who owns the table. Remember, owner names are never used to qualify objects, as of SQL Server 2005.

The beauty of schemas becomes obvious when it is time to apply permissions to the objects in the schema. Assuming that each object is equivalent from a permissions point of view, only a single grant is necessary to give a user access to every object within a schema. For instance, after the following T-SQL is run, the Alejandro user will have access to select rows from every table in the Sales schema, even if new tables are added later:

```
CREATE USER Alejandro
WITHOUT LOGIN
GO

GRANT SELECT ON SCHEMA::Sales
TO Alejandro
GO
```

It's important to note that when initially created, the owner of any object in a schema will be the same as the owner of the schema itself. The individual object owners can be changed later, but in most cases I recommend that you keep everything in any given schema owned by the same user. This is especially important for ownership chaining, covered later in this chapter. In addition, because two-part naming now references a schema rather than an object owner, the process for explicitly setting an object's owner changes with SQL Server 2005. A new command, ALTER AUTHORIZATION, is used in order to set ownership on objects. The following T-SQL shows the basics of how it is used:

```
--Create a user
CREATE USER Javier
WITHOUT LOGIN
GO

--Create a table
CREATE TABLE JaviersData
(
    SomeColumn INT
)
GO

--Set Javier as the owner of the table
ALTER AUTHORIZATION ON JaviersData
TO Javier
GO
```

As a final note on schemas, there is also a command that can be used to move objects between them. By using ALTER SCHEMA with the TRANSFER option, you can specify that a table should be moved to another schema:

```
--Create a new schema
CREATE SCHEMA Purchases
GO

--Move the SalesData table into the new schema
ALTER SCHEMA Purchases
TRANSFER Sales.SalesData
GO

--Reference the table by its new schema name
SELECT *
FROM Purchases.SalesData
GO
```

Schemas are a powerful feature in SQL Server, and I recommend their use any time you're dealing with sets of tables that are tightly related to one another. The AdventureWorks sample database that ships with SQL Server 2005 makes great use of schemas, and I highly recommend that you take a look at what Microsoft has done in that example and try to design new databases along similar lines. Legacy database applications that use multiple databases in order to create logical boundaries between objects might also benefit from schemas. The multiple databases can be consolidated to a single database that uses schemas. The benefit is that the same logical boundaries will exist, but because the objects are in the same database, they can participate in declarative referential integrity and can be backed up together.

Basic Impersonation Using EXECUTE AS

Switching to a different user's execution context has long been possible in SQL Server, using the SETUSER command. This command was only available to members of the sysadmin or db_owner roles (at the server and database levels, respectively), and was therefore not useful for setting up least-privilege scenarios.

SQL Server 2005 introduces a new command for impersonation, EXECUTE AS. This command can be used by any user, and access is controlled by a permissions setting rather than a fixed role. The other benefit over SETUSER is that EXECUTE AS automatically reverts to the original context at the end of a module. SETUSER, on the other hand, leaves the impersonated context active when control is returned to the caller. This means that it is impossible to encapsulate impersonation within a stored procedure using SETUSER and guarantee that the caller will not be able to take control of the impersonated credentials.

To show the effects of EXECUTE AS, start by creating a new user and a table owned by the user:

```
CREATE USER Tom
WITHOUT LOGIN
GO

CREATE TABLE TomsData
(
    AColumn INT
)
GO

ALTER AUTHORIZATION ON TomsData TO Tom
GO
```

Once the user is created, it can be impersonated using EXECUTE AS, and the impersonation context can be verified using the USER_NAME function:

```
EXECUTE AS USER='Tom'
GO

SELECT USER_NAME()
GO
```

The SELECT statement returns the value Tom, indicating that that is the impersonated user. Any action done after EXECUTE AS is run will use Tom's credentials. For example, the user can alter the table, since it owns it. However, an attempt to create a new table will fail, since the user does not have permission to do so:

```
--This statement will succeed
ALTER TABLE TomsData
ADD AnotherColumn DATETIME
GO
```

```
--This statement will fail
CREATE TABLE MoreData
(
    YetAnotherColumn INT
)
GO
```

Once you have completed working with the database in the context of Tom's permissions, you can return to the outer context by using the REVERT command. If you have impersonated another user inside of another context (i.e., called EXECUTE AS more than once), REVERT will have to be called multiple times in order to return context to your login. The USER_NAME function can be checked at any time to find out whose context you are executing under.

To see the effects of nested impersonation, create a second user. The user can be given the right to impersonate Tom, using GRANT IMPERSONATE:

```
CREATE USER Paul
WITHOUT LOGIN
GO

GRANT IMPERSONATE ON USER::Tom TO PAUL
GO
```

If Paul is impersonated, the session will have no privileges to select rows from the TomsData table. In order to get those permissions, Tom must be impersonated from within Paul's context:

```
EXECUTE AS USER='Paul'
GO

--Fails
SELECT *
FROM TomsData
GO

EXECUTE AS USER='Tom'
GO

--Succeeds
SELECT *
FROM TomsData
GO

REVERT
GO

--Returns 'Paul' -- REVERT must be called again to fully revert
SELECT USER_NAME()
GO
```

The most important thing to understand is that when EXECUTE AS is called, all operations will run as if you are logged in as the impersonated user. You will lose any permissions that the outer user has that the impersonated user does not have, in addition to gaining any permissions that the impersonated user has that the outer user lacks.

For logging purposes, it is sometimes important to record the actual logged in principal. Since both the USER_NAME function and the SUSER_NAME function will return the names associated with the impersonated user, the ORIGINAL_LOGIN function has been added to SQL Server to return the name of the outermost server login. Use of ORIGINAL_LOGIN will allow you to get the name of the logged-in server principal, no matter how nested your impersonation scope is.

WHAT IS A MODULE?

Each of the privilege escalation examples that follow use stored procedures to show the functionality. However, please be aware that these methods work for any kind of **module** that SQL Server supports. A module is defined as any kind of code container that can be created inside of SQL Server: a stored procedure, view, user-defined function, trigger, or CLR assembly.

Ownership Chaining

The most common method of securing SQL Server resources is to deny database users any direct access to SQL Server resources and provide access only via stored procedures or views. If a database user has access to execute a stored procedure, and the stored procedure is owned by the same database user that owns a resource being referenced within the stored procedure, the user executing the stored procedure will be given access to the resource, via the stored procedure. This is called an **ownership chain**.

To illustrate, start by creating and switching to a test database:

```
CREATE DATABASE OwnershipChain
GO

USE OwnershipChain
GO
```

Now, create two database users, Louis and Hugo:

```
CREATE USER Louis
WITHOUT LOGIN
GO

CREATE USER Hugo
WITHOUT LOGIN
GO
```

Note For this and subsequent examples in this chapter, you should connect to SQL Server using a login that is a member of the sysadmin server role.

Note that both of these users are created using the WITHOUT LOGIN option, meaning that although these users exist in the database, they are not tied to a SQL Server login and therefore no one can authenticate as one of them by logging in to the server. This option is one way of creating the kind of proxy users mentioned previously.

Once the users have been created, create a table owned by Louis:

```
CREATE TABLE SensitiveData
(
    IntegerData INT
)
GO


ALTER AUTHORIZATION ON SensitiveData TO Louis
GO
```

At this point, Hugo has no access to the table. To create an access path without granting direct permissions to the table, a stored procedure could be created, also owned by Louis:

```
CREATE PROCEDURE SelectSensitiveData
AS
BEGIN
    SET NOCOUNT ON

    SELECT *
    FROM dbo.SensitiveData
END
GO


ALTER AUTHORIZATION ON SelectSensitiveData TO Louis
GO
```

Hugo still has no permissions on the table at this point; the user needs to be given permission to execute the stored procedure:

```
GRANT EXECUTE ON SelectSensitiveData TO Hugo
```

At this point Hugo can execute the stored procedure, thereby selecting from the table. However, this only works because Louis owns both tables, and both are in the same database; if either of those conditions were not true, the ownership chain would break, and Hugo would have to be authorized another way to select from the table. The ownership chain would also fail if the execution context changed within the stored procedure. For example, ownership chaining will not work with dynamic SQL (for more information on dynamic SQL, refer to Chapter 7).

In the case of a stored procedure in one database requesting access to an object in another database, it is possible to maintain an ownership chain, but it gets quite a bit more complex, and security is much more difficult to maintain. To set up **cross-database ownership chaining**, the user that owns the stored procedure and the referenced table(s) must be associated with a server-level login, and each database must have the DB_CHAINING property set using the ALTER DATABASE command. That property tells SQL Server that either database can participate in a cross-database ownership chain, either as source or target—but there is no way to control the direction of the chain, so setting the option could open up security holes inadvertently.

I recommend that you avoid cross-database ownership chaining whenever possible, and instead call stored procedures in the remote database. Doing so will result in a more secure, more flexible solution. For example, moving databases to separate servers is much easier if they do not depend on one another for authentication. In addition, with the inclusion of schemas in SQL Server 2005, splitting objects into multiple databases is no longer as important as it once was. Consider avoiding multiple databases altogether, if at all possible.

Privilege Escalation Without Ownership Chains

Ownership chaining will not work if the object owner does not match the module owner, or if dynamic SQL is used. In these cases, you'll have to use one of the two other kinds of privilege escalation provided by SQL Server: an extension to stored procedures using the EXECUTE AS clause, or module signing using certificates.

Using the EXECUTE AS clause with stored procedures is an easy and effective method of escalating permissions, but is not nearly as flexible as what can be done using certificates. With certificates, permissions are additive rather than impersonated—the additional permissions provided by the certificate add to, rather than replace, the permissions of the calling principal.

Stored Procedures and EXECUTE AS

As described in a previous section in this chapter, the EXECUTE AS command can be used on its own in T-SQL batches in order to temporarily impersonate other users. However, EXECUTE AS is also available for stored procedures, functions, and triggers. The examples in this section only focus on stored procedures, but the same principles apply to the other object types.

To use EXECUTE AS to change the impersonation context of an entire stored procedure, add it to the CREATE PROCEDURE statement as in the following example:

```
CREATE PROCEDURE SelectSensitiveData
WITH EXECUTE AS 'Louis'
AS
BEGIN
    SET NOCOUNT ON

    SELECT *
    FROM dbo.SensitiveData
END
```

When this stored procedure is executed by a user, all operations within the procedure will be evaluated as if they are being run by the Louis user rather than by the calling user (as is the default behavior). This includes any dynamic SQL operations, or manipulation of data in tables that the Louis user has access to. When the stored procedure has completed execution, context will be automatically reverted back to that of the caller.

Keep in mind that use of EXECUTE AS does not break ownership chains, but rather can be used to add to them and create additional flexibility. For instance, consider the following two users and associated tables:

```
CREATE USER Kevin
WITHOUT LOGIN
GO
```

```
CREATE TABLE KevinsData
(
    SomeData INT
)
GO

ALTER AUTHORIZATION ON KevinsData TO Kevin
GO

CREATE USER Hilary
WITHOUT LOGIN
GO

CREATE TABLE HilarysData
(
    SomeOtherData INT
)
GO

ALTER AUTHORIZATION ON HilarysData TO Hilary
GO
```

Both users, Kevin and Hilary, own tables. A stored procedure might need to be created that accesses both tables, but using ownership chaining will not work; if the procedure is owned by Kevin, that user would need to be given access to HilarysData in order to select from that table. Likewise for Hilary and the KevinsData table.

One solution in this case is to combine EXECUTE AS with ownership chaining and create a stored procedure that is owned by one of the users, but executes under the context of the other. The following stored procedure shows how this might look:

```
CREATE PROCEDURE SelectKevinAndHilarysData
WITH EXECUTE AS 'Kevin'
AS
BEGIN
    SET NOCOUNT ON

    SELECT *
    FROM KevinsData

    UNION ALL

    SELECT *
    FROM HilarysData
END
GO

ALTER AUTHORIZATION ON SelectKevinAndHilarysData TO Hilary
GO
```

Because Hilary owns the stored procedure, ownership chaining will kick in and allow selection of rows from the `HilarysData` table. But because the stored procedure is executing under the context of the Kevin user, permissions will also cascade for the `KevinsData` table. In this way, both permission sets can be used, combined within a single module.

Unfortunately, this is about the limit of what can be done using `EXECUTE AS`. For more complex permissions scenarios, it is necessary to resort to signing stored procedures using certificates.

Stored Procedure Signing Using Certificates

As mentioned previously in the chapter, proxy logins and users can be created based on certificates. Creating a certificate-based proxy is by far the most flexible way of applying permissions using a stored procedure, as the permissions are additive. One or more certificates can be used to sign a stored procedure, and each certificate will apply its permissions to the others already present, rather than replacing the permissions as happens when impersonation is done using `EXECUTE AS`.

To create a proxy user using a certificate, first create the certificate, and then create the user using the `FOR CERTIFICATE` syntax:

```
CREATE CERTIFICATE Greg_Certificate
WITH SUBJECT='Certificate for Greg'
GO

CREATE USER Greg
FOR CERTIFICATE Greg_Certificate
GO
```

Once the proxy user is created, it can be granted permissions to any resource in the database, just like any other database user. But a side effect of having created the user based on a certificate is that the certificate itself can also be used to propagate permissions granted to the user. This is where stored procedure signing comes into play.

To illustrate this, the following table can be created, and access granted to the `Greg` user:

```
CREATE TABLE GregsData
(
    DataColumn INT
)
GO

GRANT ALL ON GregsData
TO Greg
GO
```

A stored procedure can then be created that selects from the table, but for the sake of this example, the stored procedure will be owned by a user called `Steve`, in order to break any possible ownership chain that might result from creating both the table and the stored procedure in the same default schema:

```
CREATE PROCEDURE SelectGregsData
AS
BEGIN
    SET NOCOUNT ON

    SELECT *
    FROM GregsData
END
GO

CREATE USER Steve
WITHOUT LOGIN
GO

ALTER AUTHORIZATION ON SelectGregsData TO Steve
GO
```

Even if granted permission to execute this stored procedure, a third user will be unable to successfully do so, as the stored procedure does not propagate permissions to the GregsData table:

```
CREATE USER Linchi
WITHOUT LOGIN
GO

GRANT EXECUTE ON SelectGregsData TO Linchi
GO

EXECUTE AS USER='Linchi'
GO

--This will fail -- SELECT permission denied
EXEC SelectGregsData
GO
```

In order to make the stored procedure work for the Linchi user, permissions to the GregsData table must be propagated through the stored procedure. This can be done by signing the procedure using the same certificate that was used to create the Greg user. Signing a stored procedure is done using the ADD SIGNATURE command:

```
ADD SIGNATURE TO SelectGregsData
BY CERTIFICATE Greg_Certificate
```

Once the procedure is signed with the certificate, the procedure has the same permissions that the Greg user has; in this case, that means that any user with permission to execute the procedure will be able to select rows from the GregsData table when running the stored procedure.

The flexibility of certificate signing becomes apparent when you consider that you can sign a given stored procedure with any number of certificates, each of which can be associated with different users and therefore different permission sets. This means that even in an incredibly complex system with numerous security roles, it will still be possible to write stored procedures to aggregate data across security boundaries.

Keep in mind when working with certificates that any time the stored procedure is altered, all signatures will be automatically revoked by SQL Server. Therefore, it is important to keep signatures scripted with stored procedures, such that when the procedure is modified, the permissions can be easily kept in sync.

It is also important to know how to find out which certificates, and therefore which users, are associated with a given stored procedure. SQL Server's catalog views can be queried to find this information, but getting the right query is not especially obvious. The following query, which returns all stored procedures, the certificates they are signed with, and the users associated with the certificates, can be used as a starting point:

```
SELECT
    OBJECT_NAME(cp.major_id) AS signed_module,
    c.name AS certificate_name,
    dp.name AS user_name
FROM sys.crypt_properties AS cp
INNER JOIN sys.certificates AS c ON c.thumbprint = cp.thumbprint
INNER JOIN sys.database_principals dp ON SUBSTRING(dp.sid, 13, 32) = c.thumbprint
```

This query is somewhat difficult to understand, so it is worth explaining here. The sys.crypt_properties view contains information about which modules have been signed by certificates. Each certificate has a 32-byte cryptographic hash, its *thumbprint*, which is used to find out which certificate was used to sign the module, via the sys.certificates view. Finally, each database principal has a security identifier, the final 32 bytes of which is the thumbprint if the principal was created from a certificate.

Assigning Server-Level Permissions

The previous example showed only how to assign database-level permissions using a certificate. Signing a stored procedure can also be used to propagate server-level permissions, such as BULK INSERT or ALTER DATABASE. Doing so requires creation of a proxy login from a certificate, followed by creation of a database user using the same certificate. To accomplish this, the certificate must be backed up after being created, and restored in the database in which you are creating the user. Once the database user is created, the procedure to apply permissions is the same as when propagating database-level permissions.

To begin with, create a certificate in the master database. Unlike previous examples, this certificate must include a password in its definition, in order to encrypt its private key. Once the certificate has been created, use it to create a proxy login:

```
CREATE CERTIFICATE alter_db_certificate
    ENCRYPTION BY PASSWORD = 'stR()Ng_PaSSWoRDs are?BeST!'
    WITH SUBJECT = 'ALTER DATABASE permission'
GO


CREATE LOGIN alter_db_login FROM CERTIFICATE alter_db_certificate
GO
```

This login, in case you can't tell from the name, will be used to propagate ALTER DATABASE permissions. The next step is to grant the appropriate permissions to the login:

```
GRANT ALTER ANY DATABASE TO alter_db_login
```

At this point, the next step required is to back up the certificate to a file. The certificate can then be restored from the file into the database of your choosing, and from there can be used to create a database user that will have the same permissions as the server login, by virtue of having been created using the same certificate.

```
BACKUP CERTIFICATE alter_db_certificate
TO FILE = 'C:\alter_db.cer'
WITH PRIVATE KEY
(
    FILE = 'C:\alter_db.pvk',
    ENCRYPTION BY PASSWORD = 'anOtHeR$tRoNGpaSSWoRd?',
    DECRYPTION BY PASSWORD = 'stR()Ng_PaSSWoRDs are?BeST!'
)
```

Once backed up, the certificate can be restored in a database. For the purpose of this example, a new database can be created and used to keep things simple:

```
CREATE DATABASE alter_db_example
GO

USE alter_db_example
GO

CREATE CERTIFICATE alter_db_certificate
FROM FILE = 'C:\alter_db.cer'
WITH PRIVATE KEY
(
    FILE = 'C:\alter_db.pvk',
    DECRYPTION BY PASSWORD = 'anOtHeR$tRoNGpaSSWoRd?',
    ENCRYPTION BY PASSWORD = 'stR()Ng_PaSSWoRDs are?BeST!'
)
GO
```

For more information on the CREATE CERTIFICATE statement, see Chapter 5.

It is worth noting that at this point, the certificate's physical file should probably be either deleted or backed up to a safe storage repository. Although the private key is encrypted with the password, it would certainly be possible for a dedicated attacker to crack it via brute force. And since the certificate is being used to grant ALTER DATABASE permissions, such an attack could potentially end in some damage being done—so play it safe with these files.

After the certificate has been created in the database, the rest of the process is just as before. Create a stored procedure that requires the privilege escalation, create a user based on the certificate, and sign the stored procedure with the certificate:

```
CREATE PROCEDURE SetMultiUser
AS
BEGIN
    ALTER DATABASE alter_db_example
    SET MULTI_USER
END
GO

CREATE USER alter_db_user
FOR CERTIFICATE alter_db_certificate
GO

ADD SIGNATURE TO SetMultiUser
BY CERTIFICATE alter_db_certificate
WITH PASSWORD = 'stR()Ng_PaSSWoRDs are?BeST!'
GO
```

The permissions can now be tested. In order for propagation of server-level permissions to work, the user executing the stored procedure must be associated with a valid server login, and the login must be impersonated rather than the user. So this time, CREATE USER WITHOUT LOGIN will not suffice:

```
CREATE LOGIN test_alter WITH PASSWORD = 'iWanT2ALTER!!'
GO

CREATE USER test_alter FOR LOGIN test_alter
GO

GRANT EXECUTE ON SetMultiUser TO test_alter
GO
```

Finally, the test_alter login can be impersonated, and the stored procedure executed:

```
EXECUTE AS LOGIN='test_alter'
GO

EXEC SetMultiUser
GO
```

This example was obviously quite simplistic, but it should serve as a basic template that you can adapt as necessary when you need to provide escalation of server-level privilege to database users.

Summary

SQL Server's impersonation features allow developers to create secure, granular authorization schemes. By keeping authorization layered and following a least-privilege mentality, resources in the database can be much more secure, requiring that attackers do more work in order to retrieve data they are not supposed to see. A stored procedure layer can be used to control security, delegating permissions as necessary based on a system of higher-privileged proxy users.

Schemas should be used when it is necessary to logically break apart a database into groups of objects that are similar in scope. Schemas can also be used to make assignment of permissions much easier, as permissions may not have to be maintained over time as the objects in the schema change.

The EXECUTE AS clause can be a very useful and simple way of propagating permissions based on stored procedures, but certificates provide much more flexibility and control. That said, you should try to keep systems as simple and understandable as possible, in order to avoid creating maintainability nightmares.

A final note along those lines: try not to go overboard when it comes to security. Many of the techniques laid out in this chapter are probably *not* necessary for the majority of applications. If your application does not store sensitive data, try to not go too far in creating complex privilege escalation schemes; they will only make your application more difficult to deal with.

CHAPTER 5

■■■

Encryption

Your data is often the heart of your business. Protecting this most valuable asset is a central concern for any business. Exposure of sensitive data has resulted in numerous scandals, undesirable public exposure, and costly disclosure of company secrets. Increasingly, governments are making company directors personally liable for taking "every reasonable step" to protect certain classes of sensitive data. Because of this, most new data-related initiatives consider data encryption a required component, which means that we are now tasked with understanding the encryption capabilities in SQL Server 2005.

These data encryption capabilities have generated a great deal of interest. I use the term "interest" intentionally, as it's an appropriate term for the reaction of the business and technology world to this important feature. I don't often encounter a database developer or database administrator who is "excited" to implement encryption, but many businesses are mandating encryption of the data in the database, and these developers and administrators are interested in the best methods for securing this data with the least impact to application performance.

Don't let the term "interest" minimize the importance of implementing a solution to secure sensitive data. As someone who recognizes that a significant number of systems carry my personal information, I am interested in businesses that practice proper methodologies for securing my information. I know, however, that when encryption is implemented without care, it does not really protect my personal information and is nothing more than a tool to degrade performance of the database application. Compounding this issue is that businesses may have a false sense of security when they are, in fact, still vulnerable.

I have been involved with a number of very successful implementations where data encryption has proven to be a powerful tool to help protect sensitive data. In all cases, the success of the project was due to the thoughtful analysis and planning toward application, database, and server security. The physical act of encrypting your data is very simple, but data protection is much more than applying some new functions and keys to your data tier. You must approach encryption with a proper methodology to secure all methods of accessing data while maintaining a level of scalability and performance your application demands.

The following point is very important to understand: alone will not protect your data. Encryption is a tool that can be used to add a layer of protection to your data, but data protection must be addressed with an eye on all levels of security. If you have not properly secured your instance, your database, or the encryption keys, you may be exposing your business to risk. Encrypting data will obfuscate your data such that you can only see the value when you have access to the appropriate key to decrypt the data. But if you have not properly secured your server to begin with, you may be inadvertently granting access to these keys. For instance, if your application uses an application role that has rights to decrypt the data, you may still be vulnerable to attacks if someone were to break into your database through the application. You must approach encryption with a proper methodology where you define who should have access to what data, and audit and document all users and their rights on the server, instance, and database. You must map these users and their roles to the appropriate encryption keys. The key hierarchy in SQL Server 2005 can provide a number of flexible implementations, and I highly recommend studying how the keys relate, who has access to each key, and how to lock down all levels of access to the data. Throughout this chapter, I will walk through various implementation examples, and discuss the advantages and disadvantages of each solution.

In real-world implementations, data encryption has proven to be a powerful tool to help protect sensitive data, but it has also been problematic for those environments that cannot sustain the performance degradation likely to occur after implementing encryption on existing applications. In large-scale environments, data encryption must be implemented carefully to ensure that this data protection tool does not negatively impact application performance—leading to dissatisfied customers and users. Later in this chapter, I will present some solutions that protect sensitive data while providing a proper method for searching encrypted data.

This chapter is not a definitive guide to database encryption, but rather a practical approach to implementing the concepts and tools available in SQL Server 2005. This chapter assumes that you have adequately addressed server security and are ready to protect your data through encryption. The principal focus of this chapter is toward a well-performing implementation of encryption. As you will see throughout this chapter, encrypting data is not a difficult task, but it does require sufficient planning prior to implementation. To properly implement encryption to secure your sensitive data with minimal impact to your application performance requires an architected approach, as detailed in this chapter.

What to Protect

It is common for someone who is new to database-level encryption to want to encrypt the entire database. I suspect that many of these users are familiar with PGP or other file-level encryption techniques, and apply the same concepts to database-level encryption. To clear up this misunderstanding, SQL Server 2005 data encryption is not file encryption. You are not encrypting the MDF or LDF files. You are selecting columns in your tables that contain customer-sensitive data or business-sensitive data.

Data encryption does not come free, and you will typically pay the price with degradation in database read and write performance. Before any data is encrypted, thoroughly identify the risk of data exposure, review the business requirements, define sensitive data elements, and isolate columns that require encryption to minimize the impact to the overall server performance.

Customer data or business data is defined as sensitive when it would jeopardize your business should it be exposed to outside parties. Exposure may be public, such as the countless situations where companies lose personally identifying customer or employee data. Data may also be sensitive if it could jeopardize your business should your competitors receive the information, as in pricing campaigns in retail industries. Your business may simply define the risk to your data at rest—meaning that the data is not sensitive within your environment to system or database administrators. This risk may be defined with stronger requirements where your data should not be available in decrypted form to system administrators or database owners. Data encryption is one tool to help protect this information, but the implementation will determine how successfully you meet these conditions.

Before any data is physically encrypted, you will need to review all data elements with your business and technical users. Database professionals wear many hats, and this is the time to put on your business analyst hat (or hire a BA for the job). Together with the business, classify your data elements, and determine which type of encryption is necessary for each data element that has been defined as sensitive.

Sensitive data may be a single column of data, or a combination of two or more columns. Consider multicolumn combinations where each individual column will not jeopardize your customers or business, but when exposed together could prove a threat. In these situations (which occur more often than you may realize), I recommend encryption of the columns that are less likely to be searched and do not incur risk when exposed individually.

For example, a particular customer sales database stores customer address and contact information that is considered sensitive for a business. The address information includes the business name, street address, city, state, and postal code (among other things). This data is accessed by multiple applications in the company. Management analyzes sales totals by city, state, and postal code to understand trends by geographical area. Marketing will also use this data when sending campaign promotions to certain regions. A customer service application often searches for a customer based on the city or postal code. In most cases, the applications search, group by, and sort the data based on city, state, or postal code. Each individual column in this address will not pose a risk if exposed to your competitors, but the combination of business name, street address, *and* the city, state, and postal code is considered sensitive. In this situation, the business will likely require that the business name and/or street address are encrypted.

As you identify which data elements are sensitive, you will need to indicate how the data is to be protected. Hashing may be suitable for some of your data, while other data elements may require symmetric encryption or certificate encryption. Very often, nontechnical business users and managers may not understand the performance implications of using certificates or asymmetric encryption to secure your data. These business users simply require the "most secure" method of encrypting data for all sensitive data. This is the time when you put on your database administrator hat to educate nontechnical management or business users and recommend the best solution and optimal type of encryption to address both the security requirements and the database performance requirements.

Encrypting data does not come without a cost. The greatest penalty to encrypting your data is in data access performance. The depth of the penalty depends on the type of encryption used, how much data is decrypted in normal activities, and how the data is accessed. Throughout the remainder of this chapter, I will walk through the types of encryption supported in SQL Server 2005 and discuss the performance implications for each. The final sections in this chapter will detail a solution you can implement that will improve the performance of accessing encrypted data—particularly when you require searching, grouping, and filtering of your encrypted data.

Encryption Terminology: What You Need to Know

Before we dive into the different capabilities to protect your data, let's review some of the fundamental terms and concepts covered in the remainder of the chapter. These terms will be discussed in greater length through the remainder of the chapter.

Encryption Keys An encryption key will specify an algorithm to transform data from plaintext to ciphertext and/or back to plaintext. A single key may be used to encrypt your data, decrypt your data, or both.

Ciphertext Encrypting data is achieved using one or more keys to transform the data from the original plaintext into an encrypted value, known as ciphertext. You can recover the original plaintext from the ciphertext when the appropriate key is applied to the decryption process.

Hash A hash is a one-way process that applies an algorithm to predictably transform your data into a different value, which is often much smaller than the source data. Hashing is deterministic, meaning that every time you pass the same value through the same hash algorithm, you will receive the same result. The deterministic and one-way qualities make hash values ideal for authentication purposes, such as storing passwords. Because a hash is deterministic, it is often "salted" to protect against dictionary attacks.

Salt A salt is an additional series of characters added to a value prior to hashing. A salt is like additional flavor (as the name indicates) to transform the output of the hash and make it less predictable to outsiders who do not know the salt value. Attackers may create dictionaries of possible hash values and attempt reverse lookups against your hash data (also known as a **dictionary attack**). A salt added to your data will make these attacks much more difficult, unless the attacker were to obtain the salt value.

Symmetric Encryption Symmetric encryption uses a single key to encrypt and decrypt data. Symmetric encryption is also known as **shared-key encryption** and **single-key encryption**.

Asymmetric Encryption Asymmetric encryption uses a pair of keys to protect the data. A single public key is used to encrypt the data. A separate, related private key is used to decrypt the data. Any data that is encrypted with an asymmetric public key can only be decrypted with the related private key. In many cases, the private key is strongly secured, and the public key is more widely distributed. Asymmetric encryption is also referred to as **public-key encryption**.

Certificate A certificate follows the X.509 standard and embodies a pair of keys to manage the encryption and decryption of your data while binding the public key with an identity. A certificate is typically generated by an outside certification authority (CA), although you can generate self-signed certificates in SQL Server 2005.

SQL Server 2005 Encryption Key Hierarchy

Before we talk about the types of encryption supported in SQL Server 2005, it is important to understand the function of the master keys and how these keys support your encryption implementation. As will be discussed throughout the remainder of this chapter, the relationships you choose to define between the service master key, the database master key, and the private keys of asymmetric key pairs and certificates will impact how you will implement your solution and the level of protection you are placing on the data.

■**Note** This is a light discussion of the master keys in SQL Server 2005. SQL Server Books Online details master key backup and restore functionality, and Laurentiu Cristofor's blog (http://blogs.msdn.com/lcris/default.aspx) is an excellent resource for the master keys.

Service Master Key

Each installation of SQL Server 2005 has a single **service master key**, which is created when you install SQL Server 2005. The service master key is used to protect linked server logins and credential secrets, and can be used to encrypt the database master key.

This symmetric key is stored in the master database and is protected by the Data Protection API (DPAPI) using the service account credentials and the machine credentials, as depicted in Figure 5-1. Certain common events may cause either the service account credentials or the machine credentials to become invalid. On a clustered installation, a failover will invalidate the machine credential protection. If the service account is changed, the service credential protection is invalidated. With two forms of protection, the chances that the service master key is invalidated due to an external event are greatly minimized. When the server is started, SQL Server will check both credentials, and if one of these is proven to be invalid during the startup, SQL Server will re-create the invalid key based on the other valid key.

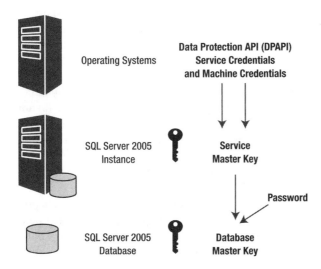

Figure 5-1. *The SQL Server 2005 master key hierarchy*

If you choose to rely on the transparent key management in SQL Server 2005, as discussed in the section "Asymmetric Key and Certificate Encryption," the service master key is the key-stone of your encryption hierarchy. As the next section will discuss, the database master key is also protected with a password, which significantly minimizes any chance that you will be unable to decrypt your data—unless the service master key is corrupt and you also forget your database master key password. The greatest risks of a corrupt or invalidated service master key are to your linked server logins and credential secrets. It is important that you have a backup of your service master key to ensure that you do not lose these entities that are protected using the service master key.

Database Master Key

Each user database can have only one **database master key**. A database master key is a symmetric key that may be used to protect the private keys of certificates and asymmetric key pairs. If your encryption implementation does not use certificates or asymmetric keys, you will not need a database master key, unless you have implemented Service Broker. If you choose to protect the private keys of certificates and asymmetric keys with a password, you may also forgo a database master key.

By default, the database master key is protected using the service master key and a password, as shown in Figure 5-1. You can choose to drop the encryption by the service master key, but the database master key must always have at least one password. If you have required password complexity on your server, SQL Server will require a strong database master key password.

```
CREATE MASTER KEY ENCRYPTION BY PASSWORD =
  'GiAFn1Blj2jxsUgmJm7Oc4Lb1dt4zLPD29GtrtJvEkBhLozTKrA4qAfOsIvS2EY'
GO
```

When the database master key is protected by the service master key, SQL Server can automatically and transparently decrypt the database master key without requiring a password from a user or application. This default nature is sufficient if your primary concern is to protect your data in the event that the files are stolen, which is known as **data at rest**. If someone were to steal the database files and attach or restore them to a different instance, he or she would need to know the database master key password to reencrypt the database master key with the service master key on the new instance. When you create a strong password, it will be extremely difficult for these evildoers to guess your password and gain access to the data. A database master key protected by the service master key is easy to implement, as you do not need to explicitly open the database master key when you open dependent private keys. Users are only granted permissions on the asymmetric keys or certificates; you do not need to grant CONTROL permissions on the database to open the database master key.

While it is easier to manage your keys when the database master key is protected by the service master key, it does expose the sensitive data and encryption keys to anyone in the sysadmin fixed server role and db_owner database role. If your business requires a higher level of data protection, you will drop the service master key protection, which will require a password to open the database master key. This will create an environment to support protecting encrypted data from the sysadmin, but a db_owner continues to have control over the database master key and associated securables. Protecting sensitive data from a db_owner will be discussed in the sections "Asymmetric Key and Certificate Encryption" and "Symmetric Key Encryption." Execute the following statement in the user database to drop the service master key protection:

```
ALTER MASTER KEY DROP ENCRYPTION BY SERVICE MASTER KEY
```

When the database master key is protected only by a password, you will explicitly open the database master key prior to using a certificate or asymmetric key that is dependent on the database master key. A user must have CONTROL permission on the database to open the key, which gives the user full rights on the database.

```
OPEN MASTER KEY DECRYPTION BY PASSWORD =
  'GiAFn1Blj2jxsUgmJm7Oc4Lb1dt4zLPD29GtrtJvEkBhLozTKrA4qAfOsIvS2EY'
```

After a key is open, it is available for use within the session. Within this session, you may change execution context to an account that does not have CONTROL permission on the database, use related asymmetric keys, and close the master key. Your biggest hurdle in this implementation will be opening the key with an elevated user account. If your security requirements dictate that the application role be a low-privileged user, you may prefer to protect your asymmetric keys and symmetric keys with a password, as I will discuss in the sections "Asymmetric Key and Certificate Encryption" and "Symmetric Key Encryption."

If you are motivated to protect the sensitive data from individuals in the sysadmin fixed server role, dropping the service master key protection is only the first step. You will need to consider how to pass the passwords from the application to open the database master key without exposing the password to the sysadmin. A sysadmin may run Profiler on an instance, which can be an issue if you are managing all database code in stored procedures. Profiler will not display text from encryption functions (as in the OPEN MASTER KEY statement), but will return any input parameter passed to a stored procedure. A sysadmin may open the text of any stored procedure, exposing any passwords hard-coded in the procedure. To properly protect sensitive data from a sysadmin, you will manage key passwords in the application code or in a configuration file where the sysadmin does not have access and open the database master key directly in the application code.

■Note Be aware that although you may be protecting your sensitive data from exposure within Profiler, machine administrators and network administrators may still have access to sensitive data and passwords using tools to access data stored in server memory or as it crosses the network.

The implementation of the database master key is directly dependent on the level of protection your business demands. If you are simply interested in protecting your data at rest, the default behavior with the database master key encrypted by the service master key is an easy implementation to provide the level of protection required. If you require a level of protection from a sysadmin, you can remove the service master key encryption and simply require a password to open the database master key. This implementation carries a number of issues, including elevated database permissions for an application user to open the database master key. As will be discussed in subsequent sections, alternative implementations will not require a database master key and will provide a more flexible implementation to secure your data from both the sysadmin and the db_owner, if required.

SQL Server 2005 Data Protection

SQL Server 2005 introduces various methods to protect your data. As discussed throughout this chapter, data encryption uses a key to create nondeterministic ciphertext (encrypted data), which can only be decrypted with the appropriate encryption key. Before we look at key-based data encryption, we will examine the HashBytes() function, which returns a deterministic representation of the input data.

HashBytes()

The HashBytes() function, new in SQL Server 2005, allows you to transform data passed into the function, but you cannot recover the original value (see Figure 5-2). This function is suitable for when you need the identifying nature of the data, but the actual value does not matter. Consider password authentication or user and customer validation; these situations require that a user submit a secret identification value, but the actual value does not need to be recovered from the database in the future. In other words, you will not need to "unhash" the data.

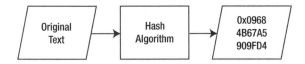

Figure 5-2. *The HashBytes() function in action*

The HashBytes() function will support the MD2, MD4, MD5, SHA, and SHA1 algorithms. In most cases, you will use the SHA1 algorithm.

```
SELECT HashBytes('SHA1', 'ClearText')
GO
```

■Note Hashing data applies a case-sensitive algorithm to deterministically transform your data into a new series of characters. It is useful for authentication, but limited in function, as you cannot later recover the plaintext value. The standard algorithms in SQL Server 2005 are theoretically vulnerable to collisions, where two distinct values passed to the same algorithm will produce the same hash output.

The beauty of this form of data protection is that it is deterministic, which is also its shortcoming. When you hash the same text using the same hash algorithm, the result will always be the same. This is very important when you want to execute equality searches on the data. You can add an index to a column that has been hashed and be confident that the database engine will properly use this index to improve the performance of queries that filter based on this data.

The deterministic output of the hash is also the greatest risk to the function. Bad guys can build a dictionary of hash results for different hash algorithms and attempt reverse lookups against your data. This poses a real threat to sensitive data. Typically, a salt is combined with the plaintext data to strengthen the hash and protect against these dictionary attacks.

In the section "Searching Encrypted Data" later in this chapter, I will explore a solution that relies on the HashBytes() function to improve performance of searching encrypted data.

Asymmetric Key and Certificate Encryption

Both certificate encryption and asymmetric encryption embody a pair of keys. Data encryption is achieved with a single public key, and decryption is achieved with a separate, mathematically related private key (see Figure 5-3). Certificate encryption and asymmetric encryption are very slow—significantly slower than symmetric key encryption. As a rule, certificate encryption or asymmetric encryption is only recommended when you need to encrypt and decrypt one or two records at a time. As noted in the next section, asymmetric keys and certificates are ideal for protecting symmetric keys.

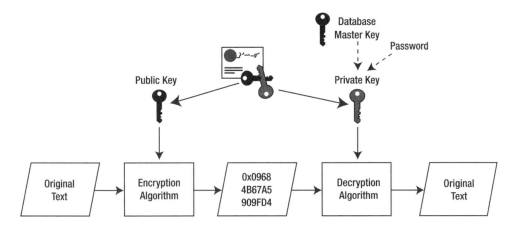

Figure 5-3. *Asymmetric encryption uses public keys on one end and private keys on the other.*

A certificate is typically a CER file that is created by an outside certification authority and imported into SQL Server. You may generate self-signed certificates in SQL Server, but these are limited with a private key length of 1024 bits. SQL Server supports private key lengths between 384 and 3456 bits on certificates that are imported from external sources. Longer private key lengths will strengthen the encryption, but will also impact the performance of decrypting and encrypting data.

An asymmetric key is also a container for a pair of keys—a public key and a private key. As with a certificate, you can import an asymmetric key from an external source. When you create an asymmetric key within SQL Server 2005, you have the option of specifying a private key length of 512, 1024, or 2048 bits.

■**Note** Both certificate and asymmetric encryption use the RSA algorithm to protect the data. Assuming equal key length, certificate encryption and asymmetric encryption will deliver the same encryption strength.

The choice between a certificate and an asymmetric key is typically one of culture. If your environment uses certificates from external certification authorities, you will probably prefer to use certificates in your SQL Server encryption implementation. If you are generating your keys in SQL Server, you may prefer to use asymmetric keys when you would like to use longer private key lengths to strengthen your encryption.

The private keys of asymmetric and certificate key pairs are protected with either the database master key or a password. By default, the private key is protected by the database master key—if you have created one. If the database master key was not created, a password is required when you create or import a certificate or asymmetric key.

As discussed in the section "Database Master Key," relying on a transparent key hierarchy will protect your data at rest and—if you remove the service master key protection—may protect your data from the sysadmin. If your principal concern is to protect your database and backup files in the event they are stolen, the default nature that protects the private key with the database master key will suffice. If you are comfortable that the individuals in the db_owner database role have access to your database master key and all dependent private keys, this default private key protection is sufficient.

In some extreme implementations, you may want to secure your data from the db_owner. If so, you will protect your private key with a password. All of the same aforementioned cautions apply where you must take care in how you are supplying the password from the application to prevent the db_owner from viewing the passwords from Profiler or directly in stored procedures.

The following example will create a self-signed certificate and an asymmetric key in SQL Server 2005:

```
CREATE CERTIFICATE MyCert
    WITH Subject = 'My Person Cert'
GO


CREATE ASYMMETRIC KEY AsymKeyPerson
    WITH Algorithm = RSA_1024
GO
```

Permissions defined on the certificate and asymmetric key will determine whether the user has access to the private key. If you would like to grant a user permission to encrypt data, but not decrypt data, the user is granted VIEW DEFINITION permission on the securable and will only have access to the public key. If the user is allowed to decrypt and encrypt data, the user is granted CONTROL permission on the securable and has access to both the public and the private key. The current permissions assume that any user who has access to decrypt data may also encrypt data. Permissions may not be set to allow a user to only decrypt data, not encrypt data.

In the following example, Pam may access the public key to encrypt data using the AsymKeyPerson asymmetric key. Tom is able to access the private key and decrypt data that was encrypted with the AsymKeyPerson key.

```
GRANT VIEW DEFINITION ON ASYMMETRIC KEY AsymKeyPerson TO Pam
GO


GRANT CONTROL ON ASYMMETRIC KEY AsymKeyPerson TO Tom
GO
```

SQL Server 2005 has introduced the EncryptByAsymKey() and EncryptByCert() functions to encrypt your data. The following example will encrypt the SocialSecurityNumber data from a table named Source using an asymmetric key named MyAsymKey and insert the encrypted data into the Person table:

```
INSERT INTO Person
(
    SocialSecurityNumber
)
SELECT
    EncryptByAsymKey(AsymKey_ID('MyAsymKey'), SocialSecurityNumber)
FROM Source
GO
```

The DecryptByAsymKey() and DecryptByCert() functions will return the varbinary representation of your decrypted data. You may need to convert the output to a meaningful format for your application. When decrypting the data, the DecryptByAsymKey() function is applied to the example as follows:

```
SELECT
    CONVERT(
        NVARCHAR(9),
        DecryptByAsymKey(
            AsymKey_ID('MyAsymKey'),
            SocialSecurityNumber))
FROM Person
GO
```

Asymmetric encryption is stronger than symmetric encryption, but performance will make it unsuitable for most data stored in tables. Asymmetric encryption is recommended for protecting symmetric keys and configuration values stored in tables. Avoid using asymmetric encryption on any column that requires filter activity on the encrypted data or decryption of more than one or two records at a time. These data requirements will perform better when encrypted with a symmetric key.

Symmetric Key Encryption

The nature of symmetric encryption uses a single key to encrypt and decrypt the data (see Figure 5-4). Symmetric encryption is significantly faster than asymmetric encryption, and it is the recommended method for encrypting data stored in user tables. In fact, it has been my experience that decrypting data that is encrypted with a symmetric key can be more than a thousand times faster than asymmetric encryption. Because of the performance differences, asymmetric keys are typically used to protect the symmetric keys that are used to encrypt data.

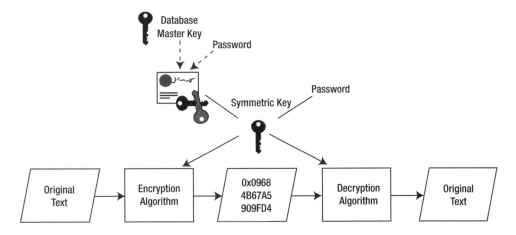

Figure 5-4. *Symmetric encryption uses the same password for both encryption and decryption.*

SQL Server 2005 symmetric encryption supports a number of algorithms. The recommended algorithms in order of key length and encryption strength are TRIPLE_DES, AES_128, AES_192, and AES_256. TRIPLE_DES is the strongest algorithm you may choose if you are running SQL Server 2005 on Windows XP. Microsoft does not recommend the RC4 or RC128 stream ciphers, as these are not salted, which results in a much weaker encryption implementation.[1]

Symmetric keys are protected by one or more of the following methods: asymmetric keys, certificates, passphrases/passwords, or other symmetric keys.

Encrypting your symmetric key with a password will generate a TRIPLE-DES key to secure your symmetric key. If you are using a stronger encryption algorithm, such as AES_256, your symmetric key is protected with a weaker algorithm. This may not be an acceptable level of protection in your business and should be considered prior to adopting this method of protection.

When you protect your symmetric key using a certificate or asymmetric key, as in Figure 5-4, you are implementing what is commonly known as the **hybrid approach** to encryption. This is the recommended approach to blend the strength of asymmetric encryption with the speed of symmetric encryption. You are ensured a stronger method of securing your symmetric key, while benefiting from the enhanced performance of symmetric encryption.

■**Note** While asymmetric keys and certificates can use only one form of protection, symmetric keys may use multiple forms of protection. If multiple forms of protection are applied to a symmetric key, you need to use only one form to open the key. A single symmetric key may be used between multiple applications, and each application will have its own password, certification, or asymmetric key to open the symmetric key.

The following example creates a symmetric key that is protected by a certificate. User Jack must have CONTROL permission on the certificate, so that the symmetric key may be decrypted. The user must also have VIEW DEFINITION permission on the symmetric key to encrypt and decrypt data using the symmetric key. Since this is a single key used for both encryption and decryption, you will not specify a different set of permissions to control each of these activities.

```
CREATE SYMMETRIC KEY MySymKey WITH ALGORITHM = AES_128
    ENCRYPTION BY CERTIFICATE MyCert
GO

GRANT CONTROL ON CERTIFICATE MyCert TO Jack
GO

GRANT VIEW DEFINITION ON SYMMETRIC KEY MySymKey TO Jack
GO
```

If you want to encrypt data with a symmetric key, you must first open—or decrypt—the key. Once the key is open, the EncryptByKey() function is used to encrypt to your data. When you are done using the symmetric key, it is a good practice to explicitly close the key—although the key is closed when the session is terminated.

---

1. See the SQL Server 2005 Books Online topic "CREATE SYMMETRIC KEY (Transact-SQL)" for Microsoft's recommended algorithms.

```
OPEN SYMMETRIC KEY MySymKey
    DECRYPTION BY CERTIFICATE MyCert;
GO

INSERT INTO Person
(
    SocialSecurityNumber
)
SELECT
    EncryptByKey(
        Key_GUID('MySymKey'),
        SocialSecurityNumber)
FROM Source
GO

CLOSE SYMMETRIC KEY MySymKey;
GO
```

Depending on how you protected your symmetric key, you will use one of a few new functions exposed by SQL Server 2005 to support data decryption. The first we will discuss is the DecryptByKey() function, which requires that you explicitly open your key. You may then pass in the Key_GUID of your symmetric key and the data to decrypt.

```
OPEN SYMMETRIC KEY MySymKey
    DECRYPTION BY CERTIFICATE MyCert;
GO

SELECT
    DecryptByKey(
        Key_GUID('MySymKey'),
        SocialSecurityNumber)
FROM Person
GO

CLOSE SYMMETRIC KEY MySymKey;
GO
```

Alternatively, if your symmetric key is protected with a certificate or asymmetric key, you can use the DecryptByKeyAutoCert() or DecryptByKeyAutoAsymKey() function to decrypt your data in a single operation. When the functions are executed, SQL Server will automatically open the symmetric key associated with the encrypted data if the user has the appropriate permission.

These functions are useful when you decrypt data from a single column where the data has been encrypted with multiple different symmetric keys. For example, we have a single table, PersonID, to store Social Security numbers and birthdates. We will create a single certificate and two separate symmetric keys that are protected with our single certificate.

```
CREATE TABLE PersonID
(
    PersonID INT IDENTITY(1,1),
    SocialSecurityNumber VARBINARY(100)
)
GO


CREATE CERTIFICATE CertPerson
    ENCRYPTION BY PASSWORD = 'pJBp4bb92548d243Ll12'
    WITH Subject = 'Person Cert',
    Expiry_Date = '01/01/2009'
GO


CREATE SYMMETRIC KEY SymKeyPerson_1
    WITH ALGORITHM = TRIPLE_DES
    ENCRYPTION BY CERTIFICATE CertPerson
GO


CREATE SYMMETRIC KEY SymKeyPerson_2
    WITH ALGORITHM = TRIPLE_DES
    ENCRYPTION BY CERTIFICATE CertPerson
GO
```

When we insert data, we specify a different symmetric key for each row. This may simulate an environment where a single table is used across multiple departments, and varying access is controlled at the row level by symmetric keys.

```
OPEN SYMMETRIC KEY SymKeyPerson_1
    DECRYPTION BY CERTIFICATE CertPerson
    WITH PASSWORD = 'pJBp4bb92548d243Ll12';
GO
INSERT INTO PersonID
SELECT
    EncryptByKey(
        Key_GUID('SymKeyPerson_1'),
        N'111111111')
GO
CLOSE SYMMETRIC KEY SymKeyPerson_1;
GO


OPEN SYMMETRIC KEY SymKeyPerson_2
    DECRYPTION BY CERTIFICATE CertPerson
    WITH PASSWORD = 'pJBp4bb92548d243Ll12';
GO


INSERT INTO PersonID
SELECT
    EncryptByKey(
```

```
        Key_GUID('SymKeyPerson_2'),
        N'222222222')
GO

CLOSE SYMMETRIC KEY SymKeyPerson_2;
GO
```

When executed, the `DecryptByKeyAutoCert()` function will automatically open the associated symmetric keys, decrypt the data, and close the symmetric keys. Because each symmetric key is protected with the same certificate, and we have permission to open all of the associated keys, we can use the `DecryptByKeyAutoCert()` function to view all of the data in a single statement.

```
SELECT
    PersonID,
    CONVERT(
        NVARCHAR(9),
        DecryptByKeyAutoCert(
            Cert_ID('CertPerson'),
            N'pJBp4bb92548d243Ll12',
            SocialSecurityNumber)
    ) AS SocialSecurityNumber
FROM PersonID;
```

The results of the preceding example are shown in Figure 5-5.

	PersonID	SocialSecurityNumber
1	1	111111111
2	2	222222222

Figure 5-5. *DecryptByKeyAutoCert()used to decrypt Social Security numbers*

The user must have `CONTROL` permission on the certificate to open the certificate and `VIEW DEFINITION` on the associated symmetric keys. If the user does not have `VIEW DEFINITION` on one of the symmetric keys, the data is not returned for those rows that depend on that symmetric key.

This is also an ideal method if you are interested in building a view to return decrypted data to the user. A user will be granted `SELECT` permission on the view, and must also have the aforementioned permissions on the certificate and symmetric key to view the encrypted data. If the user is not granted permissions on the certificates and symmetric keys, the view will return `NULL` values.

```
CREATE VIEW vw_Person
AS
SELECT
    CONVERT(
        NVARCHAR(9),
        DecryptByKeyAutoCert (
```

```
            Cert_ID('CertPerson'),
            N'pJBp4bb92548d243Ll12',
            SocialSecurityNumber)
    ) AS SocialSecurityNumber
FROM PersonID
GO
```

You can also use encryption to control which users can access data at the column level. The following example implements a solution to secure data by column for different sets of users.

■**Note** This example is not limited to symmetric encryption. You can control security to each column by encrypting the data with a certificate or an asymmetric key as well. As discussed earlier, certificate encryption and asymmetric encryption are not recommended methods of encrypting data in tables due to performance. If your business is willing to accept the significant performance difference and absolutely requires that data be encrypted with asymmetric keys or certificates, the following example may be used to secure data in a single table for different sets of users.

We will work with our PersonID table, but add another column to store BirthDate. We will use the SymKeyPerson_1 key to encrypt the SocialSecurityNumber column and the SymKeyPerson_2 key to encrypt the new BirthDate column.

```
IF  EXISTS

    (
        SELECT *
        FROM INFORMATION_SCHEMA.TABLES
        WHERE
            TABLE_NAME = 'PersonID'
    )
    DROP TABLE PersonID
GO

CREATE TABLE PersonID
(
    PersonID INT IDENTITY(1,1),
    SocialSecurityNumber VARBINARY(100),
    BirthDate VARBINARY(100)
)
GO
```

Create two users, CustomerService and HR_User. The SocialSecurityNumber column is encrypted with the SymKeyPerson_1 key, and the BirthDate column is encrypted with the SymKeyPerson_2 key. HR_User has access to all of the data in the table and is granted VIEW DEFINITION on both keys. CustomerService will only have access to the BirthDate column and is granted VIEW DEFINITION on the SymKeyPeron_2 symmetric key. Grant these users CONTROL permission on the certificate and SELECT permission on the table.

```
CREATE USER HR_User WITHOUT LOGIN
CREATE USER CustomerService WITHOUT LOGIN
GO

GRANT CONTROL ON CERTIFICATE::CertPerson TO CustomerService, HR_User
GRANT VIEW DEFINITION ON SYMMETRIC KEY::SymKeyPerson_1 TO HR_User
GRANT VIEW DEFINITION ON SYMMETRIC KEY::SymKeyPerson_2
    TO CustomerService, HR_User
GRANT SELECT ON PersonID TO CustomerService, HR_User
GO
```

Insert two rows, encrypting each column with a different symmetric key:

```
OPEN SYMMETRIC KEY SymKeyPerson_1
    DECRYPTION BY CERTIFICATE CertPerson
    WITH PASSWORD = 'pJBp4bb92548d243Ll12';
OPEN SYMMETRIC KEY SymKeyPerson_2
    DECRYPTION BY CERTIFICATE CertPerson
    WITH PASSWORD = 'pJBp4bb92548d243Ll12';
GO

INSERT INTO PersonID
SELECT
    EncryptByKey(Key_GUID('SymKeyPerson_1'), N'111111111'),
    EncryptByKey(Key_GUID('SymKeyPerson_2'), N'02/02/1977')
GO

INSERT INTO PersonID
SELECT
    EncryptByKey(Key_GUID('SymKeyPerson_1'), N'222222222'),
    EncryptByKey(Key_GUID('SymKeyPerson_2'), N'01/01/1967')
GO

CLOSE SYMMETRIC KEY SymKeyPerson_1;
CLOSE SYMMETRIC KEY SymKeyPerson_2;
GO
```

Using the new CustomerService login, execute a SELECT statement to decrypt our two columns. CustomerService has access to the SymKeyPerson_2 symmetric key and is able to see the data in the BirthDate column. The data in the SocialSecurityNumber column returns NULL values when CustomerService executes the statement. Data is available from both columns when executed as the HR_User. Notice that although the columns are using different symmetric keys, the DecryptByKeyAutoCert() is used to decrypt each column. A single set of code may be deployed to your application, and access to the data is controlled through your encryption keys.

```
EXECUTE AS USER = 'CustomerService'
GO

SELECT
    PersonID,
    CONVERT(
        NVARCHAR(9),
        DecryptByKeyAutoCert (
            Cert_ID('CertPerson') ,
            N'pJBp4bb92548d243Ll12',
            SocialSecurityNumber)
    ) AS SocialSecurityNumber,
    CONVERT(
        NVARCHAR(9),
        DecryptByKeyAutoCert (
            Cert_ID('CertPerson') ,
            N'pJBp4bb92548d243Ll12',
            BirthDate)
    ) AS BirthDate
FROM PersonID;
GO

REVERT
GO
```

Symmetric encryption and decryption is much better performing than asymmetric key or certificate encryption. Even with this better-performing type of encryption, searching a large set of encrypted data is still an issue. The results of encrypting data with a symmetric key are nondeterministic, which renders indexes less useful when searching the data. Applying filters on your encrypted data will require decrypting all data prior to applying the filter. This will result in an index or table scan, which can negatively affect server resources while seriously impacting the scalability and availability of your data for concurrent user activity. In the section "Architecting for Performance," I will detail a solution to address this issue.

EncryptByPassphrase

If ease of use is the *only* factor in determining which method of encryption to use, EncryptByPassphrase() is worth considering. It may not be the best method based on most other criteria, as I will discuss in this section.

Encrypting data with a passphrase is incredibly easy to implement. This form of encryption does not require creating or securing certificates or keys, as a symmetric key is generated at the time of encryption and stored with the encrypted data. In fact, the Triple-DES symmetric key derived by the passphrase is not stored in any system table; it is not directly accessible by anyone.

To encrypt data using a passphrase, pass the clear text followed by a passphrase into the EncryptByPassphrase() function:

```
EncryptByPassPhrase(@PassphraseEnteredByUser, 'ClearText')
```

Data is decrypted by passing the passphrase and the encrypted text into the `DecryptByPassphrase()` function. As with asymmetric and symmetric encryption, the decrypted data is returned in varbinary and may require that you convert it to a useful format for your application.

```
DecryptByPassphrase(@PassphraseEnteredByUser, 'EncryptedText')
```

Now I will address the drawbacks to using this form of encryption. First, the encrypted data can be decrypted only when passed the correct passphrase—there are no other options for decrypting the data, which introduces a level of risk. If the passphrase is lost, the data is lost. Securely storing the passphrase is vitally important to protecting your ability to decrypt the data.

`EncryptByPassphrase()` does not provide an option for using stronger keys, as with other forms of encryption. The `EncryptByPassphrase()` function will only use the `Triple-DES` symmetric key algorithm. SQL Server 2005 symmetric encryption provides stronger encryption keys, like `AES 128`, `AES 192`, and `AES 256`. Your business requirements and service-level agreements may require that the data be protected with stronger encryption algorithms with larger keys.

The `EncryptByPassphrase()` function in SQL Server 2005 will not enforce passphrase complexity. The SQL Server 2005 symmetric key and asymmetric key/certificate encryption may be protected by a password, and the `CREATE` process will check for password complexity if required on your server. If your business requires or may someday require password complexity, and you will be encrypting data using a passphrase, you will need to develop a passphrase validation routine that will check the passphrase prior to using it to encrypt the data.

Finally, while this form of encryption appears to protect the data from individuals in the sysadmin fixed server role and db_owner database role, your implementation may prove that this may not be the case without significant changes to the application, as I will discuss in the next section.

Securing Data from the DBA

Perhaps it is the increasing number of companies that outsource or offshore the DBA function, but I am regularly asked how to secure the data from the DBA who is in the sysadmin fixed server role. As I have previously discussed, you have a number of issues to consider when trying to secure your data from a sysadmin or db_owner. Some members of the community consider `EncryptByPassphrase()` to be the best way to provide this functionality. In my opinion, the better method is to architect a solution that protects an asymmetric key with a password and protects the symmetric key with this asymmetric key (hybrid approach). Even this approach is limited in what it can protect, however.

When assigned to the sysadmin fixed server role, the DBA can view, insert, update, and delete data from any table in any database in the instance. The DBA assigned to the sysadmin role can control all keys and certificates managed by SQL Server. In short, anyone assigned to the sysadmin role will inherit the rights to decrypt and encrypt any data in any database that relies on the SQL Server encryption key architecture. If you are using the SQL Server 2005 database encryption key hierarchy, you have few options for securing the data from the DBA. As discussed previously, you may decide to forgo the key hierarchy and protect the asymmetric key, certificate, or symmetric key with a password, but the sysadmin still has the authority to drop these keys, which puts your sensitive data at risk.

At first blush, EncryptByPassphrase() promises to provide a solution for this requirement: if the DBA does not have the passphrase, the DBA cannot decrypt the sensitive data. The DBA cannot drop the keys, because they do not exist in the database. You may experience key protection, but a thorough review of the way in which the data is accessed may uncover that you are not securing the passphrases from the DBA. For instance, when data is accessed through stored procedures, you may hard-code these passphrases directly in the stored procedure. The DBA has rights to view all stored procedure text and will have access to these values. As an alternative, you may input the passphrase as a parameter, as in the following example:

```
CREATE PROCEDURE GetPersonData
    @PassphraseEnteredByUser VARCHAR(100)
AS
BEGIN
    SET NOCOUNT ON

    SELECT
        CONVERT(
            NVARCHAR(9),
            DecryptByPassphrase(
                @PassphraseEnteredByUser,
                SocialSecurityNumber)
        ) AS PersonData
    FROM PersonID
END
GO
```

Any junior DBA can set up a simple trace against the database to capture all activity, including stored procedures. The DBA will see the stored procedure call coupled with the input parameter containing the passphrase.

Some experienced stored procedure aficionados are aware of a little SQL Server 2000 "trick" to hide certain procedures from Profiler and Trace. When you pass a commented-out sp_password together with the execution of the stored procedure, SQL Server will not pass the statement to Profiler:

```
EXEC GetPersonData N'Passphrase'  --sp_password
GO
```

Profiler Output
```
-- 'sp_password' was found in the text of this event.
-- The text has been replaced with this comment for security reasons.
```

This "trick" was an unintended feature in SQL Server 2000 and does not produce the same results in SQL Server 2005. As of SQL Server 2005 Service Pack 1, SQL Server does not support flagging the execution of a procedure as private to block the statement text from Trace and Profiler.

If your motivation is to protect data from anyone in the sysadmin role, using the EncryptByPassphrase() feature will require that you generate your DML statements in the application and send the batch to SQL Server. In this example, your application may store the passphrases outside of SQL Server in a configuration file or directly in the application code. Of course, the sysadmin should not have access to the source code or file location containing the passphrases. When the statement is sent to SQL Server from the application, SQL Server Profiler will not reveal text related to encryption functions. When your application code passes the DecryptByPassphrase() function coupled with the proper passphrase, Profiler will replace the text of the event with "The text has been replaced with this comment for security reasons." Navigating toward an approach to embed DML SQL statements within the application code carries a number of concerns, which are detailed in the section "The Stored Procedure vs. Ad Hoc SQL Debate" in Chapter 7.

If you protect your asymmetric keys, certificates, or symmetric keys with a password, you will open the key directly in your application code and call a stored procedure that contains the DML statements in the same session. In the previous example, we may have a stored procedure as follows:

```
CREATE PROCEDURE GET_Person
AS
    SET NOCOUNT ON

    SELECT
        CONVERT(
            NVARCHAR(9),
            DecryptByKey(SocialSecurityNumber)
        ) AS Person
    FROM Personid
GO
```

The application code will open the symmetric key and subsequently execute the GET_Person procedure. This solution will minimize the code that is embedded in your application, while providing a level of data protection from the sysadmin and db_owner. The DBA cannot change a password associated with a key or certificate without passing in the old password, which protects your passwords from malicious activity. However, this solution is still at risk if a disgruntled DBA decides to drop all keys and certificates on the server. A good backup strategy is required to address this situation.

There is no easy solution to protecting your data from the DBA. Outsourcing and offshoring such a sensitive role will require analysis of your overall server security layer; SQL Server 2005 encryption should not be considered a single approach to solving this dilemma.

Architecting for Performance

As discussed earlier, encryption will affect database performance. It will affect write performance, but given that most databases read more than they write, the biggest impact to your applications will probably be read performance. Different methods of encryption will affect performance in varying extremes. The types of algorithms used in symmetric encryption perform significantly faster than those for asymmetric encryption. Asymmetric encryption is stronger than symmetric encryption, but at a considerable cost to the decryption performance. All types of encryption are nondeterministic, which renders indexes less useful when searching or filtering on the indexed data. Even the better-performing symmetric encryption will affect the scalability of your database should you require search, filter, join, or group by activity on encrypted data.

All is not lost. The following section will walk you through an architecture design to support building a deterministic and secure hash of your sensitive data so your database application can scale while meeting the data protection requirements of the business.

Setting Up the Solution and Defining the Problem

The remainder of this chapter will work with a very simple credit card table in a Credit database to store encrypted data. Our business is primarily interested in protecting the data at rest, and will expect that the individuals assigned to the sysadmin and db_owner roles have access to the sensitive data. Our table will store an encrypted credit card number and a primary key identifier.

```
IF  NOT EXISTS
    (
        SELECT *
        FROM sys.databases
        WHERE name = N'Credit'
    )
    CREATE DATABASE Credit
GO


USE Credit
GO


IF  EXISTS
    (
        SELECT *
        FROM INFORMATION_SCHEMA.TABLES
        WHERE TABLE_NAME = 'CreditCard'
    )
    DROP TABLE CreditCard
GO


CREATE TABLE CreditCard
(
    CreditCardId INT IDENTITY(1,1) NOT NULL,
    CreditCardNumber VARBINARY(100) NOT NULL,
    CONSTRAINT PK_CreditCard
        PRIMARY KEY CLUSTERED(CreditCardId)
)
GO
```

We will create a new user to represent the users of our credit card application. This user will have access to SELECT, UPDATE, and DELETE from the CreditCard table. We will grant one additional permission on SHOWPLAN so that we may review the execution plans when executing statements as this user. A production implementation will not require this permission.

```
CREATE USER CreditCardUser WITHOUT LOGIN
GO
```

```
GRANT SELECT, UPDATE, INSERT ON CreditCard TO CreditCardUser
GO

GRANT SHOWPLAN TO CreditCardUser
GO
```

Our solution will use the hybrid approach to symmetric encryption. A symmetric key will protect our data, and the symmetric key will be protected using an asymmetric key. As discussed earlier, this hybrid approach affords us the strength of asymmetric encryption coupled with the improved performance of symmetric encryption.

Our solution will also rely on the key architecture where the private key of the asymmetric key pair is protected with the database master key, and the database master key is protected with the service master key. To set up our asymmetric key, we first create a database master key if one does not exist. Once we have our database master key, we will create the asymmetric key. The user CreditCardUser will be granted CONTROL on the asymmetric key, which will allow this user to decrypt data that was encrypted with the key.

```
IF NOT EXISTS
    (
        SELECT *
        FROM sys.Symmetric_Keys
        WHERE name LIKE '%DatabaseMasterKey%'
    )
CREATE MASTER KEY ENCRYPTION BY PASSWORD =
    'GiAFn1Blj2jxsUgmJm7Oc4Lb1dt4zLPD29GtrtJvEkBhLozTKrA4qAfOsIvS2EY'
GO

IF NOT EXISTS
    (
        SELECT *
        FROM sys.Asymmetric_Keys
        WHERE name = 'CreditCardAsymKey'
    )
CREATE ASYMMETRIC KEY CreditCardAsymKey
    WITH Algorithm = RSA_1024
GO

GRANT CONTROL ON ASYMMETRIC KEY::CreditCardAsymKey TO CreditCardUser
GO
```

Armed with our asymmetric key, we can now create the symmetric key and specify key encryption by the newly created asymmetric key. Our user will be granted the VIEW DEFINITION permission on the symmetric key. This permission will allow the user to encrypt and decrypt using the symmetric key.

```
IF NOT EXISTS
    (
        SELECT *
        FROM sys.Symmetric_Keys
```

```
        WHERE name = 'CreditCardSymKey'
    )
CREATE SYMMETRIC KEY CreditCardSymKey
    WITH ALGORITHM = TRIPLE_DES
    ENCRYPTION BY ASYMMETRIC KEY  CreditCardAsymKey
GO


GRANT VIEW DEFINITION ON SYMMETRIC KEY::CreditCardSymKey TO CreditCardUser
GO
```

We are now ready to add data to the table using our symmetric key. We will add 1,000 records to the table, which should give us a good idea of the performance impact of decryption. CreditCardUser will populate the table.

```
EXECUTE AS USER = 'CreditCardUser'
GO


OPEN SYMMETRIC KEY CreditCardSymKey
    DECRYPTION BY ASYMMETRIC KEY CreditCardAsymKey;
GO


DECLARE @i bigint
SET @i = 19999999999000


WHILE @i <= 19999999999999
BEGIN
    INSERT INTO CreditCard
    (
        CreditCardNumber
    )
    SELECT
        EncryptByKey(
            Key_GUID('CreditCardSymKey'),
            CAST(@i AS NVARCHAR(14)))

    SET @i = @i + 1
END
GO


CLOSE SYMMETRIC KEY CreditCardSymKey;
GO


REVERT
GO
```

We know that we will issue searches on CreditCardNumber, so we create an index to support this search as follows:

```
CREATE NONCLUSTERED INDEX IX_CreditCardNumber
    ON CreditCard (CreditCardNumber)
GO
```

We are finally ready to query the table. In our theoretical credit card application, a typical query will issue an equality search on the encrypted column, as shown here:

```
EXECUTE AS USER = 'CreditCardUser'
GO

DECLARE @SearchCritera NVARCHAR(14)
SET @SearchCritera = N'19999999999010'

SELECT
    CONVERT(
        NVARCHAR(50),
        DecryptByKeyAutoAsymKey(
            AsymKey_ID('CreditCardAsymKey'),
            NULL ,
            CreditCardNumber))
FROM CreditCard
WHERE
    CONVERT(
        NVARCHAR(50),
        DecryptByKeyAutoAsymKey(
            AsymKey_ID('CreditCardAsymKey'),
            NULL,
            CreditCardNumber)
    ) = @SearchCritera
GO
REVERT
GO
```

This statement will produce the execution plan depicted in Figure 5-6. SQL Server will decrypt all values in the CreditCardNumber column, which results in an index scan prior to applying the filter—even with a meaningful index on our search column.

Figure 5-6. *Searching directly on encrypted data yields a less-than-satisfactory execution plan.*

Our sample is a relatively small table, but you can imagine the performance implication when your table contains hundreds of thousands or even millions of records. Scanning the entire table will issue a shared lock on the table, which could block concurrent insert and update activity. Large scans will impact memory, and decrypting a large number of records will increase CPU utilization.

Searching Encrypted Data

The principal reason why we have a performance issue when searching encrypted data is the nondeterministic nature of the encrypted data. Encrypting the same piece of data multiple times will return different ciphertext results. To prove this, execute the following multiple times and examine the results.

```
SELECT EncryptByPassPhrase('Passphrase', 'EncryptMe')
GO
```

Consider the alternative—if encryption were deterministic, certain characteristics about your data would be exposed. Queries can be executed against the data to determine the uniqueness of the domain of data and how often a particular value may be repeated within the domain. Before you build a solution to support search, group, and join activity on your sensitive data, your business must accept the risk of exposing these data characteristics.

As demonstrated, you can create an index on an encrypted column, but the usefulness of the index is limited to index scans. The database engine will never perform an index seek on a column of encrypted data, as the data in the index will need to be decrypted prior to applying a filter, group, or join criteria. Since encryption is nondeterministic, it is not possible to encrypt search criteria with an encryption key and perform an equality search against the varbinary data stored in the table. When you are searching millions of encrypted values, index scans can be a major detriment to the scalability and performance of your database.

If your applications require search activity against encrypted data, which is often the case, you will need to architect a solution that will include a deterministic search key in addition to the encrypted data. At the same time, your solution needs to safeguard your sensitive data against dictionary attacks. An obvious solution would be to simply store a hash of the sensitive data in a separate column to use when searching. As mentioned in the section "HashBytes()," a hash is deterministic, which improves index utilization but also incurs a threat of dictionary attacks against your data. A better solution would be to extend the hash concept and build a search key based on a deterministic and secure message authentication code.

Message Authentication Code

Our search key will be built on the concept of a **message authentication code** (MAC). In this solution, we will use a MAC as a secure, deterministic value to represent a piece of encrypted data. The MAC will be the hash result of the combination of the data and a secret key. To put it simply, this is a salted hash based on a secured salt for added protection against dictionary attacks. This MAC will be stored in the same table as our encrypted data, and all search activity will be executed against the MAC column, which will enable efficient index utilization and optimal performance.

To begin creating the MAC solution, we will start by encrypting and storing a secret value in our database to be used as a salt, as depicted in Figure 5-7. The salt is decrypted and concatenated to the data. We will use the salt to alter the result of hashing a piece of data, which will make dictionary attacks nearly impossible. The concatenated result is passed through a HashBytes() function, which results in a MAC. When we add encrypted data to the database, we also add the MAC.

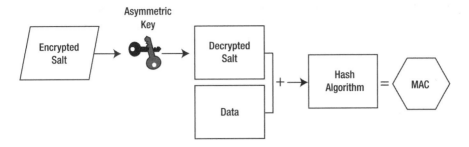

Figure 5-7. *The process of building a message authentication code*

In addition to the keys you generate to encrypt your data, this solution will require a salt stored in a separate table, a function to build the MAC, and an additional column in the table to store the MAC.

Our salt is stored in a table called MacKey. This table is a simple design for our solution, containing a single record of encrypted data.

```
IF  EXISTS
    (
        SELECT *
        FROM INFORMATION_SCHEMA.TABLES
        WHERE TABLE_NAME = 'MacKey'
    )
    DROP TABLE MacKey
GO

CREATE TABLE MacKey
(
    MacKeyID INT IDENTITY(1,1) NOT NULL,
    KeyData VARBINARY(256) NOT NULL,
    CONSTRAINT PK_MacKey
        PRIMARY KEY CLUSTERED(MacKeyID)
)
GO
```

The salt is very important to protecting our data from dictionary attacks. If an evildoer were to obtain our salt, it would be easier for him or her to build a dictionary of potential values. The salt is encrypted using an asymmetric key and stored in the KeyData column. We encrypt the salt with the same asymmetric key that is used to protect the symmetric key for encrypting our data.

■**Note** As discussed previously, asymmetric- and certificate-level encryption are best suited when decrypting a small amount of data. As we are encrypting and decrypting a single record, we can rely on a more secure method of protecting our salt with little impact to overall performance.

A strong salt value is important to ensuring that the data is protected; if the salt is broken, it exposes the data to potential dictionary attacks. Our salt is a long, unpredictable series of characters. Our encrypted salt is inserted into the MacKey table:

```
INSERT INTO MacKey
(
    KeyData
)
SELECT
    EncryptByAsymKey(
        AsymKey_ID('CreditCardAsymKey'),
        'F65rjUcXAU57YSfJf32ddWdTzlAdRMW8Ph'))
GO
```

■**Note** This same key may be used to salt multiple MAC hashes in your database, or you may decide to create a different MAC key for each encrypted column. If your business security requirements dictate that certificates and keys not be shared across multiple encrypted columns, the MacKey table may be extended with one or more additional columns indicating which application, table, and/or column each KeyValue supports. These new columns will serve as filter criteria in the BuildMac() function detailed in the upcoming text.

The next item to support the solution is a function that will concatenate the decrypted salt with the plaintext data, and build a hash on the result. Note that the input variable @PlainTextData is cast to uppercase prior to concatenating to the salt, so searches will not be case sensitive. Of course, this point is for general implementation—this example is based on numbers, so it is not affected by case sensitivity. The CreditCardUser is granted EXECUTE permission to the function.

```
CREATE FUNCTION BuildMac
(
    @PlainTextData NVARCHAR(MAX)
)
RETURNS VARBINARY(24)
AS
BEGIN
    DECLARE @return VARBINARY(24)
    DECLARE @macKey NVARCHAR(100)

    SET @return = NULL
    SET @macKey = NULL

    SET @macKey = (
        SELECT
            CONVERT(
                NVARCHAR(36),
```

```
                DecryptByAsymKey(
                    AsymKey_ID('CreditCardAsymKey'),
                    KeyData))
        FROM MacKey)

    IF(@macKey IS NOT NULL)
        SET @return = (
            SELECT
                HashBytes(
                    'SHA1',
                    UPPER(@PlainTextData) + @macKey))

    RETURN @return
END
GO


GRANT EXECUTE ON BuildMac TO CreditCardUser
GO
```

This MAC solution is ready to use. We have created a special table to store the secret key, or salt, and populated the table with a single record. We have also created a function that will be used to generate the MAC. The CreditCardUser has the necessary permission to execute the BuildMac() function.

Storing Search Data

With the salt value securely stored in the table and the function built to generate the MAC, let's turn our attention to the CreditCard table. This table will store the encrypted credit card number and the credit card number MAC. We will drop our previous table and re-create the table with the additional CreditCardMac column.

```
IF  EXISTS
    (
        SELECT *
        FROM INFORMATION_SCHEMA.TABLES
        WHERE TABLE_NAME = 'CreditCard'
    )
    DROP TABLE CreditCard
GO

CREATE TABLE CreditCard
(
    CreditCardId INT IDENTITY(1,1) NOT NULL,
    CreditCardNumber NVARCHAR(100) NOT NULL,
    CreditCardNumberMac VARBINARY(50) NOT NULL,
    CONSTRAINT PK_CreditCard
        PRIMARY KEY CLUSTERED(CreditCardId)
)
```

```
GO

GRANT SELECT, UPDATE, INSERT ON CreditCard TO CreditCardUser
GO
```

Note It may seem redundant and counterintuitive to good database design to store the same data more than once in the same table. Not only does the table require more storage, but also requires that your table inserts and data updates will need to insert and update both columns. If you update the encrypted column without also updating the MAC column, your searches will return incorrect results. This particular design is necessary, however, since the MAC value is a hash that cannot be reversed to return the original value. The cost of storing the data twice needs to be considered throughout your application design, but it should not preclude the application of this solution. When you need to search encrypted data, any cost associated with these issues is outweighed by the usefulness and performance benefits of the solution.

Before we can insert data, we need to design some triggers to ensure that the data is synchronized. A trigger will exist for new inserts, and a separate trigger for updates.

The insert trigger will return an error if an insert is attempted without a CreditCardNumber value. The trigger will insert the encrypted CreditCardNumber and the results of the BuildMac() function.

```
CREATE TRIGGER ins_CreditCard
ON CreditCard
INSTEAD OF INSERT
AS
BEGIN
    SET NOCOUNT ON

    IF EXISTS
        (
            SELECT *
            FROM inserted
            WHERE CreditCardNumber IS NULL
        )
        RAISERROR( 'Credit Card Number is required', 16, 1)
    ELSE
    BEGIN
        INSERT INTO CreditCard
        (
            CreditCardNumber,
            CreditCardNumberMac
        )
        SELECT
            EncryptByKey(
                Key_GUID('CreditCardSymKey'),
```

```
            CreditCardNumber),
        BuildMac(CreditCardNumber)
    FROM inserted
END
END
GO
```

The trigger requires that the key be open during the insert. We will issue an insert loop to populate 1,000 records.

```
EXECUTE AS USER = 'CreditCardUser'
GO

OPEN SYMMETRIC KEY CreditCardSymKey
DECRYPTION BY ASYMMETRIC KEY CreditCardAsymKey
GO

DECLARE @i BIGINT
SET @i = 19999999999000

WHILE @i <= 19999999999999
BEGIN
    INSERT INTO CreditCard
    (
        CreditCardNumber
    )
    SELECT @i

    SET @i = @i + 1
END
GO

CLOSE SYMMETRIC KEY CreditCardSymKey
GO

REVERT
GO
```

Since we are storing the CreditCardNumber in multiple columns, we will need to protect the integrity of the MAC during updates. An additional trigger is created on the table to ensure that any changes to the CreditCardNumber are applied to the CreditCardNumberMAC column. The update trigger will not allow updates directly on the CreditCardMac column.

```
CREATE TRIGGER upd_CreditCard
ON CreditCard
    INSTEAD OF UPDATE
AS
BEGIN
    SET NOCOUNT ON
```

```
    IF (UPDATE(CreditCardNumberMAC))
        RAISERROR( 'Update not allowed.', 16, 1 )
    ELSE
    BEGIN
        UPDATE cc
        SET
            CreditCardNumberMac = BuildMac(i.CreditCardNumber),
            CreditCardNumber =
                EncryptByKey(
                    Key_GUID('CreditCardSymKey'),
                    i.CreditCardNumber)
        FROM inserted i
        INNER JOIN CreditCard cc ON i.CreditCardId = cc.CreditCardId
    END
END
GO
```

Before we issue an update to test this trigger, we should build an index to support the subsequent SELECT statement to verify the trigger. This will be the same index that will support the known search path used by our theoretical application. All search activity is executed on the CreditCardNumberMac column, but we are interested in returning the decrypted CreditCardNumber value. Using the new INCLUDE feature in SQL Server 2005, we can improve the execution of queries by covering them with the index.

■**Note** When queries are covered in a single index, the database engine does not need to issue an additional seek or lookup on the data page to find the columns that are not in the index. In implementations on large tables, I have witnessed a significant performance improvement when the index covers the query.

Our index is built on CreditCardNumberMac, and the CreditCardNumber column is an included non-key column.

```
CREATE NONCLUSTERED INDEX IX_CreditCardNumberMac
    ON CreditCard (CreditCardNumberMac ASC)
    INCLUDE (CreditCardNumber)
GO
```

Armed with an index, we will test the update trigger. Because we have based our MAC on a hash value, and a hash may introduce collisions, we will always add an additional filter criterion to check for the correct decrypted CreditCardNumber value. When we issue an update on the table, the trigger will keep the columns synchronized.

```
EXECUTE AS USER = 'CreditCardUser'
GO

OPEN SYMMETRIC KEY CreditCardSymKey
    DECRYPTION BY ASYMMETRIC KEY CreditCardAsymKey
```

```
GO

UPDATE CreditCard
SET CreditCardNumber = '12345678910000'
WHERE
    BuildMac('19999999999000') = CreditCardNumberMac
    AND CONVERT(
        NVARCHAR(14),
        DecryptByKeyAutoAsymKey(
            AsymKey_ID('CreditCardAsymKey'),
            NULL,
            CreditCardNumber)
    )= N'19999999999000'
GO

CLOSE SYMMETRIC KEY CreditCardSymKey
GO

REVERT
GO
```

The following will test the update and return a single row:

```
EXECUTE AS USER = 'CreditCardUser'
GO

SELECT
    CONVERT(
        NVARCHAR(50),
        DecryptByKeyAutoAsymKey(
            AsymKey_ID('CreditCardAsymKey'),
            NULL,
            CreditCardNumber)
    ) AS CreditCardNumber
FROM CreditCard
WHERE BuildMac('12345678910000') = CreditCardNumberMac
GO

REVERT
GO
```

Equality Searches

Our solution is now complete and will now execute well-performing equality searches. To fully appreciate the difference between searching on the MAC and searching directly on the encrypted data, we will revisit the query and execution plan when searching on the encrypted data.

```
EXECUTE AS USER = 'CreditCardUser'
GO

DECLARE @SearchCritera NVARCHAR(14)
SET @SearchCritera = N'19999999999010'

SELECT
    CONVERT(
        NVARCHAR(50),
        DecryptByKeyAutoAsymKey(
            AsymKey_ID('CreditCardAsymKey'),
            NULL,
            CreditCardNumber))
FROM CreditCard
WHERE
    CONVERT(
        NVARCHAR(50),
        DecryptByKeyAutoAsymKey(
            AsymKey_ID('CreditCardAsymKey'),
            NULL,
            CreditCardNumber)
    ) = @SearchCritera
GO

REVERT
GO
```

Figure 5-8 shows the results of running the preceding execution plan.

Figure 5-8. *Using a function to search the data results in an index scan*

Apply the same search criteria using our MAC search key solution. Pass the search criteria into the BuildMac() function to generate the deterministic hash. The result of the BuildMac() function is compared against the CreditCardNumberMac column.

```
EXECUTE AS USER = 'CreditCardUser'
GO

DECLARE @SearchCritera NVARCHAR(14)
SET @SearchCritera = N'19999999999010'

SELECT
    CONVERT(
```

```
        NVARCHAR(50),
            DecryptByKeyAutoAsymKey(
                AsymKey_ID('CreditCardAsymKey'),
                NULL,
                CreditCardNumber))
FROM CreditCard
WHERE
    CreditCardNumberMac = BuildMac(@SearchCritera)
    AND CONVERT(
        NVARCHAR(14),
        DecryptByKeyAutoAsymKey(
            AsymKey_ID('CreditCardAsymKey'),
            NULL,
            CreditCardNumber)
    )= @SearchCritera
GO

REVERT
GO
```

The database engine was able to perform an index seek against the
IX_CreditCardNumberMac index, as shown in Figure 5-9. Since we covered the index by adding
the encrypted CreditCardNumber column as an INCLUDED column, the entire query is satisfied
in a single index seek.

Figure 5-9. *By using the MAC, the execution plan uses a seek instead of a scan.*

This same column can also be used to issue GROUP BY statements and serve as a surrogate
key for joining data between tables. This solution will not support range searches or substring
searches. Range searches and mid-string searches will require the data to be decrypted. In
these cases, you will need to build a customized solution to support these functions in a large-
scale environment. In the next section, I will detail how you can extend the example MAC
implementation to create a solution to support certain wildcard searches.

Wildcard Searches on Encrypted Data

You may find you need to perform wildcard searches on encrypted data. Perhaps your users
will be searching an encrypted name column for all customers whose last name begins with
a particular string. Perhaps the users will be searching data based on the last four digits of
a social security number. These cases are not uncommon, and I have often encountered situations that require some level of flexibility in the search criteria.

■**Caution** Wildcard searches may introduce a level of disclosure of your sensitive data and should be applied with care. Be cautious of the type of information on which you allow users to perform wildcard searches; you don't want sensitive data to be inferred through a series of such searches.

Hashes represent one exact piece of information; the hash built from a partial string will be completely different from the hash built on the complete string. The MAC solution developed in the previous section can only support exact matches. It is possible to architect a solution around this problem, although you will be required to define some boundaries to these search criteria.

The basic pattern of using a salted hash value as a searchable deterministic key remains the same. The difference is that the hash will now be built on a portion of the data instead of the entire value. The exact portion used to make the hash must be used consistently, and this portion must provide an adequate level of selectivity.

Returning to the credit card number example, perhaps our users wish to perform wildcard searches on the credit card numbers. The previous example built a hash on the full credit card number. To support a solution for substring searches of credit card numbers, we will require that each search include at least the last four digits of the card number. Since the last four digits will always be provided, the MAC will be built on that substring for each credit card instead of the entire number.

The substring solution will use the same `BuildMac()` function designed for the equality searches. This sample solution must support both equality searches and substring searches, so we will add a new column to store a MAC value based on our substring criteria. The original `CreditCardNumberMac` will support equality searches, and the new `CreditCardNumberSubstringMac` will support wildcard searches. We will also add an index to support the searches on the new `CreditCardNumberSubstringMac` column. Before adding data, drop and re-create the table with the new column and new index.

```
IF  EXISTS
    (
        SELECT *
        FROM INFORMATION_SCHEMA.TABLES
        WHERE TABLE_NAME = 'CreditCard'
    )
DROP TABLE CreditCard
GO

CREATE TABLE CreditCard
(
    CreditCardId INT IDENTITY(1,1) NOT NULL,
    CreditCardNumber NVARCHAR(100) NOT NULL,
    CreditCardNumberMac VARBINARY(50) NOT NULL,
    CreditCardNumberSubstringMac VARBINARY(50) NOT NULL,
    CONSTRAINT PK_CreditCard
        PRIMARY KEY CLUSTERED(CreditCardId)
)
```

```
GO

GRANT SELECT, UPDATE, INSERT ON CreditCard TO CreditCardUser
GO

CREATE NONCLUSTERED INDEX IX_CreditCardNumberSubstringMac
    ON CreditCard (CreditCardNumberSubstringMac)
    INCLUDE (CreditCardNumber)
GO
```

■**Note** A single MAC cannot support both an exact match and a wildcard MAC. If you will not be executing equality searches, your table will only require one additional column to support the substring MAC.

The insert and update triggers will use the same BuildMac() function to build the equality MAC as well as the substring MAC based on the rightmost four characters of a credit card number.

```
CREATE TRIGGER ins_CreditCard
    ON CreditCard
    INSTEAD OF INSERT
AS
BEGIN
    SET NOCOUNT ON

    IF EXISTS
        (
            SELECT *
            FROM inserted
            WHERE CreditCardNumber IS NULL
        )
        RAISERROR( 'Credit Card Number is required', 16, 1)
    ELSE
    BEGIN
        INSERT INTO CreditCard
        (
            CreditCardNumber,
            CreditCardNumberMac,
            CreditCardNumberSubstringMac
        )
        SELECT
            EncryptByKey(
                Key_GUID('CreditCardSymKey'),
                CreditCardNumber),
            BuildMac(CreditCardNumber),
            BuildMac(RIGHT(CreditCardNumber, 4))
        FROM inserted
```

```
        END
END
GO


CREATE TRIGGER upd_CreditCard
    ON CreditCard
    INSTEAD OF UPDATE
AS
BEGIN
    SET NOCOUNT ON

    IF
        (
            UPDATE(CreditCardNumberMAC)
            OR UPDATE(CreditCardNumberSubstringMac)
        )
        RAISERROR( 'Update not allowed.', 16, 1 )
    ELSE
    BEGIN
        UPDATE cc
        SET
            CreditCardNumberMac = BuildMac(i.CreditCardNumber),
            CreditCardNumberSubstringMac =
                BuildMac(RIGHT(i.CreditCardNumber, 4)),
            CreditCardNumber =
                EncryptByKey(
                    Key_GUID('CreditCardSymKey'),
                    i.CreditCardNumber)
        FROM inserted i
        INNER JOIN CreditCard cc ON i.CreditCardId = cc.CreditCardId
    END
END
GO
```

Execute the loop process to add data to the table:

```
EXECUTE AS USER = 'CreditCardUser'
GO


OPEN SYMMETRIC KEY CreditCardSymKey
    DECRYPTION BY ASYMMETRIC KEY CreditCardAsymKey
GO


DECLARE @i BIGINT
SET @i = 19999999999000


WHILE @i <= 19999999999999
BEGIN
```

```
    INSERT INTO CreditCard
    (
        CreditCardNumber
    )
    SELECT @i

    SET @i = @i + 1
END
GO


CLOSE SYMMETRIC KEY CreditCardSymKey
GO


REVERT
GO
```

As I stated earlier, this solution requires that all substring searches include at least the last four characters of a credit card number. Pass the right four characters of the search criteria into the BuildMac() function and issue an equality search against the new substring MAC.

```
WHERE
    CreditCardNumberSubstringMac = BuildMac(RIGHT(@SearchCritera, 4))
```

If the search criteria contains more than four digits, the decrypted value of the column is used in a LIKE clause. The database engine will decrypt the results from the CreditCardNumberSubstringMac exact match and compare these results against the LIKE condition.

```
AND CONVERT(
    NVARCHAR(14),
    DecryptByKeyAutoAsymKey(
        AsymKey_ID('CreditCardAsymKey'),
        NULL,
        CreditCardNumber)
    ) LIKE '%' + @SearchCritera
```

When the entire search process is executed as follows, the database engine will issue an index seek against the IX_CreditCardNumberSubstringMac index to find all records that match the last four characters of the search criteria. The results of this seek are filtered based on the LIKE condition that is applied to the decrypted CreditCardNumber. Note that SQL Server will decrypt only those records that satisfy the substring MAC filter.

```
EXECUTE AS USER = 'CreditCardUser'
GO

DECLARE @SearchCritera NVARCHAR(14)
SET @SearchCritera = N'9999456'

SELECT
    CONVERT(
```

```
            NVARCHAR(14),
            DecryptByKeyAutoAsymKey(
                AsymKey_ID('CreditCardAsymKey'),
                NULL,
                CreditCardNumber))
FROM CreditCard
WHERE
    CreditCardNumberSubstringMac = BuildMac(RIGHT(@SearchCritera, 4))
    AND CONVERT(
        NVARCHAR(14),
        DecryptByKeyAutoAsymKey(
            AsymKey_ID('CreditCardAsymKey'),
            NULL,
            CreditCardNumber)
        ) LIKE '%' + @SearchCritera
GO


REVERT
GO
```

Figure 5-10 depicts an execution plan when the data is filtered on a highly selective substring MAC. If the criteria for building the substring MAC is selective enough, we see the bulk of the work done on a quick index seek. When the substring MAC is less selective, the workload shifts to the slower filter operation.

Figure 5-10. *Substring searches on highly selective substring MACs can use index seeks.*

Keep in mind that the effectiveness of this search optimization is directly dependent on the selectivity of the substring MAC. For example, if a substring MAC is built on the last four digits of a credit card number, and a database has 10 million records that end with the same four digits, a search would have to decrypt all of those 10 million records. By the same token, if only five records in that same database end with the same four characters, the search would only decrypt those five records.

Choosing the proper rules for building a wildcard MAC is about striking a balance between the performance of your application and an acceptable number of characters. You want to have a substring MAC that is specific enough to have a high degree of selectivity in your database. At the same time, you do not want it to be so specific that users will not be able to provide enough information to perform a wildcard search at all.

Summary

Encrypting data is a powerful tool to help protect your most sensitive data, and it must be addressed with a holistic approach to securing your entire server, instance, database, and data. When used with a properly secured server, your business can be assured a greater level of protection of the precious data assets. Data protection must be considered within the context of your database application to meet the required performance and scalability of your application. Proper classification of sensitive data will reduce the number of data elements that require encryption, and designing secure data access paths using message authentication codes will address many of the performance issues of using encrypted data in your search arguments.

◼ ◼ ◼

CHAPTER 6

SQLCLR: Architecture and Design Considerations

Microsoft's announcement that it would host the common language runtime (CLR) within SQL Server 2005 was at once met by extreme resistance on the part of veteran DBAs and enthusiastic support by many developers. The only thing consistent among these two groups is that neither seemed to understand what integration would and would not actually offer. Rumors of the death of T-SQL and of developers being able to create vast worlds of DBA-impenetrable, compiled in-process data access code abounded.

The truth is that SQLCLR integration is not such a scary nor such a useful idea as many thought. And since SQL Server 2005 has been released, the fervor has, for the most part, died down. It does not appear that the CLR integration features are being heavily used, even by the same developers who were so enthusiastic about the features' potential only a year or two ago.

Those hoping to use the SQLCLR features as a wholesale replacement for T-SQL are quickly put off by the fact that writing CLR routines ends up taking a lot more code, and performance and reliability suffer due to the continual cost of marshaling data across the CLR boundaries. And for the DBAs who were not .NET developers to begin with, there is a somewhat steep learning curve involved for a feature that really doesn't have a whole lot of use cases.

Nonetheless, SQLCLR *does* have its place in a SQL Server developer's toolbox. This chapter deals with design and performance considerations for getting the most out of SQLCLR integration when you find that it is the right tool for the job at hand. It is my opinion that the primary strength of SQLCLR integration is in the ability to both move and share code between tiers— so this chapter's primary focus is on maintainability and reuse scenarios.

◼**Note** This chapter assumes that you are already familiar with SQLCLR topics, in addition to the C# programming language. You should know the basics of how to create and deploy functions, types, and aggregates, and how to deal with assembly references. For detailed coverage of these topics, refer to my chapters ".NET Integration" and "Programming Assemblies" (Chapters 5 and 6) in *Pro SQL Server 2005* (Apress, 2005).

Bridging the SQL/CLR Gap: the SqlTypes Library

The types exposed by the .NET Framework and by SQL Server are in many cases similar, but generally incompatible. A few major issues come up when dealing with SQL Server and .NET interoperability from the perspective of data types:

- First and foremost, all native SQL Server data types are nullable—that is, an instance of any given type can either hold a valid value in the domain of the type or represent an unknown (NULL). Types in .NET generally do not support this idea (note that C#'s null or VB .NET's nothing are not the same as SQL Server's NULL).

- The second difference between the type systems has to do with implementation. Format, precision, and scale of the types involved in each system differ dramatically. For example, .NET's DateTime type supports a much larger range and much greater precision than does SQL Server's DATETIME type.

- The third major difference has to do with runtime behavior of types in conjunction with operators. In SQL Server, virtually all operations involving at least one NULL instance of a type results in NULL. As the .NET Framework types are not natively nullable, this is not generally a concern for its type system. In addition to nullability, differences may result from handling overflows, underflows, and other potential errors inconsistently. For instance, adding 1 to a 32-bit integer with the value of 2147483647 (the maximum 32-bit integer value) in a .NET language may result in the value "wrapping around," producing -2147483648. In SQL Server, this behavior will never occur—instead, an overflow exception will result.

■**Note** The .NET 2.0 Framework adds something called a **nullable type**, which further muddies the waters. Nullable types allow developers to treat value type variables similarly to reference type variables in terms of the ability to dereference them. This has nothing to do with data access or database NULL values, and many developers were disappointed upon the release of .NET 2.0 to discover that ADO.NET does not accept nullable types as arguments to SQL parameters. Again, do not fall into the trap of confusing .NET's idea of null with SQL Server's idea of NULL—these are very different concepts.

In order to provide a layer of abstraction between the two type paradigms, the .NET 2.0 Framework ships with a namespace called System.Data.SqlTypes. This namespace includes a series of structures that map SQL Server types and behaviors into .NET. Each of these structures implements nullability through the INullable interface, which exposes an IsNull property that allows callers to determine whether a given instance of the type is NULL. Furthermore, these types conform to the same range, precision, and operator rules as SQL Server's native types.

Proper use of the SqlTypes types is, simply put, the most effective way of ensuring that data marshaled into and out of SQLCLR routines is handled correctly by each type system. It is my recommendation that, whenever possible, all methods exposed as SQLCLR objects use SqlTypes types as both input and output parameters, rather than standard .NET types. This will require a bit more development work upfront, but it should "futureproof" your code to some degree and help avoid type incompatibility issues.

Wrapping Code to Promote Cross-Tier Reuse

One of the primary selling points (as well as use cases) for SQLCLR integration, especially in shops that use the .NET Framework for application development, is the ability to easily move or share code between tiers when it makes sense. Unfortunately, some of the design necessities of working in the SQLCLR environment do not translate well to the application tier, and vice versa. One such example is use of the SqlTypes; although it is recommended that they be used for all interfaces in SQLCLR routines, that prescription does not make sense in the application tier, because the SqlTypes do not support the full range of operators and options that the native .NET types support. Using them for everything would make data access simple, but would rob you of the ability to do many complex data manipulation tasks, and would therefore be more of a hindrance than a helpful change.

Rewriting code or maintaining multiple versions customized for different tiers simply does not promote maintainability. In the best-case scenario, any given piece of logic used by an application should be coded in exactly one place—regardless of how many different components use the logic, or where it's deployed. This is one of the central design goals of object-oriented programming, and it's important to remember that it also applies to code being reused inside of SQL Server.

Instead of rewriting routines and types to make them compatible with the SqlTypes and implement other database-specific logic, I recommend that you get into the habit of designing wrapper methods and classes. These wrappers should map the SqlTypes inputs and outputs to the .NET types actually used by the original code, and call into the original routines via assembly references. Wrappers are also a good place to implement database-specific logic that may not exist in the original routines.

In addition to the maintainability benefits for the code itself, creating wrappers has a couple of other advantages. First of all, unit tests will not need to be rewritten—the same tests that work in the application tier will still apply in the data tier (although you may want to write secondary unit tests for the wrapper routines). Secondly—and perhaps more importantly—wrapping your original assemblies can help maintain a least-privileged coding model and help enhance security, as is discussed later in this chapter in the sections "Working with Code Access Security Privileges" and "Working with Host Protection Privileges."

A Simple Example: E-Mail Address Format Validation

It's quite common on web forms to be asked for your e-mail address, and you've no doubt encountered forms that tell you whether you've entered an e-mail address that does not comply with the standard format. This is a quicker—but obviously less effective—way to validate an e-mail address than actually sending an e-mail and waiting for a response, and it gives the user immediate feedback if something is obviously incorrect.

In addition to using this logic for front-end validation, it makes sense to implement the same thing in the database in order to drive a CHECK constraint. That way, any data that makes its way to the database—regardless of whether it already went through the check in the application—will be double-checked for correctness.

Following is a simple example method that uses a regular expression to validate the format of an address:

```
public static bool IsValidEmailAddress(string emailAddress)
{
```

```
//Validate the e-mail address
Regex r =
    new Regex(@"\w+([-+.]\w+)*@\w+([-.]\w+)*\.\w+([-.]\w+)*");

return (r.IsMatch(emailAddress));
}
```

This code could, of course, be used as-is in both SQL Server and the application tier—using it in SQL Server would simply require loading the assembly and registering the function. But this has some issues: the most obvious is the lack of proper NULL handling. As-is, this method will return an ArgumentException when a NULL is passed in. Depending on your business requirements, a better choice would probably be either NULL or false. Another potential issue is methods that require slightly different logic in the database vs. the application tier. In the case of this method, it's difficult to imagine how you might enhance the logic for use in a different tier, but for other methods, such modification would present a maintainability challenge.

The solution is to catalog the assembly containing this method in SQL Server, but not expose the method as a SQLCLR UDF. Instead, create a wrapper method that uses the SqlTypes and internally calls the initial method. This means that the initial method will not have to be modified in order to create a version that properly interfaces with the database, and the same assembly can be deployed in any tier. Following is a sample that shows a wrapper method created over the IsValidEmailAddress method, in order to expose a SQLCLR UDF version that properly supports NULL inputs and outputs. Note that I've created the inner method in a class called UtilityMethods and have also included a using statement for the namespace used in the UtilityMethods assembly.

```
[Microsoft.SqlServer.Server.SqlFunction]
public static SqlBoolean IsValidEmailAddress(
    SqlString emailAddress)
{
    //Return NULL on NULL input
    if (emailAddress.IsNull)
        return (SqlBoolean.Null);

    bool isValid = UtilityMethods.IsValidEmailAddress(emailAddress.Value);
    return (new SqlBoolean(isValid));
}
```

Note that this technique is usable not only for loading assemblies from the application tier into SQL Server, but also for going the other way—migrating logic back out of the data tier. Given the nature of SQLCLR, the potential for code mobility should always be considered, and developers should consider designing methods using wrappers even when creating code specifically for use in the database—this will maximize the potential for reuse later, when or if the same logic needs to be migrated to another tier, or even if the logic needs to be reused more than once inside of the data tier itself.

Cross-assembly references have other benefits as well, when working in the SQLCLR environment. By properly leveraging references, it is possible to create a much more robust, secure SQLCLR solution. The following sections introduce the security and reliability features that are used by the SQLCLR hosted run time, and show how you can exploit them via assembly references to manage security on a granular level.

SQLCLR Security and Reliability Features

Unlike stored procedures, triggers, UDFs, and other types of code modules that can be exposed within SQL Server, a given SQLCLR routine is not directly related to a database, but rather to an assembly **cataloged** within the database. Cataloging of an assembly is done using SQL Server's CREATE ASSEMBLY statement, and unlike their T-SQL equivalents, SQLCLR modules get their first security restrictions not via grants, but rather at the same time their assemblies are cataloged. The CREATE ASSEMBLY statement allows the DBA or database developer to specify one of three security and reliability **permission sets** that dictate what the code in the assembly is allowed to do.

The allowed permission sets are SAFE, EXTERNAL_ACCESS, and UNSAFE. Permissions granted by each set are nested to include the lower sets' permissions. The set of permissions allowed for SAFE assemblies includes limited access to math and string functions, along with data access to the host database via the context connection. The EXTERNAL_ACCESS permission set adds the ability to communicate outside of the SQL Server instance, to other database servers, file servers, web servers, and so on. And the UNSAFE permission set gives the assembly the ability to do pretty much anything—including running unmanaged code.

Although exposed as only a single user-controllable setting, internally each permission set's rights are actually enforced by two distinct methods. Assemblies assigned to each permission set are granted access to do certain operations via .NET's **Code Access Security** (CAS) technology. At the same time, access is limited to certain operations based on checks against a .NET 2.0 attribute called HostProtectionAttribute (HPA). On the surface, the difference between HPA and CAS is that they are opposites: CAS permissions dictate what an assembly can do, whereas HPA permissions dictate what an assembly cannot do. The combination of everything granted by CAS and everything denied by HPA makes up each of the three permission sets.

Beyond this basic difference is a much more important differentiation between the two access control methods. Although violation of a permission enforced by either method will result in a runtime exception, the actual checks are done at very different times. CAS grants are checked dynamically at run time via a stack walk done as code is executed. On the other hand, HPA permissions are checked at the point of just-in-time compilation—just *before* calling the method being referenced.

To observe how these differences affect the way code runs, a few test cases will be necessary. To begin with, let's take a look at how a CAS exception works. Create a new assembly containing the following CLR stored procedure:

```
[SqlProcedure]
public static void CAS_Exception()
{
    SqlContext.Pipe.Send("Starting...");

    using (System.IO.FileStream fs =
        new FileStream(@"c:\b.txt", FileMode.Open))
    {
        //Do nothing...
    }

    SqlContext.Pipe.Send("Finished...");
```

```
        return;
}
```

Catalog the assembly as `SAFE` and execute the stored procedure. This will result in the following output:

```
Starting...
Msg 6522, Level 16, State 1, Procedure CAS_Exception, Line 0
A .NET Framework error occurred during execution of user-defined routine or
aggregate "CAS_Exception":
System.Security.SecurityException: Request for the permission of type
'System.Security.Permissions.FileIOPermission, mscorlib, Version=2.0.0.0,
Culture=neutral, PublicKeyToken=b77a5c561934e089' failed.
System.Security.SecurityException:
   at System.Security.CodeAccessSecurityEngine.Check(Object demand,
StackCrawlMark& stackMark, Boolean isPermSet)
   at System.Security.CodeAccessPermission.Demand()
   at System.IO.FileStream.Init(String path, FileMode mode, FileAccess access, Int32
rights, Boolean useRights, FileShare share, Int32 bufferSize, FileOptions options,
SECURITY_ATTRIBUTES secAttrs, String msgPath, Boolean bFromProxy)
   at System.IO.FileStream..ctor(String path, FileMode mode)
   at udf_part2.CAS_Exception()
.
```

The exception thrown in this case is a `SecurityException`, indicating that this was a CAS violation (of the `FileIOPermission` type). But the exception is not the only thing that happened; notice that the first line of the output is the string "Starting...", which was output by the `SqlPipe.Send` method used in the first line of the stored procedure. So before the exception was hit, the method was entered and code execution succeeded until the actual permissions violation was attempted.

■**Note** File I/O is a good example of access to a resource—local or otherwise—that is outside of what the context connection allows. Avoiding this particular violation using the SQLCLR security buckets would require cataloging the assembly using the `EXTERNAL_ACCESS` permission.

To see how HPA exceptions behave, let's try the same experiment again, this time with the following stored procedure (again, cataloged as `SAFE`):

```
[SqlProcedure]
public static void HPA_Exception()
{
    SqlContext.Pipe.Send("Starting...");

    //The next line will throw an HPA exception...
    Monitor.Enter(SqlContext.Pipe);
```

```
    //Release the lock (if the code even gets here)...
    Monitor.Exit(SqlContext.Pipe);

    SqlContext.Pipe.Send("Finished...");

    return;
}
```

Just like before, an exception occurs. But this time, the output is a bit different:

```
Msg 6522, Level 16, State 1, Procedure HPA_Exception, Line 0
A .NET Framework error occurred during execution of user-defined routine or
aggregate "HPA_Exception":
System.Security.HostProtectionException: Attempted to perform an operation that was
forbidden by the CLR host.

The protected resources (only available with full trust) were: All
The demanded resources were: Synchronization, ExternalThreading

System.Security.HostProtectionException:
   at System.Security.CodeAccessSecurityEngine.ThrowSecurityException(Assembly asm,
PermissionSet granted, PermissionSet refused, RuntimeMethodHandle rmh,
SecurityAction action, Object demand, IPermission permThatFailed)
   at System.Security.CodeAccessSecurityEngine.ThrowSecurityException(Object
assemblyOrString, PermissionSet granted, PermissionSet refused, RuntimeMethodHandle
rmh, SecurityAction action, Object demand, IPermission permThatFailed)
   at System.Security.CodeAccessSecurityEngine.CheckSetHelper(PermissionSet grants,
PermissionSet refused, PermissionSet demands, RuntimeMethodHandle rmh, Object
assemblyOrString, SecurityAction action, Boolean throwException)
   at System.Security.CodeAccessSecurityEngine.CheckSetHelper(CompressedStack cs,
PermissionSet grants, PermissionSet refused, PermissionSet demands,
RuntimeMethodHandle rmh, Assembly asm, SecurityAction action)
   at udf_part2.HPA_Exception()
```

Unlike when executing the CAS_Exception stored procedure, this time we do not see the "Starting..." message, indicating that the SqlPipe.Send method was not called before hitting the exception. As a matter of fact, the HPA_Exception method was not ever entered at all during the code execution phase. You can verify this by attempting to set a breakpoint inside of the function and starting a debug session in Visual Studio. The reason that the breakpoint can't be hit is that the permissions check was done, and the exception thrown, immediately after just-in-time compilation.

You should also note that the wording of the exception is quite a bit different in this case. The wording of the CAS exception is a rather benign "Request for the permission ... failed." On the other hand, the HPA exception carries a much sterner warning: "Attempted to perform an operation that was *forbidden*." This difference in wording is not accidental. CAS grants are concerned with security—keep code from being able to access something protected because it's not supposed to have access. HPA permissions, on the other hand, are concerned with server reliability and keeping the CLR host running smoothly and efficiently. Threading and synchronization are considered potentially threatening to reliability and are therefore limited to assemblies marked as UNSAFE.

■**Note** Using Reflector or another .NET disassembler, it is possible to explore the Base Class Library to see how the HPA attributes are used for various classes and methods. For instance, the `Monitor` class is decorated with the following attribute that controls host access: `[ComVisible(true), HostProtection (SecurityAction.LinkDemand, Synchronization=true, ExternalThreading=true)]`.

A full list of what is and is not allowed based on the CAS and HPA models is beyond the scope of this chapter, but is well documented by Microsoft. Refer to the following MSDN topics:

- "Host Protection Attributes and CLR Integration Programming" (`http://msdn2.microsoft.com/en-us/library/ms403276.aspx`)

- "CLR Integration Code Access Security" (`http://msdn2.microsoft.com/en-us/library/ms345101.aspx`)

The Quest for Code Safety

You might be wondering why I'm covering the internals of the SQLCLR permission sets and how their exceptions differ, when fixing the exceptions is so easy: simply raise the permission level of the assemblies to EXTERNAL_ACCESS or UNSAFE and give the code access to do what it needs to do. The fact is, raising the permission levels will certainly work, but by doing so you may be circumventing the security policy, instead of working with it to make your system more secure.

As mentioned in the previous section, code access permissions are granted at the assembly level rather than the method or line level. Therefore, raising the permission of a given assembly in order to make a certain module work can actually affect many different modules contained within the assembly, giving them all enhanced access. Granting additional permissions on several modules within an assembly can in turn create a maintenance burden: if you want to be certain that there are no security problems, you must review each and every line of code in every module to make sure it's not doing anything it's not supposed to do—you can no longer trust the engine to check for you.

You might now be thinking that the solution is simple: split up your methods so that each resides in a separate assembly, and then grant permissions that way. Then, each method really will have its own permission set. But even in that case, permissions may not be granular enough to avoid code review nightmares. Consider a complex 5,000-line module that requires a single file I/O operation to read some lines from a text file. By giving the entire module EXTERNAL_ACCESS permissions, it can now read the lines from that file. But of course, you still have to check all of the remaining code to make sure it's not doing anything unauthorized.

Then there is the question of the effectiveness of manual code review. Is doing a stringent review every time any change is made enough to ensure that the code won't cause problems that would be detected by the engine if the code was marked SAFE? And do you really *want* to have to do a stringent review before deployment every time any change is made? In the following section, I will show you how to eliminate many of these problems by taking advantage of assembly dependencies in your SQLCLR environment.

Selective Privilege Escalation via Assembly References

In an ideal world, SQLCLR module permissions could be made to work like T-SQL module permissions as described in Chapter 4: outer modules would be granted the least possible privileges, but would be able to selectively and temporarily escalate their privileges in order to do certain operations that require more access. This would lessen the privileged surface area significantly, which would mean that there would be less need to do a stringent security review on outer (less-privileged) module layers, which undoubtedly constitute the majority of code written for a given system—the engine would make sure they behave.

The general solution to this problem is to split up code into separate assemblies based on permissions requirements, but to not do so without regard for both maintenance overhead and reuse. For example, consider the 5,000-line module, mentioned in the previous section, that needs to read a few lines from a text file. The entire module could be granted a high enough level of privileges to read the file, or the code to read the file could be taken out and placed into its own assembly. This external assembly would expose a method that takes a filename as input and returns a collection of lines. As I'll show in the following sections, this solution would let you catalog the bulk of the code as SAFE yet still do the file I/O operation. Plus, future modules that need to read lines from text files could reference the same assembly, and therefore not have to reimplement this logic.

The encapsulation story is, alas, not quite as straightforward as creating a new assembly with the necessary logic and referencing it. Due to the different behavior of CAS and HPA exceptions, you might have to perform some analysis of what the code is doing in order to properly encapsulate the permissions in the inner modules. In the following sections, I'll cover each of the permission types separately in order to illustrate how to design a solution.

Working with Host Protection Privileges

A fairly common SQLCLR pattern is to create static collections that can be shared among callers. However, as with any shared data set, proper synchronization is essential in case you need to update some of the data after its initial load. From a SQLCLR standpoint, this gets dicey due to the fact that threading and synchronization require UNSAFE access—granting such an open level of permission is not something to be taken lightly.

For an example of a scenario that might make use of a static collection, consider a SQLCLR UDF used to do currency conversions based on exchange rates:

```
[SqlFunction]
public static SqlDecimal GetConvertedAmount(
    SqlDecimal InputAmount,
    SqlString InCurrency,
    SqlString OutCurrency)
{
    //Convert the input amount to the base
    decimal BaseAmount =
      GetRate(InCurrency.Value) *
      InputAmount.Value;
```

```
        //Return the converted base amount
        return (new SqlDecimal(
            GetRate(OutCurrency.Value) * BaseAmount));
}
```

The GetConvertedAmount method internally makes use of another method, GetRate:

```
private static decimal GetRate(string Currency)
{
        decimal theRate;
        rwl.AcquireReaderLock(100);

        try
        {
            theRate = rates[Currency];
        }
        finally
        {
            rwl.ReleaseLock();
        }

        return (theRate);
}
```

GetRate performs a lookup in a static generic instance of Dictionary<string, decimal>, called rates. This collection contains exchange rates for the given currencies in the system. In order to protect against problems that will occur if another thread happens to be updating the rates, synchronization is handled using a static instance of ReaderWriterLock, called rwl. Both the dictionary and the ReaderWriterLock are instantiated when a method on the class is first called, and both are marked readonly in order to avoid being overwritten after instantiation:

```
static readonly Dictionary<string, decimal>
    rates = new Dictionary<string, decimal>();
static readonly ReaderWriterLock
    rwl = new ReaderWriterLock();
```

If cataloged using either the SAFE or EXTERNAL_ACCESS permission sets, this code fails due to its use of synchronization (the ReaderWriterLock), and running it produces a HostProtectionException. The solution is to move the affected code into its own assembly, cataloged as UNSAFE. Because the host protection check is evaluated at the moment of just-in-time compilation of a method in an assembly, rather than dynamically as the method is running, the check is done as the assembly boundary is being crossed. This means that an outer method can be marked SAFE and temporarily escalate its permissions by calling into an UNSAFE core.

■**Note** You might be wondering about the validity of this example, given the ease with which this system could be implemented in pure T-SQL, which would eliminate the permissions problem outright. I do feel that this is a realistic example, especially if the system needs to do a large number of currency translations on any given day. SQLCLR code will outperform T-SQL for even simple mathematical work, and caching the data in a shared collection rather than reading it from the database on every call is a huge efficiency win. I'm confident that this solution would easily outperform any pure T-SQL equivalent.

When designing the UNSAFE assembly, it is important from a reuse point of view to carefully analyze what functionality should be made available. In this case, use of the dictionary isn't causing the problem. Synchronization via the ReaderWriterLock is throwing the actual exception. However, wrapping methods around a ReaderWriterLock would probably not promote very much reuse. A better tactic, in my opinion, is to wrap the Dictionary and the ReaderWriterLock together, creating a new ThreadSafeDictionary class. This class could be used in any scenario in which a shared data cache is required.

Following is my implementation of the ThreadSafeDictionary; I have not implemented all of the methods that the generic dictionary exposes, but rather only those I commonly use:

```
using System;
using System.Collections.Generic;
using System.Text;
using System.Threading;

namespace SafeDictionary
{
    public class ThreadSafeDictionary<K, V>
    {
        private readonly Dictionary<K, V> dict = new Dictionary<K,V>();
        private readonly ReaderWriterLock theLock = new ReaderWriterLock();

        public void Add(K key, V value)
        {
            theLock.AcquireWriterLock(2000);

            try
            {
                dict.Add(key, value);
            }
            finally
            {
                theLock.ReleaseLock();
            }
        }

        public V this[K key]
        {
```

```
    get
    {
        theLock.AcquireReaderLock(2000);
        try
        {
            return (this.dict[key]);
        }
        finally
        {
            theLock.ReleaseLock();
        }
    }

    set
    {
        theLock.AcquireWriterLock(2000);
        try
        {
            dict[key] = value;
        }
        finally
        {
            theLock.ReleaseLock();
        }
    }
}

public bool Remove(K key)
{
    theLock.AcquireWriterLock(2000);
    try
    {
        return (dict.Remove(key));
    }
    finally
    {
        theLock.ReleaseLock();
    }
}

public bool ContainsKey(K key)
{
    theLock.AcquireReaderLock(2000);
    try
    {
        return (dict.ContainsKey(key));
    }
```

```
        finally
        {
            theLock.ReleaseLock();
        }
    }
  }
}
```

This class should be placed into a new assembly, which should then be compiled and cataloged in SQL Server as UNSAFE. A reference to the UNSAFE assembly should be used in the exchange rates conversion assembly, after which a few lines of the example code will have to change. First of all, the only static object that must be created is an instance of ThreadSafeDictionary:

```
static readonly ThreadSafeDictionary<string, decimal> rates =
    new ThreadSafeDictionary<string, decimal>();
```

Since the ThreadSafeDictionary is already thread safe, the GetRate method no longer needs to be concerned with synchronization. Without this requirement, its code becomes greatly simplified:

```
private static decimal GetRate(string Currency)
{
    return (rates[Currency]);
}
```

The exchange rates conversion assembly can still be marked SAFE, and can now make use of the encapsulated synchronization code without throwing a HostProtectionException. And none of the code actually contained in the assembly will be able to use resources that violate the permissions allowed by the SAFE bucket—quite an improvement over the initial implementation, from a security perspective.

■**Note** Depending on whether your database has the TRUSTWORTHY option enabled and whether your assemblies are strong named, things may not be *quite* as simple as I've implied here. The examples in both this and the next section may fail either at deployment time if your core assembly doesn't have the correct permissions or at run time if you've decided to go with a strong named assembly. See the section "Granting Cross-Assembly Privileges" later in this chapter for more information. In the meantime, if you're following along, work in a database with the TRUSTWORTHY option turned on, and forgo the strong naming for now.

Working with Code Access Security Privileges

HPA-protected resources are quite easy to encapsulate, thanks to the fact that permissions for a given method are checked when the method is just-in-time compiled. Alas, things are not quite so simple when working with CAS-protected resources, due to the fact that grants are checked dynamically at run time via a stack walk. This means that simply referencing a second assembly is not enough—the entire stack is walked each time, without regard to assembly boundaries.

To illustrate this issue, create a new assembly containing the following method, which reads all of the lines from a text file and returns them as a collection of strings:

```
public static string[] ReadFileLines(string FilePath)
{
    List<string> theLines = new List<string>();

    using (System.IO.StreamReader sr =
        new System.IO.StreamReader(FilePath))
    {
        string line;
        while ((line = sr.ReadLine()) != null)
            theLines.Add(line);
    }

    return (theLines.ToArray());
}
```

Catalog the assembly in SQL Server with the EXTERNAL_ACCESS permission set, and reference it from the assembly that contains the CAS_Exception stored procedure created in the section "SQLCLR Security and Reliability Features." Modify that stored procedure as follows:

```
[SqlProcedure]
public static void CAS_Exception()
{
    SqlContext.Pipe.Send("Starting...");

    string[] theLines =
        FileLines.ReadFileLines(@"C:\b.txt");

    SqlContext.Pipe.Send("Finished...");

    return;
}
```

Note that I created my ReadFileLines method inside a class called FileLines; reference yours appropriately depending on what class name you used. Once you've finished the modifications, redeploy the outer assembly, making sure that it is cataloged as SAFE.

Running the modified version of this stored procedure, you'll find that even though an assembly boundary is crossed, you will receive the same exception as before. The CAS grant did not change simply because a higher privileged assembly was referenced, due to the fact that the stack walk does not take into account permissions held by referenced assemblies.

Working around this issue requires taking control of the stack walk within the referenced assembly. Due to the fact that the assembly has enough privilege to do file operations, it can internally demand that the stack walk discontinue checks for file I/O permissions, even when called from another assembly that does not have the requisite permissions. This is done by using the Assert method of the IStackWalk interface, exposed in .NET's System.Security namespace.

Taking a second look at the CAS violation shown previously, note that the required permission is FileIOPermission, which is in the System.Security.Permissions namespace. The

FileIOPermission class—in addition to other "permission" classes in that namespace—implements the IStackWalk interface. To avoid the CAS exception, simply instantiate an instance of the FileIOPermission class and call the Assert method. The following code is a modified version of the ReadFileLines method that uses this technique:

```
public static string[] ReadFileLines(string FilePath)
{
    //Assert that anything File IO-related that this
    //assembly has permission to do, callers can do
    FileIOPermission fp = new FileIOPermission(
        PermissionState.Unrestricted);
    fp.Assert();

    List<string> theLines = new List<string>();

    using (System.IO.StreamReader sr =
        new System.IO.StreamReader(FilePath))
    {
        string line;
        while ((line = sr.ReadLine()) != null)
            theLines.Add(line);
    }

    return (theLines.ToArray());
}
```

This version of the method instantiates the FileIOPermission class with the PermissionState.Unrestricted enumeration, thereby enabling all callers to do whatever file I/O–related activities that the assembly has permission to do. The use of the term "unrestricted" in this context is not as dangerous as it sounds; the access is unrestricted in the sense that permission is allowed for only as much access as the assembly already has to the file system. After making the modifications shown here and redeploying both assemblies, the CAS exception will no longer be an issue.

To allow you to control things on a more granular level, the FileIOPermission class exposes other constructor overloads with different options. The most useful of these for this example uses an enumeration called FileIOPermissionAccess in conjunction with the path to a file, allowing you to limit the permissions the caller has to only specific operations on a specific file. For instance, to limit access so that the caller can only read the file specified in the input path, use the following constructor:

```
FileIOPermission fp = new FileIOPermission(
    FileIOPermissionAccess.Read,
    FilePath);
```

File I/O is only one of many kinds of permissions for which you might see a CAS exception. The important thing is being able to identify the pattern. In all cases, violations will throw a SecurityException and reference a permission class in the System.Security.Permissions namespace. Each class follows the same basic pattern outlined here, so you should be able to easily use this technique in order to design any number of privilege escalation solutions.

Granting Cross-Assembly Privileges

The examples in the preceding sections were simplified a bit in order to focus the text on a single issue at a time. There are two other issues you need to be concerned with when working with cross-assembly calls: database trustworthiness and strong naming.

The idea of a "trustworthy" database is new to SQL Server 2005, and is a direct offshoot of Microsoft's heightened awareness of security issues in recent years. Marking a database as trustworthy or not is a simple matter of setting an option using ALTER DATABASE:

```
ALTER DATABASE AdventureWorks
SET TRUSTWORTHY ON;
GO
```

Unfortunately, as simple as enabling this option is, the repercussions of this setting are far from it. Effectively, it comes down to the fact that code running in the context of a trustworthy database can access resources outside of the database more easily than code running in a database not marked as such. This means access to the file system, remote database servers, and even other databases on the same server—all of this access is controlled by this one option, so be careful.

Turning off the TRUSTWORTHY option means that rogue code will have a much harder time accessing resources outside of the database, but it also means that you as a developer will have to spend more time dealing with security issues. That said, I highly recommend leaving this turned off unless you really have a great reason to enable it. Dealing with access control in a nontrustworthy database is not too difficult; the module signing techniques discussed in Chapter 4 should be applied, which puts access control squarely in your hands and does not make life easy for code that shouldn't have access to a given resource.

In the SQLCLR world, you'll see a deploy-time exception if you catalog an assembly using the EXTERNAL_ACCESS or UNSAFE permission sets and try to catalog a referencing assembly. Following is the exception I get when trying to catalog the assembly I created that contains the GetConvertedAmount method, after setting my database to nontrustworthy mode:

```
CREATE ASSEMBLY for assembly 'CurrencyConversion' failed because
assembly 'SafeDictionary' is not authorized for PERMISSION_SET = UNSAFE.
The assembly is authorized when either of the following is true: the database
owner (DBO) has UNSAFE ASSEMBLY permission and the database has the TRUSTWORTHY
database property on; or the assembly is signed with a certificate or an asymmetric
key that has a corresponding login with UNSAFE ASSEMBLY permission.
If you have restored or attached this database, make sure the database owner is
mapped to the correct login on this server. If not, use sp_changedbowner to fix the
problem.
```

This rather verbose exception is rare and to be treasured: it describes exactly how to solve the problem! Following the steps detailed in Chapter 4, you can grant the UNSAFE ASSEMBLY permission by using certificates. To begin, create a certificate and a corresponding login in the master database, and grant the login UNSAFE ASSEMBLY permission:

```
USE master
GO

CREATE CERTIFICATE Assembly_Permissions_Certificate
```

```
ENCRYPTION BY PASSWORD = 'uSe_a STr()nG PaSSWOrD!'
WITH SUBJECT = 'Certificate used to grant assembly permission'
GO

CREATE LOGIN Assembly_Permissions_Login
FROM CERTIFICATE Assembly_Permissions_Certificate
GO

GRANT UNSAFE ASSEMBLY TO Assembly_Permissions_Login
GO
```

Next, back up the certificate to a file:

```
BACKUP CERTIFICATE Assembly_Permissions_Certificate
TO FILE = 'C:\assembly_permissions.cer'
WITH PRIVATE KEY
(
    FILE = 'C:\assembly_permissions.pvk',
    ENCRYPTION BY PASSWORD = 'is?tHiS_a_VeRySTronGP4ssWoR|)?',
    DECRYPTION BY PASSWORD = 'uSe_a STr()nG PaSSWOrD!'
)
GO
```

Now, in the database in which you're working—AdventureWorks, in my case—restore the certificate and create a local database user from it:

```
USE AdventureWorks
GO

CREATE CERTIFICATE Assembly_Permissions_Certificate
FROM FILE = 'C:\assembly_permissions.cer'
WITH PRIVATE KEY
(
    FILE = 'C:\assembly_permissions.pvk',
    DECRYPTION BY PASSWORD = 'is?tHiS_a_VeRySTronGP4ssWoR|)?',
    ENCRYPTION BY PASSWORD = 'uSe_a STr()nG PaSSWOrD!'
)
GO

CREATE USER Assembly_Permissions_User
FOR CERTIFICATE Assembly_Permissions_Certificate
GO
```

Finally, sign the assembly with the certificate, thereby granting access and allowing the assembly to be referenced:

```
ADD SIGNATURE TO ASSEMBLY::SafeDictionary
BY CERTIFICATE Assembly_Permissions_Certificate
WITH PASSWORD='uSe_a STr()nG PaSSWOrD!'
GO
```

The other issue you might encounter has to do with strong-named assemblies. Strong naming is a .NET security feature that allows you to digitally sign your assembly in order to more carefully version it and ensure its validity to users. For most SQLCLR code, strong naming is probably overkill—code running in secured, managed databases probably doesn't need the additional assurances that strong naming provides. However, vendors looking at distributing applications that include SQLCLR components will definitely want to look at strong naming.

After signing the assembly that contains the ReadFileLines method and redeploying both it and the assembly containing the CAS_Exception stored procedure, I receive the following error when I call the procedure:

```
Msg 6522, Level 16, State 1, Procedure CAS_Exception, Line 0
A .NET Framework error occurred during execution of user-defined routine or
aggregate "CAS_Exception":
System.Security.SecurityException: That assembly does not allow partially trusted
callers.
System.Security.SecurityException:
   at System.Security.CodeAccessSecurityEngine.ThrowSecurityException(Assembly asm,
PermissionSet granted, PermissionSet refused, RuntimeMethodHandle rmh,
SecurityAction action, Object demand, IPermission permThatFailed)
   at udf_part2.CAS_Exception()
.
```

The solution is to add an AllowPartiallyTrustedCallersAttribute (often seen referred to merely as APTCA in articles) to the code. This attribute should be added to a single file in the assembly, after the using declarations and before definition of any classes or namespaces. In the case of the FileLines assembly, the file looks like the following after adding the attribute:

```
using System;
using System.Data;
using System.Data.SqlClient;
using System.Data.SqlTypes;
using Microsoft.SqlServer.Server;
using System.Collections.Generic;
using System.Security.Permissions;

[assembly: System.Security.AllowPartiallyTrustedCallers]

public partial class FileLines
{
```

Once this attribute has been added, any caller can use the methods in the FileLines class, without receiving an exception. Keep in mind that this attribute must be specified for a reason, and by using it you may be allowing callers to circumvent security. If the assembly does operations that not everyone should have access to, make sure to secure things another way, such as by creating groups of assemblies with different owners in order to ensure that nongrouped assemblies cannot reference the sensitive methods.

Enhancing Service Broker Scale-Out with SQLCLR

Service Broker is frequently mentioned as an excellent choice for helping to scale out database services. One of the more compelling use cases is a Service Broker service that can be used to asynchronously request data from a remote system. In such a case, a request message would be sent to the remote data service from a local stored procedure, which could do some other work while waiting for the response—the requested data—to come back.

There are many ways to architect such a system, and given that Service Broker allows messages to be sent either as binary or XML, I wondered which would provide the best overall performance and value from a code reuse perspective.

I started working with the AdventureWorks.HumanResources.Employee table as a sample data set, imagining a remote data service requesting a list of employees along with their attributes. After some experimentation, I determined that the FOR XML RAW option is the easiest way to serialize a table in XML format, and I used the ROOT option to make the XML valid:

```
SELECT *
FROM HumanResources.Employee
FOR XML RAW, ROOT('Employees')
```

XML is, of course, known to be an extremely verbose data interchange format, and I was not surprised to discover that the data size of the resultant XML is 116KB, despite the fact that the HumanResources.Employee table itself has only 56KB of data. I experimented with setting shorter column names, but it had very little effect on the size and created what I feel to be unmaintainable code.

My first performance test, the results of which are shown in Figure 6-1, was not especially promising. Simply serializing the results was taking over 3 seconds per iteration. After some trial and error, I discovered that the TYPE option hugely improved performance, bringing average time per iteration down by over 50%, as shown in Figure 6-2.

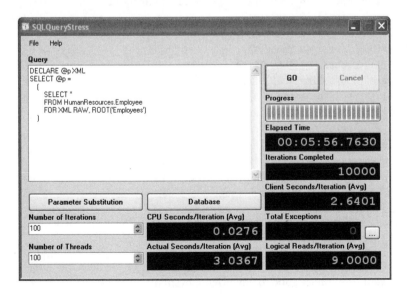

Figure 6-1. *Initial performance test of XML serialization*

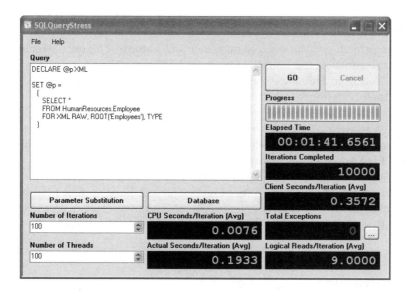

Figure 6-2. *XML serialization performed better using the TYPE directive.*

I was quite pleased with these results until I decided to test deserialization. The first problem was the code required to deserialize the XML back into a table. In order to get back the same table I started with, I had to explicitly define every column for the result set; this made the code quite a bit more complex than I'd hoped for:

```
SELECT
    col.value('@EmployeeID', 'int') AS EmployeeID,
    col.value('@NationalIDNumber', 'nvarchar(15)') AS NationalIDNumber,
    col.value('@ContactID', 'int') AS ContactID,
    col.value('@LoginID', 'nvarchar(256)') AS LoginID,
    col.value('@ManagerID', 'int') AS ManagerID,
    col.value('@Title', 'nvarchar(50)') AS Title,
    col.value('@BirthDate', 'datetime') AS BirthDate,
    col.value('@MaritalStatus', 'nchar(1)') AS MaritalStatus,
    col.value('@Gender', 'nchar(1)') AS Gender,
    col.value('@HireDate', 'datetime') AS HireDate,
    col.value('@SalariedFlag', 'bit') AS SalariedFlag,
    col.value('@VacationHours', 'smallint') AS VacationHours,
    col.value('@SickLeaveHours', 'smallint') AS SickLeaveHours,
    col.value('@CurrentFlag', 'bit') AS CurrentFlag,
    col.value('@rowguid', 'uniqueidentifier') AS rowguid,
    col.value('@ModifiedDate', 'datetime') AS ModifiedDate
FROM @p.nodes ('/Employees/row') p (col)
```

The next problem was performance. As shown in Figure 6-3, when I tested deserializing the XML, performance went from pretty good to downright abysmal.

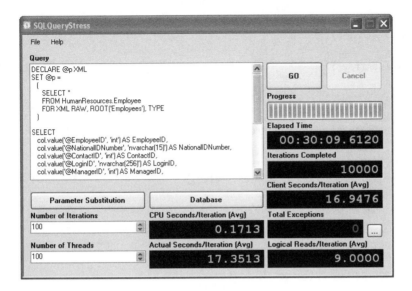

Figure 6-3. *XML deserialization performance leaves much to be desired.*

I decided to investigate SQLCLR options for solving the problem, focusing on both reuse potential and performance. My first thought was to return binary serialized DataTables, and in order to make that happen, I needed a way to return binary-formatted data from my CLR routines. This of course called for .NET's BinaryFormatter class, so I created a class called serialization_helper. The following code was cataloged in an EXTERNAL_ACCESS assembly (required for System.IO access):

```
using System;
using System.Data;
using System.Data.SqlClient;
using System.Data.SqlTypes;
using Microsoft.SqlServer.Server;
using System.Security.Permissions;
using System.Runtime.Serialization.Formatters.Binary;

public partial class serialization_helper
{
    public static byte[] getBytes(object o)
    {
        SecurityPermission sp =
            new SecurityPermission(
                SecurityPermissionFlag.SerializationFormatter);
        sp.Assert();

        BinaryFormatter bf = new BinaryFormatter();

        using (System.IO.MemoryStream ms =
            new System.IO.MemoryStream())
```

```
        {
            bf.Serialize(ms, o);

            return(ms.ToArray());
        }
    }

    public static object getObject(byte[] theBytes)
    {
        using (System.IO.MemoryStream ms =
            new System.IO.MemoryStream(theBytes, false))
        {
            return(getObject(ms));
        }
    }

    public static object getObject(System.IO.Stream s)
    {
        SecurityPermission sp =
            new SecurityPermission(
                SecurityPermissionFlag.SerializationFormatter);
        sp.Assert();

        BinaryFormatter bf = new BinaryFormatter();

        return (bf.Deserialize(s));
    }
};
```

Use of this class is fairly straightforward: to serialize an object, pass it into the getBytes
method. This method first uses an assertion to allow SAFE callers to use it, and then uses the
binary formatter to serialize the object to a Stream. The stream is then returned as a collection
of bytes. Deserialization can be done using either overload of the getObject method. I found
that depending on the scenario, I might have ready access to either a Stream or a collection of
bytes, so creating both overloads made sense instead of duplicating code to produce one from
the other. Deserialization also uses an assertion before running, in order to allow calling code
to be cataloged as SAFE.

My first shot at getting the data was to simply load the input set into a DataTable and run it through the serialization_helper methods. The following code implements a UDF called GetDataTable_Binary, which uses this logic:

```
[Microsoft.SqlServer.Server.SqlFunction(
    DataAccess = DataAccessKind.Read)]
public static SqlBytes GetDataTable_Binary(string query)
{
    SqlConnection conn =
        new SqlConnection("context connection = true;");

    SqlCommand comm = new SqlCommand();
    comm.Connection = conn;
    comm.CommandText = query;

    SqlDataAdapter da = new SqlDataAdapter();
    da.SelectCommand = comm;

    DataTable dt = new DataTable();
    da.Fill(dt);

    //Serialize and return the output
    return new SqlBytes(
        serialization_helper.getBytes(dt));
}
```

This method is used by passing in a query for the table that you'd like to get back in binary serialized form, as in the following example:

```
USE AdventureWorks
GO

DECLARE @sql NVARCHAR(4000)
SET @sql = 'SELECT * FROM HumanResources.Employee'

DECLARE @p VARBINARY(MAX)
SET @p =
    dbo.GetDataTable_Binary(@sql)
```

While I'd achieved the reuse potential I hoped for—this function can be used for any number of queries—I was disappointed to find that the output data size had ballooned to 232KB. Things looked even worse when I ran a performance test and serialization speed turned out to be dismal at best, as shown in Figure 6-4.

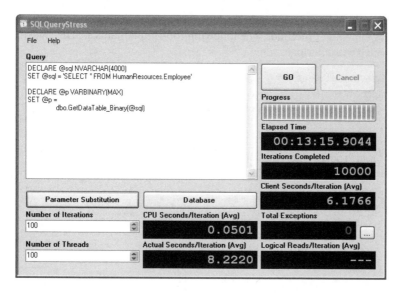

Figure 6-4. *Performance of binary serializing DataTables is far from adequate.*

The main problem, as it turned out, was the default serialization behavior of the DataTable. Even when using the BinaryFormatter, a DataTable serializes itself first to XML, and then to binary—double the work that I expected. To fix this, set the RemotingFormat property of the DataTable to Binary before serialization:

```
dt.RemotingFormat = SerializationFormat.Binary;
```

Making this change resulted in much better performance, as illustrated by the test results shown in Figure 6-5.

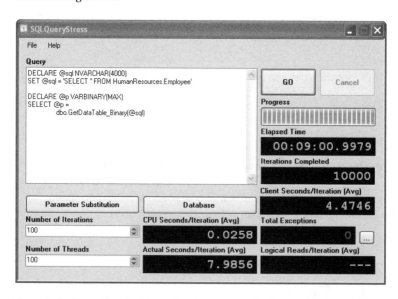

Figure 6-5. *By setting the RemotingFormat on the DataTable before serialization, performance is greatly improved.*

I still felt that I could do better, and after several more attempts that I won't bore you with the details of, I decided to forgo the DataTable altogether and focus on a class that I've found historically to be much faster: SqlDataReader. I worked on pulling the data out into object collections, and initial tests that I ran showed the data size to be much closer to what I expected. In addition to size improvements, serialization performance turned out to be far better than that of the DataTable (but not as good as XML serialization with the TYPE directive).

The advantage of a DataTable is that it's one easy-to-use unit that contains all of the data, as well as the metadata. You don't have to be concerned with column names, types, and sizes, as everything is automatically loaded into the DataTable for you. Working with a SqlDataReader requires a bit more work, since it can't be serialized as a single unit, but must instead be split up into its component parts.

Since the code I implemented is somewhat complex, I will walk you through it section by section. To begin with, I set the DataAccessKind.Read property on the SqlFunctionAttribute, in order to allow the method to access data via the context connection. A generic List is instantiated, which will hold one object collection per row of data, in addition to one for the metadata. Finally, the SqlConnection is instantiated, and the SqlCommand set up and executed:

```
[Microsoft.SqlServer.Server.SqlFunction(
    DataAccess = DataAccessKind.Read)]
public static SqlBytes GetBinaryFromQueryResult(string query)
{
    List<object[]> theList = new List<object[]>();

    using (SqlConnection conn =
        new SqlConnection("context connection = true;"))
    {
        SqlCommand comm = new SqlCommand();
        comm.Connection = conn;
        comm.CommandText = query;

        conn.Open();

        SqlDataReader read = comm.ExecuteReader();
```

The next step is to pull the metadata for each column out of the SqlDataReader. A method called GetSchemaTable is used to return a DataTable populated with one row per column. The available fields are documented in the MSDN Library, but I'm using the most common of them in the code that follows. After populating the object collection with the metadata, it is added to the output List:

```
        DataTable dt = read.GetSchemaTable();

        //Populate the field list from the schema table
        object[] fields = new object[dt.Rows.Count];
        for (int i = 0; i < fields.Length; i++)
        {
            object[] field = new object[5];
            field[0] = dt.Rows[i]["ColumnName"];
            field[1] = dt.Rows[i]["ProviderType"];
```

```
            field[2] = dt.Rows[i]["ColumnSize"];
            field[3] = dt.Rows[i]["NumericPrecision"];
            field[4] = dt.Rows[i]["NumericScale"];

            fields[i] = field;
        }

        //Add the collection of fields to the output list
        theList.Add(fields);
```

Finally, the code loops over the rows returned by the query, using the GetValues method to pull each row out into an object collection that is added to the output. The List is converted into an array of object[] (object[][], to be more precise), which is serialized and returned to the caller.

```
        //Add all of the rows to the output list
        while (read.Read())
        {
            object[] o = new object[read.FieldCount];
            read.GetValues(o);
            theList.Add(o);
        }
    }

    //Serialize and return the output
    return new SqlBytes(
        serialization_helper.getBytes(theList.ToArray()));
}
```

Once this function is created, calling it is almost identical to calling GetDataTable_Binary:

```
USE AdventureWorks
GO

DECLARE @sql NVARCHAR(4000)
SET @sql = 'SELECT * FROM HumanResources.Employee'

DECLARE @p VARBINARY(MAX)
SET @p =
    dbo.GetBinaryFromQueryResult(@sql)
```

The result: 57KB worth of binary data—quite an improvement over both the XML and DataTable methods. If using this to transfer data between Broker instances on remote servers, the decrease in network traffic can make a big difference. The serialization performance test, the results of which are shown in Figure 6-6, showed that performance is vastly improved over the DataTable attempt, while not as good as XML serialization in conjunction with the TYPE directive.

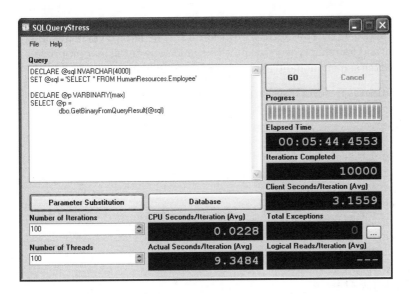

Figure 6-6. *Performance of binary serializing object collections derived from a SqlDataReader is much better than the DataTable equivalent.*

Pleased with these results, I decided to go ahead with deserialization. Continuing with my stress on reuse potential, I decided that a stored procedure would be a better choice for a UDF. A stored procedure does not have a fixed output as does a UDF, so any input table can be deserialized and returned without worrying about violating column list contracts.

The first part of the stored procedure follows:

```
[Microsoft.SqlServer.Server.SqlProcedure]
public static void GetTableFromBinary(SqlBytes theTable)
{
    //Deserialize the input
    object[] dt = (object[])(
        serialization_helper.getObject(theTable.Value));

    //First, get the fields
    object[] fields = (object[])(dt[0]);
    SqlMetaData[] cols = new SqlMetaData[fields.Length];

    //Loop over the fields and populate SqlMetaData objects
    for (int i = 0; i<fields.Length; i++)
    {
        object[] field = (object[])(fields[i]);
        SqlDbType dbType = (SqlDbType)field[1];
```

After deserializing the input bytes back into a collection of objects, the first item in the collection—which is assumed to be the column metadata—is converted into a collection of objects. This collection is looped over item-by-item in order to create the output SqlMetaData objects that will be used to stream back the data to the caller.

The trickiest part of setting this up is the fact that each SQL Server data type requires a different SqlMetaData overload. DECIMAL needs a precision and scale setting; character and binary types need a size; and for other types, size, precision, and scale are all inappropriate inputs. The following switch statement handles creation of the SqlMetaData instances:

```
//Different SqlMetaData overloads are required
//depending on the data type
switch (dbType)
{
    case SqlDbType.Decimal:
        cols[i] = new SqlMetaData(
            (string)field[0],
            dbType,
            (byte)field[3],
            (byte)field[4]);
        break;
    case SqlDbType.Binary:
    case SqlDbType.Char:
    case SqlDbType.NChar:
    case SqlDbType.NVarChar:
    case SqlDbType.VarBinary:
    case SqlDbType.VarChar:
        switch ((int)field[2])
        {
            //If it's a MAX type, use -1 as the size
            case 2147483647:
                cols[i] = new SqlMetaData(
                    (string)field[0],
                    dbType,
                    -1);
                break;
            default:
                cols[i] = new SqlMetaData(
                    (string)field[0],
                    dbType,
                    (long)((int)field[2]));
                break;
        }
        break;
    default:
        cols[i] = new SqlMetaData(
            (string)field[0],
            dbType);
        break;
}
}
```

Once population of the columns collection has been completed, the data can be sent back to the caller using the SqlPipe class's SendResults methods. After starting the stream, the remainder of the objects in the input collection are looped over, cast to object[ ], and sent back as SqlDataRecords:

```
//Start the result stream
SqlDataRecord rec = new SqlDataRecord(cols);
SqlContext.Pipe.SendResultsStart(rec);

for (int i = 1; i < dt.Length; i++)
{
    rec.SetValues((object[])dt[i]);
    SqlContext.Pipe.SendResultsRow(rec);
}

//End the result stream
SqlContext.Pipe.SendResultsEnd();
}
```

Although the serialization test had not yielded spectacular results, it turns out that deserialization of data prepared in this manner is exceptionally fast compared with the alternatives. The performance test, the results of which are shown in Figure 6-7, revealed that deserialization of the SqlDataReader data is almost an order of magnitude faster than deserialization of similar XML. Although the serialization is slightly slower, I feel that the combination of better network utilization and much faster deserialization makes this a great technique for transferring tabular data between Service Broker instances in scale-out and distributed processing scenarios.

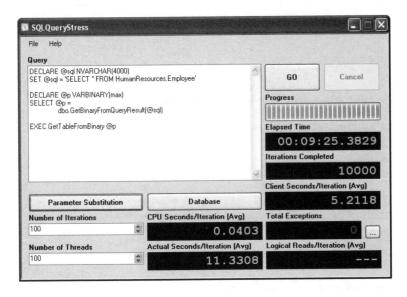

Figure 6-7. *Deserializitation of the SqlDataReader data has much less overhead than deserialization of XML.*

Extending User-Defined Aggregates

By far the most interesting SQLCLR feature is the ability to create custom aggregates. Each of the other SQLCLR features, with the possible exception of triggers, will see more use in production applications than will aggregates, but aggregates and types are the only members of the group that can help developers do things that simply were not possible before. And unlike types, for which there was some limited support in previous versions of SQL Server, aggregates bring something totally new to the table. For that reason, it's a feature that gets quite a bit of attention.

Unfortunately, the story is not so great when it comes to actually using UDAs. Developers experimenting with them for the first time are often extremely disappointed to discover the maximum size limitation imposed by the engine. To illustrate this, consider a simple aggregate designed to concatenate an input set of strings. I'll walk through it section by section in order to describe how it works.

To begin with, the `SqlUserDefinedAggregateAttribute` is used. Because strings are used internally, the format must be set to `UserDefined`. The `MaxByteSize` property is set to 8000, the maximum allowed:

```
[Serializable]
[Microsoft.SqlServer.Server.SqlUserDefinedAggregate(
    Format.UserDefined, MaxByteSize=8000)]
public struct string_concat : IBinarySerialize
{
```

A generic `List` is used to hold strings as they're sent to the aggregate, and the `List` is instantiated in the `Init` method:

```
    private List<string> theStrings;

    public void Init()
    {
        theStrings = new List<string>();
    }
```

The `Accumulate` method checks whether the input is `NULL`, and if not adds it to the `List`:

```
    public void Accumulate(SqlString Value)
    {
        if (!(Value.IsNull))
            theStrings.Add(Value.Value);
    }
```

The `Merge` method pulls all data out of the input group's collection, adding it to the local collection:

```
    public void Merge(string_concat Group)
    {
        foreach (string theString in Group.theStrings)
            this.theStrings.Add(theString);
    }
```

The Terminate method converts the List to an array, and then uses the Join method to delimit the elements in the array with commas:

```
public SqlString Terminate()
{
    string[] allStrings = theStrings.ToArray();
    string final = String.Join(",", allStrings);

    return new SqlString(final);
}
```

The final two methods are Read and Write, used for serialization and deserialization of the aggregate. Serialization occurs at two points during an aggregate's lifetime: before calling Merge and before calling Terminate. Any time the data size of the serialized instance is greater than the MaxByteSize specified in the SqlUserDefinedFunctionAttribute, an exception will be thrown and aggregation will stop. The following implementation of the Read and Write methods works by first serializing the number of members in the List, and then serializing each member:

```
#region IBinarySerialize Members

public void Read(System.IO.BinaryReader r)
{
    int count = r.ReadInt32();
    this.theStrings = new List<string>(count);

    for (; count > 0; count--)
    {
        theStrings.Add(r.ReadString());
    }
}

public void Write(System.IO.BinaryWriter w)
{
    w.Write(theStrings.Count);
    foreach (string s in theStrings)
        w.Write(s);
}

#endregion
}
```

The following T-SQL can be used to run this aggregate against the Name column of the Production.Product table in the AdventureWorks database:

```
SELECT dbo.String_Concat(Name)
FROM Production.Product
```

The expected output is a comma-delimited list of product names, but instead the following exception results due to the fact that the MaxByteSize has been exceeded:

```
Msg 6522, Level 16, State 2, Line 1
A .NET Framework error occurred during execution of user-defined routine or
aggregate "string_concat":
System.Data.SqlTypes.SqlTypeException: The buffer is insufficient. Read or write
operation failed.
System.Data.SqlTypes.SqlTypeException:
    at System.Data.SqlTypes.SqlBytes.Write(Int64 offset, Byte[] buffer, Int32
offsetInBuffer, Int32 count)
    at System.Data.SqlTypes.StreamOnSqlBytes.Write(Byte[] buffer, Int32 offset, Int32
count)
    at System.IO.BinaryWriter.Write(String value)
    at string_concat.Write(BinaryWriter w)
```

This is, to put it mildly, both frustrating and annoying. The idea of being able to produce custom aggregates, but for them to only be applicable when used for extremely limited data sets, is akin to keeping the carrot just out of the reach of the donkey.

I tried various methods of getting around this limitation, including data compression and different ways of serializing the data, all without much success. I finally realized that the key is to *not serialize the data* at all, but rather to keep it in memory between calls to the aggregate. The solution I came up with was to store the data in a static `Dictionary` between calls, but the problem was what to use as a key.

Once again, I tried several methods of solving the problem, including keying off of the caller's SPID and passing a unique key into the aggregate by concatenating it with the input data. These methods worked to some degree, but eventually I came up with the idea of generating the key—a GUID—at serialization time and serializing it instead of the data. This way, the caller never has to worry about what the aggregate is doing internally to extend its output byte size—obviously, highly desirable from an encapsulation point of view.

In order to implement this solution, I used the `SafeDictionary` described in the section "Working with HostProtection Privileges":

```
using SafeDictionary;
```

Thread safety is extremely important in this scenario, since many callers may be using the aggregate at the same time, and one caller's insert into or deletion from the `Dictionary` may affect the location of another's data in the internal tables, therefore causing a concurrency problem.

To implement this, I began with the same code as the `string_concat` method, but renamed it to `string_concat_2`. I modified the `SqlUserDefinedAggregateAttribute` to use a `MaxByteSize` of 16—the data size of a GUID—and set up a `readonly`, `static` instance of the `ThreadSafeDictionary` in addition to the local `List`:

```
[Microsoft.SqlServer.Server.SqlUserDefinedAggregate(
    Format.UserDefined, MaxByteSize=16)]
public struct string_concat_2 : IBinarySerialize
{
    readonly static ThreadSafeDictionary<Guid, List<string>> theLists =
        new ThreadSafeDictionary<Guid, List<string>>();

    private List<string> theStrings;
```

Aside from the serialization methods, the only method requiring modification was `Terminate`. Since I was using Visual Studio deployment, I had to use `SqlChars` instead of `SqlString` in order to expose output data typed as `NVARCHAR(MAX)`:

```
//Make sure to use SqlChars if you use
//VS deployment!
public SqlChars Terminate()
{
    string[] allStrings = theStrings.ToArray();
    string final = String.Join(",", allStrings);

    return new SqlChars(final);
}
```

The `Write` method creates a new GUID, which is used as a key for the local collection holding the already-accumulated strings. This GUID is then serialized so that it can be used as the key to pull the data from the `Dictionary` in the `Read` method later. Note the exception handling—one major consideration when working with shared memory in SQLCLR objects is making sure to safeguard against memory leaks whenever possible.

```
public void Write(System.IO.BinaryWriter w)
{
    Guid g = Guid.NewGuid();

    try
    {
        //Add the local collection to the static dictionary
        theLists.Add(g, this.theStrings);

        //Persist the GUID
        w.Write(g.ToByteArray());
    }
    catch
    {
        //Try to clean up in case of exception
        if (theLists.ContainsKey(g))
            theLists.Remove(g);
    }
}
```

The `Read` method deserializes the GUID and uses it to get the collection of strings from the `Dictionary`. After this, the collection is immediately removed; again, it's important to be as cautious as possible regarding memory leaks when using this technique, in order to ensure that you do not create server instability.

```
public void Read(System.IO.BinaryReader r)
{
    //Get the GUID from the stream
    Guid g = new Guid(r.ReadBytes(16));
```

```
    try
    {
        //Grab the collection of strings
        this.theStrings = theLists[g];
    }
    finally
    {
        //Clean up
        theLists.Remove(g);
    }
}
```

After deploying this modified version of the aggregate, things work the way they *should have worked from the start*. No exception occurs when aggregating every product name in the Production.Product table; instead, a delimited list is output.

I had a hunch that removing most of the serialization would also improve performance, so I decided to test the two versions against one another. I had to filter down the input set a bit in order to get string_concat to work without throwing an exception, so I added a WHERE clause and limited the input to product IDs less than 500. Figures 6-8 and 6-9 show the results of the tests of string_concat and string_concat_2, respectively. Removing the serialization reduced the overhead of the aggregation somewhat, and resulted in around a 10% performance improvement—a nice bonus.

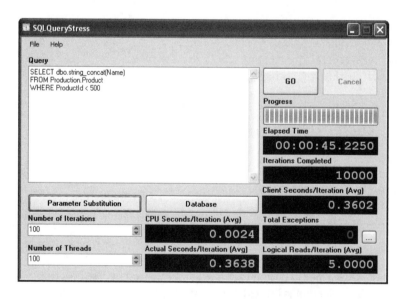

Figure 6-8. *Testing aggregation using serialization of all members of the internal collection*

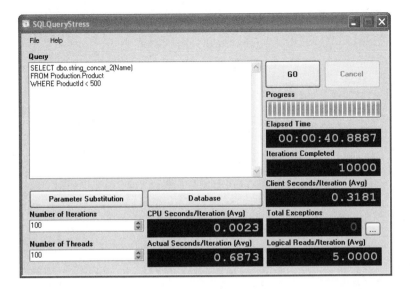

Figure 6-9. *Aggregating only the GUID is a much faster solution, in addition to offering greater functionality.*

Although I've shown a solution involving string concatenation, that is certainly not the only problem for which this technique could be used. Median and statistical variance calculation are two other areas that spring to mind, both of which require internally holding a list of inputs. In cases in which these lists can grow larger than 8000 bytes, this technique should help to provide aggregate functionality where it was previously not possible.

Keep in mind that this method does stress memory quite a bit more than the usual way of developing aggregates. Not only keeping more data in memory, but also keeping it around for a longer period of time, means that you'll use up quite a bit more of your server's resources. As with any technique that exploits the host in a way that wasn't really intended, make sure to test carefully before deploying solutions to production environments.

Summary

Getting the most out of SQLCLR routines involves a bit of thought investment. Upfront design and architecture considerations will yield great benefits in terms of security, reliability, and performance. You should also consider reuse at every stage, in order to minimize the amount of work that must be done when you need the same functionality six months or a year down the road. If you've already coded it once, why code it again?

To illustrate these concepts, I showed two examples: serializing tables using the `BinaryFormatter`, and extending user-defined aggregates. In both cases, I used a common, core set of higher-privileged utility assemblies in order to limit the outer surface area, and tried to design the solutions to promote flexibility and potential for use in many projects throughout the lifetime of the code.

CHAPTER 7

■ ■ ■

Dynamic T-SQL

When designing any application, the general goal is to create a great user experience; if users don't like the application, they won't use it, and if users won't use it, chances are it won't sell. So pleasing users is incredibly important to keeping software businesses afloat. Once this goal has been established, the question then becomes, "What do the users want?" More often than not, the answer is that users want flexible interfaces that let them control the data the way they want to. It's common for software customer support teams to receive requests for slightly different sort orders, filtering mechanisms, or outputs for data, making it imperative that applications be designed to support extensibility along these lines.

As with other data-related development challenges, such requests for flexible data output tend to fall through the application hierarchy, eventually landing on the database (and, therefore, the database developer). This is especially true in web-based application development, where client-side sortable and filterable grid controls are still a rarity, and many teams are working in a lightweight two-tier model, without a business layer to handle data caching and filtering.

Flexibility in the database can mean many things, and I have seen some very interesting approaches in applications I've worked with, usually involving creation of many stored procedures or complex, nested control-of-flow blocks. These solutions invariably seem to create more problems than they solve, and make application development much more difficult than it needs to be by introducing a lot of additional complexity in the database layer.

In this chapter, I will discuss use of dynamic SQL to solve these problems as well as to create more flexible stored procedures. Many developers seem to scorn dynamic SQL, often believing that it will cause performance, security, or maintainability problems, and many others simply don't understand how to properly use it. I believe that dynamic SQL is a powerful tool that, if used correctly, is a tremendous asset to the database developer's toolbox. There is a lot of misinformation floating around about what it is and when or why it should be used, and I hope to clear up some myths and misconceptions in these pages.

Dynamic T-SQL vs. Ad Hoc T-SQL

Before I begin a serious discussion about how dynamic SQL should be used, it's first important to establish a bit of terminology. Two terms that are often intermingled in the database world with regard to SQL are **dynamic** and **ad hoc**. I consider any batch of SQL generated dynamically by an application layer and sent to SQL Server for execution to be ad hoc SQL. Dynamic SQL, on the other hand, I define as a batch of SQL that is generated *within T-SQL* and executed

169

using the EXECUTE statement or, preferably, via the sp_executesql system stored procedure (which is covered later in this chapter).

Most of this chapter focuses on dynamic SQL and how to build effective dynamic stored procedures. However, if you are one of those working with systems that do not use stored procedures, I advise you to still read the sections "SQL Injection" and "Compilation and Parameterization" at a minimum. Both sections are definitely applicable to ad hoc scenarios and are extremely important.

All of that said, I do not recommend the use of ad hoc SQL in application development, and feel that there are a lot of problems that are solved through the use of stored procedures.

The Stored Procedure vs. Ad Hoc SQL Debate

A seemingly never-ending battle in online database forums concerns the question of whether database application development should involve the use of stored procedures or not. This question can become quite complex, with proponents of rapid software development methodologies such as Test-Driven Development (TDD) claiming that stored procedures slow down their process, and fans of Object-Relational Mapping (ORM) technologies making claims about the benefits of those technologies over stored procedures. It does not help that many of the combatants in these battles happen to have a vested interest in ORM; some of the most heated debates in recent memory were started by inflammatory claims made by vendors of ORM tools.

I highly recommend that you search the Web to find these debates and reach your own conclusions. Personally, I heavily favor the use of stored procedures, for several reasons that I will briefly discuss here.

First and foremost, stored procedures create an abstraction layer between the database and the application, hiding details about both the schema and, sometimes, the data. The encapsulation of data logic within stored procedures greatly decreases coupling between the database and the application, meaning that maintenance of or modification to the database will not necessitate changing the application accordingly. Reducing these dependencies and thinking of the database as a data API rather than a simple application persistence layer translates into a much more flexible application development process. Often, this can permit the database and application layers to be developed in parallel rather than in sequence, thereby allowing for greater scale-out of human resources on a given project. For more information on concepts such as encapsulation, coupling, and treating the database as an API, see Chapter 1.

If stored procedures are properly defined, with well-documented and consistent outputs, testing is not at all hindered—unit tests can be easily created, as shown in Chapter 2, in order to support TDD. Furthermore, support for more advanced testing methodologies also becomes easier, not more difficult, thanks to stored procedures. For instance, consider use of **mock objects**, façade methods that TDD practitioners create which return specific known values. These are then substituted for real methods in testing scenarios such that testing any given method does not test any methods that it calls (any calls made from within the method being tested will actually be a call to a mock version of the method). This technique is actually much easier to implement for testing of data access when stored procedures are used, as mock stored procedures can easily be created and swapped in and out without disrupting or recompiling the application code being tested.

Another important issue is security. Ad hoc SQL (as well as dynamic SQL) presents various security challenges, including opening possible attack vectors and making data access security much more difficult to enforce declaratively, rather than programmatically. This means that by using ad hoc SQL your application may be more vulnerable to being hacked, and you may not be able to rely on SQL Server to secure access to data. The end result is that a greater degree of testing will be required in order to ensure that security holes are properly patched and that users—both authorized and not—are unable to access data they're not supposed to see. See the section "Dynamic SQL Security Considerations" for further discussion of these points.

Finally, I will address the hottest issue that online debates always seem to gravitate toward. Of course, this is none other than the question of performance. Proponents of ad hoc SQL make the valid claim that, thanks to better support for query plan caching in SQL Server 2000 and 2005, stored procedures no longer have much of a performance benefit. (Please note, this is only true if ad hoc or dynamic SQL is properly used in either case! See the section "Why Go Dynamic?" for more information.) And although this sounds like a great argument for not having to use stored procedures, I personally believe that it is a nonissue. Given equivalent performance, I think the obvious choice is the more maintainable and secure option (i.e., stored procedures).

In the end, the stored procedure vs. ad hoc SQL question is really one of purpose. Many in the ORM community feel that the database should be used as nothing more than a very simple object persistence layer, and would probably be perfectly happy with a database that only had a single table with only two columns: a GUID to identify an object's ID and an XML column for the serialized object graph.

In my eyes, a database is much more than just a collection of data. It is also an enforcer of data rules, a protector of data integrity, and a central data resource that can be shared among multiple applications. For these reasons, I firmly believe that a decoupled, stored procedure–based design is the only way to go.

Why Go Dynamic?

As mentioned in the introduction for this chapter, dynamic SQL can help create more flexible data access layers, thereby helping to enable more flexible applications, which makes for happier users. This is a righteous goal, but the fact is that dynamic SQL is just one means by which to attain the desired end result. It is quite possible—in fact, often preferable—to do dynamic sorting and filtering directly on the client in many desktop applications, or in a business layer, if one exists to support either a web-based or client-server–style desktop application. It is also possible to not go dynamic at all, and support static stored procedures that supply optional parameters—but that's not generally recommended.

Before committing to any database-based solution, determine whether it is really the correct course of action. Keep in mind the questions of performance, maintainability, and most important, scalability. Database resources are often the most taxed of any used by a given application, and dynamic sorting and filtering of data can potentially mean a lot more load put on the database. Remember that scaling the database can often be much more expensive than scaling other layers of an application.

For example, consider the question of sorting data. In order for the database to sort data, the data must be queried. This means that it must be read from disk or memory, thereby using I/O and CPU time, filtered appropriately, and finally sorted and returned to the caller. Every time the data needs to be resorted a different way, it must be reread or sorted in memory and refiltered by the database engine. This can add up to quite a bit of load if there are hundreds or thousands of users all trying to sort data in different ways, and all sharing resources on the same database server.

Due to this issue, if the same data is resorted again and again (for instance, by a user who wants to see various high or low data points), it often makes sense to do the work in a disconnected cache. A desktop application that uses a client-side data grid, for example, can load the data only once, and then sort and resort it using the client computer's resources rather than the database server's resources. This can take a tremendous amount of strain off of the database server, meaning that it can use its resources for other data-intensive operations.

Aside from the scalability concerns, it's important to note that database-based solutions can be tricky and difficult to test and maintain. I offer some suggestions in the section "Going Dynamic: Using EXECUTE," but keep in mind that procedural code may be easier to work with for these purposes than T-SQL.

Once you've exhausted all other resources, *only then* should you look at the database as a solution for dynamic operations. In the database layer, the question of using dynamic SQL instead of static SQL comes down to issues of both maintainability and performance. The fact is, dynamic SQL can be made to perform much better than simple static SQL for many dynamic cases, but more complex (and difficult to maintain) static SQL will generally outperform maintainable dynamic SQL solutions. For the best balance of maintenance vs. performance, I always favor the dynamic SQL solution.

Compilation and Parameterization

Any discussion of dynamic SQL and performance is not possible to fully comprehend without a basic background understanding of how SQL Server processes queries and caches their plans. To that end, I will provide a brief discussion here, with some examples to help you get started in investigating these behaviors within SQL Server.

Every query executed by SQL Server goes through a compilation phase before actually being executed by the query processor. This compilation produces what is known as a *query plan*, which tells the query processor how to physically access the tables and indexes in the database in order to satisfy the query. However, query compilation can be expensive for certain queries, and when the same queries or types of queries are executed over and over, there generally is no reason to compile them each time. In order to save on the cost of compilation, SQL Server caches query plans in a memory pool called the **query plan cache**.

The query plan cache uses a simple hash lookup based on the exact text of the query in order to find a previously compiled plan. If the exact query has already been compiled, there is no reason to recompile it, and SQL Server skips directly to the execution phase in order to get the results for the caller. If a compiled version of the query is not found, the first step taken is parsing of the query. SQL Server determines which operations are being conducted in the SQL, does validation of syntax, and produces a **parse tree**, which is a structure that contains information about the query in a normalized form.[1] The parse tree is further validated and eventually compiled into a query plan, which is placed into the query plan cache for future invocations of the query.

---

1. Itzak Ben-Gan et al., *Inside Microsoft SQL Server 2005: T-SQL Querying* (Redmond, WA: Microsoft Press, 2006) pp. 35–37.

■**Note** Query compilation and plan caching are complex topics, and it's not possible to completely cover them in the scope of this chapter. For a detailed explanation of how things work, see Arun Marathe's TechNet white paper, "Batch Compilation, Recompilation, and Plan Caching Issues in SQL Server 2005," at `http://www.microsoft.com/technet/prodtechnol/sql/2005/recomp.mspx`.

The effect of the query plan cache on execution time can be seen even with simple queries. To see the amount of time spent in the parsing and compilation phase, turn on SQL Server's `SET STATISTICS TIME` option, which causes SQL Server to output informational messages about time spent in parsing/compilation and execution. For example, consider the following T-SQL, which turns on time statistics, and then queries the `HumanResources.Employee` table, which can be found in the AdventureWorks database:

```
SET STATISTICS TIME ON
GO

SELECT *
FROM HumanResources.Employee
WHERE EmployeeId IN (1, 2)
GO
```

Executing this query in SQL Server Management Studio on my system produces the following output messages the first time the query is run:

```
SQL Server parse and compile time:
   CPU time = 0 ms, elapsed time = 5 ms.

(2 row(s) affected)

SQL Server Execution Times:
   CPU time = 0 ms,  elapsed time = 1 ms.
```

This query took 5 milliseconds to parse and compile. But subsequent runs produce the following output, indicating that the cached plan is being used:

```
SQL Server parse and compile time:
   CPU time = 0 ms, elapsed time = 1 ms.

(2 row(s) affected)

SQL Server Execution Times:
   CPU time = 0 ms,  elapsed time = 1 ms.
```

Thanks to the cached plan, each subsequent invocation of the query takes 4 milliseconds less than the first invocation—not bad, when you consider that the actual execution time is less than 1 millisecond (the lowest elapsed time reported by time statistics).

■**Note** In order to simplify the output a bit, I ran SET STATISTICS TIME OFF between the two runs shown here. Otherwise, you would see additional times reported for the SET STATISTICS TIME ON statement. It's also important to note that during testing it is possible to clear out the query plan cache, and I did that on my end as well in order to show you clean output. To clear out the cache, use the DBCC FREEPROCCACHE command. Keep in mind that this command clears out the cache for the entire instance of SQL Server—doing this is not generally recommended in production environments. Another option is DBCC FLUSHPROCINDB, which has a single parameter, a database ID for which to clear the procedure cache. Since it only clears the cache for a single database, it may be a better alternative to DBCC FREEPROCCACHE. However, the command is undocumented, which means that it's not officially supported by Microsoft. Use it at your own risk, preferably only in development environments.

Auto-Parameterization

An important part of the parsing process that enables the query plan cache to be more efficient in some cases involves determination of which parts of the query qualify as parameters. If SQL Server determines that one or more literals used in the query are parameters that may be changed for future invocations of a similar version of the query, it can **auto-parameterize** the query. To understand what this means, let's first take a glance into the query plan cache, via the sys.dm_exec_cached_plans dynamic management view and the sys.dm_exec_sql_text function. The following query finds all cached queries that contain the string "HumanResources", except those that contain the name of the view itself—this second predicate is necessary so that the plan for the query to see the query plans is not returned.

```
SELECT
    ecp.objtype,
    p.Text
FROM sys.dm_exec_cached_plans AS ecp
CROSS APPLY
(
    SELECT *
    FROM sys.dm_exec_sql_text(ecp.plan_handle)
) p
WHERE
    p.Text LIKE '%HumanResources%'
    AND p.Text NOT LIKE '%sys.dm_exec_cached_plans%'
```

Querying the view after executing the previous query against HumanResources.Employee results in the output shown in Figure 7-1. The important things to note here are that the objtype column indicates that the query is being treated as ad hoc, and that the Text column shows the exact text of the executed query. Queries that cannot be auto-parameterized are classified by the query engine as "ad hoc" (obviously, this is a slightly different definition from the one I use).

	objtype	Text
1	Adhoc	SELECT * FROM HumanResources.Employee WHERE E...

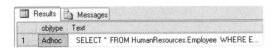

Figure 7-1. *Query text of cached ad hoc plan*

The previous example query was used to keep things simple, precisely because it could not be auto-parameterized. The following query, on the other hand, can be auto-parameterized:

```
SELECT *
FROM HumanResources.Employee
WHERE EmployeeId = 1
```

Clearing the execution plan cache, running this query, and finally querying the view again results in the output shown in Figure 7-2. In this case, two plans have been generated: an ad hoc plan for the query's exact text and a prepared plan for the auto-parameterized version of the query. Looking at the text of the latter plan, notice that the query has been normalized (the object names are bracket-delimited, carriage returns and other extraneous white space have been removed, and so on) and that a parameter has been derived from the text of the query.

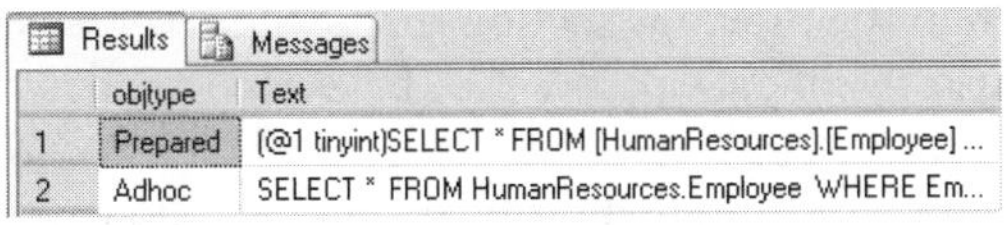

	objtype	Text
1	Prepared	(@1 tinyint)SELECT * FROM [HumanResources].[Employee]...
2	Adhoc	SELECT * FROM HumanResources.Employee WHERE Em...

Figure 7-2. *Query text of cached ad hoc and prepared plans*

The benefit of this auto-parameterization is that subsequent queries submitted to SQL Server that can be auto-parameterized to the same normalized form may be able to make use of the prepared query plan, thereby avoiding compilation overhead.

Note The auto-parameterization examples shown here were done using the AdventureWorks database with its default options set, including the "simple parameterization" option, which tells the query engine not to work too hard to auto-parameterize queries. SQL Server 2005 includes an option to turn on a more powerful form of auto-parameterization, called "forced parameterization." This option makes SQL Server work much harder to auto-parameterize queries, which means greater query compilation cost in some cases. This can be very beneficial to applications that use a lot of nonparameterized ad hoc queries, but may cause performance degradation in other cases. I recommend thoroughly reading the materials in SQL Server 2005 Books Online and carefully testing before setting this option in production environments.

Application-Level Parameterization

Auto-parameterization is not the only way that a query can be parameterized. Other forms of parameterization are possible at the application level for ad hoc SQL, or within T-SQL when working with dynamic SQL in a stored procedure. The section "sp_executesql: A Better EXECUTE," found later in this chapter, describes how to parameterize dynamic SQL, but I will briefly discuss application-level parameterization here.

Every query framework that can communicate with SQL Server supports the idea of Remote Procedure Call (RPC) invocation of queries. In the case of an RPC call, parameters are bound and strongly typed, rather than encoded as strings and passed along with the rest of the query text. Parameterizing queries in this way has one key advantage from a performance standpoint: the application tells SQL Server what the parameters are; SQL Server does not need to (and will not) try to find them itself.

To illustrate how this works, I will show you an example using the SQLQueryStress tool. SQLQueryStress uses parameterized queries to support its parameter substitution mode. This is implemented in ADO.NET by populating the `Parameters` collection on the `SqlCommand` object when preparing a query.

To see the effect of parameterization, load the tool and configure the Database options to connect to an instance of SQL Server and use AdventureWorks as the default database. Next, enter the following query into the Query textbox:

```
SELECT *
FROM HumanResources.Employee
WHERE EmployeeId IN (@EmpId1, @EmpId2)
```

This query is the same as the query shown in the previous section that SQL Server was unable to auto-parameterize. However, in this case, the literal employee IDs have been replaced with the variables `@EmpId1` and `@EmpId2`.

Once the query is in place, click the Parameter Substitution button and put the following query into the Parameter Query textbox:

```
SELECT 1 AS EmpId1, 2 AS EmpId2
```

This query returns one row, containing the values 1 and 2, which will be substituted into the outer query as parameters for the RPC call. Once this query is in the textbox, click the Get Columns button and map the `EmpId1` column to `@EmpId1` and the `EmpId2` column to `@EmpId2`. When you are finished, your column mappings should look like what's shown in Figure 7-3. Once done mapping, click OK, and then click GO to run the query (don't bother setting iterations or threads above 1—this run is not a load test).

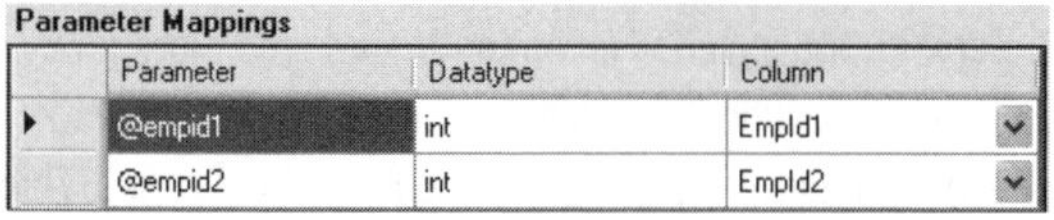

Figure 7-3. *SQLQueryStress column mappings*

Once you have run the query, go back into SQL Server Management Studio and query the `sys.dm_exec_cached_plans` view using the query from the previous section. The result should be the same as that shown in Figure 7-4. Just like with auto-parameterized queries, the plan is prepared, and the text is prefixed with the parameters. However, notice that the text of the query is not normalized. The object name is not bracket-delimited, and although it is not apparent in this screenshot, white space has not been removed. This fact is extremely important! If you were to run the same query, but with slightly different formatting, you would get a second plan—so when working with parameterized queries, make sure that the application generating the query produces the exact same formatting every time. Otherwise, you will end up wasting both the CPU cycles required for needless compilation and memory for caching the additional plans.

■Note White space is not the only type of formatting that can make a difference in terms of plan reuse. The cache lookup mechanism is nothing more than a simple hash on the query text and is case sensitive. So the exact same query submitted twice with different capitalization will be seen by the cache as different queries—even on a case-insensitive server. It's always a good idea when working with SQL Server to try to be consistent with your use of capitalization and formatting. Not only does it make your code more readable, but it may wind up improving performance!

Figure 7-4. *Cached text for a parameterized query*

Performance Implications of Parameterization and Caching

Now that all of the background information has been covered, the burning question can be answered: why should you care, and what does any of this have to do with dynamic SQL? The answer, of course, is that this has everything to do with dynamic SQL, if you care about performance (and other issues, but we'll get to those shortly).

If you're not still in SQLQueryStress from the previous section, load the tool back up and get it to the same state that it was in at the end of the section. Now, click the Parameter Substitution button, and enter the following query into the Parameter Query textbox:

```
SELECT Number, Number + 1 AS NumberPlus1
FROM master..spt_values
WHERE Type = 'P'
```

This query uses the master..spt_values table, which happens to contain every number from 0 to 2047 in a column called Number, keyed off of the Type of P. (Whatever that means—this table is undocumented and appears to be used only by one system stored procedure, also undocumented, called sp_MSobjectprivs. But it certainly does come in handy when you need some numbers, stat.)

In the Parameter Mappings section, map the Number column to @EmpId1, and NumberPlus1 to @EmpId2. When you're done, click OK and set the Number of Iterations to 2048 in order to go through every number returned by the substitution query. Once you've finished configuring, click GO to start the run. Figure 7-5 shows the output from the run on my system.

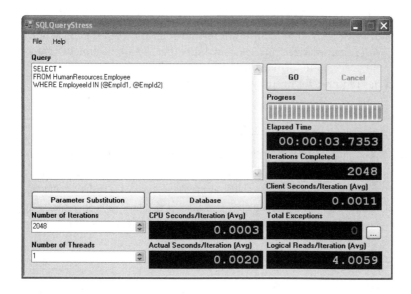

Figure 7-5. *SQLQueryStress output from parameterized run: each iteration takes around 2 ms.*

Once again, return to SQL Server Management Studio and query the sys.dm_exec_cached_ plans view, and you will see that the results have not changed. There is only one plan in the cache for this form of the query, even though it has just been run 2,048 times with different parameter values. This indicates that parameterization is working, and the server does not need to do extra work to compile the query every time a slightly different form of it is issued.

Now that a positive baseline has been established, let's investigate what happens when queries are *not* properly parameterized. Back in SQLQueryStress, enter the following query into the Query textbox:

```
DECLARE @sql VARCHAR(MAX)

SET @sql =
'SELECT *
FROM HumanResources.Employee
WHERE EmployeeId IN (' +
    CONVERT(VARCHAR, @EmpId1) + ', ' +
    CONVERT(VARCHAR, @EmpId2) + ')'

EXEC(@sql)
```

Since SQLQueryStress uses parameterized queries for its parameter substitution mode, a bit of tweaking is necessary to get it to load test nonparameterized queries with substitution. In this case, a dynamic SQL string is built using the input parameters and the resultant query executed using the EXECUTE statement (see the section "Going Dynamic: Using EXECUTE" later in this chapter if you're not familiar with it). Once you're ready, click GO to start the run. The results of the run from my system are shown in Figure 7-6.

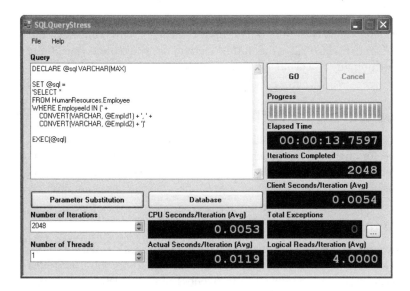

Figure 7-6. *SQLQueryStress output from nonparameterized run: performance is degraded by a factor of 5.*

The end result shown here should be enough to make you a believer in the power of parameterization. But just in case you're still not sure, jump back into SQL Server Management Studio one final time and query the sys.dm_exec_cached_plans view for a nice surprise. The abbreviated results of the query as run on my system are shown in Figure 7-7.

	objtype	Text
1	Prepared	(@empid1 int,@empid2 int)SELECT * FROM HumanResour…
2	Prepared	(@empid1 int,@empid2 int)DECLARE @sql VARCHAR(MAX…
3	Adhoc	SELECT * FROM HumanResources.Employee WHERE Em…
4	Adhoc	SELECT * FROM HumanResources.Employee WHERE Em…
5	Adhoc	SELECT * FROM HumanResources.Employee WHERE Em…
6	Adhoc	SELECT * FROM HumanResources.Employee WHERE Em…
7	Adhoc	SELECT * FROM HumanResources.Employee WHERE Em…
8	Adhoc	SELECT * FROM HumanResources.Employee WHERE Em…
9	Adhoc	SELECT * FROM HumanResources.Employee WHERE Em…
10	Adhoc	SELECT * FROM HumanResources.Employee WHERE Em…
11	Adhoc	SELECT * FROM HumanResources.Employee WHERE Em…
12	Adhoc	SELECT * FROM HumanResources.Employee WHERE Em…

Figure 7-7. *Nonparameterized queries produce one ad hoc plan per query.*

Running 2,048 nonparameterized ad hoc queries with different parameters resulted in 2,048 additional cached plans. That means not only the slowdown apparent in the average seconds per iteration counters (resulting from the additional compilation), but also that quite a bit of RAM is now wasted in the query plan cache. In SQL Server 2005, queries are aged out of the plan cache on a least-recently-used basis, and depending on the server's workload it can take quite a bit of time for unused plans to be removed.

In a large production environment, not using parameterized queries can result in gigabytes of RAM being wasted caching query plans that will never be used again. This is obviously not a good thing! So please—for the sake of all of that RAM—learn to use your connection library's parameterized query functionality and avoid falling into this trap.

Supporting Optional Parameters

The primary use case for dynamic SQL is the ability to write stored procedures that can support optional parameters for queries in an efficient, maintainable manner. Although it is quite easy to write static stored procedures that handle optional query parameters, these are generally grossly inefficient or highly unmaintainable—as a developer, you can take your pick.

Optional Parameters via Static T-SQL

Before presenting the dynamic SQL solution to the optional parameter problem, a few demonstrations are necessary to illustrate why static SQL is not the right tool for the job. There are a few different methods of varying complexity and effectiveness, but none deliver consistently.

As a baseline, consider the following query, which selects data from the `HumanResources.Employee` table in the `AdventureWorks` database:

```
SELECT
    ContactId,
    LoginId,
    Title
FROM HumanResources.Employee
WHERE
    EmployeeId = 1
    AND NationalIdNumber = N'14417807'
```

This query uses predicates to filter on both the `EmployeeId` and `NationalIdNumber` columns. Executing the query produces the execution plan shown in Figure 7-8, which has an estimated cost of 0.0032831, and which requires two logical reads. This plan involves a seek of the table's clustered index, which uses the `EmployeeId` column as its key.

Figure 7-8. *Base execution plan with seek on EmployeeId clustered index*

Since the query uses the clustered index, it does not need to do a lookup to get any additional data. Furthermore, since `EmployeeId` is the primary key for the table, the `NationalIdNumber` predicate is not used when physically identifying the row. Therefore, the following query, which uses only the `EmployeeId` predicate, produces the exact same query plan with the same cost and same number of reads:

```
SELECT
    ContactId,
    LoginId,
    Title
FROM HumanResources.Employee
WHERE
    EmployeeId = 1
```

Another form of this query involves removing EmployeeId and querying based only on NationalIdNumber:

```
SELECT
    ContactId,
    LoginId,
    Title
FROM HumanResources.Employee
WHERE
    NationalIdNumber = N'14417807'
```

This query results in a very different plan from the other two, due to the fact that a different index must be used to satisfy the query. Figure 7-9 shows the resultant plan, which involves a seek on a nonclustered index on the NationalIdNumber column, followed by a lookup to get the additional rows for the SELECT list. This plan has an estimated cost of 0.0065704, and does four logical reads.

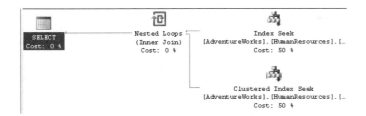

Figure 7-9. *Base execution plan with seek on NationalIdNumber nonclustered index followed by a lookup into the clustered index*

The final form of the base query has no predicates at all:

```
SELECT
    ContactId,
    LoginId,
    Title
FROM HumanResources.Employee
```

As shown in Figure 7-10, the query plan is a simple clustered index scan, with an estimated cost of 0.0080454, and nine logical reads. Since all of the rows need to be returned and no index covers every column required, a clustered index scan is the most efficient way to satisfy this query.

Figure 7-10. *Base execution plan with scan on the clustered index*

These baseline numbers will be used to compare the relative performance of various methods of creating a dynamic stored procedure that returns the same columns, but which optionally enables one or both predicates. To begin with, the query can be wrapped in a stored procedure:

```
CREATE PROCEDURE GetEmployeeData
    @EmployeeId INT = NULL,
    @NationalIdNumber NVARCHAR(15) = NULL
AS
BEGIN
    SET NOCOUNT ON

    SELECT
        ContactId,
        LoginId,
        Title
    FROM HumanResources.Employee
    WHERE
        EmployeeId = @EmployeeId
        AND NationalIdNumber = @NationalIdNumber
END
```

This stored procedure uses the parameters @EmployeeId and @NationalIdNumber to support the predicates. Both of these parameters are optional, with NULL default values. However, this stored procedure does not really support the parameters optionally; not passing one of the parameters will mean that no rows will be returned by the stored procedure at all, since any comparison with NULL in a predicate will not result in a true answer.

As a first shot at making this stored procedure optionally enable the predicates, a developer might try control of flow and rewrite the procedure as follows:

```
CREATE PROCEDURE GetEmployeeData
    @EmployeeId INT = NULL,
    @NationalIdNumber NVARCHAR(15) = NULL
AS
BEGIN
    SET NOCOUNT ON

    IF (@EmployeeId IS NOT NULL
        AND @NationalIdNumber IS NOT NULL)
    BEGIN
        SELECT
            ContactId,
```

```
            LoginId,
            Title
        FROM HumanResources.Employee
        WHERE
            EmployeeId = @EmployeeId
            AND NationalIdNumber = @NationalIdNumber
    END
    ELSE IF (@EmployeeId IS NOT NULL)
    BEGIN
        SELECT
            ContactId,
            LoginId,
            Title
        FROM HumanResources.Employee
        WHERE
            EmployeeId = @EmployeeId
    END
    ELSE IF (@NationalIdNumber IS NOT NULL)
    BEGIN
        SELECT
            ContactId,
            LoginId,
            Title
        FROM HumanResources.Employee
        WHERE
            NationalIdNumber = @NationalIdNumber
    END
    ELSE
    BEGIN
        SELECT
            ContactId,
            LoginId,
            Title
        FROM HumanResources.Employee
    END
END
```

Although executing this stored procedure produces the exact same query plans—and, therefore, the exact same performance—as the test batches, it has an unfortunate problem. Namely, taking this approach turns what was a very simple 10-line stored procedure into a 42-line monster. Consider that when adding a column to the SELECT list for this procedure, a change would have to be made in four places. Now consider what would happen if a third predicate were needed—the number of cases would jump from four to eight, meaning that any change such as adding or removing a column would have to be made in eight places. Now consider 10 or 20 predicates, and it's clear that this method has no place in the SQL Server developer's toolbox. It is simply not a manageable solution.

The next most common technique is one that has appeared in articles on several SQL Server web sites over the past few years. As a result, a lot of code has been written against it by developers who don't seem to realize that they're creating a performance time bomb. This technique takes advantage of the COALESCE function, as shown in the following rewritten version of the stored procedure:

```
CREATE PROCEDURE GetEmployeeData
    @EmployeeId INT = NULL,
    @NationalIdNumber NVARCHAR(15) = NULL
AS
BEGIN
    SET NOCOUNT ON

    SELECT
        ContactId,
        LoginId,
        Title
    FROM HumanResources.Employee
    WHERE
        EmployeeId = COALESCE(@EmployeeId, EmployeeId)
        AND NationalIdNumber = COALESCE(@NationalIdNumber, NationalIdNumber)
END
```

This version of the stored procedure looks great and is easy to understand. The COALESCE function returns the first non-NULL value passed into its parameter list. So if either of the arguments to the stored procedure are NULL, the COALESCE will "pass through," comparing the value of the column to itself—and at least in theory, that seems like it should be a no-op.

Unfortunately, because the COALESCE function uses a column from the table as an input, it cannot be evaluated deterministically before execution of the query. The result is that the function is evaluated once for every row of the table, resulting in a table scan. This means consistent results, but probably not in a good way; all four combinations of parameters result in the same query plan, a clustered index scan with an estimated cost of 0.0080454 and nine logical reads. This is over four times the I/O for the queries involving the EmployeeId column—quite a performance drain.

Similar to the version that uses COALESCE is a version that uses OR to conditionally set the parameter only if the argument is not NULL:

```
CREATE PROCEDURE GetEmployeeData
    @EmployeeId INT = NULL,
    @NationalIdNumber NVARCHAR(15) = NULL
AS
BEGIN
    SET NOCOUNT ON

    SELECT
        ContactId,
        LoginId,
        Title
    FROM HumanResources.Employee
    WHERE
        (@EmployeeId IS NULL
```

```
            OR EmployeeId = @EmployeeId)
    AND (@NationalIdNumber IS NULL
            OR @NationalIdNumber = NationalIdNumber)
END
```

This version, while similar in idea to the version that uses COALESCE, has some interesting performance traits. Depending on which parameters you use the first time you call it, you'll see vastly different results. If you're lucky enough to call it the first time with no arguments, the result will be an index scan, producing nine logical reads—and the same number of reads will result for any combination of parameters passed in thereafter. If, however, you first call the stored procedure using only the @EmployeeId parameter, the resultant plan will use only four logical reads—until you happen to call the procedure with no arguments, and it produces a massive 582 reads.

Given the surprisingly huge jump in I/O that the bad plan can produce, as well as the unpredictable nature of what performance characteristics you'll end up with, this is undoubtedly the worst possible choice.

The final method that can be used is a bit more creative, and also can result in somewhat better results. The following version of the stored procedure shows how it is implemented:

```
CREATE PROCEDURE GetEmployeeData
    @EmployeeId INT = NULL,
    @NationalIdNumber NVARCHAR(15) = NULL
AS
BEGIN
    SET NOCOUNT ON

    SELECT
        ContactId,
        LoginId,
        Title
    FROM HumanResources.Employee
    WHERE
        EmployeeId BETWEEN
            COALESCE(@EmployeeId, -2147483648)
                AND COALESCE(@EmployeeId, 2147483647)
        AND NationalIdNumber LIKE COALESCE(@NationalIdNumber, N'%')
END
```

If you're a bit confused by the logic of this stored procedure, you're now familiar with the first reason that I don't recommend this technique: it's relatively unmaintainable if you don't understand exactly how it works. Using it almost certainly guarantees that you will produce stored procedures that will stump others who attempt to maintain them in the future. And while that might be good for job security, using it for that purpose is probably not a virtuous goal.

This stored procedure operates by using COALESCE to cancel out NULL arguments by substituting in minimum and maximum conditions for the integer predicate (EmployeeId) and a LIKE expression that will match anything for the string predicate (NationalIdNumber).

If @EmployeeId is NULL, the EmployeeId predicate effectively becomes EmployeeId BETWEEN -2147483648 AND 2147483647—in other words, all possible integers. If @EmployeeId is not NULL, the predicate becomes EmployeeId BETWEEN @EmployeeId AND @EmployeeId. This is equivalent with EmployeeId=@EmployeeId.

The same basic logic is true for the NationalIdNumber predicate, although because it's a string instead of an integer, LIKE is used instead of BETWEEN. If @NationalIdNumber is NULL, the predicate becomes NationalIdNumber LIKE N'%'. This will match any string in the NationalIdNumber column. On the other hand, if @NationalIdNumber is not NULL, the predicate becomes NationalIdNumber LIKE @NationalIdNumber, which is equivalent with NationalIdNumber=@NationalIdNumber—assuming that @NationalIdNumber contains no string expressions. This predicate can also be written using BETWEEN to avoid the string expression issue (for instance: BETWEEN N'' AND REPLICATE(NCHAR(1000), 15)). However, that method is both more difficult to read than the LIKE expression and fraught with potential problems due to collation issues (which is why I only went up to NCHAR(1000) instead of NCHAR(65535) in the example).

The real question, of course, is one of performance. Unfortunately, this stored procedure manages to confuse the query optimizer, resulting in the same plan being generated for every invocation. The plan, in every case, involves a clustered index seek on the table, with an estimated cost of 0.0048592, as shown in Figure 7-11. Unfortunately, this estimate turns out to be highly inconsistent, as the number of actual logical reads varies widely based on the arguments passed to the procedure.

Figure 7-11. *Every set of arguments passed to the stored procedure results in the same execution plan.*

If both arguments are passed or @EmployeeId is passed but @NationalIdNumber is not, the number of logical reads is three. While this is much better than the nine logical reads required by the previous version of the stored procedure, it's still 50% more I/O than the two logical reads required by the baseline in both of these cases. This estimated plan really breaks down when passing only @NationalIdNumber, since there is no way to efficiently satisfy a query on the NationalIdNumber column using the clustered index. In both that case and when passing no arguments, nine logical reads are reported. For the NationalIdNumber predicate this is quite a failure, as the stored procedure does over twice as much work for the same results as the baseline.

Going Dynamic: Using EXECUTE

The solution to all of the static SQL problems is, of course, to go dynamic. Building dynamic SQL inside of a stored procedure is simple, the code is relatively easy to understand, and as I'll show, it can provide excellent performance. However, there are various potential issues to note, not the least of which being security concerns. I'll explain how to deal with these as the examples progress.

The real benefit of dynamic SQL is that the execution plans generated for each invocation of the query will be optimized for only the predicates that are actually being used at that moment. The main issue with the static SQL solutions, aside from maintainability, was that the additional predicates confused the query optimizer, causing it to create inefficient plans. Dynamic SQL gets around this issue by not including anything extra in the query.

The simplest way to implement dynamic SQL in a stored procedure is with the EXECUTE statement. This statement takes as input a string, and executes whatever SQL the string contains. The following batch shows this in its simplest—and least effective—form:

```
EXEC('SELECT
    ContactId,
    LoginId,
    Title
FROM HumanResources.Employee')
```

Note that in this example (and all other examples in this chapter), I use the truncated form of EXECUTE. This seems to be a de facto standard for SQL Server code; I very rarely see code that uses the full form with the added "UTE." Although this is only a savings of three characters, I am very used to seeing it, and for some reason it makes a lot more sense to me when reading SQL than seeing the full EXECUTE keyword.

In this case, a string literal is passed to EXECUTE, and this doesn't really allow for anything very "dynamic." For instance, to add a predicate on EmployeeId to the query, the following would not work:

```
DECLARE @EmployeeId INT
SET @EmployeeId = 1

EXEC('SELECT
    ContactId,
    LoginId,
    Title
FROM HumanResources.Employee
WHERE EmployeeId = ' + CONVERT(VARCHAR, @EmployeeId))
```

This fails (with an "incorrect syntax" exception) because of the way EXECUTE is parsed by the SQL Server engine. SQL Server does only one pass to parse the syntax, and then tries to concatenate and execute the SQL in a second step. But due to the fact that the first step does not include a stage for inline expansion, the CONVERT is still a CONVERT, rather than a literal, when it's time for concatenation.

The solution to this issue is quite simple. Define a variable and assign the dynamic SQL to it, and *then* call EXECUTE:

```
DECLARE @EmployeeId INT
SET @EmployeeId = 1

DECLARE @sql NVARCHAR(MAX)

SET @sql = 'SELECT
    ContactId,
```

```
    LoginId,
    Title
FROM HumanResources.Employee
WHERE EmployeeId = ' + CONVERT(VARCHAR, @EmployeeId)

EXECUTE(@sql)
```

The string variable, @sql, can be manipulated in any way in order to form the desired dynamic SQL string, and since it's a variable, various code paths can be created using control-of-flow statements. In other words, forming the dynamic SQL is now limited only by the tools available within the T-SQL language for string manipulation.

A first shot at optional inclusion of both the EmployeeId and NationalIdNumber predicates follows:

```
DECLARE @EmployeeId INT
SET @EmployeeId = 1

DECLARE @NationalIdNumber NVARCHAR(15)
SET @NationalIdNumber = N'14417807'

DECLARE @sql NVARCHAR(MAX)

SET @sql = 'SELECT
    ContactId,
    LoginId,
    Title
FROM HumanResources.Employee '

IF (@EmployeeId IS NOT NULL
    AND @NationalIdNumber IS NOT NULL)
BEGIN
    SET @sql = @sql +
        'WHERE EmployeeId = ' + CONVERT(NVARCHAR, @EmployeeId) +
            ' AND NationalIdNumber = N''' + @NationalIdNumber + ''''
END
ELSE IF (@EmployeeId IS NOT NULL)
BEGIN
    SET @sql = @sql +
        'WHERE EmployeeId = ' +
            CONVERT(NVARCHAR, @EmployeeId)
END
ELSE IF (@NationalIdNumber IS NOT NULL)
BEGIN
    SET @sql = @sql +
        'WHERE NationalIdNumber = N''' + @NationalIdNumber + ''''
END

EXEC(@sql)
```

If this looks sickeningly familiar, you've been doing a good job of paying attention as the chapter progressed; this example has the same maintenance issues as the first shot at a static SQL stored procedure. Adding additional parameters will create a combinatorial explosion, making this solution completely unmaintainable. In addition, the SQL statement has been broken up into two component parts, making it lack a good sense of flow. Think about how bad this might get if you had to add ORDER BY or GROUP BY clauses.

To solve this problem, I like to concatenate my dynamic SQL in one shot, using CASE expressions instead of control-of-flow statements in order to optionally concatenate sections. The following example should serve to illustrate how this works:

```
DECLARE @EmployeeId INT
SET @EmployeeId = 1

DECLARE @NationalIdNumber NVARCHAR(15)
SET @NationalIdNumber = N'14417807'

DECLARE @sql NVARCHAR(MAX)

SET @sql = 'SELECT
    ContactId,
    LoginId,
    Title
FROM HumanResources.Employee
WHERE 1=1' +
CASE
    WHEN @EmployeeId IS NULL THEN ''
    ELSE 'AND EmployeeId = ' + CONVERT(NVARCHAR, @EmployeeId)
END +
CASE
    WHEN @NationalIdNumber IS NULL THEN ''
    ELSE 'AND NationalIdNumber = N''' + @NationalIdNumber + ''''
END

EXEC(@sql)
```

In this example, the CASE expressions concatenate an empty string if one of the parameters is NULL. Otherwise, the parameter is formatted as a string and concatenated to the predicate.

Thanks to the CASE expressions, the code is much more compact, and the query is still generally formatted like a query instead of like procedural code. But the real trick here is the addition of 1=1 to the WHERE clause, in order to avoid the combinatorial explosion problem. The query optimizer will "optimize out" (i.e., discard) 1=1 in a WHERE clause, so it has no effect on the resultant query plan. What it does do is allow the optional predicates to use AND without having to be aware of whether other optional predicates are being concatenated. Each predicate can therefore be listed only once in the code, and combinations are not a problem.

The final maintainability issue with this code is one of formatting, and this is an area that I feel is extremely important when working with dynamic SQL. Careful, consistent formatting can mean the difference between quick one-minute changes to stored procedures, instead of several hours of trying to decipher messy code.

To see the problem with the way the code is currently formatted, add `PRINT @sql` to the end of the batch, to see the final string:

```
SELECT
    ContactId,
    LoginId,
    Title
FROM HumanResources.Employee
WHERE 1=1AND EmployeeId = 1AND NationalIdNumber = N'14417807'
```

Although this SQL is valid and executes as-is without exception, it has the potential for problems due to the lack of spacing between the predicates. Debugging spacing issues in dynamic SQL can be maddening, so I have developed a formatting standard that works for me to combat the issue. When I am working with dynamic SQL, I concatenate every line separately, ensuring that each line is terminated with a space. This adds a bit more complexity to the code, but I've found that it makes it much easier to debug. Following is an example of how I like to format my dynamic SQL:

```
DECLARE @EmployeeId INT
SET @EmployeeId = 1

DECLARE @NationalIdNumber NVARCHAR(15)
SET @NationalIdNumber = N'14417807'

DECLARE @sql NVARCHAR(MAX)

SET @sql = '' +
    'SELECT ' +
        'ContactId, ' +
        'LoginId, ' +
        'Title ' +
    'FROM HumanResources.Employee ' +
    'WHERE 1=1 ' +
    CASE
        WHEN @EmployeeId IS NULL THEN ''
        ELSE 'AND EmployeeId = ' + CONVERT(NVARCHAR, @EmployeeId) + ' '
    END +
    CASE
        WHEN @NationalIdNumber IS NULL THEN ''
        ELSE 'AND NationalIdNumber = N''' + @NationalIdNumber + ''' '
    END

EXEC(@sql)
```

> **Note** I developed this style when working with older versions of SQL Server, which did not have the MAX data types and therefore had stringent variable size limitations. Cutting everything up into individual tokens greatly reduced the amount of white space, meaning that I could fit a lot more code in each variable. Removal of extraneous white space is not necessary in SQL Server 2005, but I still feel that this technique is great for ensuring proper spacing.

Now that the code fragment is properly formatted, it can be transferred into a new version of the GetEmployeeData stored procedure:

```
CREATE PROCEDURE GetEmployeeData
    @EmployeeId INT = NULL,
    @NationalIdNumber NVARCHAR(15) = NULL
AS
BEGIN
    SET NOCOUNT ON

    DECLARE @sql NVARCHAR(MAX)

    SET @sql = '' +
        'SELECT ' +
            'ContactId, ' +
            'LoginId, ' +
            'Title ' +
        'FROM HumanResources.Employee ' +
        'WHERE 1=1 ' +
        CASE
            WHEN @EmployeeId IS NULL THEN ''
            ELSE 'AND EmployeeId = ' + CONVERT(NVARCHAR, @EmployeeId) + ' '
        END +
        CASE
            WHEN @NationalIdNumber IS NULL THEN ''
            ELSE 'AND NationalIdNumber = N''' + @NationalIdNumber + ''' '
        END

    EXEC(@sql)
END
```

So that's it—a dynamic stored procedure with optional parameters. At first glance, this might look like a great solution, but it is still fraught with problems.

From a performance point of view, this procedure appears to be great when taken for a few test runs. Each set of input parameters produces the same execution plan as the baseline examples, with the same estimated costs and number of reads. However, under the covers, a major issue still exists: parameterization is not occurring. To illustrate this, start with the following T-SQL, which clears the query plan cache and then runs the procedure with the same optional parameter, for three different input values:

```
DBCC FREEPROCCACHE
GO

EXEC GetEmployeeData
    @EmployeeId = 1
GO

EXEC GetEmployeeData
    @EmployeeId = 2
GO

EXEC GetEmployeeData
    @EmployeeId = 3
GO
```

Now, query the sys.dm_exec_cached_plans view, and you will see the output shown in Figure 7-12. In this image, notice that there is one cached plan for the procedure itself—which is expected for any stored procedure—and an additional ad hoc plan cached for each invocation of the stored procedure. This means that every time a new argument is passed, a compilation occurs, which is clearly going to kill performance.

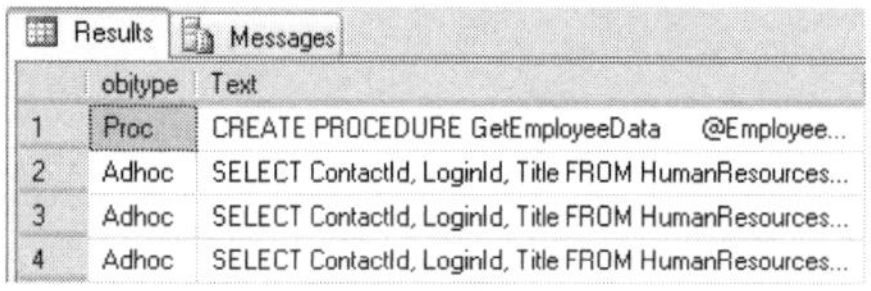

	objtype	Text
1	Proc	CREATE PROCEDURE GetEmployeeData @Employee...
2	Adhoc	SELECT ContactId, LoginId, Title FROM HumanResources...
3	Adhoc	SELECT ContactId, LoginId, Title FROM HumanResources...
4	Adhoc	SELECT ContactId, LoginId, Title FROM HumanResources...

Figure 7-12. *The dynamic query is not being parameterized and is therefore producing duplicate query plans for different arguments.*

The other issue with this stored procedure, as it currently stands, is a serious security hole. A stored procedure implemented similarly to this one but with a minor modification would open a simple attack vector that a hacker could exploit to easily pull information out of the database, or worse.

SQL Injection

Concatenating string parameters such as @NationalIdNumber directly onto queries can open your applications to considerable problems. The issue is a hacking technique called a **SQL injection attack**, which involves passing bits of semiformed SQL into textboxes in order to try to manipulate dynamic or ad hoc SQL on the other side.

The example GetEmployeeData stored procedure doesn't actually have much of a problem as-is, because @NationalIdNumber is defined as only 15 characters—this doesn't give a hacker much room to work with. But what if you were working with another stored procedure that had to be a bit more flexible? The following example procedure, which might be used to search for addresses in the AdventureWorks database, gives an attacker more than enough characters:

```
CREATE PROCEDURE FindAddressByString
    @String NVARCHAR(60)
AS
BEGIN
    SET NOCOUNT ON

    DECLARE @sql NVARCHAR(MAX)

    SET @sql = '' +
        'SELECT AddressId ' +
        'FROM Person.Address ' +
        'WHERE AddressLine1 LIKE ''%' + @String + '%'''

    EXEC(@sql)
END
```

This stored procedure can be executed with a string such as "Stone" used for the parameter value:

```
EXEC FindAddressByString
    @String = 'Stone'
```

This outputs the result set you might expect, with all of the address IDs that use that string in the AddressLine1 column. That output is shown in Figure 7-13.

Figure 7-13. *Output of searching addresses for the string "Stone"*

Consider what actually happened inside of the stored procedure. The WHERE clause for the query was concatenated, such that it literally became WHERE AddressLine1 LIKE '%Stone%'. But nothing is stopping someone from passing a string into the stored procedure that has a more profound effect. For instance, consider what happens in the following case, the output of which is shown in Figure 7-14:

```
EXEC FindAddressByString
    @String = ''' ORDER BY AddressId --'
```

After concatenation, the `WHERE` clause reads `WHERE AddressLine1 LIKE '%' ORDER BY AddressId --%'`. An `ORDER BY` clause—which was not there before—has been added to the query, and the `%'` at the end of the query has been commented out so that it will have no effect.

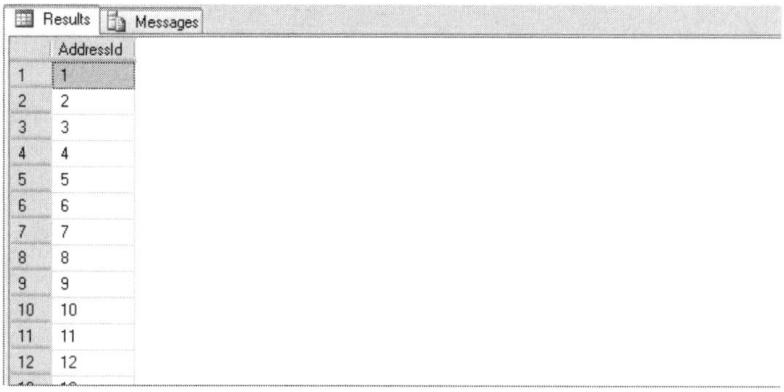

Figure 7-14. *An injected ORDER BY clause ordered the results.*

This is, of course, a fairly mundane example. How about something a bit more interesting, such as getting back the full pay history for every employee in the database?

```
EXEC FindAddressByString
    @String = ''; SELECT * FROM HumanResources.EmployeePayHistory --'
```

Assuming that the account used for the query has access to the `HumanResources.EmployeePayHistory` table, running the stored procedure produces the output shown in Figure 7-15. The fact is the attacker can do anything in the database that the authenticated account has access to do and that can be done in 60 characters (the size of the string parameter). This includes viewing data, deleting data, or inserting fake data. Such an attack can often be waged from the comfort of a web browser, and intrusion can be incredibly difficult to detect.

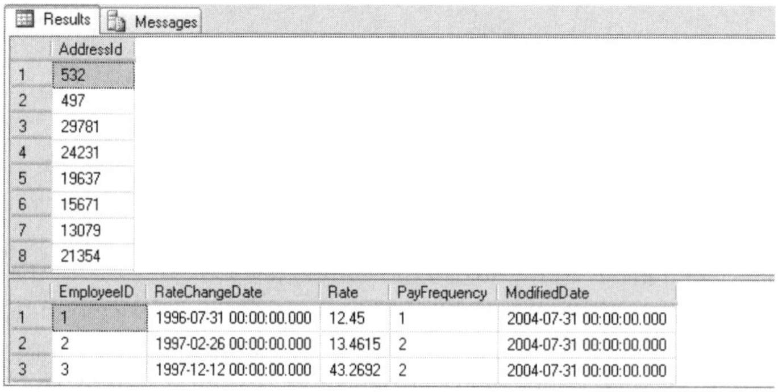

Figure 7-15. *An attacker can use SQL injection to do anything that the authenticated account has access to do.*

The solution is not to stop using dynamic SQL. Rather, it's to make sure that your dynamic SQL is *always* parameterized. Let me repeat that for effect: ***Always, always, always parameterize your dynamic SQL!*** The next section shows you how to use sp_executesql to do just that.

sp_executesql: A Better EXECUTE

In the previous sections, I identified two major problems with building dynamic SQL statements and executing them using EXECUTE: First of all, there is the issue of extraneous compilation and query plan caching, which makes performance drag and uses up valuable system resources. Second, and perhaps more important, is the threat of SQL injection attacks.

Query parameterization, mentioned earlier in this chapter in the context of application development, is the key to fixing both of these problems. Parameterization is a way to build a query such that any parameters are passed as strongly typed variables, rather than formatted as strings and appended to the query. In addition to the performance benefits this can bring by allowing SQL Server to do less work when processing the query, parameterization also has the benefit of virtually eliminating SQL injection attacks.

The first step in parameterizing a query is to replace literals with variable names. For instance, the injection-vulnerable query from the previous section could be rewritten in a parameterized manner as follows (I've removed the stored procedure creation code for simplicity):

```
DECLARE @String NVARCHAR(60)
SET @String = 'Stone'

DECLARE @sql NVARCHAR(MAX)

SET @sql = '' +
    'SELECT AddressId ' +
    'FROM Person.Address ' +
    'WHERE AddressLine1 LIKE ''%'' + @String + ''%'''
```

The only thing that has changed about this query compared to the version in the last section is two additional single quotes added such that the literal value of @String is no longer concatenated with the rest of the query. Previously, the literal value of @sql after concatenation would have been as follows:

```
SELECT AddressId FROM Person.Address WHERE AddressLine1 LIKE '%Stone%'
```

As a result of this change, the literal value after concatenation is now the following:

```
SELECT AddressId FROM Person.Address WHERE AddressLine1 LIKE '%' + @Stone + '%'
```

Due to the fact that no variables are getting formatted into strings for concatenation with the rest of the query, the type of SQL injection described in the previous section is impossible in this scenario. The only thing such an attempt would yield for a hacker is a search in which no results are returned!

Trying to execute this SQL using EXECUTE results in the following exception:

```
Msg 137, Level 15, State 2, Line 1
Must declare the scalar variable "@String".
```

The reason for this is that EXECUTE runs the SQL in a different context than that in which it was created. In the other context, the variable @String has not been declared and is therefore unknown.

The solution to this problem is to use the sp_executesql system stored procedure, which allows you to pass parameters to dynamic SQL, much as you can to a stored procedure. The parameters for sp_executesql are a Unicode (NVARCHAR or NCHAR) string containing a dynamic SQL batch, a second Unicode string that defines the data types of the variables referenced in the dynamic SQL, and a list of values or variables from the calling scope that correspond to the variables defined in the data type list. The following T-SQL shows how to execute the Person.Address query using sp_executesql:

```
DECLARE @String NVARCHAR(60)
SET @String = 'Stone'

DECLARE @sql NVARCHAR(MAX)

SET @sql = '' +
    'SELECT AddressId ' +
    'FROM Person.Address ' +
    'WHERE AddressLine1 LIKE ''%'' + @String + ''%'''

EXEC sp_executesql
    @sql,
    N'@String NVARCHAR(60)',
    @String
```

Running this batch will produce the same results as calling FindAddressByString and passing the string "Stone". The parameters to sp_executesql serve to map the @String variable from the outer scope, into the new scope spawned when the dynamic SQL is executed—without having to concatenate the literal value of the variable.

For an example that uses multiple parameters, consider again the GetEmployeeData stored procedure, now rewritten to use sp_executesql instead of EXECUTE:

```
CREATE PROCEDURE GetEmployeeData
    @EmployeeId INT = NULL,
    @NationalIdNumber NVARCHAR(15) = NULL
AS
BEGIN
    SET NOCOUNT ON

    DECLARE @sql NVARCHAR(MAX)

    SET @sql = '' +
        'SELECT ' +
            'ContactId, ' +
            'LoginId, ' +
            'Title ' +
        'FROM HumanResources.Employee ' +
        'WHERE 1=1 ' +
```

```
            CASE
                WHEN @EmployeeId IS NULL THEN ''
                ELSE 'AND EmployeeId = @EmployeeId '
            END +
            CASE
                WHEN @NationalIdNumber IS NULL THEN ''
                ELSE 'AND NationalIdNumber = @NationalIdNumber '
            END

    EXEC sp_executesql
        @sql,
        N'@EmployeeId INT, @NationalIdNumber NVARCHAR(60)',
        @EmployeeId,
        @NationalIdNumber
END
```

For multiple parameters, simply comma-delimit their data type definitions in the second parameter, and then pass as many outer parameters as necessary to define every variable listed in the second parameter. Note that you can use a string variable for the second parameter, which might make sense if you are defining a long list—but I usually keep the list in a string literal so that I can easily match the definitions with the variables passed in from the outer scope.

Another important thing to note here is that even though both parameters are optional, they will both get passed to the query every time it is executed. This is perfectly okay! There is very little overhead in passing parameters into sp_executesql, and trying to work around this issue would either bring back the combinatorial explosion problem or require some very creative use of nested dynamic SQL. Neither solution is maintainable or worth the time required, so save your energy for more interesting pursuits.

Performance Comparison

As a first step in evaluating the relative performance of the sp_executesql solution against other solutions mentioned, you can verify that sp_executesql really is reusing query plans as expected. To verify, run the same code that was used to show that the EXECUTE method was not reusing plans:

```
DBCC FREEPROCCACHE
GO

EXEC GetEmployeeData
    @EmployeeId = 1
GO

EXEC GetEmployeeData
    @EmployeeId = 2
GO

EXEC GetEmployeeData
    @EmployeeId = 3
GO
```

After running this code, query the `sys.dm_exec_cached_plans` view as before. The results should be similar to those shown in Figure 7-16. One plan is cached for the procedure itself, and one for the invocation of the dynamic query with the `@EmployeeId` parameter. Invoking the query with a different combination of parameters will result in creation of more cached plans, because the resultant query text will be different. However, the maximum number of plans that can be cached for the stored procedure is five: one for the procedure itself and one for each possible combination of parameters.

Figure 7-16. *The sp_executesql solution promotes reuse of query plans.*

To further validate performance, open up the SQLQueryStress tool for some simple load testing. But before configuring SQLQueryStress, create a renamed version of the best performing (but worst for maintenance) static SQL version of the stored procedure. Call it `GetEmployeeData_Static`:

```
CREATE PROCEDURE GetEmployeeData_Static
    @EmployeeId INT = NULL,
    @NationalIdNumber NVARCHAR(15) = NULL
AS
BEGIN
    SET NOCOUNT ON

    IF (@EmployeeId IS NOT NULL
        AND @NationalIdNumber IS NOT NULL)
    BEGIN
        SELECT
            ContactId,
            LoginId,
            Title
        FROM HumanResources.Employee
        WHERE
            EmployeeId = @EmployeeId
            AND NationalIdNumber = @NationalIdNumber
    END
    ELSE IF (@EmployeeId IS NOT NULL)
    BEGIN
        SELECT
            ContactId,
            LoginId,
            Title
        FROM HumanResources.Employee
        WHERE
            EmployeeId = @EmployeeId
    END
```

```
    ELSE IF (@NationalIdNumber IS NOT NULL)
    BEGIN
        SELECT
            ContactId,
            LoginId,
            Title
        FROM HumanResources.Employee
        WHERE
            NationalIdNumber = @NationalIdNumber
    END
    ELSE
    BEGIN
        SELECT
            ContactId,
            LoginId,
            Title
        FROM HumanResources.Employee
    END
END
```

This version produces the best possible query plans, but of course has the issue of being impossible to maintain. It also has no additional overhead associated with context switching, which may make it slightly faster than a dynamic SQL solution if the queries are very simple. For more complex queries that take longer, any context switching overhead will be overshadowed by the actual runtime of the query.

Once the stored procedure is created, enter the following into the SQLQueryStress Query textbox:

```
EXEC GetEmployeeData_Static
    @EmployeeId,
    @NationalIdNumber
```

Next, click the Database button and configure your database connection to use AdventureWorks as the default database. Once finished, click the Parameter Substitution button and enter the following T-SQL into the Parameter Query textbox:

```
SELECT EmployeeId, NationalIdNumber
FROM HumanResources.Employee

UNION ALL

SELECT NULL, NationalIdNumber
FROM HumanResources.Employee

UNION ALL

SELECT NULL, NationalIdNumber
FROM HumanResources.Employee
```

UNION ALL

SELECT NULL, NULL

This code selects one row for every possible combination of input parameters to the stored procedure, which will allow testing of every type of invocation. Click the Get Columns button, and map the EmployeeId column to @EmployeeId, and the NationalIdNumber column to @NationalIdNumber. Then, click OK to go back to the main SQLQueryStress screen.

To keep the test simple, configure the tool to use five threads and to do 8,710 iterations. Since there are 871 rows returned by the parameter substitution query, this means that each thread will run through every possible combination ten times. These numbers are somewhat arbitrary, but the point is to simply validate the solutions against each other with a consistent test, not to completely stress them until they break. The results of the test as run on my system are shown in Figure 7-17.

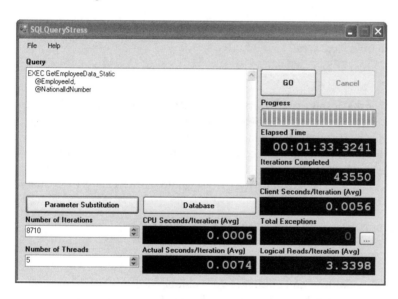

Figure 7-17. *SQLQueryStress output from the test of the static SQL solution*

Next, create a renamed version of the EXECUTE solution, called GetEmployeeData_Execute:

```
CREATE PROCEDURE GetEmployeeData_Execute
    @EmployeeId INT = NULL,
    @NationalIdNumber NVARCHAR(15) = NULL
AS
BEGIN
    SET NOCOUNT ON

    DECLARE @sql NVARCHAR(MAX)

    SET @sql = '' +
        'SELECT ' +
```

```
            'ContactId, ' +
            'LoginId, ' +
            'Title ' +
        'FROM HumanResources.Employee ' +
        'WHERE 1=1 ' +
        CASE
            WHEN @EmployeeId IS NULL THEN ''
            ELSE
                'AND EmployeeId = ' +
                CONVERT(NVARCHAR, @EmployeeId) + ' '
        END +
        CASE
            WHEN @NationalIdNumber IS NULL THEN ''
            ELSE
                'AND NationalIdNumber = N''' +
                @NationalIdNumber + ''' '
        END

    EXEC(@sql)
END
```

Testing this stored procedure against the static solution and, later, the sp_executesql
solution will create a nice means by which to compare static SQL against both parameterized
and nonparameterized dynamic SQL, and will show the effects of parameterization on performance. Back in SQLQueryStress, change the text in the Query textbox to the following:

```
EXEC GetEmployeeData_Execute
    @EmployeeId,
    @NationalIdNumber
```

Once finished, click the GO button to begin the test; do not reconfigure the parameter
substitution, number of threads, or number of iterations, in order to keep things consistent.
The results of the test as run on my system are shown in Figure 7-18.

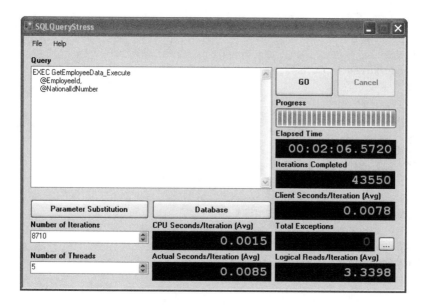

Figure 7-18. *SQLQueryStress output from the test of the EXECUTE solution*

The final stored procedure to test is, of course, the sp_executesql solution. Once again, create a renamed version of the stored procedure in order to differentiate it. This time, call it GetEmployeeData_sp_executesql:

```
CREATE PROCEDURE GetEmployeeData_sp_executesql
    @EmployeeId INT = NULL,
    @NationalIdNumber NVARCHAR(15) = NULL
AS
BEGIN
    SET NOCOUNT ON

    DECLARE @sql NVARCHAR(MAX)

    SET @sql = '' +
        'SELECT ' +
            'ContactId, ' +
            'LoginId, ' +
            'Title ' +
        'FROM HumanResources.Employee ' +
        'WHERE 1=1 ' +
        CASE
            WHEN @EmployeeId IS NULL THEN ''
            ELSE 'AND EmployeeId = @EmployeeId '
        END +
```

```
            CASE
                WHEN @NationalIdNumber IS NULL THEN ''
                ELSE 'AND NationalIdNumber = @NationalIdNumber '
            END

        EXEC sp_executesql
            @sql,
            N'@EmployeeId INT, @NationalIdNumber NVARCHAR(60)',
            @EmployeeId,
            @NationalIdNumber
END
```

In SQLQueryStress, change the text of the Query textbox to the following:

```
EXEC GetEmployeeData_sp_executesql
    @EmployeeId,
    @NationalIdNumber
```

When finished, click GO to begin the test. Figure 7-19 shows the results from my system.

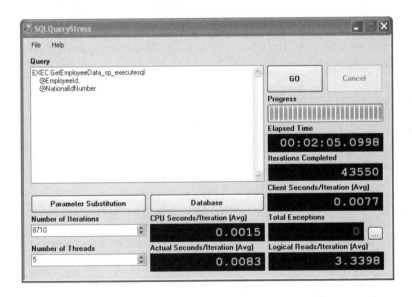

Figure 7-19. *SQLQueryStress output from the test of the sp_executesql solution*

Interestingly, the results between the two dynamic SQL solutions are very close together, with the sp_executesql solution beating the EXECUTE solution by only just over a second, even given the benefits of parameterization for performance. Runs with a lower number of iterations or against stored procedures that are more expensive for SQL Server to compile will highlight the benefits more clearly.

The static SQL version, in this case, clearly wins from a performance point of view (although all three are extremely fast). Again, more complex stored procedures with longer run times will naturally overshadow the difference between the dynamic SQL and static SQL solutions, leaving the dynamic SQL vs. static SQL question purely one of maintenance.

> **Note** When running these tests on my system, I restarted my SQL Server service between each run in order to ensure absolute consistency. Although this may be overkill for this case, you may find it interesting to experiment on your end with how restarting the service affects performance. This kind of test can also be useful for general scalability testing, especially in clustered environments. Restarting the service before testing is a technique that you can use to find out how the application will behave if a failover occurs, without having to have a clustered testing environment.

Output Parameters

Although it is somewhat of an aside to this discussion, I would like to point out one other feature that sp_executesql brings to the table compared with EXECUTE, which is often overlooked by users who are just getting started using it. sp_executesql allows you to pass parameters to dynamic SQL just like to a stored procedure—and this includes output parameters.

Output parameters become quite useful when you need to use the output of a dynamic SQL statement that perhaps only returns a single scalar value. An output parameter is a much cleaner solution than having to insert the value into a table and then read it back into a variable.

To define an output parameter, simply append the OUTPUT keyword in both the parameter definition list and the parameter list itself. The following T-SQL shows how to use an output parameter with sp_executesql:

```
DECLARE @SomeVariable INT

EXEC sp_executesql
    N'SET @SomeVariable = 123',
    N'@SomeVariable INT OUTPUT',
    @SomeVariable OUTPUT
```

As a result of this T-SQL, the @SomeVariable variable will have a value of 123.

Since this is an especially contrived example, I will add that in practice I often use output parameters with sp_executesql in search stored procedures with optional parameters. A common user interface requirement is to return the number of total rows found by the selected search criteria, and an output parameter is a quick way to get the data back to the caller.

Dynamic SQL Security Considerations

To finish up this chapter, a few words on security are important. Aside from the SQL injection example shown in a previous section, there are a couple of other security topics that are important to consider. In this section, I will briefly discuss permissions issues and a few interface rules to help you stay out of trouble when working with dynamic SQL.

Permissions to Referenced Objects

As mentioned a few times throughout this chapter, dynamic SQL is invoked in a different scope than static SQL. This is extremely important from an authorization perspective, because upon

execution, permissions for all objects referenced in the dynamic SQL will be checked. Therefore, in order for the dynamic SQL to run without throwing an authorization exception, the
user executing the dynamic SQL must either have access directly to the referenced objects or
be impersonating a user with access to the objects.

This creates a slightly different set of challenges from those you get when working with static
SQL stored procedures, due to the fact that the change of context that occurs when invoking
dynamic SQL breaks any ownership chain that has been established. If you need to manage
a permissions hierarchy such that users should have access to stored procedures that use
dynamic SQL, but not to the base tables they reference, make sure to become intimately familiar
with certificate signing and the EXECUTE AS clause, both described in detail in Chapter 4.

Interface Rules

This chapter has focused on optional parameters of the type you might pass to enable or disable a certain predicate for a query. However, there are other types of optional parameters that
developers often try to use with dynamic SQL. These parameters involve passing table names,
column lists, ORDER BY lists, and other modifications to the query itself into a stored procedure
for concatenation.

If you've read Chapter 1 of this book, you know that these practices are incredibly dangerous from a software development perspective, leading to tight coupling between the database
and the application, in addition to possibly distorting stored procedures' implied output contracts, therefore making testing and maintenance extremely arduous.

As a general rule, you should never, ever pass any database object name from an application into a stored procedure (and the application should not know the object names anyway).
If you absolutely must modify a table or some other object name in a stored procedure, try to
encapsulate the name via a set of parameters instead of allowing the application to dictate.

For instance, assume you were working with the following stored procedure:

```
CREATE PROC SelectDataFromTable
    @TableName VARCHAR(200)
AS
BEGIN
    SET NOCOUNT ON

    DECLARE @sql VARCHAR(MAX)

    SET @sql = '' +
        'SELECT ' +
            'ColumnA, ' +
            'ColumnB, ' +
            'ColumnC ' +
        'FROM ' + @TableName

    EXEC(@sql)
END
```

Table names cannot be parameterized, meaning that using sp_executesql in this case would
not help in any way. However, in virtually all cases, there is a limited subset of table names that
can (or will) realistically be passed into the stored procedure. If you know in advance that this

stored procedure will only ever use tables TableA, TableB, and TableC, you can rewrite the stored procedure to keep those table names out of the application while still providing the same functionality.

The following stored procedure is an example of how you might provide dynamic table functionality, while abstracting the names somewhat to avoid coupling issues:

```
CREATE PROC SelectDataFromTable
    @UseTableA BIT = 0,
    @UseTableB BIT = 0,
    @UseTableC BIT = 0
AS
BEGIN
    SET NOCOUNT ON

    IF (
        CONVERT(TINYINT, COALESCE(@UseTableA, 0)) +
        CONVERT(TINYINT, COALESCE(@UseTableB, 0)) +
        CONVERT(TINYINT, COALESCE(@UseTableC, 0))
        ) <> 1
    BEGIN
        RAISERROR('Must specify exactly one table', 16, 1)
        RETURN
    END

    DECLARE @sql VARCHAR(MAX)

    SET @sql = '' +
        'SELECT ' +
            'ColumnA, ' +
            'ColumnB, ' +
            'ColumnC ' +
        'FROM ' +
            CASE
                WHEN @UseTableA = 1 THEN 'TableA'
                WHEN @UseTableB = 1 THEN 'TableB'
                WHEN @UseTableC = 1 THEN 'TableC'
            END

    EXEC(@sql)
END
```

This version of the stored procedure is obviously quite a bit more complex, but it is still relatively easy to understand. The IF block validates that exactly one table is selected (i.e., the value of the parameter corresponding to the table is set to 1), and the CASE expression handles the actual dynamic selection of the table name.

If you find yourself in a situation in which even this technique is not possible, and you *absolutely must* support the application passing in object names dynamically, you can at least do a bit to protect from the possibility of SQL injection problems. SQL Server includes a function called QUOTENAME, which bracket-delimits any input string such that it will be treated as an identifier if concatenated with a SQL statement. For instance, QUOTENAME('123') returns the value [123].

By using QUOTENAME, the original version of the dynamic table name stored procedure can be modified such that there will be no risk of SQL injection:

```
CREATE PROC SelectDataFromTable
    @TableName VARCHAR(200)
AS
BEGIN
    SET NOCOUNT ON

    DECLARE @sql VARCHAR(MAX)

    SET @sql = '' +
        'SELECT ' +
            'ColumnA, ' +
            'ColumnB, ' +
            'ColumnC ' +
        'FROM ' + QUOTENAME(@TableName)

    EXEC(@sql)
END
```

Unfortunately, this does nothing to fix the interface issues, and modifying the database schema may still necessitate a modification to the application code.

Summary

Dynamic SQL can be an extremely useful tool for working with stored procedures that require flexibility. However, it is important to make sure that you are using dynamic SQL properly in order to ensure the best balance of performance, maintainability, and security. Make sure to *always* parameterize queries and *never* trust any input from a caller, lest a nasty payload is waiting, embedded in an otherwise innocent search string.

■ ■ ■

CHAPTER 8

Designing Systems for Application Concurrency

One of the amazing things about application development is how well applications tend to both behave and scale with only one concurrent user. Most developers are familiar with the wonderful feeling of checking in complex code at the end of an exhaustingly long release cycle and going home confident in the fact that everything works, and performs, to spec. Alas, that feeling can be instantly ripped away, transformed into excruciating pain, when the multitude of actual end users start hammering away at the system, and it becomes obvious that just a bit more testing of concurrent utilization might have been helpful. Unless your application will be used by only one user at a time, it simply can't be designed and developed as though it will be.

Concurrency can be one of the toughest areas in application development, because the problems that occur often depend on extremely specific timing. An issue that might cause a test run to end with a flurry of exceptions may not fire any alarms on the next run because some other module happened to take a few milliseconds longer than usual, lining up the cards just right. Even worse is when the opposite happens, and a concurrency problem pops up seemingly out of nowhere, at odd and irreproducible intervals (but *always* right in the middle of an important demo).

While it may be difficult or impossible to completely eliminate these kinds of issues from your software, proper upfront design can help you greatly reduce the number of incidents you see. The key is to understand a few basic factors:

- What kinds of activities do your users need to do that might overwrite or get in the way of activities other users are involved in?

- What features of the database (or software system) will help or hinder your users doing their work concurrently?

- What are the business rules that must be obeyed in order to make sure that concurrency is properly handled?

This chapter delves into the different types of application concurrency models you might need to implement in the database layer, the tools SQL Server offers to help you design applications that work properly in concurrent scenarios, and how to go beyond what SQL Server offers right out of the box.

The Business Side: What Should Happen When Processes Collide?

Before getting into the technicalities of dealing with concurrency, it's important to define both the basic problem areas and how they are commonly dealt with. In a database setting, concurrency issues generally take one of three forms:

- **Overwriting** of data can occur when two or more users edit the same data simultaneously. This can be a problem for a few reasons: First of all, one user's changes will be lost if overwritten by another's changes, thereby destroying both effort and, perhaps, valuable data. Secondly, time may be wasted; it might not make sense for multiple users to work on the same piece of data at the same time. And finally, in some cases, overwriting of a piece of data will lead to invalid data in the database. A simple example is a point-of-sale application that reads a stock number from a table into a variable, adds or subtracts an amount based on a transaction, and then writes the updated number back to the table. If two sales terminals are running and each processes a sale for the same product at exactly the same time, there is a chance that both terminals will retrieve the initial value and that one terminal will overwrite, instead of update, the other's change.

- **Nonrepeatable reading** is a situation that occurs when an application reads a set of data from a database and does some calculations on it, and then needs to read the same set of data again for another purpose—but the original set has changed in the interim. A common example of where this problem can manifest itself is in "drill-down" reports in analytical systems. The reporting system might present the user with an aggregate view of the data, calculated based on an initial read. As the user clicks various data points, the reporting system might return to the database and read the detail data. However, there is a chance that another user may have changed some data between the initial read and the detail read, meaning that the two sets will no longer match.

- **Blocking** may occur when one process is writing data and another tries to read or write the same data. This can be (and usually is) a good thing—it prevents many types of overwriting problems and ensures that only consistent data is read by clients. However, excessive blocking can greatly decrease an application's ability to scale, and therefore it must be carefully controlled in many cases.

There are several ways of dealing with these issues, with varying degrees of technical ease of implementation. But for the sake of this section, I'll keep the discussion at the business rules level. There are four primary methodologies that should be considered:

- **Anarchy**: Assume that collisions and inconsistent data do not matter. Do not block readers from reading inconsistent data, and do not worry about overwrites or repeatable reads. This methodology is often used in applications in which users have little or no chance of editing the same data point concurrently, and in which repeatable read issues are unimportant.

- **Pessimistic concurrency control**: Assume that collisions will be frequent; stop them from being able to occur. Block readers from reading inconsistent data, but do not necessarily worry about repeatable reads. To avoid overwrites, do not allow anyone to begin editing a piece of data that's being edited by someone else.

- **Optimistic concurrency control**: Assume that there will occasionally be some collisions, but that it's okay for them to be handled when they occur. Block readers from reading inconsistent data, and let the reader know what version of the data is being read. This enables the reader to know when repeatable read problems occur (but not avoid them). To avoid overwrites, do not allow anyone to overwrite a piece of data if the version has changed since it was read for editing by the process requesting the write.

- **Multivalue concurrency control (MVCC)**: Assume that there will be collisions, but that they should be treated as new versions rather than as collisions. Block readers both from reading inconsistent data and encountering repeatable read problems by letting the reader know what version of the data is being read and allowing the reader to reread the same version multiple times. To avoid overwrites, create a newer version of the data, but keep the old version in place.

Each of these methodologies represents a different user experience, and the choice must be made based on the necessary functionality of the application at hand. For instance, a message board application might use a more-or-less anarchic approach to concurrency, since it's unlikely or impossible that two users would be editing the same message at the same time—overwrites and inconsistent reads are acceptable.

On the other hand, many applications cannot bear overwrites. A good example of this is a source control system, where overwritten source code might mean a lot of lost work. However, the best way to handle the situation for source control is up for debate. Two popular systems, Subversion and Visual SourceSafe, each handle this problem differently. Subversion uses an optimistic scheme in which anyone can edit a given file, but you receive a collision error when you commit if someone else has edited it in the interim. Visual SourceSafe, on the other hand, uses a pessimistic model where you must check out a given file before editing it, thereby restricting anyone else from doing edits until you check it back in.

Finally, an example of a system that supports MVCC is a wiki. Although some wiki packages use an optimistic model, many allow users to make edits at any time, simply incrementing the version number for a given page to reflect each change, but still saving past versions. This means that if two users are making simultaneous edits, some changes might get overwritten. However, users can always look back at the version history to restore overwritten content—in an MVCC system, nothing is ever actually deleted.

In the sections in which I describe solutions for each of these methodologies, I will explain their role in a software system in greater detail.

A Brief Overview of SQL Server Isolation Levels

This chapter assumes that the reader has some background in working with SQL Server transactions and isolation levels, but in case some readers are not familiar with some of the terminology, this section presents a very basic introduction to the topic.

Isolation levels are set in SQL Server in order to tell the database engine how to handle locking and blocking when multiple transactions collide, trying to read and write the same data. Selecting the correct isolation level for a transaction is extremely important in many business cases, especially those that require consistency when reading the same data multiple times.

SQL Server's isolation levels can be segmented into two basic classes: those in which readers are blocked by writers, and those in which blocking of readers does not occur. The READ COMMITTED, REPEATABLE READ, and SERIALIZABLE isolation levels are all in this first class, whereas READ UNCOMMITTED and SNAPSHOT fall into the latter group. A special subclass of the SNAPSHOT isolation level, READ COMMITTED SNAPSHOT, is also included in this second, nonblocking class.

Transactions using the blocking isolation levels take shared locks when reading data, thereby blocking anyone else trying to update the same data during the course of the read. The primary differences between these three isolation levels is that the granularity and behavior of the shared locks they take changes which writes will be blocked and when.

All transactions, regardless of the isolation level used, take exclusive locks on data being updated. Transaction isolation levels do not change the behavior of locks taken at write time, but rather only those taken or honored by readers.

In order to see how the isolation levels work, a table should be created that will be accessed by multiple transactions. The following T-SQL creates a table called Blocker in TempDB and populates it with three rows:

```
USE TempDB
GO

CREATE TABLE Blocker
(
    Blocker_Id INT NOT NULL
        PRIMARY KEY
)
GO

INSERT Blocker
SELECT 1
UNION ALL
SELECT 2
UNION ALL
SELECT 3
GO
```

Once the table has been created, open two SQL Server Management Studio query windows. I will refer to the windows hereafter as **blocking window** and **blocked window**.

In each of the three blocking isolation levels, readers will be blocked by writers. To see what this looks like, run the following T-SQL in the blocking window:

```
BEGIN TRANSACTION

UPDATE Blocker
SET Blocker_Id = Blocker_Id + 1
```

Now, run the following in the blocked window:

```
SELECT *
FROM Blocker
```

This second query will not return until the transaction started in the blocking window is either committed or rolled back. In order to release the locks, roll back the transaction by running the following in the blocking window:

```
ROLLBACK
```

■Note Complete coverage of locking and blocking is out of the scope of this book. Refer to the topic "Locking in the Database Engine" in SQL Server 2005 Books Online for a detailed explanation.

The default isolation level used by SQL Server is READ COMMITTED. In this isolation level, a reader will hold its locks only for the duration of the statement doing the read, even inside of an explicit transaction. To illustrate this, run the following in the blocking window:

```
BEGIN TRANSACTION

SELECT *
FROM Blocker
```

Now run the following in the blocked window:

```
BEGIN TRANSACTION

UPDATE Blocker
SET Blocker_Id = Blocker_Id + 1
```

In this case, the update runs without being blocked, even though the transaction is still active in the blocking window. The reason is that as soon as the SELECT ended, the locks it held were released. When you're finished observing this behavior, don't forget to roll back the transactions started in both windows by executing the ROLLBACK statement in each.

Both the REPEATABLE READ and SERIALIZABLE isolation levels hold locks for the duration of an explicit transaction. The difference is that REPEATABLE READ transactions take locks at a level of granularity that ensures that data already read cannot be updated by another transaction, but that allows other transactions to insert data that would change the results. On the other hand, SERIALIZABLE transactions take locks at a higher level of granularity, such that no data can be either updated or inserted within the locked range.

To observe the behavior of a REPEATABLE READ transaction, start by running the following T-SQL in the blocking window:

```
SET TRANSACTION ISOLATION LEVEL REPEATABLE READ

BEGIN TRANSACTION

SELECT *
FROM Blocker
```

Running the following update in the blocked window will result in blocking behavior—the query will wait until the blocking window's transaction has completed:

```
BEGIN TRANSACTION

UPDATE Blocker
SET Blocker_Id = Blocker_Id + 1
```

Both updates and deletes will be blocked by the locks taken by the query. However, inserts such as the following will not be blocked:

```
BEGIN TRANSACTION

INSERT Blocker
SELECT 4

COMMIT
```

Rerun the SELECT statement in the blocking window, and you'll see the new row. This phenomenon is known as a **phantom row**, because the new data seems to appear like an apparition—out of nowhere. Once you're done investigating phantom rows, make sure to issue a ROLLBACK in both windows.

The difference between the REPEATABLE READ and SERIALIZABLE isolation levels is that while the former allows phantom rows, the latter does not. Any key—existent or not at the time of the SELECT—that is within the range predicated by the WHERE clause will be locked for the duration of the transaction if the SERIALIZABLE isolation level is used. To see how this works, first run the following in the blocking window:

```
SET TRANSACTION ISOLATION LEVEL SERIALIZABLE

BEGIN TRANSACTION

SELECT *
FROM Blocker
```

Next, try either an INSERT or UPDATE in the blocked window. In either case, the operation will be forced to wait for the transaction in the blocking window to commit, since the transaction locks all rows in the table—whether or not they exist yet. To lock only a specific range of rows, add a WHERE clause to the query, and all DML operations within the key range will be blocked for the duration of the transaction. When you're done, be sure to issue a ROLLBACK.

■**Tip** The REPEATABLE READ and SERIALIZABLE isolation levels will hold shared locks for the duration of a transaction on whatever tables are queried. However, you might wish to selectively hold locks only on specific tables within a transaction in which you're working with multiple objects. To accomplish this, you can use the HOLDLOCK table hint, applied only to the tables that you want to hold the locks on. In a READ COMMITTED transaction, this will have the same effect as if the isolation level had been escalated just for those tables to REPEATABLE READ. For more information on table hints, see SQL Server 2005 Books Online.

The nonblocking isolation levels, READ UNCOMMITTED and SNAPSHOT, each allow readers to read data without waiting for writing transactions to complete. This is great from a concurrency standpoint—no blocking means that processes spend less time waiting and therefore users get their data back faster—but can be disastrous for data consistency.

READ UNCOMMITTED transactions do not apply shared locks as data is read and do not honor locks placed by other transactions. This means that there will be no blocking, but the data being read might be inconsistent (not yet committed). To see what this means, run the following in the blocking window:

```
BEGIN TRANSACTION

UPDATE Blocker
SET Blocker_Id = 10
WHERE Blocker_Id = 1
```

This operation will place an exclusive lock on the updated row, so any readers should be blocked reading the data until the transaction completes. However, the following query will not be blocked if run in the blocked window:

```
SET TRANSACTION ISOLATION LEVEL READ UNCOMMITTED

SELECT *
FROM Blocker
```

The danger here is that because the query is not blocked, a user may see data that is part of a transaction that later gets rolled back. This can be especially problematic when users are shown aggregates that do not add up based on the leaf-level data when reconciliation is done later. I recommend that you carefully consider before using READ UNCOMMITTED (or the NOLOCK table hint) in your queries.

An alternative to READ UNCOMMITTED is SQL Server 2005's SNAPSHOT isolation level. This isolation level shares the same nonblocking characteristics as READ UNCOMMITTED, but only consistent data is shown. This is achieved by making use of a row-versioning technology that stores previous versions of rows in TempDB as data modifications occur in a database.

SNAPSHOT almost seems like the best of both worlds: no blocking, yet no danger of inconsistent data. However, this isolation level is not without its problems. First and foremost, storing the previous row values in TempDB can create a huge amount of load, causing many problems for servers that are not properly configured to handle the additional strain. And secondly, for many apps, this kind of nonblocking read does not make sense. For example, consider an application that needs to read updated inventory numbers. A SNAPSHOT read might cause the user to receive an invalid amount, because the user will not be blocked on a write and will therefore see previously committed data.

If you do decide to use either nonblocking isolation level, make sure to think carefully through the issues. There are many possible caveats with either technology, and they are not right for every app, or perhaps even most apps.

■**Note** SNAPSHOT isolation is a big topic, out of the scope of this chapter. For more information, see my chapter "T-SQL Enhancements for DBAs" (Chapter 4) in *Pro SQL Server 2005* (Apress, 2005).

Concurrency Control and SQL Server's Native Isolation Levels

Some of the same names for the business logic methodologies mentioned in the previous section—particularly **optimistic** and **pessimistic**—are often used to help describe the behavior of SQL Server's own locking and isolation rules, especially with regard to cursors. However, you should understand that these forms of concurrency control are not quite the same. From SQL Server's standpoint, the only concurrency control necessary is between two transactions that happen to hit the server at the same time—and from that point of view, its behavior works quite well. However, from a purely business-based perspective, there are no transactions—there are only users and processes trying to make modifications to the same data. In this sense, a purely transactional mindset fails to deliver enough control.

SQL Server's default isolation level, READ COMMITTED, as well as its REPEATABLE READ and SERIALIZABLE isolation levels, can be said to support a form of pessimistic concurrency. When using these isolation levels, writers are not allowed to overwrite data in the process of being written by others. However, the moment the blocking transaction ends, the data is fair game, and another session can overwrite it without even knowing that it was modified in the interim. From a business point of view, this falls quite short of the pessimistic goal of keeping two end users from ever even beginning to edit the same data at the same time.

A newer isolation level supported by SQL Server is SNAPSHOT, which is said to support a form of optimistic concurrency control. This is a far easier case to argue, even from a business point of view, than the pessimistic concurrency of the other isolation levels. With SNAPSHOT isolation, if you read a piece of data in order to make edits or modifications to it, and someone else updates the data after you've read it but before you've had a chance to write your edits, you will get an exception when you try to write. This is almost a textbook definition of optimistic concurrency, with one slight problem: SQL Server's isolation levels are *transactional*—so in order to make this work, you would have to have held a transaction open for the entire duration of the read, edit, and rewrite attempt. This doesn't scale especially well if, for instance, the application is web-enabled and the user wants to spend an hour editing the document.

Another form of optimistic concurrency control supported by SQL Server is used with updateable cursors. The OPTIMISTIC options support a very similar form of optimistic concurrency to that of SNAPSHOT isolation. However, given the rarity with which updateable cursors are actually used in properly designed production applications, this isn't an option you're likely to see very often.

Although both SNAPSHOT isolation and the OPTIMISTIC WITH ROW VERSIONING cursor options work by holding previous versions of rows in a version store, these should not be confused with MVCC. In both the case of the isolation level and the cursor option, the previous versions of the rows are only held in order to help support nonblocking reads. The rows are not available later—for instance, as a means by which to merge changes from multiple writers—which is a hallmark of a properly designed MVCC system.

Yet another isolation level that is frequently used in SQL Server application development scenarios is READ UNCOMMITTED. This isolation level implements the anarchy business methodology mentioned in the previous section, and does it quite well—readers are not blocked by writers, and writers are not blocked by readers, whether or not a transaction is active.

Again, it's important to stress that although SQL Server does not really support concurrency properly from a business point of view, it wouldn't make sense for it to do so. The goal of SQL Server's isolation levels is to control concurrency at the transactional level, helping to maintain the ACID properties so important to keeping data in a consistent state in the database.

Regardless of its inherent lack of provision for business-compliant concurrency solutions, SQL Server provides all of the tools necessary to easily build them yourself. The following sections discuss how to use SQL Server in order to help define concurrency models within database applications.

Preparing for the Worst: Pessimistic Concurrency

Imagine, for a moment, that you are tasked with building a system to help a life insurance company do data input for many years of paper-based customer profile update forms. The company sent out the forms to each of its several hundred thousand customers on a biannual basis, in order to get the customers' latest information.

Most of the profiles were filled in by hand, so OCR is out of the question—they must be keyed in manually. To make matters worse, a large percentage of the customer files were removed from the filing system by employees and incorrectly refiled. Many were also photocopied at one time or another, and employees often filed the photocopies instead of throwing them out, resulting in a massive amount of duplication. The firm has tried to remove the oldest of the forms and bring the newer ones to the top of the stack, but it's difficult because many customers didn't always send back the forms each time they were requested—for one customer 1994 may be the newest year, whereas for another the latest form is from 2006.

Back to the challenge at hand: building the data input application is fairly easy, as is finding students willing to do the data input for fairly minimal rates. The workflow is as follows: for each profile update form, the person doing the data input will bring up the customer's record based on that customer's Social Security number or other identification number. If the date on the profile form is greater than the last updated date in the system, the profile needs to be updated with the newer data. If the dates are the same, the firm has decided that the operator should scan through the form and make sure all of the data already entered is correct—since it has hired students to do the work, the firm is aware that typographical errors will be made. Each form is several pages long, and the larger ones will take hours to type in.

As is always the case in projects like this, time and money are of the essence, and the firm is concerned about the tremendous amount of profile form duplication as well as the fact that many of the forms are misfiled in the wrong order. It would be a huge waste of time for the data input operators if, for instance, one entered a customer's 1986 update form at the same time another happened to be entering the same customer's 1992 form.

This situation all but cries out for a solution involving pessimistic concurrency control. Each time a customer's Social Security number is entered into the system, the application can check whether someone else has entered the same number and has not yet persisted changes or sent back a message saying there are no changes (i.e., hit the cancel button). If another operator is currently editing that customer's data, a message can be returned to the user telling him or her to try again later—this profile is locked.

The problem then becomes a question of how best to implement such a solution. A scheme I've seen attempted several times is to create a table along the lines of the following:

```
CREATE TABLE CustomerLocks
(
    CustomerId INT NOT NULL PRIMARY KEY
        REFERENCES Customers (CustomerId),
```

```
    IsLocked BIT NOT NULL DEFAULT (0)
)
GO
```

The `IsLocked` column could instead be added to the existing `Customers` table, but that is not recommended in a highly transactional database system. I generally advise keeping locking constructs separate from actual data, in order to limit excessive blocking on core tables.

In this system, the general technique employed is to populate the table with every customer ID in the system. The table is then queried when someone needs to take a lock, using code such as the following:

```
DECLARE @LockAcquired BIT
SET @LockAcquired = 0

IF
    (
        SELECT IsLocked
        FROM CustomerLocks
        WHERE CustomerId = @CustomerId
    ) = 0
BEGIN
    UPDATE CustomerLocks
    SET IsLocked = 1
    WHERE CustomerId = @CustomerId

    SET @LockAcquired = 1
END
```

Unfortunately, this approach is fraught with issues. The first and most serious problem is that between the query in the `IF` condition and the `UPDATE`, the row's value can be changed by another writer. If two sessions ask for the lock at the same moment, the result may be that both writers will believe that they hold the exclusive lock. In order to remedy this issue, the `IF` condition should be eliminated; instead, check for the ability to take the lock at the same time as you're taking it, in the `UPDATE`'s `WHERE` clause:

```
DECLARE @LockAcquired BIT

UPDATE CustomerLocks
SET IsLocked = 1
WHERE
    CustomerId = @CustomerId
    AND IsLocked = 0

SET @LockAcquired = @@ROWCOUNT
```

This pattern fixes the issue of two readers requesting the lock at the same time, but leaves open a maintenance issue: my recommendation to separate the locking from the actual table used to store customer data means that you must now ensure that all new customer IDs are added to the locks table as they are added to the system.

To solve this issue, avoid modeling the table as a collection of lock statuses per customer. Instead, define the existence of a row in the table as indication of a lock being held. Then the table becomes as follows:

```
CREATE TABLE CustomerLocks
(
    CustomerId INT NOT NULL PRIMARY KEY
        REFERENCES Customers (CustomerId)
)
GO
```

To take a lock with this new table, you can attempt an INSERT, using a TRY/CATCH block to find out whether you've caused a primary key violation:

```
DECLARE @LockAcquired BIT

BEGIN TRY
    INSERT CustomerLocks
    (
        CustomerId
    )
    VALUES
    (
        @CustomerId
    )

    --No exception: Lock acquired
    SET @LockAcquired = 1
END TRY
BEGIN CATCH
    --Caught an exception: No lock acquired
    SET @LockAcquired = 0
END CATCH
```

Releasing the lock is a simple matter of deleting the row:

```
DELETE FROM CustomerLocks
WHERE CustomerId = @CustomerId
```

We are now getting closer to a robust solution, but are not there quite yet. Imagine that a buggy piece of code exists somewhere in the application, and instead of calling the stored procedure to take a lock, it's instead occasionally calling the stored procedure to release the lock. In the system as it's currently designed, there is no protection against this kind of issue—anyone can request a lock release at any time. This is very dangerous, as it will invalidate the entire locking scheme for the system. In addition, the way the system is implemented as shown, the caller will not know that a problem occurred and that the lock didn't exist. Both of these problems can be solved with some additions to the framework in place.

In order to help protect the locks from being prematurely invalidated, a **lock token** can be issued. This token is nothing more than a randomly generated unique identifier for the lock, and will be used as the key to release the lock instead of the customer ID. To implement this solution, the table's definition becomes the following:

```
CREATE TABLE CustomerLocks
(
    CustomerId INT NOT NULL PRIMARY KEY
        REFERENCES Customers (CustomerId),
    LockToken UNIQUEIDENTIFIER NOT NULL UNIQUE
)
GO
```

With this table in place, the insert routine becomes the following:

```
DECLARE @LockToken UNIQUEIDENTIFIER

BEGIN TRY
    --Generate the token
    SET @LockToken = NEWID()

    INSERT CustomerLocks
    (
        CustomerId,
        LockToken
    )
    VALUES
    (
        @CustomerId,
        @LockToken
    )
END TRY
BEGIN CATCH
    --Caught an exception: No lock acquired
    SET @LockToken = NULL
END CATCH
```

Now rather than checking whether @LockAcquired is 1 to find out if the lock was success-fully taken, check whether @LockToken is NULL. By using a GUID, this system greatly decreases the chance that a buggy piece of application code will cause the lock to be released by a process that does not hold it.

After taking the lock, the application should remember the lock token, passing it instead of the customer ID when it comes time to release the lock:

```
DELETE FROM CustomerLocks
WHERE LockToken = @LockToken
```

Even better, the code used to release the lock can check to find out whether the lock was not successfully released (or whether there was no lock to release to begin with) and return an exception to the caller:

```
DELETE FROM CustomerLocks
WHERE LockToken = @LockToken

IF @@ROWCOUNT = 0
    RAISERROR('Lock token not found!', 16, 1)
```

The caller should do any updates to the locked resources and request the lock release in the same transaction. That way, if the caller receives this exception, it can take appropriate action—rolling back the transaction—ensuring that the data does not end up in an invalid state.

Almost all of the issues have now been eliminated from this locking scheme: two processes will not erroneously be granted the same lock, there is no maintenance issue with regard to keeping the table populated with an up-to-date list of customer IDs, and the tokens greatly eliminate the possibility of lock release issues.

One final, slightly subtle problem remains: what happens if a user requests a lock, forgets to hit the save button, and leaves for a two-week vacation? Or in the same vein, what should happen if the application takes a lock and then crashes 5 minutes later, thereby losing its reference to the token?

Solving this issue in a uniform fashion that works for all scenarios is, unfortunately, not possible, and one of the biggest problems with pessimistic schemes is that there will always be administrative overhead associated with releasing locks that for some reason did not get properly handled. The general method of solving this problem is to add an audit column to the locks table to record the date and time the lock was taken:

```
CREATE TABLE CustomerLocks
(
    CustomerId INT NOT NULL PRIMARY KEY
        REFERENCES Customers (CustomerId),
    LockToken UNIQUEIDENTIFIER NOT NULL UNIQUE,
    LockGrantedDate DATETIME NOT NULL
        DEFAULT (GETDATE())
)
GO
```

None of the code already listed needs to be modified in order to accommodate the LockGrantedDate column, since it has a default value. An external job must be written to poll the table on a regular basis, "expiring" locks that have been held for too long. The code to do this is simple; the following T-SQL deletes all locks older than 5 hours:

```
DELETE FROM CustomerLocks
WHERE LockGrantedDate < DATEADD(hour, -5, GETDATE())
```

This code can be implemented in a SQL Server Agent job, set to run occasionally throughout the day. The actual interval depends on the amount of activity your system sees, but once every 20 or 30 minutes is sufficient in most cases.

Although this expiration process works in most cases, it's also where things can break down from both administrative and business points of view. The primary challenge is defining a timeout period that makes sense. If the average lock is held for 20 minutes, but there are certain long-running processes that might need to hold locks for hours, it's important to define the timeout to favor the later processes, even providing padding to make sure that their locks will never be automatically expired when not appropriate. Unfortunately, no matter what timeout period you choose, it will never work for everyone. There is virtually a 100 percent chance that at some point, a user will be working on a very high-profile action that must be completed quickly, and the application will crash, leaving the lock in place. The user will have no recourse available but to call for administrative support or wait for the timeout period— and, of course, if it's been designed to favor processes that take many hours, this will not be a popular choice.

Although I have seen this problem manifest itself in pessimistic concurrency solutions, it has generally not been extremely common and hasn't caused any major issues aside from a few stressed-out end users. I am happy to say that I have never received a panicked call at 2 o'clock in the morning from a user requesting a lock release, although I could certainly see it happening. If this is a concern for your system, the solution is to design the application such that it sends "heartbeat" notifications back to the database on a regular basis as work is being done. These notifications should update the lock date/time column:

```
UPDATE CustomerLocks
SET LockGrantedDate = GETDATE()
WHERE LockToken = @LockToken
```

The application can be made to send a heartbeat as often as necessary—for instance, once every 5 minutes—during times it detects user activity. This is easy even in web applications, thanks to Ajax and similar asynchronous techniques. If this design is used, the timeout period can be shortened considerably, but keep in mind that users will occasionally become temporarily disconnected while working; buffer the timeout at least a bit in order to help keep disconnection-related timeouts at bay.

■Tip As an alternative to keeping the LockGrantedDate in the locks table, you could instead model the column as a LockExpirationDate. This might improve the flexibility of the system a bit by letting callers request a maximum duration for a lock when it is taken, rather than being forced to take the standard expiration interval. Of course, this has its downside: users requesting locks to be held for unrealistically large amounts of time. Should you implement such a solution, carefully monitor usage to make sure that this does not become an issue.

Enforcing Pessimistic Locks at Write Time

A problem with this and other programmatic pessimistic concurrency schemes is the fact that the lock is generally not enforced outside of the application code. While that's fine in many cases, it is important to make sure that every data consumer follows the same set of rules with regard to taking and releasing locks. These locks do not prevent data modification, but rather only serve as a means by which to tell calling apps whether they are allowed to modify data. If an application is not coded with the correct logic, violation of core data rules may result.

It may be possible to avoid some or all of these types of problems by double-checking locks in triggers at write time, but this can be difficult to implement because you may not be able to tell which user has taken which lock for a given row, let alone make a determination about which user is doing a particular update, especially if your application uses only a single database login.

I have come up with a technique that can help get around some of these issues. To begin with, a new candidate key should be added to the CustomerLocks table, based on the CustomerId and LockToken columns:

```
ALTER TABLE CustomerLocks
ADD CONSTRAINT UN_Customer_Token
    UNIQUE (CustomerId, LockToken)
```

This key can then be used as a reference in the Customers table once a LockToken column is added there:

```
ALTER TABLE Customers
ADD
    LockToken UNIQUEIDENTIFIER NULL,
    CONSTRAINT FK_CustomerLocks
        FOREIGN KEY (CustomerId, LockToken)
        REFERENCES CustomerLocks (CustomerId, LockToken)
```

Since the LockToken column in the Customers table is nullable, it is not required to reference a valid token at all times. However, when it is actually set to a certain value, that value must exist in the CustomerLocks table, and the combination of customer ID and token in the Customers table must coincide with the same combination in the CustomerLocks table.

Once this is set up, enforcing the lock at write time, for all writers, can be done using a trigger:

```
CREATE TRIGGER tg_EnforceCustomerLocks
ON Customers
FOR UPDATE
AS
BEGIN
    SET NOCOUNT ON

    IF EXISTS
        (
            SELECT *
            FROM inserted
            WHERE LockToken IS NULL
        )
    BEGIN
        RAISERROR('LockToken is a required column', 16, 1)
        ROLLBACK
    END

    UPDATE Customers
    SET LockToken = NULL
    WHERE
        CustomerId IN
        (
            SELECT CustomerId
```

```
                FROM inserted
        )
END
GO
```

The foreign key constraint enforces that any non-NULL value assigned to the LockToken column must be valid. However, it does not enforce NULL values; the trigger takes care of that, forcing writers to set the lock token at write time. If all rows qualify, the tokens are updated back to NULL so that the locks can be released—holding a reference would mean that the rows could not be deleted from the CustomerLocks table.

This technique adds a bit of overhead to updates, as each row must be updated twice. If your application processes a large number of transactions each day, make sure to carefully test in order to ensure that this does not cause a performance issue.

Application Locks: Generalizing Pessimistic Concurrency

The example shown in the previous section can be used to pessimistically lock rows, but it requires some setup per entity type to be locked and cannot easily be generalized to locking of resources that span multiple rows, tables, or other levels of granularity supported within a SQL Server database.

Recognizing the need for this kind of locking construct, Microsoft included a feature in SQL Server called **application locks**. Application locks are programmatic, named locks, which behave much like other types of locks in the database: within the scope of a session or a transaction, a caller attempting to acquire an incompatible lock with a lock already held by another caller causes blocking and queuing.

Application locks are acquired using the sp_getapplock stored procedure. By default, the lock is tied to an active transaction, meaning that ending the transaction releases the lock. There is also an option to tie the lock to a session, meaning that the lock is released when the user disconnects. To set a transactional lock, begin a transaction and request a lock name (**resource**, in application lock parlance). You can also specify a lock mode, such as **shared** or **exclusive**. A caller can also set a wait timeout period, after which the stored procedure will stop waiting for other callers to release the lock. The following T-SQL acquires an exclusive transactional lock on the customers resource, waiting up to 2 seconds for other callers to release any locks they hold on the resource:

```
BEGIN TRAN

EXEC sp_getapplock
    @Resource = 'customers',
    @LockMode = 'exclusive',
    @LockTimeout = 2000
```

sp_getapplock does not throw an exception if the lock is not successfully acquired, but rather sets a return value. The return will be 0 if the lock was successfully acquired without waiting, 1 if the lock was acquired after some wait period had elapsed, and any of a number of negative values if the lock was not successfully acquired. As a consumer of sp_getapplock, it's important to know whether or not you actually acquired the lock you asked for—so the preceding example call is actually incomplete. The following call checks the return value to find out whether the lock was granted:

```
BEGIN TRAN

DECLARE @ReturnValue INT

EXEC @ReturnValue = sp_getapplock
    @Resource = 'customers',
    @LockMode = 'exclusive',
    @LockTimeout = 2000

IF @ReturnValue IN (0, 1)
    PRINT 'Lock granted'
ELSE
    PRINT 'Lock not granted'
```

To release the lock, you can commit or roll back the active transaction, or use the sp_releaseapplock stored procedure, which takes the lock resource name as its input value:

```
EXEC sp_releaseapplock
    @Resource = 'customers'
```

SQL Server's application locks are quite useful in many scenarios, but they suffer from the same problems mentioned previously in this chapter with regard to why concurrency modes cannot really be compared between what SQL Server offers and what the business might actually require. These locks are held only for the duration of a transaction or a session, meaning that to lock a resource and perform a long-running business transaction based on the lock, the caller would have to hold open a connection to the database the entire time. This is clearly not a scalable option, so I set out to write a replacement, nontransactional application lock framework.

My goal was to mimic most of the behavior of sp_getapplock, but for exclusive locks only—pessimistic locking schemes do not generally require shared locks on resources. I especially wanted callers to be able to queue and wait for locks to be released by other resources. Since this would not be a transactional lock, I also wanted to handle all of the caveats I've discussed in this section, including making sure that multiple callers requesting locks at the same time would not each think they'd been granted the lock, returning tokens to avoid invalid lock release scenarios, and adding lock timeout periods to ensure that orphaned locks would not be stranded until an admin removed them.

When considering the SQL Server 2005 features that would help me create this functionality, I immediately thought of **Service Broker**. Service Broker provides asynchronous queuing that can cross transactional and session boundaries, and the WAITFOR command allows callers to wait on a message without having to continually poll the queue.

___

■**Note** For a thorough background on SQL Service Broker, see *Pro SQL Server 2005 Service Broker* by Klaus Aschenbrenner (Apress, 2007) or *Rational Guide to SQL Server 2005 Service Broker* by Roger Wolter (Rational Press, 2006).

The architecture I developed to solve this problem begins with a central table used to keep track of which locks have been taken:

```
CREATE TABLE AppLocks
(
    AppLockName NVARCHAR(255) NOT NULL,
    AppLockKey UNIQUEIDENTIFIER NULL,
    InitiatorDialogHandle UNIQUEIDENTIFIER NOT NULL,
    TargetDialogHandle UNIQUEIDENTIFIER NOT NULL,
    LastGrantedDate DATETIME NOT NULL DEFAULT(GETDATE()),
    PRIMARY KEY (AppLockName)
)
GO
```

The AppLockName column stores the names of locks that users have requested, and the AppLockKey functions as a lock token. This token also happens to be the conversation handle for a Service Broker dialog, but I'll get to that shortly. The InitiatorDialogHandle and TargetDialogHandle columns are conversation handles for another Service Broker dialog, which I will also explain shortly. Finally, the LastGrantedDate column is used just as in the examples earlier, to keep track of when each lock in the table was used. As you'll see, this column is even more important in this case, because locks are reused instead of deleted in this scheme.

To support the Service Broker services, I created one message type and one contract:

```
CREATE MESSAGE TYPE AppLockGrant
VALIDATION=EMPTY
GO

CREATE CONTRACT AppLockContract (
    AppLockGrant SENT BY INITIATOR
)
GO
```

If you're wondering why there is a message used to grant locks but none used to request them, it's because this system does not use a lock request service. Service Broker is used only because it happens to provide the queuing, waiting, and timeout features I needed—a bit different from most Service Broker samples.

I created two queues to support this infrastructure, along with two services. Here is where we get closer to the meat of the system:

```
CREATE QUEUE AppLock_Queue
GO

CREATE SERVICE AppLock_Service
ON QUEUE AppLock_Queue (AppLockContract)
GO

CREATE QUEUE AppLockTimeout_Queue
GO
```

```
CREATE SERVICE AppLockTimeout_Service
ON QUEUE AppLockTimeOut_Queue
GO
```

The `AppLock_Queue` queue and its associated service are used as follows: When a lock on a given resource is requested by a caller, if no one has ever requested a lock on that resource before, a dialog is started between the `AppLock_Service` service and itself. Both the initiator and target conversation handles for that dialog are used to populate the `InitiatorDialogHandle` and `TargetDialogHandle` columns, respectively. Later, when that caller releases its lock, an `AppLockGrant` message is sent on the queue from the initiator dialog handle stored in the table. When another caller wants to acquire a lock on the same resource, it gets the target dialog handle from the table and waits on it. This way, callers can wait for the lock to be released without having to poll, and will be able to pick it up as soon as it is released if they happen to be waiting at that moment.

The `AppLockTimeout_Queue` is used a bit differently. You might notice that its associated service uses the default contract. This is because no messages—except, perhaps, Service Broker system messages—will ever be sent from or to it. Whenever a lock is granted, a new dialog is started between the service and itself, and the initiator conversation handle for the dialog becomes the lock token.

In addition to being used as the lock token, the dialog serves another purpose: when it is started, a lifetime is set. A dialog lifetime is a timer that, after its set period, sends a message to all active parties involved in the conversation—in this case, since no messages will have been sent, only the initiator will receive the message. Upon receipt, an activation procedure is used to release the lock. I found this to be a more granular way of controlling lock expirations than using a job as I did in the example in the previous section. Whenever a lock is released by a caller, the conversation is ended, thereby clearing its lifetime timer.

To allow callers to request locks, I created a stored procedure called `GetAppLock`, which I will walk through in sections in order to explain more thoroughly. To begin with, the stored procedure exposes three parameters, each required: the name of the resource to be locked, how long to wait for the lock in case someone else already has it, and an output parameter, the lock key to be used later to release the lock. Following are the first several lines of the stored procedure, ending where the transactional part of the procedure begins:

```
CREATE PROC GetAppLock
    @AppLockName NVARCHAR(255),
    @LockTimeout INT,
    @AppLockKey UNIQUEIDENTIFIER = NULL OUTPUT
AS
BEGIN
    SET NOCOUNT ON
    SET XACT_ABORT ON

    --Make sure this variable starts NULL
    SET @AppLockKey = NULL

    DECLARE @LOCK_TIMEOUT_LIFETIME INT
    SET @LOCK_TIMEOUT_LIFETIME = 18000 --5 hours
```

```
DECLARE @startWait DATETIME
SET @startWait = GETDATE()

DECLARE @init_handle UNIQUEIDENTIFIER
DECLARE @target_handle UNIQUEIDENTIFIER

BEGIN TRAN
```

The stored procedure defines a couple of important local variables. The `@LOCK_TIMEOUT_` `LIFETIME` is the amount of time to wait until expiring an orphaned lock. It is currently hard coded, but could easily be converted into a parameter in order to allow callers to specify their own estimated times of completion. This might be a more exact way of handling the lock expiration problem. The `@startWait` variable is used in order to track lock wait time, so that the procedure does not allow callers to wait longer than the requested lock timeout value.

Next, the stored procedure makes use of the very feature that I was attempting to supersede: SQL Server's native transactional application locks. There is a bit of a back story to why I had to use them. During development of this technique, I discovered that Service Broker waits are queued in reverse: the newest process waiting is the first to get a message off the queue. This is counterintuitive if you're used to working with FIFO queues, but as was explained to me by Remus Rusanu from the Service Broker team, the queues were designed this way in order to allow the minimum number of activation stored procedures to stay alive after bursts of activity. By giving the message to the newest waiting process, the older processes are forced to eventually time out and expire.

Obviously such a scheme, while extremely clever and useful in the world of activation stored procedures, does not follow the requirements of a queued lock, so I made use of a transactional application lock in order to force serialization of the waits. Following is the code used to take the lock:

```
--Get the app lock -- start waiting
DECLARE @RETURN int
EXEC @RETURN = sp_getapplock
    @resource = @AppLockName,
    @lockmode = 'exclusive',
    @LockTimeout = @LockTimeout

IF @RETURN NOT IN (0, 1)
BEGIN
    RAISERROR(
        'Error acquiring transactional lock for %s', 16, 1, @AppLockName)
    ROLLBACK
    RETURN
END
```

If the lock is successfully granted, the code will keep going; otherwise, it will roll back, and the caller will receive an error so that it knows it did not acquire the requested lock. Once inside the scope of the transactional lock, it's finally time to start thinking about the Service Broker queues. The next thing the stored procedure does is get the target conversation handle, if one exists. If so, it starts a wait on the queue for a message:

```
--Find out whether someone has requested this lock before
SELECT
    @target_handle = TargetDialogHandle
FROM AppLocks
WHERE AppLockName = @AppLockName

--If we're here, we have the transactional lock
IF @target_handle IS NOT NULL
BEGIN
    --Find out whether the timeout has already expired...
    SET @LockTimeout = @LockTimeout - DATEDIFF(ms, @startWait, GETDATE())

    IF @LockTimeout > 0
    BEGIN
        --Wait for the OK message
        DECLARE @message_type NVARCHAR(255)

        --Wait for a grant message
        WAITFOR
        (
            RECEIVE
                @message_type = message_type_name
            FROM AppLock_Queue
            WHERE conversation_handle = @target_handle
        ), TIMEOUT @LockTimeout
```

One thing to make note of in this section of the code is that the input lock timeout is
decremented by however long the stored procedure has already been waiting, based on the
@startWait variable. It's possible that a caller could ask for, say, a 2500 ms wait time, and wait
2000 ms for the transactional lock. At that point, the caller should only be made to wait up to
500 ms for the message to come in on the queue. Therefore, the decremented timeout is used
as the RECEIVE timeout on the WAITFOR command.

The procedure next checks the received message type. If it is an AppLockGrant message, all
is good—the lock has been successfully acquired. The timeout conversation is started, and the
lock token is set. If an unexpected message type is received, an exception is thrown and the
transaction is rolled back:

```
IF @message_type = 'AppLockGrant'
BEGIN
    BEGIN DIALOG CONVERSATION @AppLockKey
    FROM SERVICE AppLockTimeout_Service
    TO SERVICE 'AppLockTimeout_Service'
    WITH
        LIFETIME = @LOCK_TIMEOUT_LIFETIME,
        ENCRYPTION = OFF

    UPDATE AppLocks
    SET
```

```
                    AppLockKey = @AppLockKey,
                    LastGrantedDate = GETDATE()
                WHERE
                    AppLockName = @AppLockName
            END
            ELSE IF @message_type IS NOT NULL
            BEGIN
                RAISERROR('Unexpected message type: %s', 16, 1, @message_type)
                ROLLBACK
            END
        END
    END
END
```

The next section of code deals with the branch that occurs if the target handle acquired before entering the IF block was NULL, meaning that no one has ever requested a lock on this resource type before. The first thing this branch does is begin a dialog on the AppLock_Service service. Since the target conversation handle is required for others to wait on the resource, and since the target handle is not generated until a message is sent, the first thing that must be done is to send a message on the dialog. Once the message has been sent, the target handle is picked up from the sys.conversation_endpoints catalog view, and the sent message is picked up so that no other callers can receive it:

```
ELSE
BEGIN
    --No one has requested this lock before
    ;BEGIN DIALOG @init_handle
    FROM SERVICE AppLock_Service
    TO SERVICE 'AppLock_Service'
    ON CONTRACT AppLockContract
    WITH ENCRYPTION = OFF

    --Send a throwaway message to start the dialog on both ends
    ;SEND ON CONVERSATION @init_handle
    MESSAGE TYPE AppLockGrant;

    --Get the remote handle
    SELECT
        @target_handle = ce2.conversation_handle
    FROM sys.conversation_endpoints ce1
    JOIN sys.conversation_endpoints ce2 ON
        ce1.conversation_id = ce2.conversation_id
    WHERE
        ce1.conversation_handle = @init_handle
        AND ce2.is_initiator = 0

    --Receive the throwaway message
    ;RECEIVE
        @target_handle = conversation_handle
```

```
    FROM AppLock_Queue
    WHERE conversation_handle = @target_handle
```

After starting the lock grant dialog and initializing the target conversation handle, the time-out/token dialog can finally be started, and the lock inserted into the AppLocks table. Once that's taken care of, the stored procedure checks to find out whether the @AppLockKey variable was populated. If it was, the transaction is committed. Otherwise, a timeout is assumed to have occurred, and all work is rolled back.

```
    BEGIN DIALOG CONVERSATION @AppLockKey
    FROM SERVICE AppLockTimeout_Service
    TO SERVICE 'AppLockTimeout_Service'
    WITH
        LIFETIME = @LOCK_TIMEOUT_LIFETIME,
        ENCRYPTION = OFF

    INSERT AppLocks
    (
        AppLockName,
        AppLockKey,
        InitiatorDialogHandle,
        TargetDialogHandle
    )
    VALUES
    (
        @AppLockName,
        @AppLockKey,
        @init_handle,
        @target_handle
    )
    END

    IF @AppLockKey IS NOT NULL
        COMMIT
    ELSE
    BEGIN
        RAISERROR(
            'Timed out waiting for lock on resource: %s', 16, 1, @AppLockName)
        ROLLBACK
    END
END
GO
```

The bulk of the work required to set up these locks is done in the GetAppLock stored procedure. Luckily, the accompanying ReleaseAppLock procedure is much simpler:

```
CREATE PROC ReleaseAppLock
    @AppLockKey UNIQUEIDENTIFIER
AS
```

```
BEGIN
    SET NOCOUNT ON
    SET XACT_ABORT ON

    BEGIN TRAN

    DECLARE @dialog_handle UNIQUEIDENTIFIER

    UPDATE AppLocks
    SET
        AppLockKey = NULL,
        @dialog_handle = InitiatorDialogHandle
    WHERE
        AppLockKey = @AppLockKey

    IF @@ROWCOUNT = 0
    BEGIN
        RAISERROR('AppLockKey not found', 16, 1)
        ROLLBACK
    END

    ;END CONVERSATION @AppLockKey

    --Allow another caller to acquire the lock
    ;SEND ON CONVERSATION @dialog_handle
    MESSAGE TYPE AppLockGrant

    COMMIT
END
GO
```

The caller sends the acquired lock's token to this procedure, which first tries to nullify its value in the AppLocks table. If the token is not found, an error is raised and the transaction rolled back. Otherwise, the conversation associated with the token is ended. Finally—and most importantly—an AppLockGrant message is sent on the grant conversation associated with the lock. This message will be picked up by any other process waiting for the lock, thereby granting it.

One final stored procedure is required to support this infrastructure: an activation stored procedure that is used in case of dialog lifetime expirations on the AppLockTimeout_Queue queue. The following T-SQL creates the procedure and enables activation on the queue:

```
CREATE PROC AppLockTimeout_Activation
AS
BEGIN
    SET NOCOUNT ON
    SET XACT_ABORT ON

    DECLARE @dialog_handle UNIQUEIDENTIFIER
```

```
    WHILE 1=1
    BEGIN
        SET @dialog_handle = NULL

        BEGIN TRAN

        WAITFOR
        (
            RECEIVE @dialog_handle = conversation_handle
            FROM AppLockTimeout_Queue
        ), TIMEOUT 10000

        IF @dialog_handle IS NOT NULL
        BEGIN
            EXEC ReleaseAppLock @AppLockKey = @dialog_handle
        END

        COMMIT
    END
END
GO


ALTER QUEUE AppLockTimeout_Queue
WITH ACTIVATION
(
    STATUS = ON,
    PROCEDURE_NAME = AppLockTimeout_Activation,
    MAX_QUEUE_READERS = 1,
    EXECUTE AS OWNER
)
GO
```

This procedure waits, on each iteration of its loop, up to 10 seconds for a message to appear on the queue. Since no messages are expected other than timeout notifications, any message received is assumed to be one, and spawns a call to the ReleaseAppLock stored procedure. If no message is received within 10 seconds, the activation procedure exits.

Once this system is in place, application locks can be requested using the GetAppLock stored procedure, as in the following example:

```
DECLARE @AppLockKey UNIQUEIDENTIFIER
EXEC GetAppLock
    @AppLockName = 'customers',
    @LockTimeout = 2000,
    @AppLockKey = @AppLockKey OUTPUT
```

In this example, the stored procedure will wait up to 2 seconds for the resource to become available before returning an error. Just as with other pessimistic schemes, it's important for the application to keep the returned key in order to release the lock later, using the ReleaseAppLock stored procedure.

Note that ongoing maintenance of this approach to locks is somewhat different from the method described for row-based pessimistic locks. Once a lock has been requested once, its row in the AppLocks table as well as its associated grant dialog will not get expired. I designed the system this way in order to minimize setup and break down a large number of dialogs in a system using and reusing a lot of locks, but it is possible that due to this architecture the number of dialogs could get quite large over time. If this should become an issue, use the LastGrantedDate column to find locks that have not been recently requested, and call END CONVERSATION for both the initiator and target handles.

Hoping for the Best: Optimistic Concurrency

Compared with the complexity and overhead of pessimistic concurrency solutions, optimistic schemes feel like a wonderful alternative. Indeed, even the word "optimistic" evokes a much nicer, warm-and-fuzzy feeling, and the name is quite appropriate to the methodology. Optimistic schemes use no read-time or edit-time locks, instead only checking for conflicts just before the data is actually written to the table. This means none of the administrative overhead of worrying about orphans and other issues that can occur with pessimistic locks, but it also means that the system may not be as appropriate to many businesses.

Consider the life insurance firm described in the section "Preparing for the Worst: Pessimistic Concurrency." For that firm, an optimistic scheme would mean many hours of lost time and money—not a good idea. However, suppose that the firm had a new project: this time, instead of updating many years' worth of lengthy personal information forms, the firm merely wants some address change cards input into the system. Just like with the personal information forms, these cards have not been well managed by the employees of the insurance firm, and there is some duplication. Luckily, however, the cards were filed using a much newer system, and the repetition of data is not nearly as serious as it was for the personal information forms.

In this scenario, the management overhead associated with a pessimistic scheme is probably not warranted. The chance for collision is much lower than in the personal information form scenario, and should an operator's input happen to collide with another's, it will only cost a few minutes' worth of lost work, instead of potentially hours.

The basic setup for optimistic concurrency requires a column that is updated whenever a row gets updated. This column is used as a version marker and retrieved along with the rest of the data by clients. At update time, the retrieved value is sent back along with updates, and its value is checked to ensure that it did not change between the time the data was read and the time of the update.

There are a few different choices for implementing this column, but to begin with I'll discuss a popular option: SQL Server's ROWVERSION type. The ROWVERSION type is an 8-byte binary string that is automatically updated by SQL Server every time a row is updated in the table. For example, consider the following table:

```
CREATE TABLE CustomerNames
(
    CustomerId INT NOT NULL PRIMARY KEY,
    CustomerName VARCHAR(50) NOT NULL,
    Version ROWVERSION NOT NULL
)
GO
```

The following T-SQL, the output of which is shown in Figure 8-1, inserts two rows and then retrieves all rows from the table:

```
INSERT CustomerNames
(
    CustomerId,
    CustomerName
)
SELECT 123, 'Ron Talmage'
UNION ALL
SELECT 456, 'Andrew Kelly'
GO

SELECT *
FROM CustomerNames
GO
```

	CustomerId	CustomerName	Version
1	123	Ron Talmage	0x00000000000007D1
2	456	Andrew Kelly	0x00000000000007D2

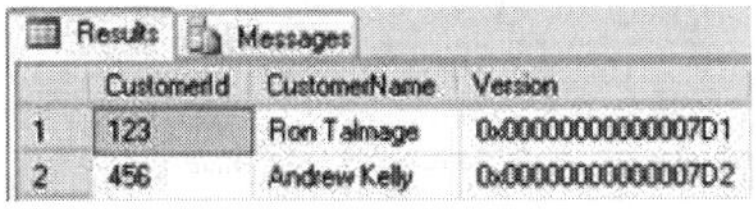

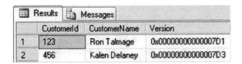

Figure 8-1. *Initial values of rows in the CustomerNames table*

Updating either row automatically updates the `ROWVERSION` column. The following T-SQL updates one of the rows and then retrieves all of the rows in the table, and its output is shown in Figure 8-2:

```
UPDATE CustomerNames
SET CustomerName = 'Kalen Delaney'
WHERE CustomerId = 456
GO

SELECT *
FROM CustomerNames
GO
```

	CustomerId	CustomerName	Version
1	123	Ron Talmage	0x00000000000007D1
2	456	Kalen Delaney	0x00000000000007D3

Figure 8-2. *Updating a row automatically causes the ROWVERSION to get updated.*

It's important to note that any committed update operation on the table will cause the `Version` column to get updated—even if you update a column with the same value. Do not assume that the version is tracking changes to the data; instead, it's tracking actions on the row.

Using a column such as this to support an optimistic scheme is quite straightforward. An effective first pass involves pulling back the Version column along with the rest of the data in the row when reading, and checking it at write time:

```
UPDATE CustomerNames
SET CustomerName = @CustomerName
WHERE
    CustomerId = @CustomerId
    AND Version = @Version

IF @@ROWCOUNT = 0
    RAISERROR('Version conflict encountered', 16, 1)
```

This is a simple method of handling optimistic concurrency, but it has a couple of problems. First of all, every update routine in the system must be made to comply with the requirements of checking the version. As with the pessimistic schemes described in the previous section, even one buggy module will cause the entire system to break down—not a good thing. Secondly, this setup does not leave you with many options when it comes to providing a nice user experience. Getting a conflict error without any means of fixing it is not especially fun—when possible, I prefer to send back enough data so that users can perform a merge if they feel like it (and the app provides that capability, of course).

The solution to both of these problems starts with a change to the version column's data type. Since columns that use ROWVERSION type are not updateable by anything except SQL Server, it makes the system difficult to control. Therefore, my first suggestion is to switch to either UNIQUEIDENTIFIER or DATETIME. Following is an updated version of CustomerNames, which uses a UNIQUEIDENTIFIER column:

```
CREATE TABLE CustomerNames
(
    CustomerId INT NOT NULL PRIMARY KEY,
    CustomerName VARCHAR(50) NOT NULL,
    Version UNIQUEIDENTIFIER NOT NULL
        DEFAULT (NEWID())
)
GO
```

To solve the potential problem of routines not following the rules, a trigger can be used to enforce the optimistic scheme. This is done by requiring that any updates to the table include an update to the Version column, which is enforced by checking the UPDATE function in the trigger. The column should be set to the value of whatever version was returned when the data was read. This way, the trigger can check the value present in the inserted table against the value in the deleted table for each row updated. If the two don't match, there is a version conflict. Finally, the trigger can set a new version value for the updated rows, thereby marking them as changed for anyone who has read the data. Following is the definition for the trigger:

```
CREATE TRIGGER tg_UpdateCustomerNames
ON CustomerNames
FOR UPDATE AS
BEGIN
    SET NOCOUNT ON

    IF NOT UPDATE(Version)
    BEGIN
        RAISERROR('Updating the Version column is required', 16, 1)
        ROLLBACK
    END

    IF EXISTS
        (
            SELECT *
            FROM inserted i
            JOIN deleted d ON i.CustomerId = d.CustomerId
            WHERE i.Version <> d.Version
        )
    BEGIN
        RAISERROR('Version conflict encountered', 16, 1)
        ROLLBACK
    END
    ELSE
        --Set new versions for the updated rows
        UPDATE CustomerNames
        SET Version = NEWID()
        WHERE
            CustomerId IN
            (
                SELECT CustomerId
                FROM inserted
            )
END
GO
```

This trigger can also be extended to help provide users with more options when they get a conflict. This is one place I find SQL Server's XML capabilities to be useful. To create an output document similar to an ADO.NET XML DiffGram, modify the IF block as follows:

```
IF EXISTS
    (
        SELECT *
        FROM inserted i
        JOIN deleted d ON i.CustomerId = d.CustomerId
        WHERE i.Version <> d.Version
    )
BEGIN
    SELECT
        (
            SELECT
                ROW_NUMBER() OVER (ORDER BY CustomerId) AS [@row_number],
                *
            FROM inserted
            FOR XML PATH('customer_name'), TYPE
        ) new_values,
        (
            SELECT
                ROW_NUMBER() OVER (ORDER BY CustomerId) AS [@row_number],
                *
            FROM deleted
            FOR XML PATH('customer_name'), TYPE
        ) old_values
    FOR XML PATH('customer_name_rows')
```

After making this modification, updating the table with an invalid version value will produce output similar to that shown in Figure 8-3. Although this doesn't exactly write the merge routine for you, I find that the XML format is very easy to work with when it comes to doing these kinds of operations.

```
<customer_name_rows>
  <new_values>
    <customer_name row_number="1">
      <CustomerId>123</CustomerId>
      <CustomerName>Peter DeBetta</CustomerName>
      <Version>D388F997-634C-4CB1-A37C-5E54201E070A</Version>
    </customer_name>
  </new_values>
  <old_values>
    <customer_name row_number="1">
      <CustomerId>123</CustomerId>
      <CustomerName>Ron Talmage</CustomerName>
      <Version>4690E83E-E3BE-49EE-86CF-886D996E1B7C</Version>
    </customer_name>
  </old_values>
</customer_name_rows>
```

Figure 8-3. *An XML DiffGram–style document represents the optimistic conflict.*

Since the document contains the newer version value that caused the conflict, you can let the end user perform a merge or choose to override the other user's change without having to go back to the database to get the new rows a second time.

A NOTE ON TRIGGERS AND PERFORMANCE

Throughout the previous two sections, update triggers were employed as a mechanism by which to control workflows around locking. Triggers are a great tool because the caller has no control over them—they will fire on any update to the table, regardless of whether it was made in a stored procedure or an ad hoc batch, and regardless of whether the caller has bothered to follow the locking rules. Unfortunately, triggers also cause problems: most notably, they can have an acute effect on performance.

The major performance problems caused by triggers generally result from lengthened transactions and the resultant blocking that can occur when low-granularity locks are held for a long period. In the case of these triggers, that's not much of an issue since they use the same rows that were already locked anyway by the updates themselves. However, these triggers will slow down updates a bit. In SQL Server 2005, the inserted and deleted tables are actually hidden temporary tables; the population of these tables does not come for free—the data must be transferred into TempDB. In addition, each of these triggers incurs additional index operations against the base table that are not necessary for a simple update.

In my testing, I've found that these triggers slow down updates by a factor of 2. However, that's generally the difference between a few milliseconds and a few more milliseconds—certainly not a big deal, especially given the value that they bring to the application. It's worth testing to make sure that these triggers don't cause severe performance issues for your application, but at the same time remember that nothing is free—and if it's a question of data integrity vs. performance, I personally would always choose the former.

Embracing Conflict: Multivalue Concurrency

While optimistic and pessimistic concurrency are focused on enabling long-running business processes to work together without mangling data that happens to be getting modified concurrently, multivalue concurrency control is based around the idea that performance is king.

MVCC is not concerned with making sure you can't overwrite someone else's data, because in an MVCC scheme there is no overwriting of data—period. Instead of updating existing rows, every change is done as an insert. This means that there's no reason to check for data collisions; no data can get lost if nothing is being updated. In an MVCC system, new rows are marked with a version number—generally a date/time column or ascending key—so that newer versions can be readily identified and queried by users.

Generally speaking, to benefit from MVCC, the cost of blocking for a given set of transactions must outweigh all other resource costs, particularly with regard to disk I/O. Since new versions of rows will be inserted as entirely new rows, the potential for massive amounts of disk utilization is quite huge. However, due to the fact that no updates are taking place, blocking becomes almost nonexistent.

Illustrating the performance gains possible from an insert-only architecture is fairly simple using a load tool. To begin with, create a table and populate it with some sample data, as shown in the following T-SQL:

```
CREATE TABLE Test_Updates
(
    PK_Col INT NOT NULL PRIMARY KEY,
    Other_Col VARCHAR(100) NOT NULL
)
GO
```

```
INSERT Test_Updates
(
    PK_Col,
    Other_Col
)
SELECT
    EmployeeId,
    Title
FROM AdventureWorks.HumanResources.Employee
```

Next, fire up SQLQueryStress and type the following into the Query window:

```
BEGIN TRAN

UPDATE Test_Updates
SET Other_Col = @Other_Col
WHERE PK_Col = @PK_Col

WAITFOR DELAY '00:00:00.25'

COMMIT
```

This code simulates an UPDATE followed by a quarter of a second of other actions taking place in the same transaction. It doesn't matter what the other actions are; the important thing is that this is a somewhat long-running transaction, and that the UPDATE will hold its locks for the duration of the transaction, which is necessary in order to guarantee consistency of the updated data.

Next, configure your database connection, and use the following as your parameter substitution query:

```
SELECT
    e1.EmployeeId,
    e1.Title
FROM AdventureWorks.HumanResources.Employee e1
CROSS JOIN AdventureWorks.HumanResources.Employee e2
WHERE
    e2.EmployeeId BETWEEN 1 AND 10
ORDER BY
    e1.EmployeeId
```

This query will return each row in the HumanResources.Employee table ten times. The rows are ordered such that the same employees will be grouped together in the output. This is done so that as the load threads read the data, they will concurrently submit requests to update the same rows, thereby highlighting the effects of collision and blocking.

Finally, map the EmployeeId column to the @PK_Col variable, and the Title column to the @Other_Col variable. Set SQLQueryStress to do 290 iterations (the number of rows in HumanResources.Employee) on 40 threads, and click the GO button. The output of this test when run on my laptop is shown in Figure 8-4.

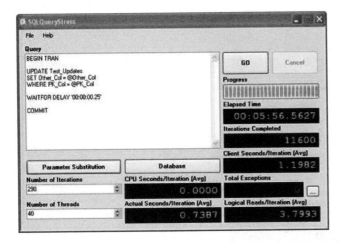

Figure 8-4. *Performance of updates is compromised due to blocking.*

To compare the relative performance of updates in a highly concurrent scenario with that of inserts, create a similar table to Test_Updates, this time designed to hold—and version—inserted rows:

```
CREATE TABLE Test_Inserts
(
    PK_Col INT NOT NULL,
    Other_Col VARCHAR(100) NOT NULL,
    Version INT IDENTITY(1,1) NOT NULL,
    PRIMARY KEY (PK_Col, Version)
)
GO
```

Use the same SQLQueryStress settings as before, except for the main query. This time, use the following:

```
BEGIN TRAN

INSERT Test_Inserts
(
    PK_Col,
    Other_Col
)
SELECT
    @PK_Col,
    @Other_Col

WAITFOR DELAY '00:00:00.25'

COMMIT
```

Start the run by clicking the GO button. The results of this test when run on my laptop are shown in Figure 8-5.

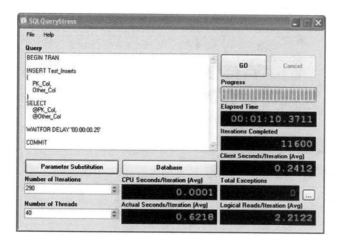

Figure 8-5. *Inserts do not block one another, thereby leading to higher concurrency.*

The results are fairly clear: when simulating a massive blocking scenario, inserts are the clear winner over updates, thanks to the fact that processes do not block each other trying to write the same rows. Admittedly, this example is contrived, but it should serve to illustrate the purported benefit of MVCC as a concurrency technique.

Of course, there is a bit more to MVCC than the idea of using inserts instead of updates. You still need to be able to retrieve a consistent view of the data. A query such as the following can be used to get the latest version of every row:

```
SELECT
    ti.PK_Col,
    ti.Other_Col,
    ti.Version
FROM Test_Inserts ti
WHERE
    Version =
    (
        SELECT MAX(ti1.Version)
        FROM Test_Inserts ti1
        WHERE
            ti1.PK_Col = ti.PK_Col
    )
```

I will not cover MVCC queries extensively in this section—instead, I will refer you to Chapter 10, which covers temporal data. The bitemporal techniques discussed in that chapter share many similarities with MVCC, but with a greater overall value proposition thanks to the fact that they take advantage of time as well as versioning, allowing you to pull back consistent views of the data based on time rather than just version.

As you might guess, MVCC, while an interesting concept, cannot be applied as described here to many real-world applications. Merging the MVCC concept with bitemporal data models can help make this a much more interesting technique for highly concurrent applications in which versioning of data collisions makes sense.

Extending Scalability Through Queuing

To finish this chapter, I'd like to discuss some recent research I've done in the area of increasing database scalability potential by introducing pipeline queues. This is an area very much tied to high concurrency, but that may not fit cleanly with the rest of the material in this chapter. Nonetheless, I feel that it's an important topic.

The idea I'll discuss in this section is how to increase an application's ability to scale on the same hardware, by putting limits on per-process resource consumption using queues. This is something I've seen done in a few applications I've worked on in the past, but it's something that was difficult to implement in SQL Server until Service Broker was added to the product.

The central motivation for pipeline queue centers around the fact that as concurrency increases, overall server resource availability drops, and resource queues start forming. As resources are taxed to their limit, every request takes longer and longer, and the server is no longer able to satisfy requests as quickly as it did with fewer concurrent users. The premise is that by introducing a queue to limit the number of concurrent requests allowed to hit the system at one time, each request will take less time, and if balanced properly, the amount of time required to get through even a fairly backed up queue will actually be less than the amount of time that would be required for each request to process if the requests were allowed to hit the server concurrently.

To test this technique, I wanted to simulate a common scenario I see in many applications: it is often the case that some of the queries that are run the most often are also the heaviest in terms of resource utilization. This makes sense; users want to get as much value as they can from the applications they use, and it's often the case that the highest-value queries in the system read the most data. In order to ensure that I would create a good amount of resource utilization without having to design a complex test case, I settled on multirow inserts and decided that each request should cause 100 rows to be inserted into a central table.

To easily simulate concurrency, I decided to use Service Broker as my test harness. I started with the following Service Broker objects in an empty database called `Pipeline_Test`:

```
CREATE MESSAGE TYPE Pipeline_Test_Msg
VALIDATION = EMPTY
GO

CREATE CONTRACT Pipeline_Test_Contract
(Pipeline_Test_Msg SENT BY INITIATOR)
GO

CREATE QUEUE Pipeline_Test_Queue
GO

CREATE SERVICE Pipeline_Test_Service
ON QUEUE Pipeline_Test_Queue
```

```
(Pipeline_Test_Contract)
GO
```

I also created two tables to be used in the testing:

```
CREATE TABLE Pipeline_Test_Rows
(
    AColumn INT,
    BColumn DATETIME DEFAULT(GETDATE())
)
GO

CREATE TABLE Pipeline_Test_Times
(
    StartTime DATETIME,
    EndTime DATETIME,
    NumberOfThreads INT
)
GO
```

The Pipeline_Test_Rows table was the central table into which rows were inserted on each test iteration, in order to stress server resources. The Pipeline_Test_Times table was used to record how long each iteration took and the number of threads (activation procedures) active during the iteration.

The job of the activation stored procedure was to wait on the queue, receiving requests as they came in. For each request, 100 rows were inserted into the Pipeline_Test_Rows table, the conversation was ended from the target end (WITH CLEANUP—I wanted to simulate the overhead of ending a conversation, but did not want to deal with checking for dialog end messages on the initiator end), and finally a row was inserted into the Pipeline_Test_Times table. Following is the activation procedure I used:

```
CREATE PROC Pipeline_Test_Activation
AS
BEGIN
    SET NOCOUNT ON

    DECLARE @handle UNIQUEIDENTIFIER
    DECLARE @start datetime

    WHILE 1=1
    BEGIN
        SET @handle = NULL

        --Wait up to five seconds for a message
        WAITFOR
        (
            RECEIVE top(1) @handle = conversation_handle
            FROM Pipeline_Test_Queue
        ), TIMEOUT 5000
```

```
        --We didn't get a handle -- abort the loop
        IF @handle IS NULL
            BREAK

        SET @start = GETDATE()

        INSERT Pipeline_Test_Rows
        (
            AColumn
        )
        SELECT TOP(100)
            Number
        FROM master..spt_values

        END CONVERSATION @handle
        WITH CLEANUP

        INSERT Pipeline_Test_Times
        (
            StartTime,
            EndTime,
            NumberOfThreads
        )
        SELECT
            @start,
            GETDATE(),
            COUNT(*)
        FROM sys.dm_broker_activated_tasks
    END
END
GO
```

I also created the following table to hold the interim test results during the course of the run:

```
CREATE TABLE FinalResults
(
    AvgIterationTime INT,
    ConcurrentThreads INT
)
GO
```

Finally, I created a loop to run each scenario from 1 to 200 readers. The start of the loop initializes the global number of threads counter and resets the state of the test database by truncating the test tables, disabling activation on the target queue, and setting the NEW_BROKER option:

```
DECLARE @counter INT
SET @counter = 1
```

```
WHILE @counter <= 200
BEGIN
    TRUNCATE TABLE Pipeline_Test_Rows
    TRUNCATE TABLE Pipeline_Test_Times

    --Alter the queue and turn on activation
    ALTER QUEUE Simple_Queue_Target
    WITH ACTIVATION
    (
        STATUS = OFF
    )

    --Reset the database
    ALTER DATABASE Pipeline_Test SET NEW_BROKER
```

Next, 200,000 messages were sent on the queue:

```
DECLARE @i INT
SET @i = 1

WHILE @i <= 200000
BEGIN
    DECLARE @h UNIQUEIDENTIFIER

    BEGIN DIALOG CONVERSATION @h
    FROM SERVICE Pipeline_Test_Service
    TO SERVICE 'Pipeline_Test_Service'
    ON CONTRACT Pipeline_Test_Contract
    WITH ENCRYPTION=OFF;

    SEND ON CONVERSATION @h
    MESSAGE TYPE Pipeline_Test_Msg

    SET @i = @i + 1
END
```

At this point, messages were sitting on the queue but were not being processed. Activation was reenabled, and the MAX_QUEUE_READERS setting set to the current value of @counter:

```
--Need dynamic SQL here because MAX_QUEUE_READERS cannot take
--a variable as input
DECLARE @sql VARCHAR(500)
SET @sql = '' +
    'ALTER QUEUE Pipeline_Test_Queue ' +
    'WITH ACTIVATION ' +
    '( ' +
        'STATUS = ON, ' +
        'PROCEDURE_NAME = Pipeline_Test_Activation, ' +
        'MAX_QUEUE_READERS = ' + CONVERT(VARCHAR, @counter) + ', ' +
```

```
        'EXECUTE AS OWNER ' +
    ')'
```

```
EXEC (@sql)
```

Finally, I set the loop to wait until all messages had been processed, as determined by polling the `Pipeline_Test_Rows` table once every 10 seconds to find out whether 200,000 insertions of 100 rows had occurred (for a total of 20,000,000 rows). If the result was positive, the average number of milliseconds per iteration was recorded in the `FinalResults` table. Note that because activation starts with only a single active procedure and ramps up from there, an additional `WHERE` clause was necessary in order to only take rows in which the maximum number of queue readers had been reached:

```
--Activation has started -- wait for everything to finish
WHILE 1=1
BEGIN
    WAITFOR DELAY '00:00:10'

    IF
        (
            SELECT COUNT(*)
            FROM Pipeline_Test_Rows WITH (NOLOCK)
        ) = 20000000
    BEGIN
        INSERT FinalResults
        (
            AvgIterationTime,
            ConcurrentThreads
        )
        SELECT
            AVG(DATEDIFF(ms, StartTime, EndTime)),
            @counter
        FROM Pipeline_Test_Times
        WHERE NumberOfThreads = @counter

        BREAK
    END
END

SET @counter = @counter + 1
END
GO
```

I ran this test on a 4-core x64 server attached to a small RAID 5 storage device. Results were just as I expected: as the number of concurrent readers increased, so did the average time per iteration. However, the amount of time required to clear the queue also went down, thanks to the fact that average time did not increase in a linear manner as the number of readers was ratcheted up.

Figure 8-6 shows my findings from this test. The dashed line shows the average time per iteration, as extracted from the `FinalResults` table. The solid line shows the maximum estimated amount of time that a reader would have to wait to get through a queue with 200 requests in front of it. This was calculated using the following algorithm: `CEILING((200 / (Number of concurrent readers)) * (Average time per iteration))`. This algorithm is somewhat naïve in its assumption that all readers will complete the task in an identical amount of time. It finds the number of "levels" in the queue, which is the number of passes that all readers must take to clear the queue. So for instance, if there are 40 readers, the queue can be said to be five levels deep, given that it will take five passes of all 40 readers working to clear the queue. A request sitting last in the queue won't get processed in this case for four passes.

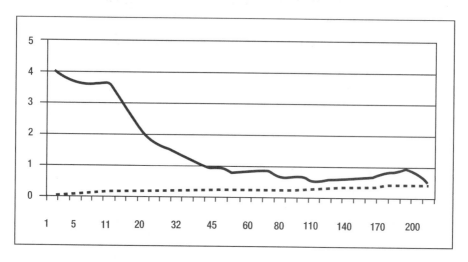

Figure 8-6. *Testing concurrency from 1 to 200 readers. The dashed line represents average time per iteration, and the solid line represents the maximum time required to get through a 200-deep queue.*

These results show that adding more readers was extremely beneficial until around 50 concurrent readers were added. At that point, additional readers improved time through the queue, but not as much. At around 115 readers, resource utilization is maxed out on the server, and adding additional readers has an inverse effect: it begins slowing down the amount of time needed for a message to get through the queue.

The conclusion that can be drawn on the surface is that if this were the only process running on your database server and you had bursts of up to 200 concurrent requests, setting a maximum number of queue readers in your pipeline to around 110 would maximize overall response time by limiting resource thrashing to a manageable level. However, I would recommend instead taking a more holistic view and considering the state of the entire server. It's clear, even without investigating performance counters, that the server is fairly stressed as the number of readers approaches 110. So it might be better—if possible—to determine the maximum acceptable response time and throttle back the maximum number of concurrent processes appropriately. In this case, since the benefit of adding additional readers steeply drops off around 80, I would tend to choose a figure in that vicinity.

This is, of course, a fairly simplified test of this technique, but it shows the potential for queuing to help limit server utilization while helping to even out response time. Thanks to Service Broker, this approach can be implemented inside of the database as a performance measure, encapsulated within a stored procedure such that the application does not even need to know that the technique is being used. Further research is clearly required to determine the best practices for using this technique in a wide variety of applications, but from a scalability and concurrency point of view, I think it's safe to say that the benefits of this technique are quite promising.

Summary

Concurrency is a complex topic, with many possible solutions. In this chapter, I introduced the various concurrency models that should be considered from a business process and data collision point of view, and explained how they differ from the similarly named concurrency models supported by the SQL Server database engine. Pessimistic concurrency is probably the most commonly used form, but it can be complex to set up and maintain. Optimistic concurrency, while much lighter weight, might not be applicable to as many business scenarios. And multivalue concurrency control, while a novel technique, might be difficult to implement in such a way that allowing collisions will help deliver value other than a performance enhancement.

Finally, I covered the impact of queuing on enhancing concurrency and scalability. Although a well-known technique in the world of application development, this is a fairly new idea inside of the database. The discussion here only scratched the surface of the potential for this technique; I feel that many applications could benefit from the introduction of pipeline queues used to limit resource utilization.

CHAPTER 9

■■■

Working with Spatial Data

One of the major new terrains for software development is that of **geospatial data**. GPS systems have rapidly advanced from military intelligence equipment to toys for the happy few to generally available household appliances. Now that these positioning systems are affordable for everyone, the market for applications for those systems is booming as well—and as a result, interest in efficient techniques for storing and retrieving geospatial data continues to increase.

The topic of **spatial data** is broader than just geospatial data. Air traffic controllers need to know altitude of a plane as well as the ground position to ensure that planes won't fly into each other, astrologists need a way to represent the locations of stellar objects in space, game developers have to maintain a list of objects in a two- or three-dimensional virtual game world, architects have to pinpoint the exact size and location of each room in the building they're designing, and so on. The list of possible examples is seemingly endless.

In this chapter, I will show that, while it is easy to *store* spatial data, actually *retrieving* and *manipulating* it efficiently can be much more challenging. I will then go on to show you several techniques to overcome these challenges. I will focus most of the discussion on the handling of geospatial data. Keep in mind that most of the techniques for storing and handling geospatial data can be applied to *all* kinds of spatial data in a two-dimensional space—not just geographical data. And with some adaptations, these techniques can even be used for three-dimensional space.

Representing Geospatial Data by Latitude and Longitude

The most common way to represent positions on earth is to use the tried and true **latitude** and **longitude** coordinate system. This scheme has many similarities to the representation of points in an arbitrary two-dimensional space based on x and y coordinates, which we all came to know and hate during high school. However, there are some important differences, due to the way the two-dimensional surface of the earth has been wrapped around a globe.

If the earth were a flat surface, 20 degrees difference in longitude would be the same distance anywhere, regardless of latitude. And the distance from Alaska (140 to 170 degrees west) to Kamchatka (approximately 160 degrees east) would be enormous (see Figure 9-1). But in reality, the earth is a globe (see Figure 9-2). This means that 20 degrees difference in longitude is not the same everywhere, and that Alaska and Kamchatka are virtually neighbors. It also means that distance calculations on earth differ from distance calculations on flat surfaces, and that, contrary to popular belief, the shortest connection between two points is not always a straight line (unless you happen to be a mole).

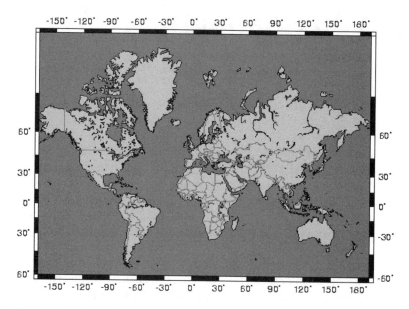

Figure 9-1. *The earth, projected on a flat surface*

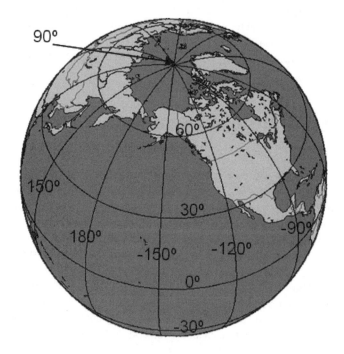

Figure 9-2. *The earth as it really is*

Setting Up Sample Data

In order to demonstrate the various techniques I want to show in this chapter, as well as to assess their relative performance, use of a fairly large sample data set is necessary. Fortunately, Microsoft has provided such a database as part of the samples that ship with SQL Server 2005.

To use this sample database, you first have to unpack the samples.[1] To do this, all you need to do is click Start ➤ All Programs ➤ Microsoft SQL Server 2005 ➤ Documentation and Tutorials ➤ Samples ➤ Microsoft SQL Server 2005 Samples (English). This will unpack the samples and install them to the default location (`C:\Program Files\Microsoft SQL Server\90\Samples`) or to another location that you can supply. It will also install a shortcut to the chosen location at Start ➤ All Programs ➤ Microsoft SQL Server 2005 ➤ Documentation and Tutorials ➤ Samples Directory.

■**Note** If you can't find the samples on your computer, chances are that they were not selected when SQL Server 2005 was installed. You can fix this by reinstalling SQL Server 2005, or by downloading the samples from `http://www.microsoft.com/downloads/details.aspx?familyid=E719ECF7-9F46-4312-AF89-6AD8702E4E6E&displaylang=en` (March 2007) and installing the downloaded package. Microsoft will periodically update the samples; if you see different results from the results listed in this chapter, it might be due to a different version of the sample database for spatial data.

Once the samples have been installed and unpacked, you can set up the sample database for geospatial data. Everything you need is located in `C:\Program Files\Microsoft SQL Server\90\Samples\Engine\Programmability\CLR\Spatial` (provided you unpacked the samples to their default location). To set up the `Spatial` database, you first need to compile and build an assembly from the CLR code for this sample. You won't be using any of this code right away, but the assembly has to exist in order for the database to be built. Navigate to the `CS` directory and double-click the `Spatial.sln` file. Once Microsoft Visual Studio has finished loading files, click Build Spatial in the Build menu. After a few seconds, you will see the message "Build succeeded" in the lower-left corner. This indicates that the assembly has been built—you can now close Microsoft Visual Studio.

The next step is to actually build the database for geospatial data and load it with a large set of sample data. First, you need to check whether you already have a database called `Spatial` on your server. If you have one, rename or delete it. Then find and double-click the `BuildSpatialDatabase.bat` file in the `Scripts` directory. This will create a new database called `Spatial`, set up some tables, and load them with data.

---

1. Unpacking the samples has to be done only once. If you or someone else have already unpacked the samples on your computer, there is no need to do it again—unless you suspect that someone has messed up the samples and you want to restore to the original samples.

Note There are in fact two scripts in the `Scripts` directory. The `BuildSpatialDatabase.bat` file is used to create all objects, load the assembly, and bulk insert the data from the `.dat` files in the `Data` directory. The other script, `AttachSpatialDatabase.bat`, simply attaches the prebuilt database `Spatial.mdf` in the `Data` directory. This should be a bit faster—but if you have followed security best practices when setting up SQL Server, this script will fail. The `ATTACH` operation will attempt to allocate the log file in the same directory as the data file, and the SQL Server service user should not have any write permissions to that folder. You can, of course, assign extra privileges or copy the files to another location, but I would recommend not bothering—the `BuildSpatialDatabase.bat` script works, and runs fast enough (at least on my computer).

The table we will be working with hereafter is the table `Place`. This table contains data for almost 23,000 cities and towns in the United States of America. Following is a peek at its contents:

```
SELECT
    PlaceName,
    State,
    Lat,
    Lon
FROM Place;
GO
```

This code results in the following output:

```
PlaceName                State Lat                Lon

Merrill                  WI    45.182023          -89.703459
Tomahawk                 WI    45.473409          -89.724151
Crystal Falls            MI    46.097305          -88.327727
...
Rio Dell                 CA    40.500822          -124.10633
Ferndale                 CA    40.579486          -124.260625

(22993 row(s) affected)
```

There are a few more columns in the table, but I won't use them for now.

Calculating the Distance Between Two Points

The most basic operation on two points is the calculation of the distance between them. The formulas shown here may look complex, but it is not important for you to fully understand them unless you're especially interested in math. More important is an understanding of the processes involved and when to use each given formula.

For points that are on a flat surface, the Pythagorean theorem can be used, and the distance between two points (x1, y1) and (x2, y2) can be calculated with the following algorithm:

$$Distance = \sqrt{(x2-x1)^2 + (y2-y1)^2}$$

Since the earth is not a flat surface, a different formula is needed for geographical distance calculation, except when dealing with extremely short distances, where using the Pythagorean theorem will yield results that are only insignificantly off. The formulas for the correct distance between two points on earth are rather more complex. Here is one possible way to compute this distance:

$$Distance = 2 * \arcsin(\sqrt{\sin(\frac{lat1 - lat2}{2})^2 + \cos(lat1) * \cos(lat2) * \sin(\frac{lon1 - lon2}{2})^2})$$

■**Note** This formula, plus many other useful formulas for working with geospatial data, can be found on the web site `http://williams.best.vwh.net/avform.htm`. Also note that all inputs and the result are all measured in radians.

For extremely long distances, the results of this formula will be slightly incorrect. That is because the shape of the earth is not an exact sphere; it bulges slightly at the equator.

MEASURING LONGITUDE AND LATITUDE IN DEGREES AND RADIANS

Most people are familiar with using degrees as a measurement for angles. The basic idea is to divide a full circle into 360 equal parts, called **degrees**. That makes an angle of 90 degrees a square angle, an angle of 180 degrees a straight line, any angle of less than 90 degrees an acute angle, and any angle of over 90 but less than 180 degrees an obtuse angle.

For latitude, degrees are used as well. The way this works is that a straight line is projected from the center of the earth through the equator. Another straight line is projected from the center of the earth through your chosen location. The angle at which these two imaginary lines intersect at the center of the earth is the number of degrees north or south for the location. For the North Pole and South Pole, the lines intersect at a square angle so they are 90 degrees north and 90 degrees south. The equator itself is at 0 degrees, of course.

The exact same technique is used to get a longitude in degrees, except that in this case, the first line is projected from the center of the earth through a location with the same latitude as the chosen location on the Greenwich meridian, the line connecting the North Pole to the South Pole that runs straight through Greenwich, a village near London, Great Britain.

While the use of degrees to measure angles, longitude, and latitude is widespread and relatively easy for normal humans to understand, mathematicians prefer to use another measure: **radians**. This preference is caused by that fact that many formulas are simpler when angles are measured in radians.

The idea behind radians is very much like that of degrees. In fact, the only difference is the number of units in a full circle (and therefore the number of units in any given angle). Whereas a whole circle measures 360 degrees, that same whole circle measures 2 * π radians. (Note that π is the Greek letter pi, a symbol used in mathematics for a constant that is roughly equal to 3.14159265.)

Converting between degrees and radians is very easy—to convert from degrees, simply divide by 360 and multiply by 2 * π (or, divide by 180 and multiply by π). And to convert back from radians to degrees, reverse the process: divide by π and multiply by 180. I will use this method for conversion in the .NET code later in this chapter; in the T-SQL code, I simply call the built-in functions `RADIANS()` and `DEGREES()`.

The following T-SQL function implements the algorithm to calculate the distance between two points on the earth, either in kilometers or in miles:

```
CREATE FUNCTION Distance
(
    @Lat1 FLOAT,
    @Lon1 FLOAT,
    @Lat2 FLOAT,
    @Lon2 FLOAT,
    @Unit CHAR(2) = 'km'
)
RETURNS FLOAT
AS
BEGIN;
    DECLARE
        @Lat1R FLOAT,
        @Lon1R FLOAT,
        @Lat2R FLOAT,
        @Lon2R FLOAT,
        @DistR FLOAT,
        @Dist  FLOAT;

    -- Convert from degrees to radians
    SET @Lat1R = RADIANS(@Lat1);
    SET @Lon1R = RADIANS(@Lon1);
    SET @Lat2R = RADIANS(@Lat2);
    SET @Lon2R = RADIANS(@Lon2);

    -- Calculate the distance (in radians)
    SET @DistR =
        2 * ASIN(SQRT(
            POWER(SIN((@Lat1R - @Lat2R) / 2), 2) +
            (COS(@Lat1R) * COS(@Lat2R) * POWER(SIN((@Lon1R - @Lon2R) / 2), 2))));

    -- Convert distance from radians to kilometers or miles
    -- Convert distance from km/mi to radians
    -- Note: DistR = Distance in nautical miles * (pi / (180 * 60))
    --               One nautical mile is 1.852 kilometers, thus:
    --       DistR =(DistKM / 1.852) * pi / (180 * 60)
    --   or: DistR = DistKM * pi / (180 * 60 * 1.852)
```

```
    IF @Unit = 'km'
        SET @Dist = @DistR * 20001.6 / PI();
    ELSE
        SET @Dist = @DistR * 20001.6 / PI() / 1.609344;

    RETURN @Dist;
END;
GO
```

Using this function, we can answer a variety of basic spatial questions. For instance, the following T-SQL can be used to find the distance between Seattle, WA, and Redmond, WA, both in kilometers and in miles:

```
WITH Seattle AS
(
    SELECT Lat, Lon
    FROM Place
    WHERE
        PlaceName = 'Seattle'
        AND State = 'WA'
)
,Redmond AS
(
    SELECT Lat, Lon
    FROM Place
    WHERE
        PlaceName = 'Redmond'
        AND State = 'WA'
)
SELECT
    dbo.Distance(s.Lat, s.Lon, r.Lat, r.Lon, 'km') AS DistInKilometers,
    dbo.Distance(s.Lat, s.Lon, r.Lat, r.Lon, 'mi') AS DistInMiles
FROM Seattle AS s
CROSS JOIN Redmond AS r;
GO
```

This query returns the following result set, from which we can learn that Redmond is 18½ kilometers (or 11½ miles) from Seattle.

```
DistInKilometers        DistInMiles
---------------------   ----------------------
18.5680519862199        11.5376526002023
```

COMPARING THE ALGORITHMS

In case you are wondering whether it's really necessary to implement this complicated formula rather than using the much simpler algorithm based on the Pythagorean theorem, run the following code to see the difference between the two.

```
DECLARE @State CHAR(2);
SET @State = 'FL';

WITH TwoCalculations
AS
(
    SELECT
        dbo.Distance(a.Lat, a.Lon, b.Lat, b.Lon, 'km') AS Correct,
        SQRT (POWER(a.Lat - b.Lat, 2)
            + POWER(a.Lon - b.Lon, 2)) * 111.12 AS Approx
    FROM Place AS a
    INNER JOIN Place AS b ON b.HtmID >= a.HtmID²
    WHERE
        a.State = @State
        AND b.State = @State
)
SELECT
    Correct,
    Approx,
    Approx - Correct AS Diff,
    (Approx - Correct) * 100.0 / NULLIF(Correct, 0.0) AS Perc
FROM TwoCalculations
ORDER BY Perc DESC;
GO
```

If you inspect the results, you will see that even in Florida, relatively near to the equator, the difference can be as much as 16% or more. Now change the second line to SET @State = 'WA'; and run the query again. You'll see that as you approach the polar regions, the error in the approximation based on the Pythagorean theorem gets worse, causing results to be off by over 50%!

If you want, you can also remove the WHERE clause from this query to calculate the difference between the two formulas for all places in the USA—but be prepared to leave the computer running overnight, since you'll be effectively running a cross join between two copies of a 23,000-row table.

---

2. The primary key column HtmID is used here to prevent double results. Without this filter, each combination would appear twice in the results, as City1 compared to City2, and as City2 compared to City1. For more information about the values in this column, see the section "Representing Geospatial Data by Using the Hierarchical Triangular Mesh."

Moving from Point to Point

Another basic operation is to find a new point, based on a starting position, a distance, and a direction. I'll skip the algorithm for the theoretical flat earth, knowing how far off from the truth answers based on those calculations are, and move straight to the formulas for the real earth.

The stored procedure that follows takes a point (@Lat1, @Lon1), a distance (@Dist) in kilometers or miles, and a direction (@Dir) in degrees, and calculates a new point (@Lat2, @Lon2) by moving the specified distance in the specified direction. I have implemented this as a stored procedure so that I can return latitude and longitude in one call. Implementing this as a user-defined function won't work, because a user-defined function can return only a single scalar value.

■**Note** You could implement a CLR user-defined type for storing points and use that instead of the methods shown here. Doing so would allow you to use a user-defined function with a single scalar output. In that case, you might want to use a CLR user-defined function instead of a T-SQL one, or you might want to implement this logic as a method on the type itself. However, both of these are left as an exercise for you to try on your own.

The formula used in the following procedure, like the formula for the distance calculation, is found on http://williams.best.vwh.net/avform.htm.

```
CREATE PROCEDURE Move
    @Lat1 FLOAT,
    @Lon1 FLOAT,
    @Dist FLOAT,
    @Dir  FLOAT,
    @Lat2 FLOAT OUTPUT,
    @Lon2 FLOAT OUTPUT,
    @Unit CHAR(2) = 'km'
AS
BEGIN;
    DECLARE
        @Lat1R FLOAT,
        @Lon1R FLOAT,
        @Lat2R FLOAT,
        @Lon2R FLOAT,
        @DLonR FLOAT,
        @DistR FLOAT,
        @DirR  FLOAT;

    -- Convert from degrees to radians
    SET @Lat1R = RADIANS(@Lat1);
    SET @Lon1R = RADIANS(@Lon1);
    SET @DirR  = RADIANS(@Dir);
```

```
    -- Convert distance from km/mi to radians
    -- Note: DistR = Distance in nautical miles * (pi / (180 * 60))
    --                One nautical mile is 1.852 kilometers, thus:
    --    or: DistR =(DistKM / 1.852) * pi / (180 * 60)
    --    or: DistR = DistKM * pi / (180 * 60 * 1.852)
    --    or: DistR = DistKM * pi / 20001.6
    -- Since one mile is 1.609344 kilometers, the formula for miles is:
    --        DistR =(DistMI * 1.609344) * pi / 20001.6
    --    or: DistR = DistMI * pi / (20001.6 / 1.609344)
    --    or: DistR = DistMI * pi / 12428.4180386542591267000071581961
    IF @Unit = 'km'
        SET @DistR = @Dist * PI() / 20001.6;
    ELSE
        SET @DistR = @Dist * PI() / 12428.4180386542591267000071581961;

    -- Calculate latitude of new point
    SET @Lat2R = ASIN(SIN(@Lat1R) * COS(@DistR)
                    + COS(@Lat1R) * SIN(@DistR) * COS(@DirR));

    -- Calculate longitude difference.
    SET @DLonR = ATN2(SIN(@DirR)  * SIN(@DistR) * COS(@Lat1R),
                    COS(@DistR) - SIN(@Lat1R) * SIN(@Lat2R));
    -- Calculate longitude of new point - ensure result is between -PI and PI.
    SET @Lon2R = (CAST(@Lon1R - @DLonR + PI() AS DECIMAL(38,37))
                % CAST(2*PI() AS DECIMAL(38,37)))
                - PI();

    -- Convert back to degrees
    SET @Lat2 = DEGREES(@Lat2R);
    SET @Lon2 = DEGREES(@Lon2R);
END;
GO
```

■**Note** The direction parameter (Dir) should be specified as an angle, in degrees, with 0 degrees being straight north, 90 degrees straight west, 180 degrees straight south, and 270 degrees (or –90 degrees, both can be used) straight east. To move northwest, use a direction of 45 degrees; for southeast, use 225 (or –135) degrees; and so forth.

With this stored procedure, it's easy to determine where you end up if you travel 100 kilometers northeast (–45 or 315 degrees) from Seattle.

```
DECLARE
    @Lat1 FLOAT,
    @Lon1 FLOAT,
```

```
    @Lat2 FLOAT,
    @Lon2 FLOAT;

SELECT
    @Lat1 = Lat,
    @Lon1 = Lon
FROM Place
WHERE
    PlaceName = 'Seattle'
    AND State = 'WA';

EXEC Move
    @Lat1,
    @Lon1,
    100,            -- Distance
    -45,            -- Direction
    @Lat2 OUTPUT,
    @Lon2 OUTPUT,
    'km';

SELECT
    @Lat2 AS Lat,
    @Lon2 AS Lon;
GO
```

When this query is executed, the results are as follows:

```
Lat                    Lon
--------------------   --------------------
48.2542113748429       -121.394599203379
```

Since the procedure Move is computation-intensive, I have also tried implementing it as a CLR stored procedure. This turned out to be a bad idea, though—my tests showed that the CLR version of Move is almost twice as slow as the T-SQL version (4.753 vs. 2.453 seconds for 100,000 executions on my laptop). The reason for this slowness is that SQL Server always assumes that you're going to do data access from a CLR stored procedure, so you incur the overhead of setting up the environment for that data access. Here's the CLR version of the code anyway, just in case you want to try it for yourself:

```
using System;
using System.Data;
using System.Data.SqlClient;
using System.Data.SqlTypes;
using Microsoft.SqlServer.Server;
```

```
public partial class StoredProcedures
{
    [Microsoft.SqlServer.Server.SqlProcedure]
    public static void MoveCLR
                (SqlDouble Lat1, SqlDouble Lon1,
                 SqlDouble Dist, SqlDouble Dir,
                 out SqlDouble Lat2, out SqlDouble Lon2,
                 SqlString Unit)
    {
        // This is just a wrapper for the T-SQL interface.
        // Call the proc that does the real work.
        double Lat2d;
        double Lon2d;
        SpatialMove(Lat1.Value, Lon1.Value,
                    Dist.Value, Dir.Value,
                    (Unit.Value.Equals("mi")),
                    out Lat2d, out Lon2d);
        Lat2 = new SqlDouble(Lat2d);
        Lon2 = new SqlDouble(Lon2d);
    }

    public static void SpatialMove
                (double Lat1, double Lon1,
                 double Dist, double Dir,
                 bool Miles,
                 out double Lat2, out double Lon2)
    {
        // Convert degrees to radians
        double Lat1R = Lat1 * Math.PI / 180;
        double Lon1R = Lon1 * Math.PI / 180;
        double DirR = Dir * Math.PI / 180;

        // Convert distance from km/mi to radians
        // Note: DistR = Distance in nautical miles * (pi / (180 * 60))
        //               One nautical mile is 1.852 kilometers, thus:
        //    or: DistR =(DistKM / 1.852) * pi / (180 * 60)
        //    or: DistR = DistKM * pi / (180 * 60 * 1.852)
        //    or: DistR = DistKM * pi / 20001.6
        // Since one mile is 1.609344 kilometers, the formula for miles is:
        //         DistR =(DistMI * 1.609344) * pi / 20001.6
        //    or: DistR = DistMI * pi / (20001.6 / 1.609344)
        //    or: DistR = DistMI * pi / 12428.418038654259126700071581961
        double DistR = Dist * Math.PI
                    / (Miles ? 12428.418038654259126700071581961 : 20001.6);

        // Calculate new latitude
        double Lat2R = Math.Asin(Math.Sin(Lat1R) * Math.Cos(DistR)
```

```
                        + Math.Cos(Lat1R) * Math.Sin(DistR) * Math.Cos(DirR));
            // Convert results back to degrees
            Lat2 = Lat2R * 180 / Math.PI;

            // Calculate longitude difference
            double DLonR = Math.Atan2(Math.Sin(DirR)
                                * Math.Sin(DistR) * Math.Cos(Lat1R),
                                  Math.Cos(DistR)
                                - Math.Sin(Lat1R) * Math.Sin(Lat2R));
            // Calculate new longitude - ensure result is between -PI and PI
            double Lon2R = ((Lon1R - DLonR + Math.PI) % (2 * Math.PI)) - Math.PI;
            // Convert results back to degrees
            Lon2 = Lon2R * 180 / Math.PI;
    }
};
```

■**Note** Splitting the procedure into a wrapper procedure and a separate procedure that does the real work isn't really required in this case, but it makes it easier to reuse the "real work" procedure from other CLR components later. See Chapter 6 for more information.

Searching the Neighborhood

You have probably seen a large number of web sites that allow you to search for all hotels, restaurants, or video rental stores within a set radius of a specific location. Using the table of places in the USA and the user-defined function for distance calculation, you can now do the same (except that you won't find anything useful, like restaurants, since none are loaded into the sample database). Here's a query to find all places that exist within a 10-kilometer radius from a specific location:

```
DECLARE
    @Lat FLOAT,
    @Lon FLOAT,
    @MaxDist FLOAT;

SET @Lat = 47.622;
SET @Lon = -122.35;
SET @MaxDist = 10.0;

WITH PlacePlusDistance
AS
(
    SELECT
        PlaceName,
        State,
        dbo.Distance (Lat, Lon, @Lat, @Lon, 'km') AS Dist
```

```
    FROM Place
)
SELECT
    PlaceName,
    State,
    CAST(Dist AS decimal(6,4)) AS Distance
FROM PlacePlusDistance
WHERE Dist < @MaxDist
ORDER BY Dist ASC;
GO
```

The results from this query are as follows:

```
PlaceName                State Distance
--------------------     ----- ------------
Seattle                  WA    0.0330
Medina                   WA    8.5230
Hunts Point              WA    9.3639
Clyde Hill               WA    9.9352
```

Unfortunately, this query is not very efficient. On my laptop, the query takes on average 254.2 ms. That might seem fairly speedy, but when you consider that a database of hotels will hold millions of rows instead of just 23,000, you'll understand that this spells trouble. A quick look at the execution plan (see Figure 9-3) reveals that a full table scan is used. Not surprising, considering that there's only one filter in the WHERE clause, which filters on a very non-sargable calculation result.

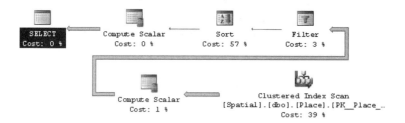

Figure 9-3. *Finding places within a radius requires a clustered index scan.*

Inlining the User-Defined Function

Most SQL Server users probably know that whereas a user-defined function is great for isolating the complexity of the code, it is not so nice for performance. A first attempt to improve performance would be to replace the call to the user-defined function with an inline expression. This results in a horrible query from a readability perspective, but better performance. Running the following "query from hell" on my laptop reduces the average execution time to 65.0 ms, and also results in a simpler execution plan (see Figure 9-4); but it can't prevent the table scan.

```
DECLARE
    @Lat FLOAT,
    @Lon FLOAT,
    @MaxDist FLOAT;

SET @Lat = 47.622;
SET @Lon = -122.35;
SET @MaxDist = 10.0;

WITH PlacePlusDistance
AS
(
    SELECT
        PlaceName,
        State,
        2 * ASIN(SQRT(POWER(SIN((RADIANS(Lat) - RADIANS(@Lat)) / 2), 2)
                    + (COS(RADIANS(Lat)) * COS(RADIANS(@Lat))
                      * POWER(SIN((RADIANS(Lon) - RADIANS(@Lon)) / 2), 2)
                      ))) * 20001.6 / PI() AS Dist
    FROM Place
)
SELECT
    PlaceName,
    State,
    CAST(Dist AS decimal(6,4)) AS Distance
FROM PlacePlusDistance
WHERE Dist < @MaxDist
ORDER BY Dist ASC;
GO
```

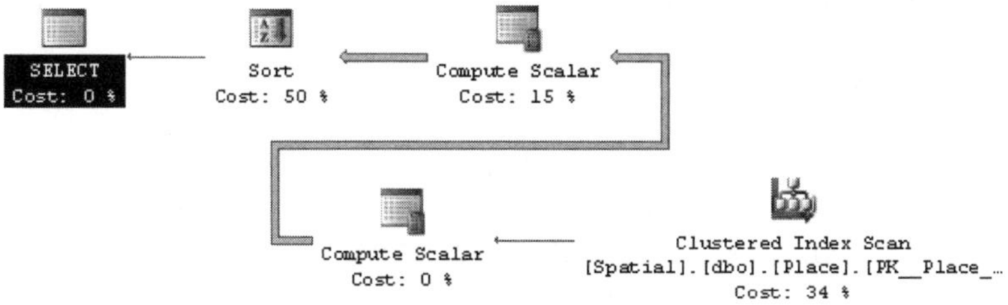

Figure 9-4. *Inlining the calculation simplifies the query plan, but it doesn't get rid of the clustered index scan.*

Employing the CLR

The last option for improving performance of the distance calculation is to implement the function as a CLR user-defined function. Since there is no data access done in the user-defined function, SQL Server doesn't have to set up the environment for data access, unlike within a CLR stored procedure. As a result of this lack of additional overhead, the user-defined function nibbles yet another bit off the execution time.

```csharp
using System;
using System.Data;
using System.Data.SqlClient;
using System.Data.SqlTypes;
using Microsoft.SqlServer.Server;

public partial class UserDefinedFunctions
{
    [Microsoft.SqlServer.Server.SqlFunction(IsDeterministic=true)]
    public static SqlDouble DistCLR
                (SqlDouble Lat1, SqlDouble Lon1,
                 SqlDouble Lat2, SqlDouble Lon2, SqlString Unit)
    {
        // This is just a wrapper for the T-SQL interface.
        // Call the function that does the real work.
        double Dist = SpatialDist(Lat1.Value, Lon1.Value,
                                  Lat2.Value, Lon2.Value,
                                  (Unit.Value.Equals("mi")));
        return new SqlDouble(Dist);
    }


    public static double SpatialDist
                (double Lat1, double Lon1,
                 double Lat2, double Lon2, bool Miles)
    {
        // Convert degrees to radians
        double Lat1R = Lat1 * Math.PI / 180;
        double Lon1R = Lon1 * Math.PI / 180;
        double Lat2R = Lat2 * Math.PI / 180;
        double Lon2R = Lon2 * Math.PI / 180;

        // Calculate distance
        double DistR =
            2 * Math.Asin(Math.Sqrt(Math.Pow(Math.Sin((Lat1R - Lat2R) / 2), 2)
              + (Math.Cos(Lat1R) * Math.Cos(Lat2R)
                * Math.Pow(Math.Sin((Lon1R - Lon2R) / 2), 2))));

        // Convert from radians to kilometers or miles
        double Dist = DistR
                    * (Miles ? 20001.6 / 1.609344 : 20001.6)
                    / Math.PI;

        return Dist;
    }
};
```

With the following query, which uses the CLR user-defined function instead of the T-SQL version, I saw a reduction in the average execution time to only 62.7 ms. This shows that for complex calculations such as these, CLR routines often outperform their T-SQL counterparts.

```
DECLARE
    @Lat FLOAT,
    @Lon FLOAT,
    @MaxDist FLOAT;
SET @Lat = 47.622;
SET @Lon = -122.35;
SET @MaxDist = 10.0;

WITH PlacePlusDistance
AS
(
    SELECT
        PlaceName,
        State,
        dbo.DistCLR (Lat, Lon, @Lat, @Lon, 'km') AS Dist
    FROM Place
)
SELECT
    PlaceName,
    State,
    CAST(Dist AS decimal(6,4)) AS Distance
FROM PlacePlusDistance
WHERE Dist < @MaxDist
ORDER BY Dist ASC;
GO
```

Unfortunately, even the CLR version can't avoid the table scan and thus is still calculating the distance for every single place in the table, as shown in Figure 9-5. The bounding box technique explained in the section "The Bounding Box" enables an index seek (and thus vastly reduces the number of calculations required).

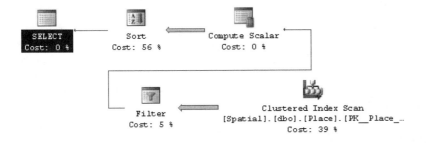

Figure 9-5. *Using the CLR distance function, I'm still getting a table scan.*

The Unavoidable Table Scan

Reducing average execution time from 254.2 ms to 62.7 ms is good, of course—but utterly useless without also finding a way to get rid of the table scan. Don't forget that our test table holds only a mere 23,000 rows. Imagine having to execute this query against a table holding the positions of all pine trees in America. Or worse: all Starbucks locations!

One of the first things I always look into when optimizing queries is the potential for using covering indexes. In this case, there's not much to be gained. Not only because all the longer columns are used in the query, so that the number of bytes per row for the covering index would be only slightly less than that of the clustered index, but also because most of the 60.0 ms execution time is spent in calculating the distance. The only way to really reduce the execution time is to ensure that the optimizer can produce a plan with a seek operator instead of a scan operator, so that the number of rows passed into the distance calculation can be reduced.

Of course, the optimizer can only produce a plan with a seek operator if the query has at least one sargable filter—a filter in the form of `indexed-column >= expression` or such. None of the queries already shown have such a filter, so the formula has to be rewritten. With all the trigonometric expressions in the formula, this is no easy task, so I tried rewriting it using the simpler Pythagorean theorem–based method first (see the sidebar "Rewriting the Pythagorean Theorem"). As it turns out, this won't help us here. The minimum and maximum values for latitude depend on the longitude, and vice versa—just as the minimum and maximum values of x depend on the actual value of y in a two-dimensional space.

REWRITING THE PYTHAGOREAN THEOREM

Earlier in this chapter, I explained how the Pythagorean theorem can be used for distance calculations on flat surfaces and for short distances on the earth's surface. When used for a neighborhood search, this formula suffers the same problem as the geospatial formula used in this chapter: when used as given, it doesn't result in a sargable filter in the WHERE clause. It has to be rewritten to the form of x2 >= (expression) AND x2 <= (expression). Remember that the distance between two points (x1, y1) and (x2, y2) is

$$Distance = \sqrt{(x2 - x1)^2 + (y2 - y1)^2}$$

This means that for any given point (x1, y1), all points with a maximum distance D satisfy this equation:

$$\sqrt{(x2 - x1)^2 + (y2 - y1)^2} \leq D$$

Square both sides to get

$$(x2 - x1)^2 + (y2 - y1)^2 \leq D^2$$

Now subtract (y2 − y1)^2 from both sides.

$$(x2 - x1)^2 \leq D^2 - (y2 - y1)^2$$

Take the square root of both sides—remember that a square root can be negative as well!

$$-\sqrt{D^2 - (y2 - y1)^2} \leq x2 - x1 \leq \sqrt{D^2 - (y2 - y1)^2}$$

Finally, add x1 to both sides to get

$$x1 - \sqrt{D^2 - (y2 - y1)^2} \le x2 \le x1 + \sqrt{D^2 - (y2 - y1)^2}$$

This can be translated to the following T-SQL expression:

```
WHERE
    x2 >= x1 - SQRT(POWER(D, 2) - POWER(y2 - y1, 2))
    AND x2 <= x1 + SQRT(POWER(D, 2) - POWER(y2 - y1, 2))
```

Unfortunately, this rewrite won't help us get an index seek operator in the execution plan, even though the filter now abides by the form requirements for sargable filters. The reason is that the expressions on the right-hand side of the predicate are not constant; their value changes with each row in the table, which makes them unsuitable for use in a seek operator.

This actually makes sense when you think about what we're trying to do. All points at a maximum distance D of point (x1, y1) are in a circle with (x1, y1) at the center and radius equal to D. This means that the minimum and maximum values for x2 depend on the y2 value, but the minimum and maximum values for y2 in turn depend on the x2 value. Due to this mutual dependency between x2 and y2, it is in fact impossible to rewrite the distance filter into a sargable expression.

The Bounding Box

Now that I have established the impossibility of writing the maximum distance filter as a sargable expression, it's time to explore the alternative: finding a way to limit the number of points that have to be passed to the distance calculation function. Creating a square that encloses the circular area to be searched is the most efficient way to limit the input set. If you imagine a square just outside of the circle (see Figure 9-6), you'll note that each point that is within the circle will also be within the square (though the reverse is not always true).

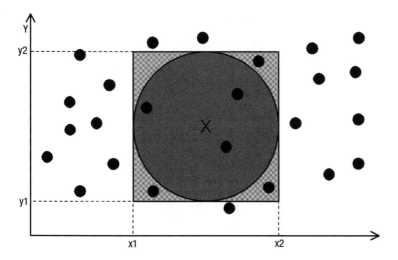

Figure 9-6. *Using the bounding box to limit the number of points to review*

Figure 9-6 shows a total of 25 points. Normally, the distance for each of those 25 would have to be calculated to determine whether the point is within the maximum distance of the start point of the search (marked X in Figure 9-6). A lot of work can be saved by precalculating the minimum and maximum values of x and y (x1, x2, y1, and y2 in Figure 9-6). With those values, it is trivial to test whether a point is within the **bounding box** (X between x1 and x2, and Y between y1 and y2). The full distance calculation is then needed for only the six points that satisfy this preliminary test, after which 3 out of the 6 points will be left as the result of the search.

Though the surface of our planet is curved rather than flat, the same principle can still be applied. To leverage this for use in our queries, we need to find a way to determine the minimum and maximum values for the longitude and latitude. That's actually quite easy—just use the Move stored procedure that we implemented earlier to move the maximum distance north, south, east, and west from the starting point to find the boundaries of the bounding box.

■**Note** Special case handling is needed if the bounding box spans the North Pole, the South Pole, or the 180th meridian. Because that's not a standard requirement, adding code for these special cases is left as an exercise for you to try on your own.

The optimized algorithm for searching the neighborhood consists of two steps. The first step is to find the minimum and maximum values for longitude and latitude; the second step uses one of the queries already presented, but with the bounding box as an additional filter in the WHERE clause, in order to limit the number of rows for which the distance calculation is carried out. Here's the T-SQL code required to implement this two-step implementation:[3]

```
DECLARE
    @Lat FLOAT,
    @Lon FLOAT,
    @MaxDist FLOAT;

SET @Lat = 47.622;
SET @Lon = -122.35;
SET @MaxDist = 10.0;

DECLARE
    @LatMin FLOAT,
    @LatMax FLOAT,
    @LonMin FLOAT,
    @LonMax FLOAT,
    @Dummy  FLOAT;
```

---

3. Remember to use the T-SQL version for the Move procedure and the CLR version for the Distance function, since these are the fastest.

```
-- Determine minimum and maximum latitude and longitude
EXEC Move
    @Lat,
    @Lon,
    @MaxDist,
    0,                 -- North
    @LatMax OUTPUT,
    @Dummy  OUTPUT,    -- Don't need this
    'km';

EXEC Move
    @Lat,
    @Lon,
    @MaxDist,
    90,                -- West
    @Dummy  OUTPUT,    -- Don't need this
    @LonMin OUTPUT,
    'km';

EXEC Move
    @Lat,
    @Lon,
    @MaxDist,
    180,               -- South
    @LatMin OUTPUT,
    @Dummy  OUTPUT,    -- Don't need this
    'km';

EXEC Move
    @Lat,
    @Lon,
    @MaxDist,
    -90,               -- East
    @Dummy  OUTPUT,    -- Don't need this
    @LonMax OUTPUT,
    'km';

WITH PlacePlusDistance
AS
(
    SELECT
        PlaceName,
        State,
        dbo.DistCLR (Lat, Lon, @Lat, @Lon, 'km') AS Dist
    FROM Place
```

```
    WHERE
        Lat BETWEEN @LatMin AND @LatMax
        AND Lon BETWEEN @LonMin AND @LonMax
)
SELECT
    PlaceName,
    State,
    CAST(Dist AS decimal(6,4)) AS Distance
FROM PlacePlusDistance
WHERE Dist < @MaxDist
ORDER BY Dist ASC;
GO
```

There are no indexes defined for Place that can be used here, so this query yet again results in a table scan—but because places outside of the bounding box can be discarded before the distance is calculated, the execution time still drops significantly. The average execution time is now down to 3.82 ms.

To *really* leverage the bounding box, you have to add an index on either one or both of the longitude and latitude columns. I tried various permutations and found that the following index yields the best performance for the examples covered thus far:

```
CREATE INDEX ix_LonLat ON Place(Lon,Lat)
INCLUDE(State, PlaceName);
```

This index permits the query optimizer to compile a plan with an index seek, based on the longitude. The latitude is then used to further reduce the number of rows for which the distance has to be calculated. The included columns make this index covering for the query: since all columns used in the query are included in the index itself, no clustered index lookup is required to obtain the rest of the data.

After creating this index and rerunning the preceding code, the execution plan reveals that I am finally rid of the table scan (see Figure 9-7). This results in another tremendous boost to performance, taking average execution time down to a mere 0.973 ms.

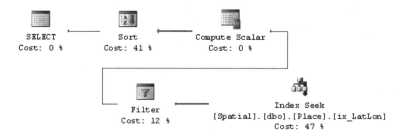

Figure 9-7. *Thanks to the bounding box, I now have an index seek.*

Encapsulating the Code

The preceding code is so complex that it just begs to be included in a single unit. There are basically two options for this encapsulation: a stored procedure or a table-valued user-defined function.

The first option, the stored procedure, is so trivial that I won't waste any words on how to achieve it. Unfortunately, this option lacks flexibility—it's not possible to use the results of a stored procedure directly in a query, and it's also not possible to call a stored procedure for each row in a query without using row-by-row processing. For example, getting a list of all cities in Texas that are more than 5 but less than 10 kilometers apart from each other would require both a cursor (to loop over all of the cities in Texas) and a temporary table (to hold the neighbors for each given city). Embedding the code to find neighbors in a user-defined function would be much nicer, since you could then achieve the same task in a single query, by using the CROSS APPLY operator as follows:

```
SELECT
    p.PlaceName AS pPlace,
    p.State AS pState,
    n.PlaceName,
    n.State,
    n.Dist
FROM Place AS p
CROSS APPLY dbo.GetNeighbors(p.Lat, p.Lon, 10, 'km') AS n
WHERE
    p.State = 'TX'
    AND n.State = 'TX'
    AND n.Dist > 5;
GO
```

Unfortunately, there is one big hurdle that prevents me from just enclosing the preceding code in the definition of a table-valued user-defined function: SQL Server 2005 disallows executing stored procedures from within a user-defined function. So, what are the options?

1. Change the Move stored procedure to a user-defined function. This is only possible after implementing a user-defined type for storing latitude and longitude of a single point as a single scalar value. This is definitely a good option—but as mentioned before, it is out of the scope of this chapter.

2. Copy and paste the code in the Move stored procedure inside the user-defined function GetNeighbors. Since the stored procedure has to be called four times, that will result in four copies of the code in the function—certainly not great from a maintainability point of view.

3. Implement the complete user-defined function as a CLR user-defined table-valued function.

I will explore the two other options in the following sections.

Encapsulating in T-SQL

Without implementing a user-defined type for points, the only way to implement a table-valued function to leverage the bounding box technique requires the duplication of the code from Move inside the function, no less than four times. The good news is that the longitude calculation can be left out for two of the four repetitions. The bad news is that, even after that simplification, the resulting code is still quite ugly:

```
CREATE FUNCTION dbo.GetNeighbors
(
    @Lat FLOAT,
    @Lon FLOAT,
    @MaxDist FLOAT,
    @Unit CHAR(2) = 'km'
)
RETURNS @Neighbors TABLE
(
    PlaceName VARCHAR(100) NOT NULL,
    State CHAR(2) NOT NULL,
    Dist FLOAT NOT NULL
)
AS
BEGIN
    DECLARE
        @LatMin FLOAT,
        @LatMax FLOAT,
        @LonMin FLOAT,
        @LonMax FLOAT,
        @Lat1R FLOAT,
        @Lon1R FLOAT,
        @Lat2R FLOAT,
        @Lon2R FLOAT,
        @DLonR FLOAT,
        @MaxDistR FLOAT,
        @DirR  FLOAT;

    -- Convert from degrees to radians
    SET @Lat1R = RADIANS(@Lat);
    SET @Lon1R = RADIANS(@Lon);

    IF @Unit = 'km'
        SET @MaxDistR = @MaxDist * PI() / 20001.6;
    ELSE
        SET @MaxDistR = @MaxDist * PI() / 12428.418038654259126700071581961;

    -- Determine minimum and maximum latitude and longitude
    -- Calculate latitude of north boundary
    SET @DirR  = RADIANS(0e0);
    SET @Lat2R = ASIN( SIN(@Lat1R) * COS(@MaxDistR)
                    + COS(@Lat1R) * SIN(@MaxDistR) * COS(@DirR));
    -- Convert back to degrees
    SET @LatMax = DEGREES(@Lat2R);

    -- Calculate longitude of west boundary
    SET @DirR  = RADIANS(90e0);
```

```
-- Need latitude first
SET @Lat2R = ASIN( SIN(@Lat1R) * COS(@MaxDistR)
                 + COS(@Lat1R) * SIN(@MaxDistR) * COS(@DirR));
-- Calculate longitude difference.
SET @DLonR = ATN2(SIN(@DirR)  * SIN(@MaxDistR) * COS(@Lat1R),
                  COS(@MaxDistR) - SIN(@Lat1R) * SIN(@Lat2R));
-- Calculate longitude of new point - ensure result is between -PI and PI.
SET @Lon2R = ( CAST(@Lon1R - @DLonR + PI() AS DECIMAL(38,37))
             % CAST(2*PI() AS DECIMAL(38,37)))
             - PI();
-- Convert back to degrees
SET @LonMin = DEGREES(@Lon2R);


-- Calculate latitude of south boundary
SET @DirR  = RADIANS(180e0);
SET @Lat2R = ASIN( SIN(@Lat1R) * COS(@MaxDistR)
                 + COS(@Lat1R) * SIN(@MaxDistR) * COS(@DirR));
-- Convert back to degrees
SET @LatMin = DEGREES(@Lat2R);


-- Calculate longitude of west boundary
SET @DirR  = RADIANS(-90e0);
-- Need latitude first
SET @Lat2R = ASIN( SIN(@Lat1R) * COS(@MaxDistR)
                 + COS(@Lat1R) * SIN(@MaxDistR) * COS(@DirR));
-- Calculate longitude difference.
SET @DLonR = ATN2(SIN(@DirR)  * SIN(@MaxDistR) * COS(@Lat1R),
                  COS(@MaxDistR) - SIN(@Lat1R) * SIN(@Lat2R));
-- Calculate longitude of new point - ensure result is between -PI and PI.
SET @Lon2R = ( CAST(@Lon1R - @DLonR + PI() AS DECIMAL(38,37))
             % CAST(2*PI() AS DECIMAL(38,37)))
             - PI();
-- Convert back to degrees
SET @LonMax = DEGREES(@Lon2R);


-- Search neighborhood within boundaries
WITH PlacePlusDistance
AS
(
    SELECT
        PlaceName,
        State,
        dbo.DistCLR (Lat, Lon, @Lat, @Lon, @Unit) AS Dist
    FROM Place
    WHERE
        Lat BETWEEN @LatMin AND @LatMax
        AND Lon BETWEEN @LonMin AND @LonMax
)
```

```
        INSERT INTO @Neighbors
        (
            PlaceName,
            State,
            Dist
        )
        SELECT
            PlaceName,
            State,
            Dist
        FROM PlacePlusDistance
        WHERE Dist < @MaxDist;
        RETURN;
END;
GO
```

Once this table-valued user-defined function is created, we can use it like this:

```
SELECT
    PlaceName,
    State,
    CAST(Dist AS decimal(6,4)) AS Distance
FROM dbo.GetNeighbors (@Lat, @Lon, @MaxDist, 'km')
ORDER BY Dist ASC;
GO
```

This is much cleaner than having to repeat the complete bounding box logic each time neighbors have to be found. It does incur a slight performance loss, though. The average execution time for this user-defined function drops from 0.973 ms to 0.980 ms for the single test location. Finding cities in Texas that are more than 5 but less than 10 kilometers apart from each other (see earlier for query) takes 428 ms.

Encapsulating Using the CLR

Another way to encapsulate the code is by using a CLR user-defined table-valued function. The code for such a function, called CLRNeighbors, follows. In this function, I reuse the SpatialMove and SpatialDist functions that I implemented earlier.

```
using System;
using System.Data;
using System.Data.SqlClient;
using System.Data.SqlTypes;
using Microsoft.SqlServer.Server;
using System.Collections;
using System.Collections.Generic;

public partial class UserDefinedFunctions
{
    public struct BBox
```

```
{
    public SqlString PlaceName;
    public SqlString State;
    public SqlDouble Dist;
    public BBox(SqlString PlaceName, SqlString State, SqlDouble Dist)
    {
        PlaceName = PlaceName;
        State = State;
        Dist = Dist;
    }
}

[Microsoft.SqlServer.Server.SqlFunction(IsDeterministic = true,
  DataAccess = DataAccessKind.Read, FillRowMethodName = "FillRow",
  TableDefinition = "PlaceName NVARCHAR(100), State NCHAR(2), Dist FLOAT")]
public static IEnumerable CLRNeighbors(SqlDouble LatIn, SqlDouble LonIn,
                                       SqlDouble MaxDistIn, SqlString Unit)
{
    double Lat = LatIn.Value, Lon = LonIn.Value, MaxDist = MaxDistIn.Value;
    double LatMax, LatMin, LonMax, LonMin, Dummy;
    bool Miles = (Unit.Value.Equals("mi"));
    // Calculate minimum and maximum longitude and latitude
    StoredProcedures.SpatialMove(Lat, Lon, MaxDist, 0,    // North
                                 Miles, out LatMax, out Dummy);
    StoredProcedures.SpatialMove(Lat, Lon, MaxDist, 90,   // West
                                 Miles, out Dummy, out LonMin);
    StoredProcedures.SpatialMove(Lat, Lon, MaxDist, 180,  // South
                                 Miles, out LatMin, out Dummy);
    StoredProcedures.SpatialMove(Lat, Lon, MaxDist, -90,  // East
                                 Miles, out Dummy, out LonMax);

    List<BBox> BBdata = new List<BBox>();

    using (SqlConnection conn =
        new SqlConnection("context connection = true"))
    {
        SqlCommand comm =
            new SqlCommand("" +
                "SELECT " +
                    "PlaceName, " +
                    "State, " +
                    "Lat, " +
                    "Lon " +
                "FROM Place " +
                "WHERE " +
                    "Lat BETWEEN @LatMin AND @LatMax " +
                    "AND Lon BETWEEN @LonMin AND @LonMax", conn);
```

```
                comm.Parameters.Add("@LatMin", SqlDbType.Float);
                comm.Parameters[0].Value = LatMin;
                comm.Parameters.Add("@LatMax", SqlDbType.Float);
                comm.Parameters[1].Value = LatMax;
                comm.Parameters.Add("@LonMin", SqlDbType.Float);
                comm.Parameters[2].Value = LonMin;
                comm.Parameters.Add("@LonMax", SqlDbType.Float);
                comm.Parameters[3].Value = LonMax;

                conn.Open();
                SqlDataReader reader = comm.ExecuteReader();

                while (reader.Read())
                {
                    double Lat2 = reader.GetDouble(2);
                    double Lon2 = reader.GetDouble(3);
                    double Dist = SpatialDist(Lat, Lon, Lat2, Lon2, Miles);
                    if (Dist <= MaxDist)
                    {
                        SqlString PlaceName = reader.GetSqlString(0);
                        SqlString State = reader.GetSqlString(1);
                        BBox BBnew = new BBox(PlaceName,
                                              State,
                                              (SqlDouble)Dist);
                        BBdata.Add(BBnew);
                    }
                }
            }

            return (IEnumerable)BBdata;
        }

        public static void FillRow(Object obj, out SqlString PlaceName,
                            out SqlString State, out SqlDouble Dist)
        {
            BBox bb = (BBox)obj;
            PlaceName = bb.PlaceName;
            State = bb.State;
            Dist = bb.Dist;
        }
};
```

The code to invoke this CLR user-defined function is almost identical to the code to invoke the T-SQL version of the function:

```
SELECT
    PlaceName,
    State,
```

```
    CAST(Dist AS decimal(6,4)) AS Distance
FROM dbo.CLRNeighbors (@Lat, @Lon, @MaxDist, 'km')
ORDER BY Dist ASC;
GO
```

Since the CLR version of the function is invoked in exactly the same way as its T-SQL counterpart, the only possible reasons to choose one or the other would be personal preference or performance. *My* personal preference would be the CLR version, because I hate duplicating code, as is done in the T-SQL version, even in a function that I code once and expect to never have to look at again. And fortunately, the CLR version results in better performance as well.[4] The preceding code takes on average 0.957 ms with the index, 2.3% faster than the T-SQL version of the function. And the Texan city list runs in 388 milliseconds with the CLR implementation, a 9% improvement.

■**Tip** The CLR version of the function can get even faster by not reading PlaceName and State from SQL Server, storing them in the List<BBox> and returning them in the function results. Instead, the function can read, store, and return only the primary key of the Place table, the BIGINT HtmID. This shaves off about 10% of the execution time—but to get the output I need (using human-readable state and place names instead of the HtmID code), I have to add another join. And because SQL Server can't predict the number of rows the function will return, I also have to add an optimizer hint to help it pick a good execution plan. With the hint, the performance gain of the user-defined function can sometimes exceed the additional cost of this join, resulting in a net performance gain—but only if the number of rows returned from the function is very small. My tests showed this alternative to be detrimental to my standard neighborhood search test (with average execution time up to 1.05 ms), but beneficial to the Texas test (execution time down to 345 ms).

The Bottom Line

Searching all locations within a given distance from a point can be achieved efficiently, but only when implemented with care. My first attempt to search the neighborhood of a point took over a quarter of a second for a single search in a relatively small (22,993 rows) table. After moving some of the calculations to the CLR, employing the bounding box technique and adding a covering index, the execution time decreased to less than a millisecond, but the code became very complex.

Good application design requires complex code to be encapsulated. I have shown two ways to achieve this, one in T-SQL and the other using the CLR. In both cases, encapsulating the code reduced efficiency somewhat, but execution time was still submillisecond. The CLR version turned out to be slightly faster than the T-SQL version.

---

4. Thanks to SQL Server MVPs Alejandro Mesa, Adam Machanic, and Simon Sabin, who went to great lengths to help me turn my sloppy and sluggish original code into the great end product you see here.

GETTING RELIABLE PERFORMANCE MEASUREMENTS

In both this section and the next one, I mention a lot of average execution times. Getting reliable measurements for these posed several problems. The first problem was the easiest to solve: since I used a fairly limited test set of only 23,000 rows, many of the queries lasted only a single millisecond or less—well below the accuracy of 3.33 milliseconds for SQL Server's DATETIME data type. I solved this by putting the query in a loop (sending the results to a temporary table, of course, to prevent any client slowness from hampering the measurements) and executing it 10, 100, or even 1,000 times in a row, to get the total execution time in the range of one to a few seconds. And as a bonus, I would also average out the usual random dips and peaks in activity on my laptop. At least, that was what I thought. I turned out to be wrong when I reexecuted some tests. Most queries used approximately the same execution time, with only a few percent difference, but not all. The worst offender of the bunch displayed execution times for 1,000 executions ranging from 890 up to 2,516 milliseconds! So I built another loop around the first loop. Each test would be executed 10, 100, or 1,000 times and the execution times would be stored in a table—and then the whole process would start over again. After 1,000 repetitions, I discarded the 100 slowest and the 100 fastest executions of each query and calculated the average of the remaining execution times. Those are the figures you see in these sections.

```
WITH RankedResults
AS
(
    SELECT
        TestGroup,
        TestName,
        CONVERT(FLOAT, Duration) / Repetitions AS AvgDuration,
        ROW_NUMBER () OVER (
            PARTITION BY TestGroup, TestName
            ORDER BY CONVERT(FLOAT, Duration) / Repetitions
        ) AS rn,
        COUNT(*) OVER (
            PARTITION BY TestGroup, TestName
        ) AS cnt
    FROM TestResults
)
SELECT
    TestGroup,
    TestName,
    AVG(AvgDuration) AS AvgDur,
    MAX(AvgDuration) AS MaxDur,
    MIN(AvgDuration) AS MinDur,
    (MAX(AvgDuration) - MIN(AvgDuration)) / AVG(AvgDuration) AS MaxDiff
FROM RankedResults
WHERE
    rn BETWEEN FLOOR((cnt + 10) * 0.1)
    AND CEILING(cnt * 0.9)
GROUP BY
    TestGroup,
    TestName
```

```
ORDER BY
    TestGroup,
    AvgDur ASC;
GO
```

Finding the Nearest Neighbor

Another common requirement is to find the single nearest neighbor. Examples of this requirement include answering questions such as "What is the nearest hotel to Kennedy Airport,"
"For each movie theater, where is the nearest pub," or "Which pickup truck is closest to each
of our customers with a pending pickup request?" This problem is closely related to the neighborhood search covered previously, but with two differences. First, the number of rows to be
returned is always one for each input row (except, possibly, in the case of ties). And second,
there is no information known in advance about what the maximum distance will be. This
means that we can't use the bounding box technique, as that technique relies on knowing the
distance to be searched (in order to actually build the bounding sides).

The Straightforward Approach

Suppose that my manager walks into my office and says that he needs a report showing the
nearest other place for each place in America, with no additional constraints. What is the best
way to solve this problem? I can of course use the fastest of the neighborhood search techniques
without the bounding box technique, remove the filter on maximum distance and replace it
with a TOP(1) expression to return only the lowest distance. Here's how that query looks:

```
SELECT
    f.PlaceName AS PlaceFrom,
    f.State AS StateFrom,
    t.PlaceName AS PlaceTo,
    t.State AS StateTo,
    t.Dist
FROM Place AS f
OUTER APPLY
(
    SELECT TOP (1)
        PlaceName,
        State,
        dbo.DistCLR (f.Lat, f.Lon, p.Lat, p.Lon, 'km') AS Dist
    FROM Place AS p
    WHERE
        -- Place is always nearest to itself - exclude this row
        p.HtmID <> f.HtmID
        -- Filter below is only to speed up testing
        AND p.State = 'IL'
    ORDER BY Dist
) AS t
```

```
-- Filter below is only to speed up testing
WHERE f.State = 'IL';
GO
```

To speed up testing, I have added a filter to restrict the operation to just the places in the state of Illinois. Even for these 1,308 places, finding the nearest neighbor for each place takes over 7.2 seconds. Since performance degrades exponentially as the number of rows increases, I expect the query to run for at least half an hour if I remove the filter on State to process all 22,993 rows in the sample table. For a real application with hundreds of thousands or even millions of rows in the table, execution time would easily run into days, if not weeks. This is unacceptable, especially when the data you are dealing with is prone to change—for instance, when the table holds the current locations of all UPS delivery vehicles worldwide. For more static data, you could perhaps schedule the query to run during off hours and save the result, but run time would still be quite slow.

■**Note** I have also tried a query that uses the RANK() function and filters on the value 1 rather than using the proprietary TOP(1) syntax. Unfortunately, this version turned out to run almost twice as slow as the version presented here.

Why the Bounding Box Won't Work

Since the straightforward approach results in unacceptable performance, I clearly have to identify a better technique. I have already found that the bounding box technique will result in a dramatic improvement of performance for neighborhood searches. The only problem is that in order to use the bounding box, I have to set a maximum distance for the search. In this case, my manager has asked me to list the nearest neighbor without specifying this distance.

If I still want to use the bounding box technique, I will have to come up with a maximum distance myself. To get an idea of what a sensible maximum distance might be, I started from the earlier query to find nearest neighbors in Illinois and ordered the results by distance. The maximum distance between two nearest neighbors turns out to be a little over 17.6 kilometers (in case it ever comes up in a trivia quiz—that's the distance from Marshall to Martinsville). So it would seem in this case that setting the maximum distance to 20 kilometers should be enough. That results in the following query:

```
DECLARE @MaxDist FLOAT;
SET @MaxDist = 20.0;

SELECT
    f.PlaceName AS PlaceFrom,
    f.State AS StateFrom,
    t.PlaceName AS PlaceTo,
    t.State AS StateTo,
    t.Dist
FROM Place AS f
CROSS APPLY
(
```

```
SELECT TOP (1)
    n.PlaceName,
    n.State,
    n.Dist
FROM dbo.CLRNeighbors (f.Lat, f.Lon, @MaxDist, 'km') AS n
WHERE
    -- Place is always nearest to itself - exclude this row
    n.Dist <> 0
    -- Filter below is only to speed up testing
    AND n.State = 'IL'
ORDER BY n.Dist
) AS t
-- Filter below is only to speed up testing
WHERE f.State = 'IL';
GO
```

With the filter to reduce the search to just the state of Illinois in place, this query finishes in 0.885 seconds. This is greater than an 87% improvement over my previous attempt. Even better news is that after introducing the boundary box, performance now degrades linearly rather than exponentially as the number of rows increases. If I remove the filters, so as to find the nearest neighbor for each place in the USA, the results are returned in just 12.4 seconds.

Unfortunately, the results returned are not only fast, but also incomplete. The result set has 22,056 rows, rather than the expected 22,993. So where are the other 937 rows? Why are they not listed? The answer is simple—they were omitted because for these places, there was not a single neighbor within 20 kilometers. That causes the result of CLRNeighbors to be empty, hence the row is omitted. If I had used OUTER APPLY rather than CROSS APPLY, I would have gotten all 22,997 rows in my result set, but with NULL in the PlaceTo, StateTo, and Dist columns.

So clearly a 20 kilometer maximum distance is not enough to get the nearest neighbor for each place in our table. If I want to pursue this technique, I'll have to increase the maximum distance. For my next experiment, I increased @MaxDist to 40 kilometers. Since this results in a larger bounding box, the function CLRNeighbors will have to calculate the distance for more places. This has a severe impact on performance—the time needed to find the nearest neighbor for all places in the table goes from 12.4 to 25.3 seconds. And the list is still not complete: I now have 22,853 rows in the result set, which means that there are still 140 rows missing.

I can of course continue to increase @MaxDist, but with each increment, I will lose more performance. Once I set @MaxDist to 120—and waited over two minutes—the query finally returned the nearest neighbor for each of the 22,993 rows in the table. However, one should not forget that the @MaxDist of 120 is valid for *this* data only! As soon as people start changing data, this distance might not be sufficient any longer, again causing rows to be left out of the result of the query for the nearest neighbor. As an extreme example, let's assume that management decides that the capitol of each country in the world has to be added to the table. Distances between capitols are of course much bigger than between cities and towns in the United States, so I'd probably have to set @MaxDist to well over a thousand kilometers—and it would perform almost as bad, or maybe even worse, than the straightforward approach covered in the previous section.

The Dynamic Bounding Box

The reason that the bounding box technique doesn't work is that a fixed maximum distance is used to calculate the boundaries. This maximum distance has to be big enough to ensure that the nearest neighbor is found in even the sparsest populated areas, but this big maximum distance causes way too many places to fall inside the boundaries (and hence way too many distance calculations to be performed) in more densely populated areas.

An ideal solution would be to change the distance of the boundaries based on how densely populated a region is. The only problem here is that I have to find a way to get a reasonable approximation of the maximum distance to use without spending too much computer time on it.

You may recall that I have created a covering index to speed up the neighborhood search several pages ago. To save you the hassle of flipping pages, here's the definition of that index once more:

```
CREATE INDEX ix_LonLat ON Place(Lon,Lat)
INCLUDE(State, PlaceName);
```

Since Lon is the first column in this index, it is ideally suited for finding the place that has the lowest higher (or the highest lower) longitude from a give place. We can, of course, be sure that this place is never nearer than the nearest neighbor. We could be extremely lucky and find that this place actually *is* the nearest neighbor, or at least very close to it. Or we could be unlucky and find a place with almost the same longitude on the Canadian border, whereas we're searching for the nearest neighbor of a place near Mexico.

If we don't stop at one, but instead examine several places just a bit to the east and a few places just a bit to the west of a given place, there's a fair chance that at least one of those places will be reasonably close on the North-South axis as well, so it will be reasonably close to the nearest neighbor. For example, consider Seattle. If I take one town in the US that's just to the west of Seattle, I might get lucky and catch another town in Washington, or I might get unlucky and find a town in California. In the latter case, the bounding box would be way too big. If, on the other hand, I examine the 20 places just to the west of Seattle, chances are that at least one of them will be in Washington, and probably even quite close to Seattle.

And that's the key to the dynamic bounding box algorithm. Before I get to the code, here's the pseudo-code for the algorithm to get the nearest neighbor of a place P:

1. Find a number[5] of places with the lowest longitude greater than P's longitude.

2. Find a number of places with the highest longitude less than P's longitude.

3. Calculate distance to P for all places found.

4. Find neighbors of P with @MaxDist set to the lowest calculated distance.

5. Return the neighbor with the minimum distance.

---

5. The ideal number of places to use here will have to be determined by trial and error.

> **■Note** I have chosen to have longitude before latitude in the index, and to base the search for the boundaries of the dynamic bounding box on longitude, because the sample data is based on the USA. The maximum east-to-west distance in the USA is higher than the maximum north-to-south distance. Therefore, the selectivity for longitude is higher as the selectivity for latitude. For a country where the north-south distances exceed the east-west distances (such as Japan, Italy, or Argentina), performance would improve when basing the boundary search on the closest latitude and supporting it with an index on (`Lat`, `Lon`).

The T-SQL Implementation

The pseudo-code for the dynamic bounding box presented earlier is thoroughly algorithmic in nature. And while it would certainly be possible to implement it as described in T-SQL, it would probably not yield the best performance. After all, SQL Server is optimized toward giving the best performance for set-based queries.

In order to get a set-based implementation of the dynamic bounding box, I'll look at the individual steps. The first two steps are finding the places just to the east and just to the west of a starting point and calculating their distances to that starting point. The following query does exactly that (returning only the calculated distance, as that's the only thing I'm interested in at the moment) for the eastern side:

```
SELECT TOP(@top)
    dbo.DistCLR(@Lat, @Lon, Lat, Lon, 'km') AS Dist
FROM Place
WHERE Lon > @Lon
ORDER BY Lon ASC;
GO
```

For the western side, the same query can be used, except that the longitude now has to be less than the input longitude, and the `ORDER BY` that qualifies the `TOP(@top)` clause has to be reversed. Getting all the distances of places near the starting point is a simple matter of combining these two queries with `UNION ALL`—except that both have to be enclosed in their own derived table construction, as otherwise the optimizer uses the last `ORDER BY` to order the results after applying the `UNION ALL` operator, instead of using it to qualify the second `TOP(@top)` clause.

```
SELECT Dist
FROM
(
    SELECT TOP(@top)
        dbo.DistCLR(@Lat, @Lon, Lat, Lon, 'km') AS Dist
    FROM Place
    WHERE Lon > @Lon
    ORDER BY Lon ASC
) AS East

UNION ALL
```

```
SELECT Dist
FROM
(
    SELECT TOP(@top)
        dbo.DistCLR(@Lat, @Lon, Lat, Lon, 'km') AS Dist
    FROM Place
    WHERE Lon < @Lon
    ORDER BY Lon DESC
) AS West;
GO
```

All that is left to do now is to wrap the preceding query in yet another derived table construction and do a SELECT MIN(Dist) from it, and the result is the value to use as maximum distance for the bounding box. But unfortunately, this is just the value for one place. To get the dynamic bounding box distance for each place, we have to transform this into a correlated subquery and replace @Lat and @Lon with references to Lat and Lon in the outer query. This results in the following query, which lists place, state, latitude, longitude, and bounding box distance for each place in the Place table:

```
SELECT
    p.PlaceName,
    p.State,
    p.Lat,
    p.Lon,
    (
        SELECT MIN(Dist)
        FROM
        (
            SELECT Dist
            FROM
            (
                SELECT TOP(@top)
                    dbo.DistCLR(p.Lat, p.Lon, Lat, Lon, 'km') AS Dist
                FROM Place
                WHERE Lon > p.Lon
                ORDER BY Lon ASC
            ) AS East

            UNION ALL

            SELECT Dist
            FROM
            (
                SELECT TOP(@top)
                    dbo.DistCLR(p.Lat, p.Lon, Lat, Lon, 'km') AS Dist
                FROM Place
                WHERE Lon < p.Lon
                ORDER BY Lon DESC
```

```
              ) AS West
          ) AS Near
      ) AS MaxDist
FROM Place AS p;
GO
```

The result set of this query is exactly what I need for the dynamic bounding box. All that's left to do is to define a common table expression on the preceding query and use that, instead of `Place`, in the bounding box query used earlier. The final result looks like this:

```
DECLARE @top int;
SET @top = 31;
WITH PlacePlusMaxDist
AS
(
    SELECT
        p.PlaceName,
        p.State,
        p.Lat,
        p.Lon,
        (
            SELECT MIN(Dist) + 0.0001
            FROM
            (
                SELECT Dist
                FROM
                (
                    SELECT TOP(@top)
                        dbo.DistCLR(p.Lat, p.Lon, Lat, Lon, 'km') AS Dist
                    FROM Place
                    WHERE Lon > p.Lon
                    ORDER BY Lon ASC
                ) AS East

                UNION ALL

                SELECT Dist
                FROM
                (
                    SELECT TOP(@top)
                        dbo.DistCLR(p.Lat, p.Lon, Lat, Lon, 'km') AS Dist
                    FROM Place
                    WHERE Lon < p.Lon
                    ORDER BY Lon DESC
                ) AS West
            ) AS Near
        ) AS MaxDist
    FROM Place AS p
)
```

```
SELECT
    f.PlaceName AS PlaceFrom,
    f.State AS StateFrom,
    t.PlaceName AS PlaceTo,
    t.State AS StateTo,
    t.Dist
FROM PlacePlusMaxDist AS f
CROSS APPLY
(
    SELECT TOP (1)
        n.PlaceName,
        n.State,
        n.Dist
    FROM dbo.CLRNeighbors (f.Lat, f.Lon, f.MaxDist, 'km') AS n
    -- Place is always nearest to itself - exclude this row
    WHERE n.Dist <> 0
    ORDER BY n.Dist
) AS t;
GO
```

■**Note**   I made one small but important change to the query in the common table expression: adding a tiny amount (0.0001) to MIN(Dist). The reason for this is that the values in this query, being of the FLOAT data type, can be subject to small rounding errors. It is possible that one of the places in the East or West derived tables happens to be the nearest neighbor. In that case, a tiny rounding error in Dist might result in this place itself being discarded because the calculated distance for this place in CLRNeighbors rounds to just a tiny fraction more than the rounded MaxDist. Adding a tiny amount to MaxDist prevents this.

The preceding query will always return the nearest neighbor for each place in Place. The value of @top does not affect the results, but it does impact performance. After trying several values, I found that 31 is the best value *for this table*. Getting the nearest neighbor for every place in the USA with the dynamic bounding box algorithm now takes me only 13.7 seconds.

The CLR Implementation

If performance matters and the code to optimize uses lots of computations, you should always try to see whether a CLR implementation is faster. So that's exactly what I'll do here. But first, let's review the pseudo-code to implement:

1. Find a number of places with the lowest longitude greater than P's longitude.

2. Find a number of places with the highest longitude less than P's longitude.

3. Calculate distance to P for all places found.

4. Find neighbors of P with @MaxDist set to the lowest calculated distance.

5. Return the neighbor with the minimum distance.

Since this code is very algorithmic, it's fairly easy to implement it exactly as written in a .NET assembly. But that would not be the best choice! Think about it for a minute—if I were to ask you to calculate (by hand) a bounding box size by calculating 62 distances, and the third distance you calculate happens to be only 4.2 km, would you still calculate the other 59 distances or would you accept 4.2 km as "good enough"? Back to the Seattle example, for something more concrete: suppose you had to find the dynamic bounding box size using 25 places to the west and 25 places to the east of Seattle. The first place you try happens to be in California, so the result is around 1,000 kilometers. The second place you try happens to be Clyde Hill, less than 10 kilometers from Seattle. Would you still calculate the other 48 distances, or would you deem 10 km to be good enough? I wouldn't calculate the other 48—and that's exactly how I want the CLR version of the nearest-neighbor algorithm to behave. So without further ado, here's the code. Note that this code reuses the BBox struct and the FillRow method; both are defined in the code for the CLRNeighbors user-defined function earlier.

```
[Microsoft.SqlServer.Server.SqlFunction(
    IsDeterministic = true,
    DataAccess = DataAccessKind.Read,
    FillRowMethodName = "FillRow",
    TableDefinition = "PlaceName NVARCHAR(100), State NCHAR(2), Dist FLOAT")]
public static IEnumerable CLRDynamicBB(
    SqlDouble LatIn,
    SqlDouble LonIn,
    SqlString Unit)
{
    double Lat = LatIn.Value, Lon = LonIn.Value, MaxDist = 100000;
    double LatMax, LatMin, LonMax, LonMin, Dummy;
    bool Miles = (Unit.Value.Equals("mi"));
    double Lat2, Lon2, Dist;
    BBox[] BBdata = new BBox[1];

    // Find MaxDist to use; try 26 locations east and west,
    //                       but stop at a threshold value of 8.5.
    using (SqlConnection conn = new SqlConnection("context connection = true"))
    {
        conn.Open();

        // Sample some places
        SqlCommand comm1 = new SqlCommand("" +
            "SELECT Lat, Lon " +
            "FROM " +
            "( " +
                "SELECT TOP(26) " +
                    "Lat, Lon " +
                "FROM Place WHERE Lon > @Lon " +
                "ORDER BY Lon ASC " +
            ") AS East " +
            "UNION ALL " +
            "SELECT Lat, Lon " +
```

```
                "FROM " +
                "( " +
                    "SELECT TOP(26) +
                        "Lat, Lon " +
                    "FROM Place " +
                    "WHERE Lon < @Lon " +
                    "ORDER BY Lon DESC " +
                ") AS West", conn);
        comm1.Parameters.Add("@Lon", SqlDbType.Float);
        comm1.Parameters[0].Value = Lon;

        using (SqlDataReader reader = comm1.ExecuteReader())
        {
            // Bail out when below threshold
            while ((MaxDist > 8.5) && (reader.Read()))
            {
                Lat2 = reader.GetDouble(0);
                Lon2 = reader.GetDouble(1);
                Dist = SpatialDist(Lat, Lon, Lat2, Lon2, Miles);
                if (Dist <= MaxDist)
                    MaxDist = Dist;
            }
        }


        // Add tiny bit to MinDist to fence off rounding errors
        MaxDist += 0.001;
        // Calculate minimum and maximum longitude and latitude for MaxDist
        StoredProcedures.SpatialMove(Lat, Lon, MaxDist, 0,    // North
                                     Miles, out LatMax, out Dummy);
        StoredProcedures.SpatialMove(Lat, Lon, MaxDist, 90,   // West
                                     Miles, out Dummy, out LonMin);
        StoredProcedures.SpatialMove(Lat, Lon, MaxDist, 180,  // South
                                     Miles, out LatMin, out Dummy);
        StoredProcedures.SpatialMove(Lat, Lon, MaxDist, -90,  // East
                                     Miles, out Dummy, out LonMax);


        // Fetch rows within the dynamic bounding box
        SqlCommand comm2 = new SqlCommand("" +
                "SELECT " +
                    "PlaceName, " +
                    "State, " +
                    "Lat, " +
                    "Lon " +
                "FROM Place " +
                "WHERE " +
                    "Lat BETWEEN @LatMin AND @LatMax " +
                    "AND Lon BETWEEN @LonMin AND @LonMax", conn);
```

```csharp
comm2.Parameters.Add("@LatMin", SqlDbType.Float);
comm2.Parameters[0].Value = LatMin;
comm2.Parameters.Add("@LatMax", SqlDbType.Float);
comm2.Parameters[1].Value = LatMax;
comm2.Parameters.Add("@LonMin", SqlDbType.Float);
comm2.Parameters[2].Value = LonMin;
comm2.Parameters.Add("@LonMax", SqlDbType.Float);
comm2.Parameters[3].Value = LonMax;

using (SqlDataReader reader = comm2.ExecuteReader())
{
    // Find place with lowest nonzero distance
    double MinDist = MaxDist;

    while (reader.Read())
    {
        Lat2 = reader.GetDouble(2);
        Lon2 = reader.GetDouble(3);
        if ((Lat2 != Lat) || (Lon2 != Lon))
        {
            Dist = SpatialDist(Lat, Lon, Lat2, Lon2, Miles);
            if (Dist < MinDist)
            {
                MinDist = Dist;
                BBdata[0].PlaceName = reader.GetSqlString(0);
                BBdata[0].State = reader.GetSqlString(1);
            }
        }
    }
    BBdata[0].Dist = MinDist;
}
}

return (IEnumerable)BBdata;
}
```

My first version of this function had two more parameters, Top and Threshold. Top was supplied as the value for the two TOP() clauses in the query, and Threshold was the highest distance value deemed low enough to stop calculating distances early. Extensive testing showed that the best overall performance was achieved with a value of 26 for Top, and a value of 8.5 for Threshold. Let me stress once again that these values are optimal for *this* data only—you will have to conduct your own tests on your own data to find the best values for your database. But since I planned to use this particular version of the function only on the sample database on my laptop, I decided to hard-code the values into the function and remove the parameters. You may wish to convert these hard-coded values into parameters when utilizing this function for your applications.

You may also notice that I did not call the CLRNeighbors function to find the neighbors in the bounding box, but instead used a slightly changed copy, optimized to make use of the knowledge that we'll always find and return exactly one neighbor.

Finding the nearest neighbor for all of the 22,993 places in the table is now as simple as running this query:

```
SELECT
    f.PlaceName AS PlaceFrom,
    f.State AS StateFrom,
    t.PlaceName AS PlaceTo,
    t.State AS StateTo,
    t.Dist
FROM Place AS f
CROSS APPLY dbo.CLRDynamicBB(f.Lat, f.Lon, 'km') AS t;
GO
```

This is not only easy, but fast as well—though not as fast as the T-SQL implementation presented previously. Total average execution time of the preceding query is 16.9 seconds, almost 25% slower than the pure T-SQL version. This goes to prove that, if performance matters, you should always test all variants extensively and not focus only on what you expect to be fastest. You might be surprised by the results ... I know I was, in this case. I had expected the additional threshold functionality to result in a performance advantage, since fewer distance calculations have to be done. But apparently, the disadvantage that the row-by-row processing of the CLR code has compared to set-based T-SQL offsets this.

■**Note** In the section "Encapsulating Using the CLR," I mentioned an alternative implementation where the CLR user-defined function returns the primary key (HtmID) instead of PlaceName and State. The additional cost of an extra join to the Place table, which increases as more rows are returned by the function, often exceeds the time saved by a faster function. But in this case, since only one row will ever be returned, this version of the function will indeed result in a net performance gain. Execution time for the dynamic bounding box function, for instance, drops from 16.9 to 14.9 seconds. A nice gain, but still not enough to beat the T-SQL version.

The Bottom Line

I have shown that the dynamic bounding box is a great extension to the regular bounding box algorithm if your application requires finding the nearest place, but you have no idea how close or far this nearest place will be. You can also leverage this technique to improve performance for a nearest-neighbor search where a maximum distance is known, but is much higher than the distance between most places. In the case of the Place table on my laptop, the dynamic bounding box was slightly slower than the 20 km bounding box, but much faster than a 40 km bounding box.

If you intend to implement the dynamic bounding box algorithm in your database, you should carefully consider a number of key factors that can make this algorithm succeed or crumble. The first is whether to use T-SQL or CLR to implement the algorithm. If you want the best performance, you really should implement and test both.

Another important step is determining whether to use the east-west axis (as in the examples in this chapter) or the north-south axis (based on latitude values) to find the places to use in the distance calculation. In general, you should use the axis that the region in your table is spread out over most. For example, use the east-west axis for the USA, Russia, or Venezuela; switch to the north-south axis for Japan, Italy, or Argentina. And remember that it never hurts to experiment, even if you think that the best decision is obvious.

The third key factor is the number of places to the east and west (or to the north and south) to examine. If you examine too few places, you'll have a high likelihood that the closest place of all places examined is still quite far away, resulting in a bounding box that's way too large. But examining too many places will just add more distance calculations to the workload without providing any actual gain in return. Determining the best number is a balancing act, especially since it also depends very much on the data in the table. Prepare for lots of testing before you know the optimal value in your database. The best value will probably be different for each table (and might even change over time if the data in your table is subject to frequent changes). Don't forget to repeat the tests after a major change to the data in the tables. For example, if a company extends its activities from the USA only to the USA plus Canada and adds all Canadian cities to the database, there's a fair chance that the optimal number of places to examine to get the size of the dynamic bounding box changes.

And the final factor to consider, but only if you implement the dynamic bounding box algorithm in the CLR, is the threshold value to use for shortcutting the process of calculating distances. Note that the number of places to examine and the threshold should be considered in combination, not each on their own. Changing one value also changes the optimal value of the other value; to get the truly optimal performance, you should try to find the best combination. Other than that, the same considerations apply as for the number of places to examine.

Conclusion

Representing spatial data by latitude and longitude is easy, since this method has been used to represent spatial data since well before computers and databases were invented. The inherent slowness of this method can easy be fixed by adding the proper indexes and choosing the algorithms with care.

The main disadvantage of using latitude and longitude is that many formulas break down when locations on or near one of the poles or on the junction between 180 degrees east and 180 degrees west come into play. Working around these limitations will make the code much more complex, and slower as a result.

■Tip One way to work around these limitations is to use a custom latitude/longitude notation, using a different origin. Having the equator at 0 degrees north/south and Greenwich at 0 degrees east/west is a choice that we all once chose to agree on, but not one that you *have* to implement in your database. If, for example, your data contains locations spread out over North America, Russia, and the northern polar region, you might choose to create your own custom "latitude" and "longitude" coordinate system such that the origin of these coordinates is somewhere in Alaska. Just don't forget to convert these custom "latitude" and "longitude" numbers back into the real latitude and longitude before outputting them! Your custom coordinate system will of course have its own "poles" and its own 180 degree "east/west" transition, so this trick won't help you if your data covers the entire world.

Representing Geospatial Data by Using the Hierarchical Triangular Mesh

The main advantage of using latitude and longitude to represent geospatial data is that it matches the system humans prefer. The disadvantage is that it is not ideal for indexing. A truly effective index would order locations that are close together on earth close together in the index as well, and locations that are far apart on earth far apart in the index. An index on longitude meets the first criterion for most of the earth (locations that are near each other will have almost the same longitude, except for locations near the North Pole or South Pole or near the 180 degrees east/180 degrees west line), but not the second (for instance, Cape Town in South Africa has almost the same longitude as Tromsö in Norway). An index on latitude suffers the same problems, and due to how indexes work, an index can only be effective for searching on either latitude or longitude, even if both columns are included in the index. SQL Server does know how to combine two indexes, for instance to search on both longitude and latitude at once, but the overhead of such operations often exceeds the gain.

It would be great to have an alternative scheme for geospatial data that meets both criteria for effective indexing: locations that are close in reality will also be close in the representation, and locations that are far removed are also far removed in the representation. An index on such a scheme would really speed up the neighborhood searches discussed earlier. Unfortunately, the very fact that SQL Server's indexes are one dimensional in nature, whereas the surface of the earth is two dimensional, makes this impossible.

That has never stopped researchers from trying to devise a representation for geospatial data that comes as close as possible to the ideal. One of those representations, the **Hierarchical Triangular Mesh** (HTM), has been used to implement a huge database for searching stellar objects (SkyServer—see `http://SkyServer.Sdss.Org/`). Several white papers describing this method, as well as the code used to implement it in SQL Server, are included in the samples that come with SQL Server. In fact, this is the very example that I have already used to demonstrate the latitude and longitude representation in the preceding section. The white papers describing the Hierarchical Triangular Mesh are located in `C:\Program Files\Microsoft SQL Server\ 90\Samples\Engine\Programmability\CLR\Spatial\docs` (provided you unpacked the samples to their default location).

A Simplified Description of HTM

The Hierarchical Triangular Mesh is a complex method. And since the researchers tried to make their description precise and complete, the white papers mentioned earlier are quite complex, which can be off-putting to laymen. In order to help you understand the Hierarchical Triangular Mesh, I will provide a simplified description. If you dislike simplifications and have no trouble reading complex scientific texts, feel free to skip this section and read the white papers instead.

The basic idea of the Hierarchical Triangular Mesh is to take the earth, divide it into small triangles (called **trixels**), and give each trixel a unique code, the so-called `HtmID`. The system used to create the triangles and their codes is such that *most* trixels that are close on the earth are also close when ordered by code, and that *all* trixels that are far removed from each other on earth will also be far removed from each other when ordered by code. Since the method is recursive (i.e., each trixel can be subdivided into several smaller trixels, as often as needed), it can be used to represent position with a very high granularity.

The First Steps

The algorithm for the Hierarchical Triangular Mesh starts by dividing the earth into its two hemispheres. These are called **N** (for the northern hemisphere) and **S** (for the southern hemisphere).

Each of the two hemispheres is then further subdivided into four roughly triangular areas, numbered from 0 to 3. The HtmID for each area is found by appending that number to the one-letter code for the hemisphere. Figure 9-8 illustrates how the northern hemisphere is divided into the four trixels N0, N1, N2, and N3. The same principle applies for the southern hemisphere.

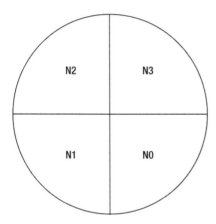

Figure 9-8. *A top-down view of the northern hemisphere, illustrating the first steps of the Hierarchical Triangular Mesh algorithm*

Subdividing the Trixels

Each of the eight trixels the first steps results in can be subdivided into four more trixels by connecting the midpoints of the three lines surrounding the triangles. These four new, smaller trixels are again numbered from 0 to 3, and the HtmID for each of the new trixels is again obtained by appending the number to the HtmID of the bigger trixel. For example, trixel N0 is subdivided into N00, N01, N02, and N03; and trixel S2 subdivided into S20, S21, S22, and S23. Since each of the four trixels on each hemisphere are subdivided into four new trixels, this results in a total of sixteen trixels on the northern hemisphere (illustrated by Figure 9-9), and another sixteen on the southern hemisphere.

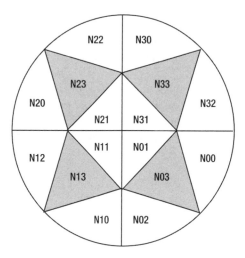

Figure 9-9. *Subdividing each of the four initial trixels into four new trixels*

This method of subdividing a trixel into four new trixels can be repeated for the resulting trixels. Figure 9-10 illustrates how trixel N03 is subdivided in N030, N031, N033, and N032, the latter of which is further subdivided in N0320, N0321, N0322, and N0323. Figure 9-11 illustrates how this looks on a projection of the earth.

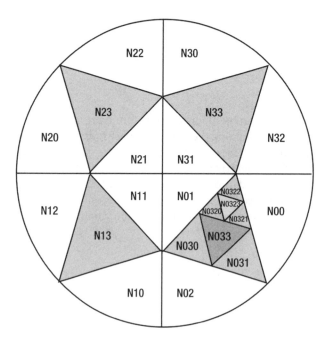

Figure 9-10. *Repeating the process of subdividing trixels in more, smaller trixels*

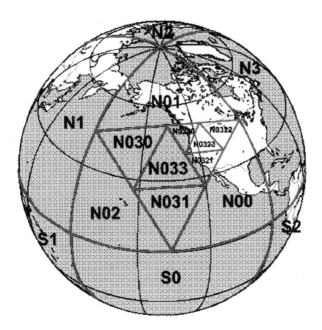

Figure 9-11. *The Hierarchical Triangular Mesh, projected on the earth*

The End Result

The subdivision of trixels can be repeated as often as needed. Each iteration will increase the number of trixels by a factor of four and decrease the size of individual trixels by the same factor. It only takes 14 iterations to get the average trixel size below a square kilometer. Add 10 more iterations, and the average trixel size is less than 1 m². And if I want to describe the exact location of a single key on my laptop's keyboard, I'd have to use a total of 30 iterations (resulting in a trixel size of 2.2 cm²).

Note that the trixels are not all the same size. However, the smallest trixel will always be at least half the size of the biggest one. This is a lot better than when using longitude, since the same single degree of longitude that represents 111.12 kilometers at the equator, represents only 20 centimeters when sufficiently near the North Pole or South Pole.

It is of course also possible to use more iterations for trixels in densely populated areas and fewer in empty areas, so as to get a more or less uniform distribution of objects over the trixels, rather than roughly equal-sized trixels. Looking at Figure 9-11, it's easy to predict that trixel N0323 will contain more cities than trixel N02, even though the latter is much larger. This could be useful for a database storing the locations of cities. Of course, for a database that holds the position of ships, you'd want to divide N033 further and leave N032 undivided.

To assess the potential of using the HtmID in an index, I'll use the same criteria I applied earlier to indexes on longitude or latitude: a truly effective index orders locations that are close together on earth near each other in the index ordering, while ordering locations that are far apart on earth far apart in the index. The HtmID easily meets the latter criterion—any two places on earth that are far removed will have a difference in either the starting letter or any of the first few digits of the HtmID, setting them far apart in the index ordering. But the former criterion does not always hold. Sure, many places that are close enough are in the same trixel or (if the trixels get smaller) in a trixel that only differs in one of the last digits of the HtmID. But there are notable exceptions—for instance, locations on either side of the equator will be very far removed because their trixels start with a different letter, even if the locations themselves are almost adjacent. The same holds, to a somewhat lesser extent, for locations on either side of the dividing lines of the eight starting trixels or of the trixels obtained in one of the first few iterations.

An interesting observation is that an index on the HtmID exposes the opposite properties of an index on longitude or latitude—the latter is great in ensuring that locations that are near each other in reality are near each other in the index as well, but fails to put far removed locations far apart in the index, whereas the former will always locate far removed locations in very different parts of the index, but fails to store all nearby locations close to each other in the index. In the rest of this chapter, I will show how to leverage the HtmID in neighborhood-search and nearest-neighbor queries. You will see that the algorithms based on the Hierarchical Triangular Mesh beat the first versions of the algorithms using latitude and longitude, but that the optimized versions of the latter are best—at least for the kind of queries that are used in this chapter.

Implementing the HtmID

Implementing the HtmID in your own databases is very easy, since Microsoft has released all code required for it as part of the samples for SQL Server 2005. If you have installed the sample database Spatial that I have used throughout this chapter for the sample data, you already have everything you need. The only difference between the sample database and your database is that the HtmID of all locations has already been calculated in the sample database, whereas you will have to use one of the conversion functions that follow to calculate it. The best way to implement it would be to add the HtmID as a persisted computed column.

Some Implementation Details

One of the columns in the sample table Place that I have not used so far is the column HtmID. With this name, you can of course expect it to hold the HtmID of the places stored in the table. However, the data in this column doesn't look at all like the HtmID explained previously:

```
SELECT
    PlaceName,
    State,
    Lat,
    Lon,
    HtmID
FROM Place;
GO
```

WORKING WITH SPATIAL DATA

The data returned by this query looks like this:

PlaceName	State	Lat	Lon	HtmID
Merrill	WI	45.182023	-89.703459	13537744123272
Tomahawk	WI	45.473409	-89.724151	13537801957369
Crystal Falls	MI	46.097305	-88.327727	13537808664315
...				
Rio Dell	CA	40.500822	-124.10633	15350232015014
Ferndale	CA	40.579486	-124.260625	15350234072514

```
(22993 row(s) affected)
```

The reason that the HtmID column doesn't look like the previously explained HtmID codes is that the code in the Spatial database adds one extra step to the algorithm. This step translates the alphanumeric version of the HtmID to a completely numeric code in order to save storage space and gain performance. The translation is carried out as follows:

1. The numeric HtmID is formed as a binary number, the first digit of which is always set to 1. This is to prevent having to code around issues that can arise from suppressing leading zeros.

2. The second bit of the binary HtmID is 0 if the string version of the HtmID starts with an N, or 1 if it starts with an S.

3. Each numeric position of the string version of the HtmID is replaced by its binary equivalent. Since these numeric positions can be either 0, 1, 2, or 3, the replacement is two bits (00, 01, 10, and 11, respectively).

4. The final step in the algorithm is to calculate the decimal equivalent of the binary HtmID.

The code in the Spatial database stores the HtmID as a BIGINT, which has a capacity of 8 bytes or 64 bits. This is sufficient to store a 31-level deep HtmID, which yields an average trixel size of less than 0.55 cm^2. The code supplied in the Spatial database stops at 21 levels, though (enough for an average trixel size of 58 m^2). You can change this by changing this constant declaration in the source code file Sql.cs:

```
const int level = 20;           // 20-deep htm is our standard.
```

Note Obviously, the programmers who created this code felt the need to prove they are true C# geeks that start to count at zero, instead of starting at one as all normal human beings do.

If you need more precision, or if you can afford to lose some precision in order to gain some speed, you can modify this constant and recompile the code. Note that I have not tried this myself, so I can't guarantee that the programmers have always used the constant rather than magic numbers. If you do change this, remember that a depth of more than 31 (i.e., setting the constant level to 31 or more) will cause overflow errors, and also take heed of the warning in the white papers that the floating-point representation and transcendental functions used in the code may lose precision near level 25.

Functions in the Spatial Database

The Spatial database contains many functions that can be used to work with HtmID data. Most of them come in three varieties, based on three possible kinds of input: longitude and latitude; x, y, and z coordinates in a three-dimensional system; or celestial right ascension and declination (another scheme for representing locations, not covered here). Following are the longitude/latitude versions of some of the functions; for a complete listing of all the functions, you can consult the white papers included with the sample.

Conversion Functions

The conversion functions will simply transform input data between the different representations of locations, without accessing the tables in the Spatial database at all.

```
dbo.fHtmLatLon(@Lat,@Lon)
```

This function takes a latitude and a longitude (both of data type FLOAT) and returns a BIGINT value holding the HtmID of the denoted location.

```
dbo.fHtmToString(@HtmID)
```

This function takes an HtmID (data type BIGINT) and returns an NVARCHAR(32) value holding the string representation of the HtmID.

```
DECLARE
    @Lat FLOAT,
    @Lon FLOAT;
SET @Lat = 47.622;
SET @Lon = -122.35;
SELECT
    dbo.fHtmLatLon(@Lat,@Lon) AS "HtmID numeric",
    dbo.fHtmToString(dbo.fHtmLatLon(@Lat,@Lon)) AS "HtmID string";
GO
```

Here are the results from this query:

HtmID numeric	HtmID string
15289295797168	N132133101002313232300

Calculating the Distance Between Two Points

Although most of the functions contained in the Spatial database use the HtmId, the database does include a function to calculate distance between two locations that are specified by latitude and longitude:

```
dbo.fDistanceLatLon(@Lat1,@Lon1,@Lat2,@Lon2)
```

All four input parameters and the result are of data type FLOAT. The result is specified in nautical miles; you'll have to multiply by 1.852 to get a distance in kilometers, or multiply by 1.852 and then divide by 1.609344 to get a result in miles. The following query reports the exact same distance between Seattle and Redmond, using the Distance function that is supplied as part of the Spatial database.

```
WITH Seattle AS
(
    SELECT Lat, Lon
    FROM Place
    WHERE
        PlaceName = 'Seattle'
        AND State = 'WA'
)
,Redmond AS
(
    SELECT Lat, Lon
    FROM Place
    WHERE
        PlaceName = 'Redmond'
        AND State = 'WA'
)
SELECT
    dbo.fDistanceLatLon(s.Lat,s.Lon,r.Lat,r.Lon) * 1.852 AS DistKilometers,
    dbo.fDistanceLatLon(s.Lat,s.Lon,r.Lat,r.Lon) * 1.852 / 1.609344 AS DistMiles
FROM Seattle AS s
CROSS JOIN Redmond AS r;
GO
```

In order to compare the performance of this distance calculation function to the CLR version I presented in the beginning of the chapter, I wrote, ran, and timed a query to calculate the average distance between any place in Michigan and any place in another state:

```
DECLARE @Start DATETIME;
SET @Start = CURRENT_TIMESTAMP;

SELECT AVG(dbo.fDistanceLatLon(a.Lat,a.Lon,b.Lat,b.Lon) * 1.852) AS MaxDistKm
FROM Place AS a
CROSS JOIN Place AS b
WHERE
    a.State = 'MI'
    AND b.State <> 'MI';

SELECT DATEDIFF(ms, @Start, CURRENT_TIMESTAMP);
GO
```

This query took 26,686 ms. After replacing the call to fDistanceLatLon with a call to DistCLR, the execution time increased to 34,093 ms. This means that the fDistanceLatLon version is over 20% faster than my best attempt. From this, I can conclude that

- All queries that I presented in the first part of this chapter can be made to go faster, simply by using fDistanceLatLon instead of DistCLR.

- My C# skills are far below my SQL skills!

Searching the Neighborhood

It probably won't come as a surprise that the Spatial database also exposes a function to perform a neighborhood search:

```
dbo.fHtmNearbyLatLon(@type,@Lat,@Lon,@r)
```

The input parameter @type is of data type CHAR(1) and is used to specify which table you want to search: Place (P) or Station (S).[6] The other parameters are all of data type FLOAT, and specify latitude, longitude, and radius or maximum distance. The radius has to be specified in nautical miles, so you have to divide the maximum distance in kilometers by 1.852 to get the value to pass in to this function. The result of this function is a table with a row for each location found, with columns for HtmID; Lat and Lon; x, y, and z; ObjID (object ID, always equal to HtmID for places); and distance (in nautical miles) of the location.

This function searches the neighborhood using a two-step algorithm. The first step is to get a list of all trixels that are completely or partly inside a circle of radius @r around the center point given by @Lat and @Lon. This list is not returned as a long list of HtmID values, but as a much shorter list of ranges of consecutive HtmID values. The second step is to calculate the distance to the center point for each location in the list of trixels; this is to make sure that no locations are returned that are in a trixel that is partly in the circle, but where the location itself is just outside the requested range.

With this function, I can now also use this code to find all places in a 10-kilometer radius from a specific location:

```
DECLARE
    @Lat FLOAT,
    @Lon FLOAT,
    @MaxDist FLOAT;

SET @Lat = 47.622;
SET @Lon = -122.35;
SET @MaxDist = 10.0;

-- Convert max distance to nautical miles.
DECLARE @MaxDistNM FLOAT;
SET @MaxDistNM = @MaxDist / 1.852;

SELECT
    PlaceName,
    State,
```

---

6. The Station table holds the location of all 17,000 stream gauges as published by the US Geological Survey. This table is also included in the Spatial sample database, but not used in any of the examples in this chapter.

```
      CAST(distance * 1.852 AS decimal(6,4)) AS Dist
FROM dbo.fHtmNearbyLatLon('P', @Lat, @Lon, @MaxDistNM) AS I
INNER JOIN Place ON I.HtmID = Place.HtmID
ORDER BY Dist ASC;
GO
```

And the query to get a list of all cities in Texas that are more than 5 but less than 10 kilometers apart can use this function as follows:

```
-- Convert min and max distance to nautical miles.
DECLARE
     @MinDistNM FLOAT,
     @MaxDistNM FLOAT;
SET @MinDistNM = 5.0 / 1.852;
SET @MaxDistNM = 10.0 / 1.852;

SELECT
     p.PlaceName AS pPlace,
     p.State AS pState,
     n.PlaceName,
     n.State,
     i.distance * 1.852 AS Dist
FROM Place AS p
CROSS APPLY dbo.fHtmNearbyLatLon('P', p.Lat, p.Lon, @MaxDistNM) AS i
INNER JOIN Place AS n ON i.HtmID = n.HtmID
WHERE
     p.State = 'TX'
     AND n.State = 'TX'
     AND i.distance > @MinDistNM;
GO
```

These queries turn out to be rather slow compared to the best versions I tested in the section "Representing Geospatial Data by Latitude and Longitude." The 10-kilometer radius search has an average execution time of 1.544 milliseconds (almost twice as slow as the CLR implementation of the bounding box), and the Texas city list takes a full 1,417 milliseconds (over 3.5 times as slow as the CLR version).

It should be noted that the comparison between these two functions is skewed. The function fHtmNearbyLatLon doesn't use the table Place, but rather SpatialIndex. This table holds the HtmID of each location in Place and each location in Station, plus some extra precalculated columns to represent the Cartesian x, y, and z coordinates. The addition of the 17,000 stream gauge locations means that more rows have to be read when using this table. On the other hand, according to the comments in the code, the precalculated x, y, and z values result in some performance gain over using latitude and longitude for all calculations. But the most important difference is that SpatialIndex doesn't hold state and place name, so that an extra join to the Place table is required to return these columns; this is probably the major cause of the performance difference.

Since the code for all functions included in the Spatial database is available, it is also possible to modify it. Checking fHtmNearbyLatLon, I found that this is a T-SQL user-defined function. This function uses the CLR function fHtmCoverCircleXyz, which returns the HtmID ranges of all trixels in the area searched (without accessing any table data); this result is then joined to SpatialIndex. It was easy to replace the latter with Place; since there are no precalculated x, y, and z columns in this table, I replaced the CLR function used with its latitude/longitude equivalent, fHtmCoverCircleLatLon. This resulted in the following user-defined function, which is specifically tweaked for the performance testing queries used in this chapter:

```
CREATE FUNCTION dbo.fHtmNearbyLatLon2
(
    @Lat FLOAT,
    @Lon FLOAT,
  . @MaxDist FLOAT,
    @Unit CHAR(2) = 'km'
)
RETURNS @Neighbors TABLE
(
    PlaceName VARCHAR(100) NOT NULL,
    State CHAR(2) NOT NULL,
    Dist FLOAT NOT NULL
)
AS
BEGIN
    -- Convert max distance to nautical miles.
    DECLARE @MaxDistNM FLOAT;
    IF @Unit = 'km'
        SET @MaxDistNM = @MaxDist / 1.852;
    ELSE
        SET @MaxDistNM = @MaxDist * 1.609344 / 1.852;

    -- Search all trixels in circular area around center
    WITH PlacePlusDistance
    AS
    (
        SELECT
            p.PlaceName,
            p.State,
            dbo.DistCLR (p.Lat, p.Lon, @Lat, @Lon, @Unit) AS Dist
        FROM dbo.fHtmCoverCircleLatLon(@Lat, @Lon, @MaxDistNM) AS c
        INNER JOIN Place AS p
            ON p.HtmID BETWEEN c.HtmIDStart AND c.HtmIDEnd
    )
    INSERT INTO @Neighbors
    (
        PlaceName,
        State,
        Dist
    )
    SELECT
```

```
        PlaceName,
        State,
        Dist
    FROM PlacePlusDistance
    WHERE Dist < @MaxDist;

    RETURN;
END;
GO
```

After creating this function, I changed the test queries to use it. Here's the new version of the 10-kilometer radius search:

```
DECLARE
    @Lat FLOAT,
    @Lon FLOAT,
    @MaxDist FLOAT;
SET @Lat = 47.622;
SET @Lon = -122.35;
SET @MaxDist = 10;

SELECT
    PlaceName,
    State,
    CAST(Dist AS decimal(6,4)) AS Distance
FROM dbo.fHtmNearbyLatLon2(@Lat,@Lon,@MaxDist,'km')
ORDER BY Dist ASC;
GO
```

And here's the adapted version of the Texas city list:

```
SELECT
    p.PlaceName AS pPlace,
    p.State AS pState,
    n.PlaceName,
    n.State,
    n.Dist
FROM Place AS p
CROSS APPLY dbo.fHtmNearbyLatLon2(p.Lat, p.Lon, 10, 'km') AS n
WHERE
    p.State = 'TX'
    AND n.State = 'TX'
    AND n.Dist > 5;
GO
```

Performance testing revealed an average execution time of 0.001323 seconds for the 10-kilometer radius search, and 1.189 seconds for the Texas query. That's better than the versions that use the SpatialIndex table and an extra join to Place, but still much slower than the CLR version that utilizes the bounding box technique.

OPTIMIZING THE ALGORITHM

If you execute the function fHtmCoverCircleLatLon (which is used in this algorithm) by itself, you'll notice that it returns a list of trixel ranges. Often, one or a few ranges enclose thousands of trixels, and the rest enclose only a few of them. And due to how the HTM algorithm dishes out the HtmID trixel names, the gaps are often fairly small. The following query and results, for instance, represent a circle with a radius of 0.5 nautical miles around Denver, CO:

```
SELECT
    dbo.fHtmToString(HtmIDStart) AS HtmIDStart,
    dbo.fHtmToString(HtmIDEnd) AS HtmIDEnd,
    HtmIDEnd - HtmIDStart + 1 AS NumberOfTrixels
FROM dbo.fHtmCoverCircleLatLon(39.768035,-104.872655,0.5);
```

This is the list of trixel ranges returned by this query:

```
HtmIDStart             HtmIDEnd               NumberOfTrixels
---------------------  ---------------------  -------------------
N132023131110200000000 N132023131110233333333 65536
N132023131110301000000 N132023131110301000333 64
N132023131110301002000 N132023131110301002333 64
N132023131110301003100 N132023131110301003103 4
N132023131110301003112 N132023131110301003112 1
N132023131110301003130 N132023131110301003133 4
N132023131110312000000 N132023131110312033333 1024
N132023131110312100000 N132023131110312133333 1024
N132023131110312320000 N132023131110312320333 64
N132023131110332000000 N132023131110332000333 64


(10 row(s) affected)
```

If you take a look at the execution plan for the key query in the user-defined function fHtmNearbyLatLon2 (see the following figure), you'll notice that a clustered index seek in Place has to be performed for each row in the preceding result set.

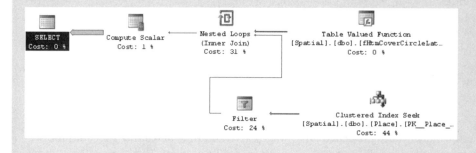

To check if the overhead of initiating ten (in this case) index seeks outweighs the overhead of scanning more unneeded data and calculating more unneeded distances, I also tested a variation where I processed all rows between the lowest and the highest numbered trixel in the circle:

```
CREATE FUNCTION dbo.fHtmNearbyLatLon3
(
    @Lat FLOAT,
    @Lon FLOAT,
    @MaxDist FLOAT,
    @Unit CHAR(2) = 'km'
)
RETURNS @Neighbors TABLE
(
    PlaceName VARCHAR(100) NOT NULL,
    State CHAR(2) NOT NULL,
    Dist FLOAT NOT NULL
)
AS
BEGIN
    -- Convert max distance to nautical miles.
    DECLARE @MaxDistNM FLOAT;
    IF @Unit = 'km'
        SET @MaxDistNM = @MaxDist / 1.852;
    ELSE
        SET @MaxDistNM = @MaxDist * 1.609344 / 1.852;

    -- Search all trixels in circular area around center
    WITH PlacePlusDistance
    AS
    (
        SELECT
            p.PlaceName,
            p.State,
            dbo.DistCLR (p.Lat, p.Lon, @Lat, @Lon, @Unit) AS Dist
        FROM
        (
            SELECT
                MIN(HtmIDStart) AS HtmIDStart,
                MAX(HtmIDEnd) AS HtmIDEnd
            FROM dbo.fHtmCoverCircleLatLon(@Lat, @Lon, @MaxDistNM)
        ) AS c
        INNER JOIN Place AS p
            ON p.HtmID BETWEEN c.HtmIDStart AND c.HtmIDEnd
    )
```

```
            INSERT INTO @Neighbors
            (
                PlaceName,
                State,
                Dist
            )
            SELECT
                PlaceName,
                State,
                Dist
            FROM PlacePlusDistance
            WHERE Dist < @MaxDist;

            RETURN;
END;
```

When my first tests showed an increase of execution time to over 1,400 milliseconds for the Texas city list query, I decided not to pursue this idea any further. But if you have a database with spatial data that has to be optimized, you might want to check whether you get better results when employing this technique in your database, since your data distribution will be different than that found in the Spatial sample database.

Finding the Nearest Neighbor

The syntax for the function to return the single nearest neighbor, regardless of actual distance, is very similar to the function for neighborhood search:

dbo.fHtmNearestLatLon(@type,@Lat,@Lon)

The input parameter @type is of data type CHAR(1) and specifies the table to search: Place (P) or Station (S). The other parameters are of data type FLOAT and specify latitude and longitude. The result of this function is a table that will always contain a single row, with columns for HtmID; Lat and Lon; x, y, and z; ObjID (object ID, always equal to HtmID for places); and distance—again, in nautical miles.

The algorithm chosen for this nearest-neighbor function is exceedingly simple. The query used is the exact same query used in the function for neighborhood search, with a fixed maximum distance of 1 nautical mile and with a TOP(1) clause added to return only the nearest neighbor. If no rows are found, the maximum distance is multiplied by 4 and the query is executed again. This is repeated (with maximum distances of 16, 64, and so on nautical miles) until a result is obtained.

There is one important difference between this function and the algorithms I have given previously for nearest-neighbor search based on latitude and longitude: this algorithm will not exclude the center point location itself from the search. This can be fine for some applications ("Where is the nearest pizza takeaway?" "Duh, you're standing right in it!"), but others might require the starting point of the search to be excluded. The query I used to demonstrate the various previously presented nearest-neighbor algorithms and to conduct performance tests falls in the latter category. So I took the code of the fHtmNearestLatLon function, added the following WHERE clause, and created a new function, fHtmNearestLatLonNot0.

```
WHERE Lat <> @Lat OR Lon <> @Lon
```

I then used this modified version of the HTM nearest-neighbor function in this query to find the nearest neighbor for each of the 22,993 locations in the Place table:

```
SELECT
    f.PlaceName AS PlaceFrom,
    f.State AS StateFrom,
    t.PlaceName AS PlaceTo,
    t.State AS StateTo,
    i.distance * 1.852 AS Dist
FROM Place AS f
CROSS APPLY dbo.fHtmNearestLatLonNot0('P', f.Lat, f.Lon) AS i
INNER JOIN Place AS t ON i.HtmID = t.HtmID;
GO
```

The results of performance testing this query were pretty dramatic. The average execution time was 47.5 seconds—almost 3.5 times the 13.7 seconds that the T-SQL implementation of the dynamic bounding box takes. But since this functions works the same way as the HTM implementation of the neighborhood search, all the remarks I made earlier apply here as well.

In order to get a better performance comparison, I also created an adapted version of this function to use the Place table and return the required columns without needing an extra join. Here's the code:

```
CREATE FUNCTION dbo.fHtmNearestLatLon2
(
    @Lat FLOAT,
    @Lon FLOAT,
    @Unit CHAR(2) = 'km'
)
RETURNS @Neighbors TABLE
(
    PlaceName VARCHAR(100) NOT NULL,
    State CHAR(2) NOT NULL,
    Dist FLOAT NOT NULL
)
AS
BEGIN
    -- Try first with a maximum distance of 1 nautical mile.
    -- Try distance = 1, 4, 16,.... till you find a nonnull set.
    DECLARE
        @MaxDistNM FLOAT,
        @MaxDist FLOAT;
    SET @MaxDistNM = 1;
```

```
retry:
    -- Convert nautical miles to kilometers or miles.
    IF @Unit = 'km'
        SET @MaxDist = @MaxDistNM * 1.852;
    ELSE
        SET @MaxDist = @MaxDistNM * 1.852 / 1.609344;

    WITH PlacePlusDistance
    AS
    (
        SELECT
            p.PlaceName,
            p.State,
            dbo.DistCLR (p.Lat, p.Lon, @Lat, @Lon, @Unit) AS Dist
        FROM dbo.fHtmCoverCircleLatLon(@Lat, @Lon, @MaxDistNM) AS c
        INNER JOIN Place AS p
            ON p.HtmID BETWEEN c.HtmIDStart AND c.HtmIDEnd
        -- Place is always nearest to itself - exclude this row
        WHERE
            p.Lat <> @Lat
            OR p.Lon <> @Lon
    )
    INSERT INTO @Neighbors
    (
        PlaceName,
        State,
        Dist
    )
    SELECT TOP (1)
        PlaceName,
        State,
        Dist
    FROM PlacePlusDistance
    WHERE Dist < @MaxDist
    ORDER BY Dist;

    -- If no rows are found, try again with larger radius.
    IF @@ROWCOUNT = 0
    BEGIN
        SET @MaxDistNM = @MaxDistNM * 4;
        GOTO retry;
    END;
    RETURN;
END;
GO
```

Note It's tempting to remove `WHERE Dist < @MaxDist` from the query in this code. After all, the `@MaxDist` variable is not a hard limit, but an aid to avoid calculating the distance for all rows in the table. If a location happens to be just outside the range, but in a trixel that is partly within the range, why exclude it? Either the query also finds another location that is closer (and in that case, the `TOP (1)` clause excludes this location), or it doesn't (and in that case, not excluding it saves me an extra iteration before finding the closest location). But let's not forget the possibility that one trixel is partly in range (for instance, spanning distances from 0.99 nautical miles to 1.013 nautical miles), and another trixel that is just outside that range (spanning distances ranging from 1.001 to 1.026 nautical miles). If the first trixel contains a place at a range of 1.01 nautical miles and the second contains a place at a distance of 1.005 nautical miles, removing the `WHERE` clause would result in the first place being found in the first iteration, whereas the second place (which will be found in the second iteration) is actually closer.

The SQL to use this function can now be simplified as follows:

```
SELECT
    f.PlaceName AS PlaceFrom,
    f.State AS StateFrom,
    t.PlaceName AS PlaceTo,
    t.State AS StateTo,
    t.Dist
FROM Place AS f
CROSS APPLY dbo.fHtmNearestLatLon2(f.Lat, f.Lon, 'km') AS t;
GO
```

Now that this code uses the same table as the dynamic bounding box algorithm, I can make a legitimate performance comparison—and it doesn't bode well for the HTM algorithm. Finding the nearest neighbor for every place in the United States takes 46.4 seconds; slightly better than the original version of the HTM algorithm, but still well over three times as slow as the T-SQL implementation of the dynamic bounding box.

Conclusion

When I first read about the Hierarchical Triangular Mesh, I was pretty excited. It sounded like a great way to improve performance for searches in spatial data. I was surprised and disappointed to find that both the neighborhood scan and the nearest-neighbor search turned out to be slower when using the Hierarchical Triangular Mesh as opposed to the algorithms using latitude and longitude. If your spatial data manipulation needs are covered by the examples given so far, you're well advised to avoid using the Hierarchical Triangular Mesh for now, and stick to latitude and longitude instead.

That does not mean that I consider the Hierarchical Triangular Mesh to be a bad idea. I still think that the idea is promising. Storing and searching lots of spatial data is a relatively new application of databases; I am sure that much more research in this field will be done over the years to come. The Hierarchical Triangular Mesh might turn out to be the starting point of a development that eventually brings us a way to store and manipulate spatial data that does outperform the latitude/longitude method.

Other Types of Spatial Data

Most of this chapter is focused around two-dimensional, geospatial data. But there are other kinds of spatial data as well. I don't have room in this book to cover these subjects as extensively as that of geospatial data, but I will mention a few other applications of spatial data briefly in the following sections.

Three-Dimensional Data

All the examples in this chapter have concentrated on location on the earth surface, without taking the altitude into account. For many applications, the altitude is not relevant—if you are hungry, you want to find the nearest restaurant, and you don't care whether it's uphill or downhill.

Other applications might store the altitude of locations as an attribute of the location; this will not change any of the algorithms covered before. The query a geologist would use to search for mountain tops at least 3 kilometers above sea level is not that much different from the query a sociologist would use to search for cities with at least one million inhabitants.

But there are also applications where altitude becomes a key attribute. Air traffic control is a prime example—there is no problem if two planes are at the exact same latitude and longitude, as long as their altitude differs by at least the height of the planes. And architects will also want to include altitude (probably represented by floor number) in their databases.

For these kinds of applications, the algorithms for distance calculation, neighborhood scan, and nearest-neighbor search can be easily modified to incorporate the altitude as well. The bounding box, for instance, can be converted into a three-dimensional bounding cube.

Astronomical Data

Representing the location of astronomical data is challenging by itself, because all objects in space move. The earth revolves around the sun, but the sun itself circles around the center of the Milky Way, which in turn is slowly moving away from all other milky ways. There is no obvious fixed point to use as a basis of measuring and representing locations, and even if there was, locations would have to be updated continually.

Fortunately, the speed of movement of objects in space is very slow in relation to their distance. As long as we only look at other stars through our telescopes instead of actually trying to get there, we can get away with ignoring the movement of the sun, the Milky Way, and the other objects. The effects of the movement of the earth can be negated by specifying the locations of objects as seen from the earth of a specific date and time.

Astronomers use several representations to specify locations of stellar objects relative to the position of the earth: latitude, longitude, and distance; right ascension, declination, and distance (J2000); or x, y, and z coordinates in a Cartesian space centered around the center of the earth. The code included in the sample database Spatial supports all three systems.

Virtual Space

The virtual worlds of online multiplayer games are getting larger by the day. The builders of those applications see themselves faced with the same problems that people face when trying to search locations on the real earth—how to store and efficiently search this data.

Since the virtual worlds usually assume a truly flat surface, distance calculations can be performed using the Pythagorean theorem. And for neighborhood scans and nearest-neighbor search algorithms, the special case handling for the North Pole, the South Pole, and the transition from 180 degrees west to 180 degrees east (which I left out of the code in this chapter but that really should be included in a real application) is not needed in these virtual worlds.

Representing Regions As Polygons

One area of spatial data that is often associated with using polygon arithmetic is that of the virtual game worlds just mentioned. Many objects in a game are represented by a combination of their location in the virtual world, combined with some description of the exact outline of the object. Determining whether a bullet hits an enemy is done by checking whether the point that represents the bullet is inside or outside of the polygon representing the enemy; checking to see whether two asteroids collide is done by searching for an intersection of the polygons representing the asteroids; and if the game implements laser weapons, you can expect an algorithm to calculate the intersection of a line and a polygon to be implemented in the game.

But do not make the mistake of thinking that polygons are exclusively limited to the virtual worlds of computer games. You can use the same algorithms to determine in which state a given location is, provided you have stored the state boundaries as polygons. Or you can store the exact form of a shoe sole as a polygon and use that to find a way to cut as many soles from a hide, minimizing the cut loss.

You can find quite a bit of information about polygons, and especially about algorithms to determine whether a point is inside a polygon, at http://www.acm.org/pubs/tog/editors/erich/ptinpoly/, plus some additional information at http://www.visibone.com/inpoly/. And you can also read the white papers included with the Spatial sample database to see how the Hierarchical Triangular Mesh can be used to work with polygons.

Summary

The number of databases that store and manipulate (geo)spatial data is increasing, and will probably continue to increase. Even if you don't use any spatial data yet, you should expect this to change shortly, and prepare yourself for it.

The combination of latitude and longitude is the easiest way to represent locations on the earth's surface. With this representation, searching a database that holds a lot of locations can be painstakingly slow—but proper indexing and clever use of techniques to limit the amount of data to be searched, such as the bounding box and the dynamic bounding box, can speed up these queries by huge factors.

The Hierarchical Triangular Mesh is an alternative method used to store locations in such a way that searching the data can be made to go faster. And though this technique does indeed return results faster than a database that uses latitude and longitude *without* proper indexing and smart query techniques, it is not (yet?) able to beat conventional algorithms in a properly designed database.

CHAPTER 10

∎∎∎

Working with Temporal Data

It's probably fair to assert that time is a central component of every possible database of any interest to anyone. Imagining a database that lacks a time component is tantamount to imagining life without time passing; it simply doesn't make sense. Without a time axis, it is impossible to describe the number of purchases made last month, the average temperature of the warehouse during the night in July, or the maximum duration that callers were required to hold the line when calling in for technical support.

Although utterly important to our data, few developers commit to really thinking in depth about the intricacies required to process temporal data successfully. Unfortunately, working with time-based data in SQL databases can be troublesome even in the best of cases. And as SQL Server developers, we must be especially clever, as the DBMS leaves out a few of the better temporal features specified in the ANSI standard.

In this chapter, I will delve into the ins and outs of dealing with time in SQL Server. I will explain some of the different types of temporal requirements you might encounter and describe how best to tackle some common—and surprisingly complex—temporal queries.

Representing More Than Just Time

When thinking of "temporal" data in SQL Server, the usual idea that springs to mind is a column typed as DATETIME, representing the time that some action took (or will take) place. However, this is merely one of several possible ways that temporal data can be implemented. Temporal data can be segmented into the following categories:

- **Instance-based data** is typified by the typical DATETIME column that you might think of when you hear the term "temporal." Scenarios in which you might model an instance include the moment a customer walks into a store, the moment a customer makes a purchase, or the moment any other kind of event takes place that you might need to record, or log, into the database. The key factor to recognize is that you're describing a specific instant in time, based on the precision of the data type you use.

- **Interval-based data** extends on the idea of an instance, describing a start point and an end point. A subset of interval-based data is the idea of a duration. Depending on your requirements, intervals may be modeled using two DATETIME columns, a DATETIME column and another column (usually numeric) that represents the amount of time that passed, or only a column representing an amount of time.

- **Period-based data** is similar to interval-based data, but the questions it answers are slightly different. When working with an interval or duration, the question is, "How long?" whereas for a period the question is, "When?" Examples of periods include "next month," "yesterday," "Labor Day," and "the holiday season." Although these are similar to—and can be represented by—intervals, the mindset of working with periods is slightly different, and it is therefore important to realize that other options exist for modeling them. For more information on periods, see the section "Defining Periods Using Calendar Tables" later in this chapter.

- **Bitemporal data** is temporal data that falls into any of the preceding categories, but also includes a separate time component (known as a **valid time** or, more loosely, an **as-of date**) indicating when the data was considered to be valid. This data pattern is commonly used in data warehouses, both for slowly changing dimensions and for updating semi-additive fact data. When querying the database bitemporally, the question transforms from "On a certain day, what happened?" to "As of a certain day, what did we think happened on a certain (other) day?" The question might also be phrased as "What is the most recent idea we have of what happened on a certain day?" This mindset can take a bit of thought to really get; see the section "Managing Bitemporal Data" later in this chapter for more information.

SQL Server's Date/Time Data Types

The first requirement for successfully dealing with temporal data in SQL Server is an understanding of what the DBMS offers in terms of native date/time data types. SQL Server offers two data types: DATETIME and SMALLDATETIME. The DATETIME data type is a fixed 8-byte type, with a resolution of 3.33 milliseconds, and a range from January 1, 1753 through December 31, 9999. The SMALLDATETIME type, on the other hand, only takes up 4 bytes per instance, but has a resolution of 1 minute and a much smaller range: January 1, 1900 through June 6, 2079.

Rattling off date ranges and storage requirements that are available in the product's documentation is great; however, working with these types involves quite a bit more than that. What developers actually need to understand when working with SQL Server's date/time types is what input and output formats should be used, and how to manipulate the types in order to create various commonly needed queries. This section covers both of these issues.

Before continuing, it's important to stress the number-one key thing that you absolutely must realize if you want to be successful with SQL Server's date/time types: These types include *both* a date *and* a time component. There is no such thing as inputting "just" a date in SQL Server. All instances of the native date/time types have both components, even if the time is set at its default value of midnight. Keeping this fact in mind will make things much easier to understand when working with these types.

Input Date Formats

There is really only one rule to remember when working with SQL Server's date/time types, when accepting data from a client: always, always, *always*, avoid ambiguous date formats! The unfortunate fact is that every date does not necessarily mean the same thing to any given two people. For instance, consider the following date:

01/02/03

If you've been living in the U.S., you probably immediately thought "January 2, 2003!" However, those faring from European nations would read this as "February 1, 2003." And if you're from one of various Asian countries (Japan, for instance), you probably think that this date signifies "February 3, 2001." Much like the inhabitants of these locales, SQL Server tries to follow local format specifications when handling input date strings, meaning that on occasion users do not get the date they expect from the input.

Luckily, there is a solution to this problem. Just as with many other classes of problems in which lack of standardization is an issue, the International Standards Organization (ISO) has come to the rescue. ISO 8601 is an international standard date/time format, which SQL Server (and other software) will automatically detect and use, independent of the local server settings. The full ISO format is specified as follows:

```
yyyy-mm-ddThh:mi:ss.mmm
```

yyyy is the four-digit year, which is key to the format; any time SQL Server sees a four-digit year first, it knows that the ISO format is being used. mm and dd are month and day, respectively, and hh, mi, ss, and mmm are hours, minutes, seconds, and milliseconds. A few further notes on this format: the dashes and the T are both optional, but the T is only optional if the dashes are not present.

As with any other date/time format used by SQL Server, the time or date itself is always optional. If the time portion is not specified, SQL Server will use midnight as the default; if the date portion is not specified, SQL Server will use January 1st 1900 as the date.

Each of the following are valid ISO date/time strings:

```
--Date without dashes, and time
20060501 13:45:03

--Date with dashes, and time specified with T
2006-05-01T13:45:03

--Date only
20060501

--Time only
13:45:03
```

Note that the following is valid according to the ISO format, but not treated as such by SQL Server:

```
--Date with dashes, and time--but no T
2006-05-01 13:45:03
```

By always using the ISO format—and always making sure that clients send dates according to the ISO format—you can ensure that the correct dates will always be used by SQL Server. Remember that SQL Server does not store the input date string; the date is converted into a binary format. So if invalid dates do end up in the database, there will be no way of reconstituting them from just the data.

Unfortunately, it's not always possible to get data in exactly the right format before it hits the database. SQL Server provides two primary mechanisms that can help when dealing with non-standard date/time formats: an extension to the CONVERT function that allows specification of a date "style," and a runtime setting called DATEFORMAT.

To use CONVERT to create an instance of DATETIME or SMALLDATETIME from a nonstandard date, use the third parameter to the function to specify the date's format. The following code block shows how to do this for the "British/French" and "U.S." styles:

```
--British/French style
SELECT CONVERT(DATETIME, '01/02/2003', 103)

--U.S. style
SELECT CONVERT(DATETIME, '01/02/2003', 101)
```

Style 103 produces the date "February 1, 2003," whereas style 101 produces the date, "January 2, 2003." By using these styles, you can more easily control how date/time input is processed, and explicitly tell SQL Server how to handle input strings. There are over 20 different styles documented; see the topic "CAST and CONVERT (Transact-SQL)" in SQL Server 2005 Books Online for a complete list.

The other commonly used option for controlling the format of input date strings is the DATEFORMAT setting. DATEFORMAT allows you to specify the input date format's order of month, day, and year, using the specifiers M, D, and Y. The following T-SQL is equivalent to the previous example that used CONVERT:

```
--British/French style
SET DATEFORMAT DMY
SELECT CONVERT(DATETIME, '01/02/2003')

--U.S. style
SET DATEFORMAT MDY
SELECT CONVERT(DATETIME, '01/02/2003')
```

There is really not much of a difference between using DATEFORMAT and CONVERT to correct nonstandard inputs. DATEFORMAT may be cleaner in some cases as it only needs to be specified once per connection, but CONVERT offers slightly more control due to the number of styles that are available. In the end, you should choose whichever one makes the particular code you're working on more easily readable, testable, and maintainable.

■**Note** Using SET DATEFORMAT within a stored procedure will cause a recompile to occur whenever the procedure is executed. This may cause a performance problem in some cases, so make sure to test carefully before deploying solutions to production environments.

Output Date Formatting

The CONVERT function is not only useful for specification of input date/time string formats. A much more common use for it is formatting dates for output.

Before continuing, I feel that a quick disclaimer is in order: it's probably not a good idea to do formatting work in the database. By formatting dates into strings in the data layer, you may reduce the ease with which stored procedures can be reused. This is because it may force applications that require differing date/time formats to convert the strings back into native date/time objects, and then reformat them as strings again. Such additional work on the part of the application is probably unnecessary, and there are very few occasions in which it really makes sense to send dates back to an application formatted as strings. The main example that springs to mind is when doing data binding to a grid or other object that doesn't support the date format you need—but of course, that is a rare situation.

Just like when working with input formatting, the main T-SQL function used for date/time output formatting is CONVERT. The same set of styles that can be used for input can also be used for output formats; the only difference is that the function is converting from an instance of a date/time type into a string, rather than the other way around. The following T-SQL shows how to format the current date as a string in both U.S. and British/French styles:

```
--British/French style
SELECT CONVERT(VARCHAR(50), GETDATE(), 103)

--U.S. style
SELECT CONVERT(VARCHAR(50), GETDATE(), 101)
```

The set of styles available for the CONVERT function is somewhat limited, and may not be enough for all situations. In addition, those coming from an Oracle background often complain of the lack of a function similar to Oracle's TO_CHAR, in SQL Server.

SQL Server 2005's CLR integration provides a solution to these problems. .NET's System.DateTime class includes extremely flexible string-formatting capabilities, which can be harnessed using a CLR scalar user-defined function. The following method exposes the necessary functionality:

```
public static SqlString FormatDate(
    SqlDateTime Date,
    SqlString FormatString)
{
    DateTime theDate = Date.Value;
    return new SqlString(theDate.ToString(FormatString.ToString()));
}
```

This UDF converts the SqlDateTime instance into an instance of System.DateTime, and then uses the overloaded ToString method to format the date/time as a string. The method accepts a wide array of formatting directives, all of which are fully documented in the Microsoft MSDN Library. As a quick example, the following invocation of the method formats the current date/time with the month part first, followed by a four-digit year, and finally the day:

```
SELECT dbo.FormatDate(GETDATE(), 'MM yyyy dd')
```

Keep in mind that the ToString method's formatting overload is case sensitive. MM, for instance, is not the same as mm, and you may get unexpected results if you are not careful.

Efficiently Querying Date/Time Columns

Knowing how to format dates for input and output is a good first step, but the real goal of any database system is to allow the user to query the data to answer business questions. Querying date/time data in SQL Server has some interesting pitfalls, but for the most part they're easily avoidable if you understand how the DBMS treats temporal data.

To start things off, create the following table:

```
USE TempDB
GO

CREATE TABLE VariousDates
(
    ADate DATETIME NOT NULL,
    PRIMARY KEY (ADate) WITH (IGNORE_DUP_KEY = ON)
)
GO
```

Note that I've created the table in `TempDB`, since this is just a throw-away table that will be used for these examples. Now insert some data into the table. The following T-SQL will insert 85,499 rows into the table, with dates spanning from February through November of 2006 (but don't worry about the logic of this T-SQL right now, unless you're particularly interested in sample data generation):

```
;WITH Numbers
AS
(
    SELECT DISTINCT
        number
    FROM master..spt_values
    WHERE number BETWEEN 1001 AND 1256
)
INSERT VariousDates
(
    ADate
)
SELECT
    CASE x.n
        WHEN 1 THEN
            DATEADD(millisecond,
                POWER(a.number, 2) * b.number,
                DATEADD(day, a.number-1000, '20060201'))
        WHEN 2 THEN
            DATEADD(millisecond,
                b.number-1001,
                DATEADD(day, a.number-1000, '20060213'))
    END
FROM Numbers a
CROSS JOIN Numbers b
```

```
CROSS JOIN
(
    SELECT 1
    UNION ALL
    SELECT 2
) x (n)
GO
```

Once the data has been inserted, the next logical step is, of course, to query it. You might first want to ask the question "What is the minimum date value in the table?" The following query uses the MIN aggregate to answer that question:

```
SELECT MIN(ADate)
FROM VariousDates
```

This query returns one row, with the value 2006-02-13 14:36:43.000. But perhaps you'd like to know what other times from February 13, 2006 are in the table. A first shot at that query might be something like the following:

```
SELECT *
FROM VariousDates
WHERE ADate = '20060213'
```

If you run this query, you might be surprised to find out that instead of seeing all rows for February 13, 2006, zero rows are returned. The reason for this is that, as stated earlier, all dates in SQL Server *must* include a time component. When this query is evaluated and the search argument ADate = '20060213' is processed, SQL Server sees that the ADate column, which is typed as DATETIME, is being compared to the date string, which is typed as VARCHAR. Based on SQL Server's rules for data type precedence,[1] the string is converted to DATETIME before being compared; and because the string includes no time portion, the default time of 00:00:00.000 is used. To see this conversion in action, try the following T-SQL:

```
SELECT CONVERT(DATETIME, '20060213')
```

When this code is run, the default time portion is automatically added, and the output of this SELECT is the value 2006-02-13 00:00:00.000. Clearly, querying based on the implicit conversion between this string and the DATETIME type is ineffective—unless you only want values for midnight.

To solve this problem, the conversion must be controlled in a slightly different way. Many developers' first reaction is to try to avoid the conversion of the string to an instance of DATETIME altogether, by converting the column itself and using a conversion style that eliminates the time portion. The following query is an example of one such way of doing this:

```
SELECT *
FROM VariousDates
WHERE CONVERT(VARCHAR(20), ADate, 112) = '20060213'
```

---

1. This is fully documented in SQL Server 2005 Books Online in the topic "Data Type Precedence (Transact-SQL)."

Running this query, you will find that the correct data is returned; you'll see all rows from February 13, 2006. While getting back correct results is a wonderful thing, there is unfortunately a major problem that might not be too obvious with the small sample data used in this example. The table's index on the ADate column is based on ADate as it is natively typed—in other words, as DATETIME. The table does not have an index for ADate converted to VARCHAR(20) using style 112 (or any other style or conversion, for that matter). As a result, this query is unable to seek an index, and SQL Server is forced to scan every row of the table, convert each ADate value to a string, and then compare it to the date string. This produces the execution plan shown in Figure 10-1, which has an estimated cost of 0.229923.

Figure 10-1. *Converting the date/time column to a string does not result in a good execution plan.*

In order to be able to effectively use the index to satisfy the query, we need to supply SQL Server with a search argument that doesn't involve converting the data already in the table. The solution is to think slightly outside of the realm of using an exact match to satisfy the query. Another way to ask for dates from February 13, 2006 is to ask for any rows where the date/time value is between February 13, 2006 at midnight and February 14, 2006 at midnight. Any instant recorded within that interval is a valid date for February 13, 2006.

The following query is a first shot at querying a range instead of an exact match:

```
SELECT *
FROM VariousDates
WHERE ADate BETWEEN '20060213' AND '20060214'
```

This query performs much better, producing the execution plan shown in Figure 10-2, which has an estimated cost of 0.0033718 (1/68 the estimated cost of the previous version!).

Figure 10-2. *Querying date/time columns using ranges allows the query engine to take advantage of indexes.*

Unfortunately, although this query performs a lot better than the version that uses string conversion, it has a subtle problem. The BETWEEN operator is *inclusive* on either end, meaning that X BETWEEN Y AND Z expands to X >= Y AND X <= Z. For the sake of this query, that means that the search argument, with times included (the implicit conversion will add those back in), will become the following:

```
ADate >= '20060213 00:00:00.000' AND ADate <= '20060214 00:00:00.000'
```

That means this query can potentially return an incorrect result, if there happens to be a row for February 14, 2006 at midnight (and the data in the sample table does indeed include such a row). Luckily, solving this problem is easy; simply don't use BETWEEN. Instead, always use the fully expanded version, inclusive of the start of the interval, and *exclusive* of the end value:

```
SELECT *
FROM VariousDates
WHERE
    ADate >= '20060213'
    AND ADate < '20060214'
```

This pattern can be used to query any kind of date range and is actually quite flexible. In the next section, you will learn how to extend this pattern to find all of "today's" rows, "this month's" rows, and other similar requirements.

Date/Time Calculations

The query pattern presented in the previous section works and returns the correct results, but is rather overly static as-is. Expecting all date range queries to have hard-coded values for the input dates is neither a realistic expectation nor a very maintainable solution. By using SQL Server's date calculation functions, input dates can be manipulated in order to dynamically come up with whatever ranges are necessary for a given query.

The two primary functions that are commonly used to perform date/time calculations are DATEDIFF and DATEADD. The first returns the difference between two dates; the second adds (or subtracts) time from an existing date. Each of these functions takes granularity as a parameter and can operate at any level between milliseconds and years.

DATEDIFF takes three parameters: the time granularity that should be used to compare the two input dates, the start date, and the end date. For example, to find out how many hours elapsed between midnight on February 13, 2006, and midnight on February 14, 2006, the following query could be used:

```
SELECT DATEDIFF(hour, '20060113', '20060114')
```

The result, as you might expect, is 24. Note that I mentioned that this query compares the two dates, both at midnight, even though neither of the input strings contains a time. Again, I want to stress that any time you use a string as an input where a date/time type is expected, it will be implicitly converted by SQL Server.

It's also important to note that DATEDIFF maintains the idea of "start" and "end" times, and the result will change if you reverse the two. Changing the previous query so that February 14 is passed before February 13 results in the output of -24.

The DATEADD function takes three parameters: the time granularity, the amount of time to add, and the input date. For example, the following query adds 24 hours to midnight on February 13, 2006, resulting in an output of 2006-01-14 00:00:00.000:

```
SELECT DATEADD(hour, 24, '20060113')
```

DATEADD can also deal with negative amounts and will subtract instead of add in that case.

The first step in doing date/time calculations in SQL Server is to learn to combine DATEDIFF and DATEADD to truncate date/time values. Understanding how it's done takes a bit of a logical jump, so I'll break the process down into its component parts:

1. Truncation is essentially the same as rounding down, so you must first decide which date/time component you'd like to use to do the rounding. The component you'll use to do the rounding should be one level of granularity above whatever data you need to truncate. For instance, if you want to remove the seconds and milliseconds, you'd round down using minutes. Likewise, to remove the entire time portion, you'd round down using days.

2. Once you've decided on a level of granularity, pick a reference date/time. For basic truncation, this date/time can be any within the range of the data type you're working with. I generally use 0, which corresponds to 1900-01-01 at midnight for both SMALLDATETIME and DATETIME.

3. Using the DATEDIFF function, find the difference between the reference date/time and the date/time you want to truncate, at the level of granularity you've picked.

4. Finally, use DATEADD to add the output from the DATEDIFF function to the same reference date/time that you used to find the difference. The result will be the truncated value of the original date/time.

Walking through an example should make this a bit clearer. Assume that you want to start with 2006-04-23 13:45:43.233 and truncate the time portion (in other words, come out with 2006-04-23 at midnight). The granularity used will be days, since that is the lowest level of granularity above the time granularities (milliseconds, seconds, minutes, and hours). The following T-SQL can be used to determine the number of days between the reference date of 0 and the input date:

```
DECLARE @InputDate DATETIME
SET @InputDate = '2006-04-23 13:45:43.233'

SELECT DATEDIFF(day, 0, @InputDate)
```

Running this T-SQL, we discover that 38828 days passed between the reference date and the input date. Using DATEADD, that number can be added to the reference date:

```
SELECT DATEADD(day, 38828, 0)
```

The result of this operation is the desired truncation: 2006-04-23 00:00:00.000. Because only the number of days was added back to the reference date—with no time portion—the date was rounded down and the time portion eliminated. Of course, you don't have to run this T-SQL step by step; in a stored procedure, you'd probably combine everything into one inline statement:

```
SELECT DATEADD(day, DATEDIFF(day, 0, @InputDate), 0)
```

Once you understand this basic pattern, you can modify it to come up with any combination of dates. For instance, finding the first of the month is a simple matter of changing the granularity:

```
SELECT DATEADD(month, DATEDIFF(month, 0, @InputDate), 0)
```

Finding the last day of the month requires just a bit more thought; find the first day of the month, add an additional month, and subtract 1 day:

```
SELECT DATEADD(day, -1, DATEADD(month, DATEDIFF(month, 0, @InputDate)+1, 0))
```

Another way to find the last day of the month is to use, as a reference date, any date that is the last day of a month. For instance, 1900-12-31:

```
SELECT DATEADD(month, DATEDIFF(month, '19001231', @InputDate), '19001231')
```

Note that the month you choose is important in this case. I chose a 31-day month; what this T-SQL is actually doing is finding the same day as the reference date, on the month in question. But if the month does not have 31 days, SQL Server will automatically round down to the closest date. Had I used February 28 instead of December 31 for the reference date, the output any time this query was run would be the 28th of the month.

Other more interesting combinations are also possible. For example, a common requirement in many applications is to do calculations based on time periods such as "every day between last Friday and today." By modifying the truncation pattern a bit, finding "last Friday" is fairly simple. The main trick is to start with a well-known reference date. In this case, to find a day on Friday, the reference date should be any Friday. We know that the number of days between any Friday and any other Friday is divisible by seven, and can use that knowledge to truncate the current date down to the nearest Friday.

The following T-SQL finds the number of days between the reference Friday, January 7, 2000, and the input date, February 9, 2006:

```
DECLARE @Friday DATETIME
SET @Friday = '20000107'

SELECT DATEDIFF(day, @Friday, '20060209')
```

The result is 2225, which of course is an integer. Taking advantage of SQL Server's integer math properties, dividing the result by 7, and then multiplying it by 7 again will round it down to the nearest number divisible by seven, 2219:

```
SELECT (2225 / 7) * 7
```

Adding 2219 days to the original reference date of January 7, 2000 results in the desired output, the "last Friday" before February 9, 2006, which was on February 3, 2006:

```
SELECT DATEADD(day, 2219, '20000107')
```

As with the previous example, this can be simplified (and clarified) by combining everything inline:

```
DECLARE @Friday DATETIME
SET @Friday = '20000107'

SELECT DATEADD(day, ((DATEDIFF(day, @Friday, @InputDate) / 7) * 7), @Friday)
```

A further simplification of the second statement is also possible. Once the result of the inner DATEDIFF is divided by 7, its granularity is in weeks until it is multiplied by 7 again to produce days. But there is no reason to do the second multiplication, and the code becomes a bit cleaner if the result is simply treated as weeks for the final calculation:

```
SELECT DATEADD(week, (DATEDIFF(day, @Friday, @InputDate) / 7), @Friday)
```

Note that these examples return the input date itself (with the time portion truncated), if the input date is a Friday. If you really want to return the "last" Friday every time, and never the input date itself—even if it is a Friday—a small modification is required. To accomplish this, you must use two reference dates: one for any Friday and one for any day within a week of the original reference date (I recommend the next day, for simplicity). By using the next day as the inner reference date, the result of the division will be one week lower if the input date is a Friday, meaning that the result will be the previous Friday. The following T-SQL does this for a given input date:

```
DECLARE @Friday DATETIME
SET @Friday = '20000107'
DECLARE @Saturday DATETIME
SET @Saturday = '20000108'

SELECT DATEADD(week, (DATEDIFF(day, @Saturday, @InputDate) / 7), @Friday)
```

By using this pattern and switching the reference date, you can easily find the last of any day of the week given an input date. To find the "next" one of a given day (e.g., "next Friday"), simply add one week to the result of the inner calculation before adding it to the reference date:

```
SELECT DATEADD(week, (DATEDIFF(day, @Friday, GETDATE()) / 7)+1, @Friday)
```

As a final example of what you can do with date/time calculations, a slightly more complex requirement is necessary. Say that you're visiting the Boston area and want to attend a meeting of the New England SQL Server Users Group. The group meets on the second Thursday of each month.[2] Given an input date, how do you find the date of the next meeting?

To find the second Thursday of the month of the input date, first find the fourteenth day of the month, and then use it to find "last Thursday." The fourteenth has significance because if the first of the month is a Thursday, the second Thursday will be the eighth day of the month. On the other hand, if the first of the month is a Friday, the second Thursday will be the fourteenth. So for any given month, the "last Thursday" (as of and including the fourteenth) will be the second Thursday of the month. The following T-SQL does exactly that:

```
DECLARE @Thursday DATETIME
SET @Thursday = '20000914'

DECLARE @FourteenthOfMonth DATETIME
SET @FourteenthOfMonth =
    DATEADD(month, DATEDIFF(month, @Thursday, @InputDate), @Thursday)

SELECT DATEADD(week, (DATEDIFF(day, @Thursday, @FourteenthOfMonth) / 7), @Thursday)
```

---

2. You can find more information at http://www.nesql.org.

Of course, this doesn't find the *next* meeting; it finds the meeting for the month of the input date. To find the next meeting, a CASE expression will be necessary, in addition to an observation about second Thursdays: if the second Thursday of a month falls on the eighth, ninth, or tenth, the next month's second Thursday is five weeks away. Otherwise, the next month's second Thursday is four weeks away. To find the day of the month represented by a given date/time instance, use T-SQL's DATEPART function, which takes the same date granularity inputs as DATEADD and DATEDIFF. The following T-SQL combines all of these techniques to find the next date for a New England SQL Server Users Group meeting, given an input date:

```
DECLARE @Thursday DATETIME
SET @Thursday = '20000914'

DECLARE @FourteenthOfMonth DATETIME
SET @FourteenthOfMonth =
    DATEADD(month, DATEDIFF(month, @Thursday, @InputDate), @Thursday)

DECLARE @SecondThursday DATETIME
SET @SecondThursday =
    DATEADD(week, (DATEDIFF(day, @Thursday, @FourteenthOfMonth) / 7), @Thursday)

SELECT
    CASE
        WHEN @InputDate <= @SecondThursday
        THEN @SecondThursday
    ELSE
        DATEADD(
            week,
            CASE
                WHEN DATEPART(day, @SecondThursday) <= 10 THEN 5
                ELSE 4
            END,
            @SecondThursday)
    END
```

Finding complex dates like the second Thursday of a month is not a very common requirement unless you're writing a scheduling application. More common are requirements along the lines of "find all of today's rows." Combining the range techniques discussed in the previous section with the date/time math seen here, it becomes easy to design stored procedures that both efficiently and dynamically query for required time periods. For instance, the following T-SQL always returns rows for the given day, no matter what the day is:

```
SELECT *
FROM VariousDates
WHERE
    ADate >= DATEADD(day, DATEDIFF(day, 0, GETDATE()), 0)
    AND ADate < DATEADD(day, DATEDIFF(day, 0, GETDATE())+1, 0)
```

The first search argument uses the calculation to find "today" with the time part truncated, and the second search argument adds 1 to the difference in days between the current day and the reference date, to return "tomorrow" with the time part truncated. The result is all rows between today at midnight, inclusive, and tomorrow at midnight, exclusive.

As a final example of date/time calculations in T-SQL, consider a seemingly simple task: find out how many years old you are as of today. The obvious answer is, of course, the following:

```
SELECT DATEDIFF(year, @YourBirthday, GETDATE())
```

Unfortunately, this answer—depending on the current day—is wrong. Consider someone born on March 25, 1965. On March 25, 2006, that person's forty-first birthday should be celebrated. Yet, according to SQL Server, that person was already 41 on March 24, 2006:

```
SELECT DATEDIFF(year, '19650325', '20060324')
```

As a matter of fact, according to SQL Server, this person was already 41 throughout the year of 2006, starting on January 1. Happy New Year and Happy Birthday—combined, thanks to the magic of SQL Server? Probably not; the discrepancy is due to the way SQL Server calculates date differences. Only the date/time component being differenced is considered, and any components below are truncated. This feature makes the previous date/time truncation examples work, but makes age calculations fail because when differencing years, days and months are not taken into account.

To get around this problem, a CASE expression must be added that subtracts one year if the day and month of the current date is less than the day and month of the input date. The following T-SQL, which both accomplishes the primary goal and takes leap years into consideration, was created by Steve Kass:[3]

```
SELECT
    DATEDIFF (
        YEAR,
        @YourBirthday,
        GETDATE()) -
    CASE
        WHEN 100 * MONTH(GETDATE()) + DAY(GETDATE())
            < 100 * MONTH(@YourBirthday) + DAY(@YourBirthday) THEN 1
        ELSE 0
    END
```

Note that this T-SQL uses the MONTH and DAY functions, which are shorthand for DATEPART(month, <date>) and DATEPART(day, <date>), respectively.

---

3. ASPFAQ, "Given two dates, how do I determine an age?" http://classicasp.aspfaq.com/date-time-routines-manipulation/given-two-dates-how-do-i-determine-an-age.html, accessed September 1, 2006.

Defining Periods Using Calendar Tables

Given the complexity of doing date/time calculations in order to query data efficiently, it makes sense to seek alternative techniques in some cases. For the most part, using the date/time calculation and range-matching techniques discussed in the previous section will yield the best possible performance. However, in some cases ease of user interaction may be more important than performance. It is quite likely that more technical business users will request direct access to query key business databases, but very unlikely that they will be savvy enough with T-SQL to be able to do complex date/time calculations.[4]

In these cases, as well as a few others that will be discussed in this section, it makes sense to predefine the time periods that will get queried. A lookup table can be created that allows users to easily derive any number of named periods from the current date. These tables, not surprisingly, are referred to as **calendar tables**, and they can be extremely useful.

The basic calendar table has a date/time column that acts as the primary key and several columns that describe time periods. Each date in the range of dates covered by the calendar will have one row inserted into the table, which can be used to reference all of the associated time periods. A standard example might look something like the following:

```
CREATE TABLE Calendar
(
    [Day] SMALLDATETIME NOT NULL PRIMARY KEY,
    [Year] TINYINT NOT NULL,
    [Month] TINYINT NOT NULL,
    DayOfYear SMALLINT NOT NULL,
    DayOfMonth TINYINT NOT NULL,
    WeekOfYear TINYINT NOT NULL,
    WeekOfMonth TINYINT NOT NULL,
    ...
)
```

By querying the table, users can quickly and easily set up queries for various time periods, without having to know too much about date/time calculations. Obviously, this can make life much easier.

The most difficult part about working with these tables is creating them. And while doing so is probably a great exercise in learning all about the kind of calculations covered previously in this chapter, it's a total waste of time. Hidden within SQL Server's companion toolset is a ready-made calendar table creation engine. This book does not discuss the Microsoft Business Intelligence suite, but for the sake of this exercise, a quick trip into that area is necessary.

To begin, open up Business Intelligence Development Studio and create a new project. Select Business Intelligence Projects and Analysis Services Project, as shown in Figure 10-3.

---

4. But if they want to try, they're more than welcome to purchase a copy of this book!

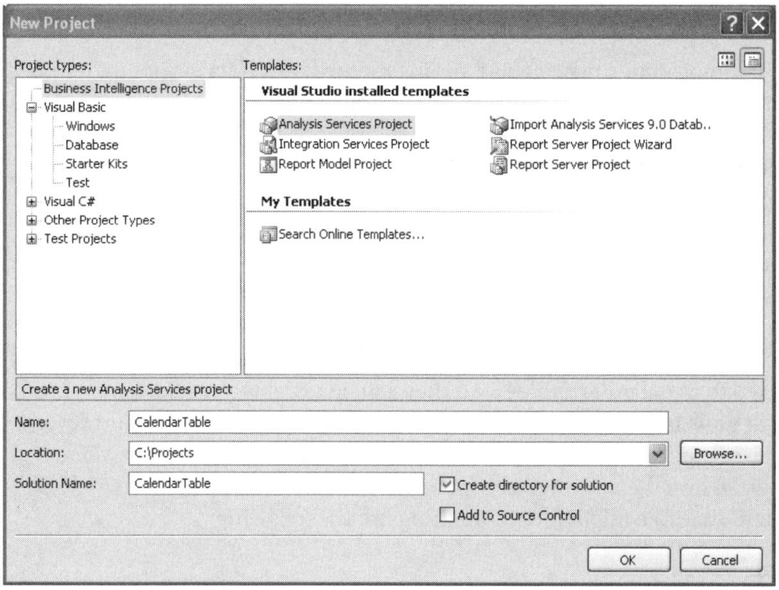

Figure 10-3. *Creating a new Analysis Services Project*

Once the project is created, you need to tell it where to find the database that you'd like the calendar table created in. Right-click Data Sources as shown in Figure 10-4, and enter the connection information for the database of your choice.

Figure 10-4. *Adding database connection information*

The next step is to bring up the Dimension Wizard, by right-clicking Dimensions and selecting New Dimension as shown in Figure 10-5. This wizard is used to define reference tables (known as **dimensions** in OLAP contexts). To set up a calendar-type table, select Build the dimension without using a data source, and then select the Date Template, as shown in Figure 10-6.

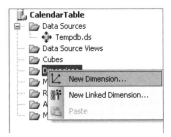

Figure 10-5. *Creating a new dimension*

Figure 10-6. *Selecting the Date dimension template*

Once the Date template has been selected, you can specify which named time periods you'd like included in the table, as shown in Figure 10-7. These will be the periods that users will be able to most easily find and work with based on the calendar table. Since selecting each of these will not add too much space to the table, it's probably not a bad idea to err on the side of too much when making selections here. However, keep in mind that additional columns may make the table more confusing for less-technical users.

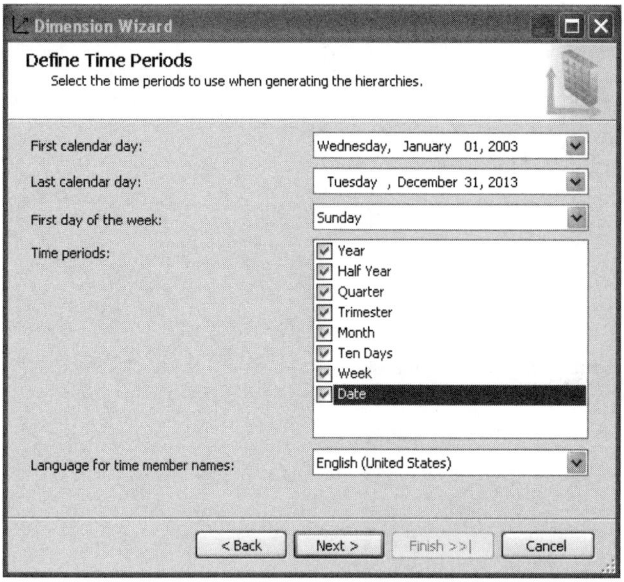

Figure 10-7. *Defining time periods for the calendar*

At the top of this screen, you'll see an option for selecting the range of days that will be included in the calendar. I recommend going as far back as the data you'll be working with goes, and at least 10 years into the future. Although this sounds like it will potentially produce a lot of rows, keep in mind that every 10 years' worth of data will only require around 3,652 rows. Considering that it's quite common to see tables with hundreds of millions of rows, such a small number should be easily manageable.

On the next screen, shown in Figure 10-8, you have the option of adding additional time periods for a few specific calendar types used in various business scenarios. Refer to the Analysis Services documentation for more details on these options.

Figure 10-9 shows the next screen in the wizard, where you can name the dimension. Keep in mind that whatever name you pick will be the name of the table in your database. Check the Generate schema now checkbox, and click Finish to move on to the next step, in which Business Intelligence Development Studio will actually create the table you've just specified.

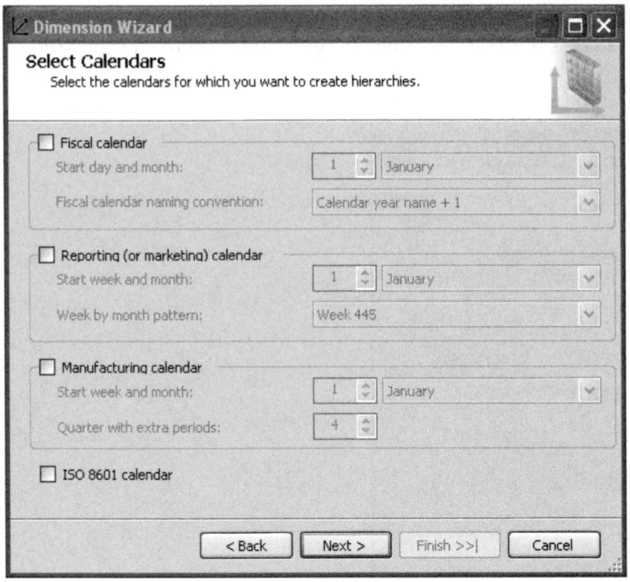

Figure 10-8. *Choosing business-related calendar periods*

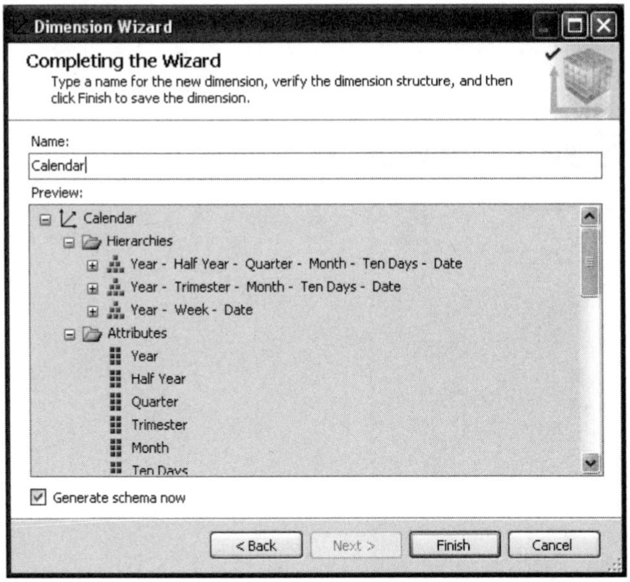

Figure 10-9. *Naming the calendar table*

On the next screen, shown in Figure 10-10, select the data source defined at the beginning and click Next. The screen shown in Figure 10-11 will appear next. Specify a schema that your table should belong to (in this case, I've chosen to put my calendar table into a new schema called `Temporal`), and check all of the checkboxes. Make sure that the Populate option is set; this option specifies that the table will be created with rows for all of the days in the selected time period.

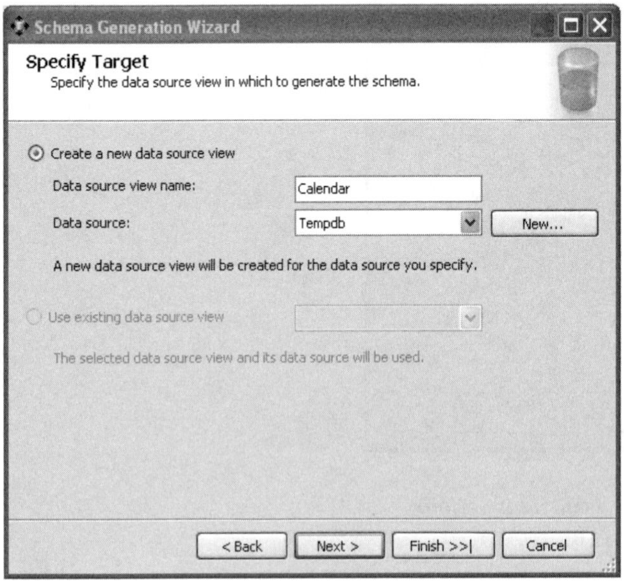

Figure 10-10. *Selecting the target data source*

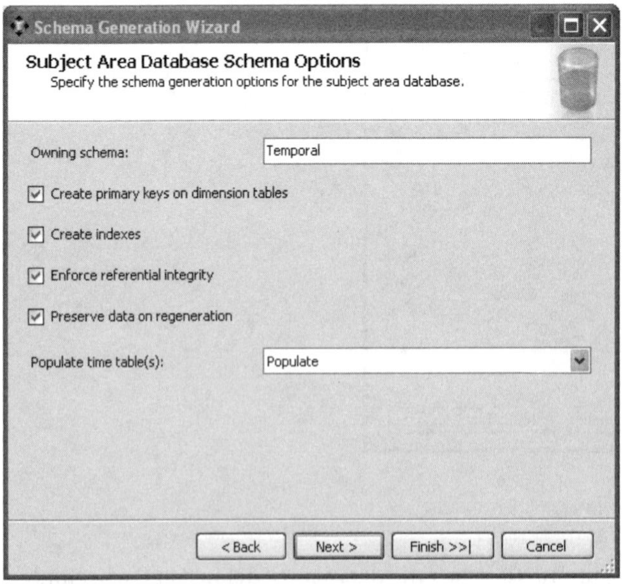

Figure 10-11. *Defining the owning schema, index, and data population options*

After clicking Finish, a screen like that shown in Figure 10-12 should appear, letting you know that the table has been created. At this point, you can delete the Analysis Services project you've created; it has served its purpose, which was to create a relational calendar table.

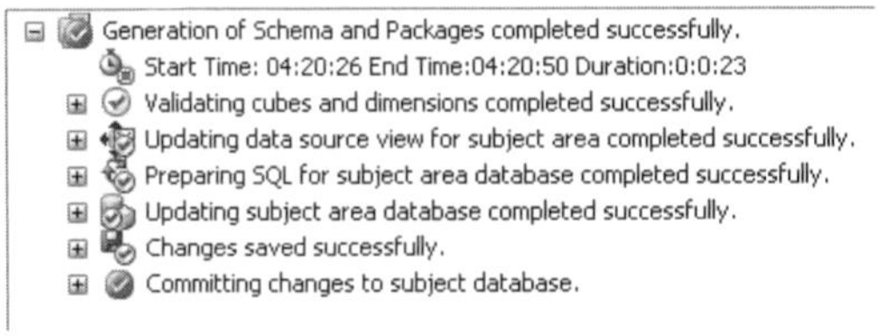

Figure 10-12. *The calendar table was successfully created.*

Once the calendar table has been created, it can be used for many of the same calculations covered in the last section, as well as for many other uses. First, a reminder: the calendar table generated by Business Intelligence Development Studio has one row per day, and each day is keyed using a DATETIME value for that day, with its time set to midnight. Therefore, in order to find "today's row," you must truncate the time portion from the GETDATE function:

```
SELECT *
FROM Temporal.Calendar AS Today
WHERE Today.PK_Date = DATEADD(day, DATEDIFF(day, 0, GETDATE()), 0)
```

Once you've identified "today," it's simple to find other days. For example, "Last Friday" is the most recent Friday with a PK_Date value less than today:

```
SELECT TOP(1) *
FROM Temporal.Calendar LastFriday
WHERE
    LastFriday.PK_Date < DATEADD(day, DATEDIFF(day, 0, GETDATE()), 0)
    AND LastFriday.Day_of_Week = 6
ORDER BY PK_Date DESC
```

Note that I selected the default setting of Sunday as first day of the week when I created my calendar table. If you select a different first day of the week, you'll have to change the Day_of_Week value specified. It is advisable to modify your calendar table and add English (or another language, if English is not your native tongue) names instead of using the numeric values. That way, if your business treats Monday instead of Sunday as the first day of the week, users will not have to know which number to use; they can query based on the name. The following T-SQL adds and populates Day_Description and Month_Description columns to the table:

```
ALTER TABLE Temporal.Calendar
ADD
    Day_Description VARCHAR(15) NULL,
    Month_Description VARCHAR(15) NULL
```

```
UPDATE Temporal.Calendar
SET
    Day_Description = DATENAME(weekday, PK_Date),
    Month_Description = DATENAME(month, PK_Date)

ALTER TABLE Temporal.Calendar
ALTER COLUMN Day_Description VARCHAR(15) NOT NULL

ALTER TABLE Temporal.Calendar
ALTER COLUMN Month_Description VARCHAR(15) NOT NULL
```

The columns are populated using the DATENAME function, which behaves similarly to DATEPART, but returns a localized character string in some cases (e.g., for days and months). Keep in mind that running this code on servers with different locale settings may produce different results.

Since the calendar table contains columns that define various periods such as the current year and the week of the year, it becomes easy to answer questions such as "What happened this week?" To find the first and last days of "this week," the following query can be used:

```
SELECT
    MIN(ThisWeek.PK_Date) AS FirstDayOfWeek,
    MAX(ThisWeek.PK_Date) AS LastDayOfWeek
FROM Temporal.Calendar AS Today
JOIN Temporal.Calendar AS ThisWeek ON
    ThisWeek.Year = Today.Year
    AND ThisWeek.Week_of_Year = Today.Week_of_Year
WHERE
    Today.PK_Date = DATEADD(day, DATEDIFF(day, 0, GETDATE()), 0)
```

A similar question might deal with adjacent weeks. For instance, you may wish to identify "Friday of last week." The following query is a first attempt at doing so:

```
SELECT FridayLastWeek.*
FROM Temporal.Calendar AS Today
JOIN Temporal.Calendar AS FridayLastWeek ON
    Today.Year = FridayLastWeek.Year
    AND Today.Week_Of_Year - 1 = FridayLastWeek.Week_Of_Year
WHERE
    Today.PK_Date = DATEADD(day, DATEDIFF(day, 0, GETDATE()), 0)
    AND FridayLastWeek.Day_Description = 'Friday'
```

Unfortunately, this code has an edge problem that will cause it to be somewhat nonfunctional around the first of the year in certain cases. The issue is that the Week_of_Year value resets to 1 on the first day of a new year, regardless of what day it falls on. The query also joins on the Year column, making the situation doubly complex.

Working around the issue using a CASE expression may be possible, but it will be difficult, and the goal of the calendar table is to simplify things. A good alternative solution is to add a Week_Number column that numbers every week consecutively for the entire duration represented by the calendar. The first step in doing this is to alter the table and add the column, as shown by the following T-SQL:

```
ALTER TABLE Temporal.Calendar
ADD Week_Number INT NULL
```

Next, a temporary table of all of the week numbers can be created, using the following T-SQL:

```
;WITH StartOfWeek (PK_Date)
AS
(
    SELECT MIN(PK_Date)
    FROM Temporal.Calendar

    UNION

    SELECT PK_Date
    FROM Temporal.Calendar
    WHERE Day_of_Week = 1
),
EndOfWeek (PK_Date)
AS
(
    SELECT PK_Date
    FROM Temporal.Calendar
    WHERE Day_of_Week = 7

    UNION

    SELECT MAX(PK_Date)
    FROM Temporal.Calendar
)
SELECT
    StartOfWeek.PK_Date AS Start_Date,
    (
        SELECT TOP(1)
            EndOfWeek.PK_Date
        FROM EndOfWeek
        WHERE EndOfWeek.PK_Date >= StartOfWeek.PK_Date
        ORDER BY EndOfWeek.PK_Date
    ) AS End_Date,
    ROW_NUMBER() OVER (ORDER BY StartOfWeek.PK_Date) AS Week_Number
INTO #WeekNumbers
FROM StartOfWeek
```

The logic of this T-SQL should be explained a bit. The StartOfWeek CTE selects each day from the calendar table where the day of the week is 1, in addition to the first day in the table, in case that day is not the first day of a week. The EndOfWeek CTE uses similar logic to find the last day of every week, in addition to the last day represented in the table. The SELECT list includes the PK_Date represented for each row of the StartOfWeek CTE, the lowest PK_Date value from the EndOfWeek CTE that's greater than the StartOfWeek value (which is the end of the week), and a week number generated using the ROW_NUMBER function. The results of the query are inserted into a temporary table called #WeekNumbers. Once this T-SQL has been run, the calendar table's new column can be populated and set to be nonnullable, using the following code:

```
UPDATE Temporal.Calendar
SET Week_Number =
    (
        SELECT WN.Week_Number
        FROM #WeekNumbers AS WN
        WHERE
            Temporal.Calendar.PK_Date BETWEEN WN.Start_Date AND WN.End_Date
    )


ALTER TABLE Temporal.Calendar
ALTER COLUMN Week_Number INT NOT NULL
```

Using the Week_Number column, finding "Friday of last week" becomes almost trivially simple:

```
SELECT FridayLastWeek.*
FROM Temporal.Calendar AS Today
JOIN Temporal.Calendar AS FridayLastWeek ON
    Today.Week_Number = FridayLastWeek.Week_Number + 1
WHERE
    Today.PK_Date = DATEADD(day, DATEDIFF(day, 0, GETDATE()), 0)
    AND FridayLastWeek.Day_Description = 'Friday'
```

The query may be easier to read—especially for beginning T-SQL users—if a subquery is used instead of a join:

```
SELECT FridayLastWeek.*
FROM Temporal.Calendar AS FridayLastWeek
WHERE
    FridayLastWeek.Day_Description = 'Friday'
    AND FridayLastWeek.Week_Number =
    (
        SELECT Today.Week_Number - 1
        FROM Temporal.Calendar AS Today
        WHERE Today.PK_Date = DATEADD(day, DATEDIFF(day, 0, GETDATE()), 0)
    )
```

Of course, one key problem still remains: finding the date of the next New England SQL Server Users Group meeting, on the second Thursday of the month. There are a couple of ways that a calendar table can be used to address this dilemma. The first method, of course, is to query the calendar table and come up with the right query. The following T-SQL is one way of doing so:

```
;WITH NextTwoMonths
AS
(
    SELECT
        Year,
        Month_of_Year
    FROM Temporal.Calendar
    WHERE
        PK_Date IN
        (
            DATEADD(day, DATEDIFF(day, 0, GETDATE()), 0),
            DATEADD(month, 1, DATEADD(day, DATEDIFF(day, 0, GETDATE()), 0))
        )
),
NumberedThursdays
AS
(
    SELECT
        Thursdays.*,
        ROW_NUMBER() OVER (PARTITION BY Month ORDER BY PK_Date) AS ThursdayNumber
    FROM Temporal.Calendar Thursdays
    JOIN NextTwoMonths ON
        NextTwoMonths.Year = Thursdays.Year
        AND NextTwoMonths.Month_of_Year = Thursdays.Month_of_Year
    WHERE
        Thursdays.Day_Description = 'Thursday'
)
SELECT TOP(1)
    NumberedThursdays.*
FROM NumberedThursdays
WHERE
    NumberedThursdays.PK_Date >= DATEADD(day, DATEDIFF(day, 0, GETDATE()), 0)
    AND NumberedThursdays.ThursdayNumber = 2
ORDER BY NumberedThursdays.PK_Date
```

If you find this T-SQL to be just a bit on the confusing side, that's probably a good sign that you haven't gone too far off the deep end yet, as can happen after years of working with databases too much. Here's how it works: First, the code finds the month and year for the current month and the next month, using the NextTwoMonths CTE. Then, in the NumberedThursdays CTE, every Thursday for those two months is identified and numbered sequentially. Finally, the lowest Thursday with a number of 2 (meaning that it's a second Thursday), which falls on a day on or after "today," is returned.

Luckily, such complex T-SQL can often be made obsolete using calendar tables. You may have noticed that the calendar table is already representing a variety of named days and time periods. There is, of course, no reason that you can't add your own columns to create named periods specific to your business requirements. Asking for the next second Thursday would have been much easier had there simply been a prepopulated column representing user group meeting days.

A much more common requirement is figuring out which days are business days. This information is essential for determining work schedules, metrics relating to service-level agreements, and other common business needs. Although you could simply count out the weekend days, this would fail to take into account national holidays, state and local holidays that your business might observe, and company retreat days or other days off that might be specific to your firm.

To address all of these issues in one shot, simply add a column to the table called `Holiday_Description`:

```
ALTER TABLE Temporal.Calendar
ADD Holiday_Description VARCHAR(50) NULL
```

This column can be populated for any holiday, be it national, local, firm-specific, or a weekend day. This makes it easy to answer questions such as "How many business days do we have this month?" The following T-SQL answers that one:

```
SELECT COUNT(*)
FROM Temporal.Calendar AS ThisMonth
WHERE
    Holiday_Description IS NULL
    AND EXISTS
    (
        SELECT *
        FROM Temporal.Calendar AS Today
        WHERE
            Today.PK_Date = DATEADD(day, DATEDIFF(day, 0, GETDATE()), 0)
            AND Today.Year = ThisMonth.Year
            AND Today.Month_Of_Year = ThisMonth.Month_of_Year
    )
```

If your business is seasonally affected, try adding a column that helps you identify various seasonal time periods, such as "early spring," "mid summer," or "the holiday season," to help with analytical queries based on these time periods. Or, you might find that several additional columns are necessary to reflect all of the time periods that are important to your queries.

Using calendar tables can make time period–oriented queries quite a bit easier, but remember that they require ongoing maintenance. Make sure to document processes for keeping defined time periods up to date, as well as for adding additional days to the calendar to make sure that your data doesn't overrun the scope of the available days. You may want to add an additional year of days on the first of each year, in order to maintain a constant 10-year buffer.

Designing and Querying Temporal Data Stores

Given the commonality of the requirement in virtually every possible application to store temporal data, it's not surprising how involved a discussion of techniques for dealing with the data can become. Depending on the business requirements, systems may need to be able to deal with users in disparate time zones, logically deal with time intervals, or work within the possibility of late-arriving updates to data that changes the facts about what happened days or weeks prior.

T-SQL includes very limited facilities to help developers deal with temporal data, but with proper design and a bit of forethought, it should not be a problem. This section discusses various temporal data design issues, and shows both how to set up your database to store various types of temporal data and how to effectively query the data once it's been stored.

Dealing with Time Zones

One of the consequences of moving into a global economy is the complexity that doing business with people in different areas brings to the table. Language barriers aside, the most important issues revolve around the problems of time variance. Essentially, any system that needs to work with people simultaneously residing in different areas must be able to properly handle the idea that these people do not all have their watches set the same way.

In 1884, 24 standard time zones were defined at a meeting of delegates in Washington, D.C., for the International Meridian Conference. Each of these time zones represents a 1-hour offset, which is determined in relation to the *prime meridian*, the time zone of Greenwich, England.[5] This central time zone is referred to either as GMT (Greenwich Mean Time) or UTC (Universale Temps Coordinee, French for "Coordinated Universal Time").

The net effect of defining these zones is that, if they know each others' offsets and are synchronized to the same UTC-specific clock, everyone on Earth can figure out what time it is anywhere else on Earth where the standard time zones are used.

As I write these words, it's just after 4:15 a.m. I'm writing in the UTC-5 zone (Eastern United States), but since we're currently observing daylight savings time, the zone is actually UTC-4 at the moment. Using the offset, I can instantly deduce that it is currently 8:15 a.m. in Greenwich and 3:15 p.m. in Bangkok, Thailand, which uses an offset of UTC+7. Unfortunately, not all of the countries in the world use the standard zones. For instance, it is 12:45 p.m. in Mumbai, India right now; India uses a nonstandard offset of UTC+5.5. Time zones, as it turns out, are really just as much about political boundaries as they are about keeping the right time globally.

There are three central issues to worry about when writing time zone–specific software:

- When a user sees data presented by the application, any dates should be rendered in the user's local time zone (if known), unless otherwise noted, in which case data should generally be rendered in UTC to avoid confusion.

- When a user submits new data or updates existing data, thereby altering date/time data in the database, the database should convert the data from the user's time zone to a standard time zone (again, this will generally be UTC). All date/time data in the database should be standardized to a specific zone so that, based on known offsets, it can be easily converted to users' local times. It can also be important to store both the original zone and the local time in that zone, in which a given event occurred, for greater control and auditability. Given that start and end dates for daylight savings times occasionally change, it can be difficult to derive the original local times from a time stored only in UTC or only with an offset. If you will need to report or query based on local times in which events occurred, consider persisting them as-is in addition to storing the times standardized to UTC.

5. Greenwich Mean Time, "Time Zones History," http://wwp.greenwichmeantime.com/info/time-zones-history.htm, accessed September 16, 2006.

- When a user asks a temporally based question, it's important to decide whether the dates used to ask the question will be used as-is (possibly in the user's local time zone) or converted to the standard time zone first. Consider a user in New York asking the question, "What happened between 2:00 p.m. and 5:00 p.m. today?" If date/time data in the database is all based in the UTC zone, it's unclear whether the user is referring to 2:00 p.m. to 5:00 p.m. EST or UTC—very different questions! The actual requirements here will vary based on business requirements, but it is a good idea to put a note on any screen in which this may be an issue to remind the user of what's going on.

Dealing with these issues is not actually too difficult, but it does require a good amount of discipline and attention to detail, not to mention some data about time zone offsets and daylight savings changes in various zones. It's a good idea to handle as much of the work as possible in the application layer, but some (or sometimes all) of the responsibility will naturally spill into the data layer. The basic technique I recommend is to maintain time zone settings for each user of the system so that when they log in, you can find out what zone you should treat their data as native to. Any time you need to show the user dates and times, convert them to the user's local zone; and any time the user enters dates or times into the application for either searching or as data points, convert them into UTC before they hit the database. However, if you can't do some or all of the work in the application layer, you'll obviously have to do the necessary date/time calculations in the database.

This all sounds easy enough, except that there is no standard way of converting dates and times between zones in SQL Server, and many programming platforms (including the .NET Framework) also lack this seemingly basic functionality. The other problem is getting the data to even implement such functionality; while you could scrape it off of a web site, that's probably not something most developers want to deal with. And luckily, you really don't have to; although not part of the .NET Framework itself, a solution in the form of a code sample has already been created by Microsoft's .NET team.

The good news is that all of the data necessary for dealing with time zone issues is already in your computer, stored in your registry. Remember when you installed Windows and were asked what time zone you were in? That data is still available—it just needs to be exposed in a better format. The bad news is that because time zones are made-up political entities, they are subject to change, and by using Microsoft's data you have to trust that Microsoft will update it from time to time as necessary—or try hacking your registry to fix the data yourself, should you find it to be less than satisfactory.

The TimeZoneSample code sample is based around a C# type called TimeZoneInfo that exposes time zone information and a method called GetTimeZonesFromRegistry that pulls all of the time zone data out of the registry and puts it into a collection of TimeZoneInfo objects.[6] The sample also includes two key methods for working with time zones: ConvertTimeZoneToUtc and ConvertUtcToTimeZone. These methods convert instances of DateTime to and from UTC, based on time zone offsets and even taking daylight savings changes into account. Essentially, this is all that's needed to manage time zone issues either in the application layer or in the database (thanks, of course, to SQLCLR integration).

---

6. The TimeZoneSample code is available here: http://download.microsoft.com/download/4/5/5/4555538c-6002-4f04-8c58-2b304af92402/converttimezone.exe.

■**Note** Daylight savings time start and end dates sometimes change—remember that they're nothing more than geopolitical constructs and are essentially set within any given time zone at the whim of government agencies charged with determining the best way to handle time changes. Unfortunately, Microsoft operating systems prior to Windows Vista supported only one "version" of daylight savings time for each given time zone. Since the TimeZoneSample uses the data in the Windows registry, data may not be consistently convertible back to local time from UTC as daylight savings changes occur. Windows Vista introduces a feature called **Dynamic Time Zone Support**, which allows the operating system to keep track of multiple versions for each zone, thereby fixing this problem—but at least as of the time of this writing, the TimeZoneSample does not yet support that feature. This is further reason that you should consider persisting a standardized version of the time in which an event occurred in addition to the actual local time.

Building a reusable class framework around the sample, which can be exploited from either application code or inside of the database, is fairly easy—all of the hard work has already been done inside of the sample. The first step is to set up a call to read the time zone data from the registry via the GetTimeZonesFromRegistry method. That requires nothing more than the following:

```
TimeZoneInfo[] tz =
    TimeZoneInfo.GetTimeZonesFromRegistry();
```

Once the TimeZoneInfo collection has been built, the next step is to find the necessary time zone and use it to convert a date either to or from UTC. However, before I get into that, I'd like to point out a performance issue: during testing, I noticed that these calls to retrieve the data from the registry were taking up to a tenth of a second each. Since this data changes very infrequently and might need to be read millions of times a day in busy applications, I decided that use of a cache was in order. So the first step to creating the class is to set up a static member to hold this data between calls and a static constructor to fill the data on the first invocation of the class:

```
public class TimeZoneData
{
    private static readonly Dictionary<int, TimeZoneInfo> timeZones =
        new Dictionary<int, TimeZoneInfo>();

    static TimeZoneData()
    {
        TimeZoneInfo[] tz =
            TimeZoneInfo.GetTimeZonesFromRegistry();

        foreach (TimeZoneInfo info in tz)
        {
            timeZones.Add(info.Index, info);
        }
    }
}
```

I've used a generic `Dictionary` to hold the `TimeZoneInfo` instances and set it up so that they can be retrieved based on the unique "index" that each time zone in the registry is given. This index is the most likely candidate for use as a key to store users' time zone preferences in the database. By using this cache, subsequent calls to retrieve the data have a tiny overhead— 1 millisecond or less on my machine.

■**Note** `GetTimeZonesFromRegistry` does exactly that; it reads from the registry. The area it reads from is, by default, accessible to all system users, so permissions are not an issue. However, if you use these samples from within SQL Server, be aware that you'll have to use the `EXTERNAL_ACCESS` permission set or your assembly will not be allowed to read from the registry.

Once the cache is set up, the next step is to create a method to pull back each time zone's name and index. This data is necessary in order to give users a way of choosing time zones. You may want to store this data in a table in the database, but I would not advise doing so, as you'll have to worry about keeping the table up to date when and if the data changes. By reading the data dynamically from the cache, you can be certain that the data will be updated either immediately when it changes or on the next system restart or cache clear thereafter. A table-valued function that retrieves the time zone names and indexes from the cache follows:

```
[Microsoft.SqlServer.Server.SqlFunction(
    FillRowMethodName="FillZoneTable",
    TableDefinition="TimeZoneName NVARCHAR(100), TimeZoneIndex INT")]
public static IEnumerable GetTimeZoneIndexes()
{
    return (timeZones.Values);
}

public static void FillZoneTable(
    object obj,
    out SqlString TimeZoneName,
    out SqlInt32 TimeZoneIndex)
{
    TimeZoneInfo tz = (TimeZoneInfo)obj;
    TimeZoneName = new SqlString(tz.DisplayName);
    TimeZoneIndex = new SqlInt32(tz.Index);
}
```

Once users have selected time zone settings, you'll have to deal with conversions. The following method first retrieves the necessary instance of `TimeZoneInfo` from the cache, and then calls the `ConvertTimeZoneToUtc` method found in the sample in order to do the conversion of the input time to UTC:

```
public static DateTime TimeZoneToUtc(
    DateTime time,
    int TimeZoneIndex)
```

```
{
    TimeZoneInfo tzInfo = null;

    try
    {
        //Get the TimeZoneInfo instance from the cache
        tzInfo = timeZones[TimeZoneIndex];
    }
    catch (KeyNotFoundException e)
    {
        //No time zone has that index
    }

    if (tzInfo != null)
    {
        //Convert the input DateTime to UTC
        DateTime convertedTime =
            TimeZoneInfo.ConvertTimeZoneToUtc(time, tzInfo);

        return (convertedTime);
    }
    else
    {
        //The value of TimeZoneIndex does not correspond to a time zone
        throw (new ArgumentOutOfRangeException("TimeZoneIndex"));
    }
}
```

This method throws an ArgumentOutOfRange exception if the input time zone index is not found. To use this method from within SQL Server, you should wrap it in a CLR UDF to both protect the type interfaces and handle the exception. In the following implementation, I return NULL if an invalid index is passed in:

```
[Microsoft.SqlServer.Server.SqlFunction]
public static SqlDateTime ConvertTimeZoneToUtc(
    SqlDateTime time,
    SqlInt32 TimeZoneIndex)
{
    try
    {
        DateTime convertedTime =
            TimeZoneToUtc(time.Value, TimeZoneIndex.Value);

        return (new SqlDateTime(convertedTime));
    }
```

```
    catch (ArgumentOutOfRangeException e)
    {
        return (SqlDateTime.Null);
    }
}
```

A similar wrapper should be created for the ConvertUtcToTimeZone method (not included here for brevity—the method signature is the same, so only a single line of code in each method has to be modified).

From a SQL Server standpoint, much of the work is done at this point. The remaining tasks are getting the UDFs into service where necessary and ensuring that any data in the database uses UTC rather than local time. Anywhere in the database code that the GETDATE function is used to insert data, you should instead use the GETUTCDATE function, which returns the current date/time in Greenwich.

Keep in mind that the GETDATE to GETUTCDATE conversion rule only applies unconditionally for inserts; if you're converting a database from local time to UTC, a blind find/replace-style conversion from GETDATE to GETUTCDATE may not yield the expected results. For instance, consider the following stored procedure, which selects "today's" orders from the AdventureWorks Sales.SalesOrderHeader table:

```
CREATE PROCEDURE GetTodaysOrders
AS
BEGIN
    SET NOCOUNT ON

    SELECT
        OrderDate,
        SalesOrderNumber,
        AccountNumber,
        TotalDue
    FROM Sales.SalesOrderHeader
    WHERE
        OrderDate >= DATEADD(day, DATEDIFF(day, 0, GETDATE()), 0)
        AND OrderDate < DATEADD(day, DATEDIFF(day, 0, GETDATE())+1, 0)
END
```

Assume that you've already updated the Sales.SalesOrderHeader table, converting all of the date/time values to UTC, by using the ConvertTimeZoneToUtc function. It might seem like changing the GETDATE calls in this code to GETUTCDATE is a natural follow-up move. However, what if your application is hosted in New York, and the majority of your users are used to seeing and dealing with times synchronized to Eastern Standard Time? This change would, in effect, break the application in two different ways:

- First of all, all of the data will be 4 or 5 hours "ahead" of where it was previously (depending on the particular value of the daylight savings setting for that time of year). Yet the date truncation methods called on GETUTCDATE will return the same exact value as if called on GETDATE, most of the day. Remember, GETUTCDATE still returns an instance of DATETIME; it's just a different time. So this change will cause you to lose the first four or 5 hours' worth of data for any given day . . . but that's true only if this code is used early enough in the day.

- The second issue is what happens if this code is called after 7:00 or 8:00 p.m. EST (again, depending on the time of year). In that case, GETUTCDATE will return a date/time that, for people in the eastern United States, is "tomorrow." The time portion will be truncated, and the query won't return any of "today's" data at all—at least, not if you're expecting things to work using Eastern Standard Time rules.

To correct these issues, use GETUTCDATE to find the current date/time in Greenwich, and convert it to the user's local time. After it is converted to local time, *then* truncate the time portion. Finally, convert the date back to UTC, and use the resultant date/time to search the table of UTC values. In order to accomplish this, the stored procedure would be modified as follows:

```
CREATE PROCEDURE GetTodaysOrders
    @TimeZoneIndex = 35
AS
BEGIN
    SET NOCOUNT ON

    DECLARE @TodayUtc DATETIME
    SET @TodayUtc = dbo.ConvertUtcToTimeZone(GETUTCDATE(), @TimeZoneIndex)
    SET @TodayUtc = DATEADD(day, DATEDIFF(day, 0, @TodayUtc), 0)
    SET @TodayUtc = dbo.ConvertTimeZoneToUtc(@TodayUtc, @TimeZoneIndex)
    SELECT @TodayUtc

    SELECT
        OrderDate,
        SalesOrderNumber,
        AccountNumber,
        TotalDue
    FROM Sales.SalesOrderHeader
    WHERE
        OrderDate >= @TodayUtc
        AND OrderDate < DATEADD(day, 1, @TodayUtc)
END
```

The @TimeZoneIndex parameter can be used to pass in the user's specified local time zone, but it has been defaulted to 35 (EST) in order to preserve the interface for existing code paths. Depending on whether or not you've handled it in your application code, a further modification would be to call ConvertUtcToTimeZone on the OrderDate column in the SELECT list, in order to return the data in the user's local time zone.

Time zone issues can become quite complex, but they can be solved by carefully evaluating the necessary changes to the code and even more carefully testing once changes have been implemented. The most important thing to remember is that consistency is key when working with time-standardized data; any hole in the data modification routines that inserts nonstandardized data can cause ambiguity that may be impossible to fix. Once inserted, there is no way to ask the database whether a time was supposed to be in UTC or a local time zone.

Working with Intervals

Very few real-world events happen in a single moment. Time is continuous, and any given state change has a clearly defined start time and end time. For example, you might say, "I drove from Stockbridge to Boston at 10:00 o'clock." But you really didn't drive only at 10:00 o'clock, unless you happen to be in possession of some futuristic time/space-folding technology (and that's clearly beyond the scope of this chapter).

When working with databases, we often consider only the start or end time of an event, rather than the full interval. A column called OrderDate is an almost ubiquitous feature in databases that handle orders; but this column only stores the date/time that the order ended—when the user submitted the final request. It does not reflect how long the user spent browsing the site, filling the shopping cart, and entering credit card information. Likewise, every time we check our e-mail, we see a Sent Date field, which captures the moment that the sender hit the send button, but does not help identify how long that person spent thinking about or typing the e-mail, activities that constitute part of the "sending" process.

The fact is we don't often see this extended data because it's generally unnecessary. For most sites, it really doesn't matter for the purpose of order fulfillment how long the user spent browsing (although that information may be useful to UI designers and other user experience people). And it doesn't really matter, once an e-mail is sent, how much effort went into sending it. The important thing is, it was sent (and later received, another data point that many e-mail clients don't expose).

Despite these examples to the contrary, for many applications, both start and end times are necessary for a complete analysis. Take, for instance, your employment history. As you move from job to job, you carry intervals during which you had a certain title, were paid a certain amount, or had certain job responsibilities. Failing to include both the start and end dates with this data can create some interesting challenges.

Modeling and Querying Continuous Intervals

If a table uses only a starting time or an ending time (but not both) to represent intervals, all of the rows in that table can be considered to belong to one continuous interval that spans the entire time period represented. Each row in this case would represent a subinterval during which some status change occurred. Let's take a look at some simple examples to clarify this. Start with the following table and rows:

```
CREATE TABLE JobHistory
(
    Company VARCHAR(100),
    Title VARCHAR(100),
    Pay DECIMAL(9, 2),
    StartDate SMALLDATETIME
)
```

```
GO

INSERT JobHistory
(
    Company,
    Title,
    Pay,
    StartDate
)
SELECT 'Acme Corp', 'Programmer', 50000.00, '1995-06-26'
UNION ALL
SELECT 'Software Shop', 'Programmer/Analyst', 62000.00, '1998-10-05'
UNION ALL
SELECT 'Better Place', 'Junior DBA', 82000.00, '2001-01-08'
UNION ALL
SELECT 'Enterprise', 'Database Developer', 95000.00, '2005-11-14'
GO
```

A note on this table: I am not going to get into the question of primary keys and how to constrain this data just yet, as the examples that follow will clarify that issue. However, I would like to take this opportunity to point out a way that you can make life somewhat easier when working with this and similar temporal data. In this case, you'll notice that each of the dates uses a default time component. No one—except the worst micromanager—cares, looking at a job history record, if someone got in to work at 8:00 a.m. or 8:30 a.m. on the first day. What matters is that the date in the table is the start *date*. Encoding this rule can make querying the data a bit simpler—no need for the range queries discussed earlier in this chapter. The following check constraint can be added to make times other than midnight illegal:

```
ALTER TABLE JobHistory
ADD CONSTRAINT CK_StartDate_Midnight
    CHECK (StartDate = DATEADD(day, DATEDIFF(day, 0, StartDate), 0))
```

The data in the JobHistory table is easy enough to transform into a more logical format; to get the full subintervals we can assume that the end date of each job is the start date of the next. The end date of the final job, it can be assumed, is the present date (or, if you prefer, NULL). Converting this into a start/end report based on these rules requires T-SQL along the following lines:

```
SELECT
    J1.*,
    COALESCE((
        SELECT MIN(J2.StartDate)
        FROM JobHistory AS J2
        WHERE J2.StartDate > J1.StartDate),
        GETDATE()
    ) AS EndDate
FROM JobHistory AS J1
```

The outer query gets the job data and the start times, and the subquery finds the first start date after the current row's start date. If no such start date exists, the current date is used. Of course, an obvious major problem here is lack of support for gaps in the job history. This table may, for instance, hide the fact that the subject was laid off from Software Shop in July 2000. This is why I stressed the continuous nature of data modeled in this way.

Despite the lack of support for gaps, let's try a bit more data and see what happens. As the subject's career progressed, he received various title and pay changes during the periods of employment with these different companies:

```
INSERT JobHistory
(
    Company,
    Title,
    Pay,
    StartDate
)
SELECT 'Acme Corp', 'Programmer', 55000.00, '1996-09-01'
UNION ALL
SELECT 'Acme Corp', 'Programmer 2', 58000.00, '1997-09-01'
UNION ALL
SELECT 'Acme Corp', 'Programmer 3', 58000.00, '1998-09-01'
UNION ALL
SELECT 'Software Shop', 'Programmer/Analyst', 62000.00, '1998-10-05'
UNION ALL
SELECT 'Software Shop', 'Programmer/Analyst', 67000.00, '2000-01-01'
UNION ALL
SELECT 'Software Shop', 'Programmer', 40000.00, '2000-03-01'
UNION ALL
SELECT 'Better Place', 'Junior DBA', 84000.00, '2002-06-01'
UNION ALL
SELECT 'Better Place', 'DBA', 87000.00, '2004-06-01'
```

This data, shown in full along with the previous data in Table 10-1, follows the subject along a path of relative job growth. A few raises and title adjustments—including one title adjustment with no associated pay raise—and an unfortunate demotion along with a down-sized salary, just before getting laid off in 2000 (the gap which, as mentioned, is not able to be represented here). Luckily, after studying databases while laid off, the subject bounced back with a much better salary and, of course, a more satisfying career track!

Table 10-1. *The Subject's Full Job History, with Salary and Title Adjustments*

Company	Title	Pay	StartDate
Acme Corp	Programmer	50000.00	1995-06-26
Acme Corp	Programmer	55000.00	1996-09-01
Acme Corp	Programmer 2	58000.00	1997-09-01
Acme Corp	Programmer 3	58000.00	1998-09-01
Software Shop	Programmer/Analyst	62000.00	1998-10-05

Company	Title	Pay	StartDate
Software Shop	Programmer/Analyst	62000.00	1998-10-05
Software Shop	Programmer/Analyst	67000.00	2000-01-01
Software Shop	Programmer	40000.00	2000-03-01
Better Place	Junior DBA	82000.00	2001-01-08
Better Place	Junior DBA	84000.00	2002-06-01
Better Place	DBA	87000.00	2004-06-01
Enterprise	Database Developer	95000.00	2005-11-14

Ignoring the gap, let's see how one might answer a resume-style question using this data. As a modification to the previous query, show the start and end date of tenure with each company, along with the maximum salary earned at the company, and what title was held when the highest salary was being earned.

The first step commonly taken in tackling this kind of challenge is to use a correlated subquery to find the rows that have the maximum value per group. In this case, that means the maximum pay per company:

```
SELECT
    Pay,
    Title
FROM JobHistory AS J2
WHERE
    J2.Pay =
    (
        SELECT MAX(Pay)
        FROM JobHistory AS J3
        WHERE J3.Company = J2.Company
    )
```

One key modification that must be made is to the basic query that finds start and end dates. Due to the fact that there are now multiple rows per job, the MIN aggregate will have to be employed to find the real start date, and the end date subquery modified to look not only at date changes, but also company changes. The following T-SQL finds the correct start and end dates for each company:

```
SELECT
    J1.Company,
    MIN(J1.StartDate) AS StartDate,
    COALESCE((
        SELECT MIN(J2.StartDate)
        FROM JobHistory AS J2
        WHERE
            J2.Company <> J1.Company
            AND J2.StartDate > MIN(J1.StartDate)),
        GETDATE()
    ) AS EndDate
```

```
FROM JobHistory AS J1
GROUP BY J1.Company
ORDER BY StartDate
```

A quick note: this query would not work properly if the person had been hired back by the same company after a period of absence during which he was working for another firm. To solve that problem, you might use a query similar to the following, in which a check is done to ensure that the "previous" row (based on StartDate) does not have the same company name (meaning that the subject switched firms):

```
SELECT
    J1.Company,
    J1.StartDate AS StartDate,
    COALESCE((
        SELECT MIN(J2.StartDate)
        FROM JobHistory AS J2
        WHERE
            J2.Company <> J1.Company
            AND J2.StartDate > J1.StartDate),
        GETDATE()
    ) AS EndDate
FROM JobHistory AS J1
WHERE
    J1.Company <>
    COALESCE((
        SELECT TOP(1)
            J3.Company
        FROM JobHistory J3
        WHERE J3.StartDate < J1.StartDate
        ORDER BY J3.StartDate DESC),
        '')
GROUP BY
    J1.Company,
    J1.StartDate
ORDER BY
    J1.StartDate
```

This example complicates things a bit too much for the sake of this chapter, but I feel that it is important to point this technique out in case you find it necessary to write these kinds of queries in production applications. This pattern is useful in many scenarios, especially when logging the status of an automated system and trying to determine downtime statistics or other metrics.

Getting back to the primary task at hand, showing the employment history along with peak salaries and job titles, the next step is to merge the query that finds the correct start and end dates with the query that finds the maximum salary and associated title. The simplest way of accomplishing this is with the CROSS APPLY operator, which behaves similarly to a correlated subquery but returns a table rather than a scalar value. The following T-SQL shows how to accomplish this:

```
SELECT
    x.Company,
    x.StartDate,
    x.EndDate,
    p.Pay,
    p.Title
FROM
(
    SELECT
        J1.Company,
        MIN(J1.StartDate) AS StartDate,
        COALESCE((
            SELECT MIN(J2.StartDate)
            FROM JobHistory AS J2
            WHERE
                J2.Company <> J1.Company
                AND J2.StartDate > MIN(J1.StartDate)),
            GETDATE()
        ) AS EndDate
    FROM JobHistory AS J1
    GROUP BY J1.Company
) x
CROSS APPLY
(
    SELECT
        Pay,
        Title
    FROM JobHistory AS J2
    WHERE
        J2.StartDate >= x.StartDate
        AND J2.StartDate < x.EndDate
        AND J2.Pay =
        (
            SELECT MAX(Pay)
            FROM JobHistory AS J3
            WHERE J3.Company = J2.Company
        )
) p
ORDER BY x.StartDate
```

This T-SQL correlates the CROSS APPLY subquery using the StartDate and EndDate columns from the outer query in order to find the correct employment intervals that go along with each position. The StartDate/EndDate pair for each period of employment is a **half-open interval** (or **semiopen**, depending on which mathematics textbook you're referring to); the StartDate end of the interval is **closed** (inclusive of the end point), and the EndDate is **open** (exclusive). This is because the EndDate for one interval is actually the StartDate for the next interval, and these intervals do not overlap.

Although the query does work, it has an issue; the CROSS APPLY subquery will return more than one row if a title change was made at the maximum pay level, without an associated pay increase (as happens in this data set), thereby producing duplicate rows in the result. The solution is to select the appropriate row by ordering the result by the Pay column, descending. The modified subquery, which will return only one row per position, is as follows:

```
SELECT TOP(1)
    Pay,
    Title
FROM JobHistory AS J2
WHERE
    J2.StartDate >= x.StartDate
    AND J2.StartDate < x.EndDate
ORDER BY Pay DESC
```

The important things that I hope you can take away from these examples are the patterns used for manipulating the intervals, as well as the fact that modeling intervals in this way may not be sufficient for many cases.

In terms of query style, the main thing to notice is that in order to logically manipulate this data, some form of an "end" for the interval must be synthesized within the query. Any time you're faced with a table that maps changes to an entity over time but uses only a single date/time column to record the temporal component, try to think of how to transform the data so that you can work with the start and end of the interval. This will make querying much more straightforward.

From a modeling perspective, this setup is clearly deficient. I've already mentioned the issue with gaps in the sequence, which are impossible to represent in this table. Another problem is overlapping intervals. What if the subject took on some after-hours contract work during the same time period as one of the jobs? Trying to insert that data into the table would make it look as though the subject had switched companies.

This is not to say that no intervals should be modeled this way. There are many situations in which gaps and overlaps may not make sense, and the extra bytes needed for a second column will be a waste. A prime example is a server uptime monitor. Systems are often used by IT departments that ping each monitored server on a regular basis and record changes to their status. Following is a simplified example table and a few rows:

```
CREATE TABLE ServerStatus
(
    ServerName VARCHAR(50),
    Status VARCHAR(15),
    StatusTime DATETIME
)
GO

INSERT ServerStatus
(
    ServerName,
    Status,
    StatusTime
)
```

```
SELECT 'WebServer', 'Available', '2005-04-20 03:00:00.000'
UNION ALL
SELECT 'DBServer', 'Available', '2005-04-20 03:00:00.000'
UNION ALL
SELECT 'DBServer', 'Unavailable', '2005-06-12 14:35:23.100'
UNION ALL
SELECT 'DBServer', 'Available', '2005-06-12 14:38:52.343'
UNION ALL
SELECT 'WebServer', 'Unavailable', '2005-06-15 09:16:03.593'
UNION ALL
SELECT 'WebServer', 'Available', '2005-06-15 09:28:17.006'
GO
```

Applying almost the exact same query as was used for start and end of employment periods, we can find out the intervals during which each server was unavailable:

```
SELECT
    S1.ServerName,
    S1.StatusTime,
    COALESCE((
        SELECT MIN(S2.StatusTime)
        FROM ServerStatus AS S2
        WHERE
            S2.StatusTime > S1.StatusTime),
        GETDATE()
    ) AS EndTime
FROM ServerStatus AS S1
WHERE S1.Status = 'Unavailable'
```

Some systems will send periodic status updates if the system status does not change. The monitoring system might insert additional "unavailable" rows every 30 seconds or minute until the target system starts responding again. As-is, this query would report each interim status update as a separate interval starting point. To get around this problem, the query could be modified as follows:

```
SELECT
    S1.ServerName,
    MIN(S1.StatusTime) AS StartTime,
    p.EndTime
FROM ServerStatus AS S1
CROSS APPLY
(
    SELECT
        COALESCE((
            SELECT MIN(S2.StatusTime)
            FROM ServerStatus AS S2
            WHERE
                S2.StatusTime > S1.StatusTime
                AND S2.Status = 'Available'
```

```
            ),
            GETDATE()
        ) AS EndTime
    ) p
WHERE S1.Status = 'Unavailable'
GROUP BY
    S1.ServerName,
    p.EndTime
```

This new version finds the first "available" row that occurs after the current "unavailable" row; that row represents the actual end time for the full interval during which the server was down. The outer query uses the `MIN` aggregate to find the first reported "unavailable" time for each `ServerName`/`EndTime` combination.

Modeling and Querying Independent Intervals

As mentioned previously, modeling intervals as a start time/end time combination may make more sense in many cases. With both a start and end time, each subinterval has no direct dependence on any other interval or subinterval. Therefore, both gaps and overlaps can be represented. The remainder of this section details how to work with intervals modeled in that way.

Going back to the employment example, assume that a system is required for a company to track internal employment histories. Following is a sample table, simplified for this example:

```
CREATE TABLE EmploymentHistory
(
    Employee VARCHAR(50) NOT NULL,
    Title VARCHAR(50) NOT NULL,
    StartDate SMALLDATETIME NOT NULL,
    EndDate SMALLDATETIME NULL,
    CONSTRAINT CK_Start_End CHECK (StartDate < EndDate)
)
GO
```

The main thing I've left out of this example is proper data integrity. Ignore the obvious need for a table of names and titles to avoid duplication of that data—that would overcomplicate the example. The holes I'm referring to deal with the employment history-specific data that the table is intended for. The primary issue is that although I did include one `CHECK` constraint to make sure that the `EndDate` is after the `StartDate` (we hope that the office isn't so bad that people are quitting on their first day), I failed to include a primary key.

Deciding what constitutes the primary key in this case requires a bit of thought. `Employee` alone is not sufficient, as employees would not be able to get new titles during the course of their employment (or at least it would no longer be a "history" of those changes). The next candidate might be `Employee` and `Title`, but this also has a problem. What if an employee leaves the company for a while, and later comes to his senses and begs to be rehired with the same title? The good thing about this table is that such a gap *can* be represented; but constraining on both the `Employee` and `Title` columns will not allow that situation to happen.

Adding `StartDate` into the mix seems like it would fix the problem, but in actuality it creates a whole new issue. An employee cannot be in two places (or offices) at the same time, and the combination of the three columns would allow the same employee to start on the same day with two different titles. And although it's common in our industry to wear many different hats, that fact is generally not reflected in our job title.

As it turns out, what we really need to constrain in the primary key is an employee starting on a certain day; uniqueness of the employee's particular title is not important in that regard. The following key can be added:

```
ALTER TABLE EmploymentHistory
ADD PRIMARY KEY (Employee, StartDate)
```

This primary key takes care of an employee being in two places at once on the same day, but how about different days? Even with this constraint in place, the following two rows would be valid:

```
INSERT EmploymentHistory
(
    Employee,
    Title,
    StartDate,
    EndDate
)
SELECT 'Jones', 'Developer', '2006-01-01', NULL
UNION ALL
SELECT 'Jones', 'Senior Developer', '2006-06-01', NULL
```

According to this data, Jones is *both* Developer and Senior Developer, as of June 1, 2006—quite a bit of stress for one person! The first idea for a solution might be to add a unique constraint on the `Employee` and `EndDate` columns. In SQL Server, unique constraints allow for one `NULL`-valued row—so only one `NULL` `EndDate` would be allowed per employee. That would fix the problem with these rows, but it would still allow the following rows:

```
INSERT EmploymentHistory
(
    Employee,
    Title,
    StartDate,
    EndDate
)
SELECT 'Jones', 'Developer', '2006-01-01', '2006-07-01'
UNION ALL
SELECT 'Jones', 'Senior Developer', '2006-06-01', NULL
```

Now, Jones was both Developer and Senior Developer for a month. Again, this is probably not what was intended.

Fixing this problem will require more than some combination of primary and unique key constraints, and a bit of background is necessary before I present the solution. Therefore, I will return to this topic in the next section, which covers overlapping intervals.

To finish off this section, a few notes on basic queries on intervals represented with both start and end points. The main benefit of this type of model over the single-date model, beside support for overlaps, is support for gaps. Ignore for a moment the lack of proper constraints, and consider the following rows (which would be valid even with the constraints):

```
INSERT EmploymentHistory
(
    Employee,
    Title,
    StartDate,
    EndDate
)
SELECT 'Jones', 'Developer', '2004-01-05', '2004-09-01'
UNION ALL
SELECT 'Jones', 'Senior Developer', '2004-09-01', '2005-09-01'
UNION ALL
SELECT 'Jones', 'Principal Developer', '2005-09-01', '2005-10-07'
UNION ALL
SELECT 'Jones', 'Principal Developer', '2006-02-06', NULL
```

The scenario shown here is an employee named Jones, who started as a developer in January 2004 and was promoted to Senior Developer later in the year. Jones was promoted again to Principal Developer in 2005, but quit a month later. However, a few months after that he decided to rejoin the company and has not yet left or been promoted again.

The two main questions that you can pose when dealing with intervals that represent gaps are "What intervals are covered by the data?" and "What holes are present?" These types of questions are ubiquitous when working with any kind of interval data. Real-world scenarios include such requirements as tracking of service-level agreements for server uptime and managing worker shift schedules—and of course, employment history.

In this case, the questions can be phrased as "During what periods did Jones work for the firm?" and the opposite, "During which periods was Jones not working for the firm?" To answer the first question, the first requirement is to find all subinterval start dates—dates that are not connected to a previous end date. The following T-SQL accomplishes that goal:

```
SELECT
    theStart.StartDate
FROM EmploymentHistory theStart
WHERE
    theStart.Employee = 'Jones'
    AND NOT EXISTS
    (
        SELECT *
        FROM EmploymentHistory Previous
        WHERE
            Previous.EndDate = theStart.StartDate
            AND theStart.Employee = Previous.Employee
    )
```

This query finds rows for Jones (remember, there could be rows for other employees in the table), and then filters them down to rows where there is no end date for a Jones subinterval that matches the start date of the row. The start dates for these rows are the start dates for the intervals covered by Jones's employment.

The next step is to find the ends of the covering intervals. The end rows can be identified similarly to the starting rows; they are rows where the end date has no corresponding start date in any other rows. To match the end rows to the start rows, find the first end row that occurs after a given start row. The following T-SQL finds start dates using the preceding query and end dates using a subquery that employs the algorithm just described:

```
SELECT
    theStart.StartDate,
    (
        SELECT
            MIN(EndDate)
        FROM EmploymentHistory theEnd
        WHERE
            theEnd.EndDate > theStart.StartDate
            AND theEnd.Employee = theStart.Employee
            AND NOT EXISTS
            (
                SELECT *
                FROM EmploymentHistory After
                WHERE
                    After.StartDate = theEnd.EndDate
                    AND After.Employee = theEnd.Employee
            )
    ) AS EndDate
FROM EmploymentHistory theStart
WHERE
    theStart.Employee = 'Jones'
    AND NOT EXISTS
    (
        SELECT *
        FROM EmploymentHistory Previous
        WHERE
            Previous.EndDate = theStart.StartDate
            AND theStart.Employee = Previous.Employee
    )
```

Finding noncovered intervals (i.e., holes) is a bit simpler. First, find all end dates using the same syntax used to find end dates in the covered intervals query. These dates are the start of noncovered intervals. Make sure to filter out rows where the EndDate is NULL—these subintervals have not yet ended, so it does not make sense to include them as holes. In the subquery for the end of the hole, find the first start date (if one exists) after the beginning of the hole—this is, in fact, the end of the hole. The following T-SQL finds these noncovered intervals:

```
SELECT
    theStart.EndDate AS StartDate,
    (
        SELECT MIN(theEnd.StartDate)
```

```
            FROM EmploymentHistory theEnd
            WHERE
                theEnd.StartDate > theStart.EndDate
                AND theEnd.Employee = theStart.Employee
        ) AS EndDate
FROM EmploymentHistory theStart
WHERE
        theStart.Employee = 'Jones'
        AND theStart.EndDate IS NOT NULL
        AND NOT EXISTS
        (
            SELECT *
            FROM EmploymentHistory After
            WHERE After.StartDate = theStart.EndDate
        )
```

Overlapping Intervals

Backing up a bit: the final benefit (or drawback, depending on what's being modeled) of using both a start and end date for intervals is the ability to work with overlapping intervals. Understanding how to work with overlaps is necessary either for doing overlap-related queries ("How many employees worked for the firm between August 2004 and September 2005?") or for constraining in order to avoid overlaps, as is necessary in the single-employee example started in the previous section.

To begin with, a bit of background on overlaps is necessary. Figure 10-13 shows the types of interval overlaps that are possible. Interval A is overlapped by each of the other intervals B through E. Interval B starts within interval A and ends after interval A. Interval C is the opposite, starting before interval A and ending within. Interval D both starts and ends within interval A. Finally, interval E both starts before and ends after interval A.

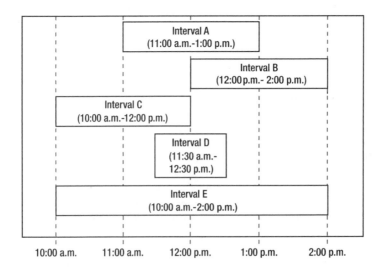

Figure 10-13. *The types of overlapping intervals*

Assuming that each interval has a `StartTime` property and an `EndTime` property, the relationships between each of the intervals B through E and interval A can be formalized in SQL-like syntax as follows:

```
B.StartDate >= A.StartDate AND B.StartDate < A.EndDate AND B.EndDate > A.EndDate
C.StartDate < A.StartDate AND C.EndDate > A.StartDate AND C.EndDate <= A.EndDate
D.StartDate >= A.StartDate AND D.EndDate <= A.EndDate
E.StartDate < A.StartDate AND E.EndDate > A.EndDate
```

Substituting the name X for all intervals B through E, we can start simplifying things a bit to create a generalized algorithm for detecting overlaps:

- `X.StartDate >= A.StartDate` is true for both intervals B and D. Combining the rest of the logic, we get `X.StartDate >= A.StartDate AND ((X.StartDate < A.EndDate AND X.EndDate > A.EndDate) OR X.EndDate <= A.EndDate)`. The `X.EndDate > A.EndDate` part can be eliminated, since knowing that `X.StartDate < A.EndDate` is sufficient in that case to constitute an overlap. This leaves us with `X.Startdate >= A.StartDate AND (X.StartDate < A.EndDate OR X.EndDate <= A.EndDate)`. The second OR'd expression is not necessary to help determine an overlap, because `X.EndDate > X.StartDate`. Therefore, if `X.EndDate <= A.EndDate`, it must be true that `X.StartDate < A.EndDate`. The final expression is `X.StartDate >= A.StartDate AND X.StartDate < A.EndDate`.

- For both intervals C and E, we can start with `X.StartDate < A.StartDate` and follow a similar path. Much like with interval B's second part, the `C.EndDate <= A.EndDate` part can be eliminated for interval C, thereby yielding the following combined Boolean expression: `X.StartDate < A.StartDate AND (X.EndDate > A.StartDate OR X.EndDate > A.EndDate)`. The second OR'd expression is unnecessary in this case, because `A.StartDate < A.EndDate`. Therefore, if `X.EndDate > A.StartDate`, it must also be true that `X.EndDate > A.EndDate`. The final expression is `X.StartDate < A.StartDate AND X.EndDate > A.StartDate`.

Rephrasing the final expressions in English, we get "If X starts after A starts and before A ends, X overlaps A" and "If X starts before A starts and X ends after A starts, X overlaps A." Essentially, what this means is that if either interval starts within the boundaries of the other interval, the intervals overlap.

One final simplification of these expressions is possible. By merging the two expressions, we find that any combination of `X.StartDate` and `A.StartDate` will make the first parts of each expression true (since `X.StartDate` will always be either `>=` or `< A.StartDate`), so that can be dropped. The resultant expression is `X.StartDate < A.EndDate AND X.EndDate > A.StartDate`. If X starts before A ends and X ends after A starts, X overlaps A. This is illustrated in Figure 10-14.

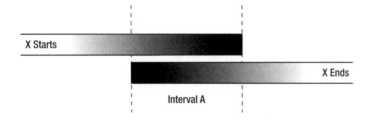

Figure 10-14. *If X starts before A ends and X ends after A starts, the two intervals overlap.*

Getting back to the EmploymentHistory table and its lack of proper constraints, it's clear that the real issue at hand is that it is not constrained to avoid overlap. A single employee cannot have two titles simultaneously, and the only way to ensure that does not happen is to make sure each employee's subintervals are unique.

Unfortunately, this logic cannot be embedded in a constraint, since in order to determine whether a row overlaps another, all of the other rows in the set must be evaluated. The following query finds all overlapping rows for Jones in the EmploymentHistory table, using the final overlap expression:

```
SELECT *
FROM EmploymentHistory E1
JOIN EmploymentHistory E2 ON
    E1.Employee = E2.Employee
    AND (
        E1.StartDate < COALESCE(E2.EndDate, '2079-06-06')
        AND COALESCE(E1.EndDate, '2079-06-06') > E2.StartDate)
    AND E1.StartDate <> E2.StartDate
WHERE
    E1.Employee = 'Jones'
```

Note that in order to avoid showing rows overlapping with themselves, the E1.StartDate <> E2.StartDate expression was added. Thanks to the primary key on the Employee and StartDate columns, we know that no two rows can share the same StartDate, so this does not affect the overlap logic. In addition, because of the open-ended (NULL) EndDate values, COALESCE is used to treat the ends of those intervals as the maximum SMALLDATETIME value. This avoids the possibility of inserting an interval starting in the future, while a current interval is still active.

This logic must be evaluated every time an insert or update is done on the table, making sure that none of the rows resulting from the insert or update operation creates any overlaps. Since this logic can't go into a constraint, there is only one possibility—a trigger. The trigger logic is fairly straightforward; instead of joining EmployeeHistory to itself, the base table will be joined to the inserted virtual table. The following T-SQL shows the trigger:

```
CREATE TRIGGER No_Overlaps
ON EmploymentHistory
FOR UPDATE, INSERT
AS
BEGIN
    IF EXISTS
    (
        SELECT *
        FROM inserted i
        JOIN EmploymentHistory E2 ON
            i.Employee = E2.Employee
            AND (
                i.StartDate < COALESCE(E2.EndDate, '2079-06-06')
                AND COALESCE(i.EndDate, '2079-06-06') > E2.StartDate)
            AND i.StartDate <> E2.StartDate
    )
```

```
    BEGIN
        RAISERROR('Overlapping interval inserted!', 16, 1)
        ROLLBACK
    END
END
```

The final examples for this section deal with a scenario in which you might want to know about (and query) overlapping intervals: when monitoring performance of concurrent processes in a database scenario.

To start setting up this example, load SQL Server Profiler, start a new trace, and connect to a test server. Uncheck all of the events except for SQL:BatchCompleted and leave the default columns selected.

Start the trace and load SQLQueryStress. Set up your database connection information and enter the following query into the Query textbox:

```
SELECT * FROM sys.Databases
```

Once that's completed, set the tool to do 100 iterations on 100 threads, and click the GO button. The run should take approximately 1 minute and will produce 20,000 Profiler events— one per invocation of the query, and one for the tool to set up its statistics collection. When the run has finished, click File, Save As, and then Trace Table in Profiler, and save the data to a table called Overlap_Trace.

Profiler trace tables include two StartTime and EndTime columns, both of which are populated for many of the events—including SQL:BatchCompleted and RPC:Completed. By treating these columns as an interval and working with some of the following query patterns, you can manipulate the data to do things such as correlate the number of concurrent queries with performance degradation of the database server.

The first and most basic query is to find out which time intervals represented in the table had the most overlaps. In other words, during the run time of a certain query, how many other queries were run? To answer this question, the intervals of every query in the table must be compared against the intervals of every other query in the table. The following T-SQL does this using the previously discussed overlap algorithm:

```
SELECT
    O1.StartTime,
    O1.EndTime,
    COUNT(*)
FROM Overlap_Trace O1
JOIN Overlap_Trace O2 ON
    (O1.StartTime < O2.EndTime AND O1.EndTime > O2.StartTime)
    AND O1.SPID <> O2.SPID
GROUP BY
    O1.StartTime,
    O1.EndTime
ORDER BY COUNT(*) DESC
```

Much like the EmploymentTable example, we need to make sure that no false positives are generated by rows overlapping with themselves. Since a SPID can't run two queries simultaneously,[7] that column works for the purpose in this case.

Running this query on an unindexed table is a painful experience. It is agonizingly slow, and in the sample table on my machine required 1,043,775 logical reads. Creating the following index on the table helped a small amount:

```
CREATE NONCLUSTERED INDEX IX_StartEnd
ON Overlap_Trace (StartTime, EndTime, SPID)
```

However, I noticed that the index was still not being effectively used; evaluating the query plan showed an outer table scan with a nested loop for an inner table scan—one table scan for every row of the table. Going back and looking at the original two algorithms before merging them, I noticed that they return exclusive sets of data. The first algorithm returns overlaps of intervals B and D, whereas the second algorithm returns overlaps of intervals C and E. I also noticed that each algorithm on its own is more index friendly than the combined version. The solution to the performance issue is to merge the two algorithms, not into a single expression, but rather using UNION ALL, as follows:

```
SELECT
    x.StartTime,
    x.EndTime,
    SUM(x.theCount)
FROM
(
SELECT
    O1.StartTime,
    O1.EndTime,
    COUNT(*) AS theCount
FROM Overlap_Trace O1
JOIN Overlap_Trace O2 ON
    (O1.StartTime >= O2.StartTime AND O1.StartTime < O2.EndTime)
    AND O1.SPID <> O2.SPID
GROUP BY
    O1.StartTime,
    O1.EndTime

UNION ALL

SELECT
    O1.StartTime,
    O1.EndTime,
    COUNT(*) AS theCount
FROM Overlap_Trace O1
```

---

7. Except if you're working with SQL Server's multiple active result sets feature.

```
JOIN Overlap_Trace O2 ON
    (O1.StartTime < O2.StartTime AND O1.EndTime > O2.StartTime)
    AND O1.SPID <> O2.SPID
GROUP BY
    O1.StartTime,
    O1.EndTime
) x
GROUP BY
    x.StartTime,
    x.EndTime
ORDER BY SUM(x.theCount) DESC
OPTION(HASH GROUP)
```

This query is logically identical to the previous one. It merges the two exclusive sets based on the same intervals and sums their counts, which is the same as taking the full count of the interval in one shot. Note that I was forced to add the HASH GROUP option to the end of the query to make the query optimizer make better use of the index. Once that hint was in place, the total number of reads done by the query dropped to 125,884—a huge improvement.

Another way to slice and dice overlapping intervals is by splitting the data into periods and looking at the activity that occurred during each. For instance, to find out how many employees worked for a firm each month of the year, you could find out which employees' work date intervals overlapped January 1 through January 31, again for February 1 through February 28, and so on.

Although it's easy to ask those kinds of questions for dates by using a calendar table, it's a bit trickier when you need to do it with times. Prepopulating a calendar table with every time, in addition to every date, for the next ten or more years would cause a massive increase in I/O required to read the dates, and would therefore seriously cut down on the table's usefulness. Instead, I recommend dynamically generating time tables as you need them. The following UDF takes an input start and end date and outputs periods for each associated subinterval:

```
CREATE FUNCTION TimeSlice
(
    @StartDate DATETIME,
    @EndDate DATETIME
)
RETURNS @t TABLE
(
    DisplayDate DATETIME NOT NULL,
    StartDate DATETIME NOT NULL,
    EndDate DATETIME NOT NULL,
    PRIMARY KEY (StartDate, EndDate) WITH (IGNORE_DUP_KEY=ON)
)
WITH SCHEMABINDING
AS
BEGIN
    IF (@StartDate > @EndDate)
        RETURN
```

```
DECLARE @TruncatedStart DATETIME
SET @TruncatedStart =
    DATEADD(second, DATEDIFF(second, '20000101', @StartDate), '20000101')

DECLARE @TruncatedEnd DATETIME
SET @TruncatedEnd =
    DATEADD(second, DATEDIFF(second, '20000101', @EndDate), '20000101')

--Insert start and end date/times first
--Make sure to match the same start/end interval passed in
INSERT @t
(
    DisplayDate,
    StartDate,
    EndDate
)
SELECT
    @TruncatedStart,
    @StartDate,
    CASE
        WHEN
            DATEADD(second, 1, @TruncatedStart) > @EndDate THEN @EndDate
        ELSE
            DATEADD(second, 1, @TruncatedStart)
    END
UNION ALL
SELECT
    @TruncatedEnd,
    CASE
        WHEN
            @TruncatedEnd < @StartDate THEN @StartDate
        ELSE
            @TruncatedEnd
    END,
    @EndDate

SET @TruncatedStart =
    DATEADD(second, 1, @TruncatedStart)

--Insert one time unit for each subinterval
WHILE (@TruncatedStart < @TruncatedEnd)
BEGIN
    INSERT @t
    (
        DisplayDate,
        StartDate,
        EndDate
    )
```

```
        VALUES
        (
            @TruncatedStart,
            @TruncatedStart,
            DATEADD(second, 1, @TruncatedStart)
        )

        SET @TruncatedStart =
            DATEADD(second, 1, @TruncatedStart)
    END

    RETURN
END
```

This function is currently hard coded to use seconds as the subinterval length, but it can easily be changed to any other time period by modifying the parameters to DATEDIFF and DATEADD.

As an example of using the function, consider the following call:

```
SELECT *
FROM dbo.TimeSlice('2006-01-02 12:34:45.003', '2006-01-02 12:34:48.100')
```

The output, as shown in Table 10-2, is one row per whole second range in the interval, with the start and end points constrained by the interval boundaries.

Table 10-2. *TimeSlicing a Few Seconds*

DisplayDate	StartDate	EndDate
2006-01-02 12:34:45.000	2006-01-02 12:34:45.003	2006-01-02 12:34:46.000
2006-01-02 12:34:46.000	2006-01-02 12:34:46.000	2006-01-02 12:34:47.000
2006-01-02 12:34:47.000	2006-01-02 12:34:47.000	2006-01-02 12:34:48.000
2006-01-02 12:34:48.000	2006-01-02 12:34:48.000	2006-01-02 12:34:48.100

To use the function to look at the number of overlapping queries during each subinterval over the course of the sample trace, first find the start and end points of the trace using the MIN and MAX aggregates. Then, slice the interval into 1-second periods using the function. The following T-SQL shows how to do that:

```
SELECT
    Slices.DisplayDate
FROM
(
    SELECT MIN(StartTime), MAX(EndTime)
    FROM Overlap_Trace
) StartEnd (StartTime, EndTime)
```

```
CROSS APPLY
(
    SELECT *
    FROM dbo.TimeSlice(StartEnd.StartTime, StartEnd.EndTime)
) Slices
```

The output of the TimeSlice function can then be used to find the number of overlapping queries that were running during each period, by using the CROSS APPLY operator again in conjunction with the interval overlap expression:

```
SELECT
    Slices.DisplayDate,
    OverLaps.thecount
FROM
(
    SELECT MIN(StartTime), MAX(EndTime)
    FROM Overlap_Trace
) StartEnd (StartTime, EndTime)
CROSS APPLY
(
    SELECT *
    FROM dbo.TimeSlice(StartEnd.StartTime, StartEnd.EndTime)
) Slices
CROSS APPLY
(
    SELECT COUNT(*) AS theCount
    FROM Overlap_Trace OT
    WHERE
        Slices.StartDate < OT.EndTime
        AND Slices.EndDate > OT.StartTime
) Overlaps
```

This data, in conjunction with a performance monitor trace, can be used to correlate spikes in counters at certain times to what was actually happening in the database. This can be especially useful for tracking sudden increases in blocking, which often will not correspond to increased utilization of any system resources, which can make them difficult to identify. By adding additional filters to the preceding query, you can look at concurrent runs of specific queries that are prone to blocking one another, in order to find out whether they might be causing performance issues.

Modeling Durations

Durations are very similar to intervals, in that they represent a start time and an end time. In many cases, therefore, it makes sense to model durations as intervals and determine the actual duration for reporting or aggregate purposes by using DATEDIFF. However, in some cases the resolution offered by SQL Server's native date/time types is not sufficient. In addition, it can be difficult to format durations for output, requiring intricate string manipulation.

There are several examples of cases when you might want to model durations rather than intervals. A common situation is databases that need to store information about timed scientific trials, which often require microsecond or even nanosecond precision. Another example is data that may not require a date/time component at all. For instance, a table containing times for runners doing the 300-yard dash may not need a start time. The exact starting moment of the run does not matter; the only important fact is how long the runner took to travel the 300 yards.

The most straightforward solution to the issue of inadequate resolution is to store a start date, along with an integer column to represent the actual duration:

```
CREATE TABLE Events
(
    EventId INT,
    StartTime DATETIME,
    DurationInMicroseconds INT
)
```

Using this table, it is possible to find the approximate end time of an event using DATEADD; just divide the duration by 1,000 to get milliseconds. For the 300-yard dash or other scenarios where starting time does not matter, that column can simply be dropped, and only the duration itself maintained.

What this table does not address is the issue of formatting, should you need to output this data rendered as a human-readable string. Once again I should stress that formatting is best done in a client tier. However, if you do need to format data in the database tier (and you have a *very* good reason to do so), there is a simple way to handle this scenario: a SQLCLR UDF that wraps .NET's TimeSpan type.

The TimeSpan type represents a duration of time, which can be manipulated at the granularity of hours, minutes, seconds, milliseconds, or **ticks**. 10,000,000 ticks make up each second, so dividing by 1,000 yields higher granularity: 10,000 ticks per millisecond, and 10 ticks per microsecond.

TimeSpan has a ToString method with no overloads, which returns the data in the format HH:MM:SS if the duration spans an exact number of seconds, and HH:MM:SS.TTTTTTT (the Ts representing ticks) if the duration does not divide evenly into seconds. The following UDF can be used to return the string format using TimeSpan.ToString:

```
[Microsoft.SqlServer.Server.SqlFunction]
public static SqlString FormatDuration(SqlInt32 TimeInMicroseconds)
{
    //Ticks == Microseconds * 10
    //There are 10,000,000 ticks per second
    long ticks = TimeInMicroseconds.ToSqlInt64().Value * 10;

    //Create the TimeSpan based on the number of ticks
    TimeSpan ts = new TimeSpan(ticks);

    //Format the output
    return new SqlString(ts.ToString());
}
```

The UDF can be used to format data at different levels of granularity—down to 1/10 of a microsecond—by changing the multiplier on the first line.

Managing Bitemporal Data

A central truth that we need to embrace to be successful as database developers is that not all data is as great as it could be (or as we might wish it to be). Sometimes, we're forced to work with incomplete or incorrect data, and correct things later as a more complete picture of reality becomes available.

Modifying data in the database is simple enough in and of itself—a call to a DML statement and the work is done. But in systems that require advanced logging and reproducibility of reports between runs for auditing purposes, a straightforward update, insert, or delete may be counterproductive. Doing such a data modification can destroy the possibility of re-creating the same output on consecutive runs of the same query.

To get around doing a simple update in the case of invalid data, some systems use the idea of **offset transactions**. An offset transaction uses the additive nature of summarization logic to fix the data in place. For example, assume that part of a financial reporting system has a table that describes customer transactions. The following table is a highly simplified representation of what such a table might look like:

```
CREATE TABLE Transactions
(
    TransactionId INT,
    Customer VARCHAR(50),
    TransactionDate DATETIME,
    TransactionType VARCHAR(50),
    TransactionAmount DECIMAL(9,2)
)
```

On June 12, 2005, customer Smith deposited $500. However, due to a teller's key error that was not caught in time, by the time the reporting data was loaded, the amount that made it into the system was $5,000:

```
INSERT Transactions
VALUES
(1001, 'Smith', '2005-06-12', 'DEPOSIT', 5000.00)
```

The next morning, the erroneous data was detected. Although the transaction row itself could be updated in place, this would destroy the audit trail, so an offset transaction must be issued. There are a few ways of handling this scenario. The first method is to issue an offset transaction dated the same as the incorrect transaction:

```
INSERT Transactions
VALUES
(1001, 'Smith', '2005-06-12', 'OFFSET', -4500.00)
```

Back-dating the offset fixes the problem in summary reports that group any dimension (transaction number, customer, date, or transaction type), but fails to keep track of the fact that the error was actually caught on June 13. Properly dating the offset record is imperative for data auditing purposes:

```
INSERT Transactions
VALUES
(1001, 'Smith', '2005-06-13', 'OFFSET', -4500.00)
```

Unfortunately, proper dating does not fix all of the issues—and introduces new ones. After properly dating the offset, a query of the data for customer Smith for all business done through June 12 does not include the correction. Only by including data from June 13 would the query return the correct data. And although a correlated query could be written to return the correct summary report for June 12, the data is in a somewhat-strange state when querying for ranges after June 12 (e.g., June 13 through 15. The offset record is orphaned if June 12 is not considered in a given query along with June 13.

To get around these and similar issues, a **bitemporal** model is necessary. In a bitemporal table, each transaction has two dates: the actual date that the transaction took place and a "valid" date, which represents the date that we know the updated data to be correct. The following, modified version of the Transactions table shows the new column:

```
CREATE TABLE Transactions
(
    TransactionId INT,
    Customer VARCHAR(50),
    TransactionDate DATETIME,
    TransactionType VARCHAR(50),
    TransactionAmount DECIMAL(9,2),
    ValidDate DATETIME
)
```

When inserting the data for Smith on June 12, a valid date of June 12 is also applied:

```
INSERT Transactions
VALUES
(1001, 'Smith', '2005-06-12', 'DEPOSIT', 5000.00, '2005-06-12')
```

Effectively, this row can be read as "As of June 12, we believe that transaction 1001, dated June 12, was a deposit for $5,000.00." On June 13, when the error is caught, no offset record is inserted. Instead, a corrected deposit record is inserted, with a new valid date:

```
INSERT Transactions
VALUES
(1001, 'Smith', '2005-06-12', 'DEPOSIT', 500.00, '2005-06-13')
```

This row indicates that as of June 13, transaction 1001 has been modified. But the important difference is the transaction still maintains its correct date—so running a report for transactions that occurred on June 13 would show no rows for June 12. In addition, this model eliminates the need for offset transactions. Rather than use an offset, queries should always find the last update for any given transaction, within the valid range.

To understand this a bit more, consider a report run on August 5, looking at all transactions that occurred on June 12. The person running the report wants the most "correct" version of the data; that is, all available corrections should be applied. This is done by taking the transaction data for each transaction from the row with the maximum valid date:

```
SELECT
    T1.TransactionId,
    T1.Customer,
    T1.TransactionType,
```

```
            T1.TransactionAmount
FROM Transactions AS T1
WHERE
        T1.TransactionDate = '2005-06-12'
        AND T1.ValidDate =
        (
            SELECT MAX(ValidDate)
            FROM Transactions AS T2
            WHERE T2.TransactionId = T1.TransactionId
        )
```

By modifying the subquery, it is possible to get "snapshot" reports based on data before updates were applied. For instance, assume that this same report was run on the evening of June 12. The output for Smith would show a deposit of $5,000.00 for transaction 1001. To reproduce that report on August 5 (or any day after June 12), change the ValidDate subquery:

```
SELECT
        T1.TransactionId,
        T1.Customer,
        T1.TransactionType,
        T1.TransactionAmount
FROM Transactions AS T1
WHERE
        T1.TransactionDate = '2005-06-12'
        AND T1.ValidDate =
        (
            SELECT MAX(ValidDate)
            FROM Transactions AS T2
            WHERE
                T2.TransactionId = T1.TransactionId
                AND ValidDate <= '2005-06-12'
        )
```

Note that in this case, the subquery could have been eliminated altogether, and the search argument could have become AND T1.ValidDate = '2005-06-12'. However, the subquery is needed any time you're querying a range of dates, so it's a good idea to leave it in place for ease of maintenance of the query.

Using this same pattern, data can also be booked in the future, before it is actually valid. It's common when doing wire transfers, credit card payments, and other kinds of electronic funds transactions to be able to set the "posting date" on which the business will actually be executed. By working with the valid date, Smith can make a request for an outgoing transfer on June 14, but ask that the transfer actually take place on June 16:

```
INSERT Transactions
VALUES
(1002, 'Smith', '2005-06-16', 'TRANSFER', -1000.00, '2005-06-14')
```

Since the transaction date is June 16, a report dealing with transactions that occurred between June 1 and June 15 will not show the transfer. But a business manager can query on

June 15 to find out which transactions will hit in the coming days or weeks, and audit when the data entered the system.

Modeling data bitemporally allows for an auditable, accurate representation of historical or future knowledge as data is updated. This can be tremendously useful in many scenarios—especially in the realm of financial reconciliation when you can be forced to deal with backdated contracts that change the terms of previous transactions and business booked in the future to avoid certain types of auditing issues.

■**Note** When modeling bitemporal data, you may want to investigate the possibility of implementing cutoff date rules, after which changes to transactions cannot be made. For example, the system may have a policy whereby transactions are said to be closed after 90 days. In this case, a simple CHECK constraint would do the trick, to ensure that the ValidDate is within 90 days of the TransactionDate. Another example would be data that has been used to generate an official report, such as for a government agency. In that case, you'd want a rule so that no transaction can be back-dated to before the report was run (lest it change the data in the report). In that case, a trigger would be needed in order to verify the date against a table containing the report run history.

Summary

Virtually all data has some form of a temporal component, and every database developer will have to deal with times and dates again and again. Managing temporal data successfully begins with an understanding of the different types of temporal data: instance-based, interval-based, period-based, and bitemporal. By applying knowledge of how SQL Server's native date/time types work, you can intelligently and efficiently do calculations and queries based on temporal data models.

■ ■ ■

CHAPTER 11

Trees, Hierarchies, and Graphs

Our world is filled with nested classifications, both those defined by nature and by man. The universe itself is hierarchical in nature, made up of galaxies, stars, and planets, each classified by the outermost set. One of the more obvious hierarchies here on Earth is probably the food chain that exists in the wild; a lion can certainly eat a zebra, but alas, a zebra will probably never dine on lion flesh. And of course, we're all familiar with corporate management hierarchies—which some companies try to kill off in favor of matrixes, which are not hierarchical at all . . . but more on that later!

We strive to describe our existence based on connections—or lack thereof—and that's what trees, hierarchies, and graphs help us do at the mathematical and data levels. The majority of databases are at least mostly hierarchical, with a central table or set of tables at the root, and all other tables branching from there via foreign key references. However, many times the database hierarchy needs to be designed at a more granular level, using intratable hierarchies. For example, you wouldn't design a management database that required one table per employee in order to support the hierarchy. Rather, you'd put all of the employees into a single table and create references between the rows.

This chapter discusses methodologies for working with these intertable hierarchies and graphs. Database developers are often surprised to discover that there are a few different techniques for designing hierarchies, each with their own virtues depending on the situation. I will describe each of the major techniques possible within SQL Server and show you how to effectively query and manage your hierarchical data.

Terminology: Everything Is a Graph

Mathematically speaking, trees and hierarchies are both different types of **graphs**. A graph is defined as a set of **nodes** (or **vertices**) connected by **edges**. Beyond that there are further classifications. The edges in a graph can be **directed** or **undirected**, meaning that they are either one-way (a directed edge) or traversing between the nodes can be done in either direction. If all of the edges in a graph are directed, the graph itself is said to be directed (sometimes referred to as a **digraph**). Graphs can also have **cycles**, sets of nodes/edges that when traversed in order bring you back to the same initial node. A graph without cycles is called an **acyclic** graph. Figure 11-1 shows some simple examples of the basic types of graphs.

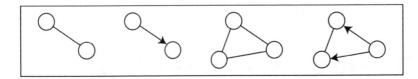

Figure 11-1. *Undirected, directed, undirected cyclic, and directed acyclic graphs*

The most immediately recognizable example of a graph is a street map. Each intersection can be thought of as a node, and each street an edge. One-way streets are directed edges, and if you drive around the block, you've illustrated a cycle. Therefore, a street system can be said to be a cyclic, directed graph. In the manufacturing world, a common graph structure is a bill of materials, or parts explosion, which describes all of the necessary component parts of a given product. And in software development, we typically work with class and object graphs, which form the relationships between the component parts of an object-oriented system.

A **tree** is defined as an undirected, acyclic graph in which exactly one path exists between any two nodes. Figure 11-2 shows a simple tree.

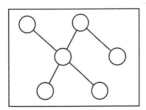

Figure 11-2. *Exactly one path exists between any two nodes in a tree.*

■**Note** Borrowing from the same agrarian terminology that was used to define a type of graph as a tree, we can also refer to multiple trees as a **forest**.

A **hierarchy** is a special subset of a tree, and it is probably the most common graph structure that developers need to work with. It has all of the qualities of a tree but is also directed and **rooted**. This means that a certain node is designated as the **root**, and all other nodes are said to be **subordinates** (or **descendants**) of that node. In addition, each nonroot node must have exactly one **parent** node—a node that directs into it. Multiple parents are not allowed, nor are multiple root nodes. Hierarchies are extremely familiar when it comes to describing most business relationships; manager/employee, contractor/subcontractor, and firm/division associations all come to mind. Figure 11-3 shows a hierarchy in which the root node has three children.

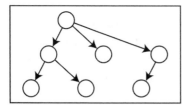

Figure 11-3. *A hierarchy must have exactly one root node, and each nonroot node must have exactly one parent.*

The parent/child relationships found in hierarchies are often classified more formally using the terms **ancestor** and **descendant**, although this terminology can get a bit awkward in software development settings. Another important term is **siblings**, which describes nodes that share the same parent. Other terms used to describe familial relationships are also routinely applied to trees and hierarchies, but I've personally found that it can get confusing trying to figure out which node is the **cousin** of another, and so have abandoned most of this terminology.

The Basics: Adjacency Lists and Graphs

The most common graph data model—and the one that can be seen in Microsoft's sample databases—is called an **adjacency list**. In an adjacency list, the graph is modeled as pairs of nodes, each representing an edge. This is an extremely flexible way of modeling a graph; any kind of graph, hierarchy, or tree can fit into this model. However, it can be problematic from the perspectives of query complexity, performance, and data integrity. In this section, I will show you how to work with adjacency lists and point out some of the issues that you should be wary of when designing solutions around them.

The simplest of graph tables contains only two columns, X and Y:

```
CREATE TABLE Edges
(
    X INT NOT NULL,
    Y INT NOT NULL,
    PRIMARY KEY (X, Y)
)
GO
```

The combination of columns X and Y constitutes the primary key, and each row in the table represents one edge in the graph. Note that X and Y are assumed to be references to some valid table of nodes. This table only represents the edges that connect the nodes. It can also be used to reference unconnected nodes; a node with a path back to itself but no other paths can be inserted into the table for that purpose.

Note When modeling unconnected nodes, some data architects prefer to use a nullable Y column rather than having both columns point to the same node. The net effect is the same, but in my opinion the nullable Y column makes some queries a bit messier, as you'll be forced to deal with the possibility of a NULL. The examples in this chapter, therefore, do not follow that convention—but you should use whatever you are most comfortable with in your production apps.

Constraining the Edges

As-is, this table can be used to represent any graph, but semantics are important, and none are implied by the columns. It's difficult to know whether each edge is directed or undirected. Traversing the graph, one could conceivably go either way, so the following two rows may or may not be logically identical:

```
INSERT Edges VALUES (1, 2)
INSERT Edges VALUES (2, 1)
```

If the edges in the graph are supposed to be directed, there is no problem. If you need both directions for a certain edge, simply insert them both, and don't insert both for directed edges. If, on the other hand, all edges are supposed to be undirected, a constraint is necessary in order to enforce that two identical paths are not inserted.

The primary key is clearly not sufficient, since it treats every combination as unique. The most obvious solution to this problem is to create a trigger that checks the rows when inserts or updates take place. Since the primary key already enforces that duplicate directional paths cannot be inserted, the trigger must only check for the opposite path:

```
CREATE TRIGGER CheckForDuplicates
ON Edges
FOR INSERT, UPDATE
AS
BEGIN
    IF EXISTS
    (
        SELECT *
        FROM Edges e
        WHERE
            EXISTS
            (
                SELECT *
                FROM inserted i
                WHERE
                    i.x = e.y
                    AND i.y = e.x
            )
    )
    BEGIN
        ROLLBACK
```

```
        END
END
GO
```

A slightly more clever way of constraining the uniqueness of the paths is to make use of an indexed view. You can take advantage of the fact that an indexed view has a unique index, using it as a constraint in cases like this where a trigger seems awkward. In order to create the indexed view, you will need a table called Numbers, with a single column, Number, which is the primary key. I like to prime mine with every number between 1 and 8000:

```
SELECT TOP (8000)
    IDENTITY(int, 1, 1) AS Number
INTO Numbers
FROM master..spt_values a
CROSS JOIN master..spt_values b

ALTER TABLE Numbers
ADD PRIMARY KEY (Number)
GO
```

The master..spt_values table is simply a random system table chosen because it has enough rows that, when cross-joined with itself, the output will be more than 8000 rows.

A table of numbers is incredibly useful in many cases in which you might need to do inter-row manipulation and look-ahead logic, especially when dealing with strings. However, in this case, its utility is fairly simple: the rows with the numbers 1 and 2 will be used to duplicate the rows in the table, and a CASE expression will be used to reverse the paths in the query depending on the row. The following view encapsulates this logic:

```
CREATE VIEW DuplicateEdges
WITH SCHEMABINDING
AS
    SELECT
        CASE n.Number
            WHEN 1 THEN e.X
            ELSE e.Y
        END X,
        CASE n.Number
            WHEN 1 THEN e.Y
            ELSE e.X
        END Y
    FROM dbo.Edges e
    CROSS JOIN dbo.Numbers n
    WHERE
        n.Number BETWEEN 1 AND 2
GO
```

Once the view has been created, it can be indexed in order to constrain against duplicate paths:

```
CREATE UNIQUE CLUSTERED INDEX IX_NoDuplicates
ON DuplicateEdges (X,Y)
GO
```

Since the view logically contains both paths as they were inserted into the table, as well as the reverse paths, the unique index serves to constrain against duplication. Both techniques have similar performance characteristics, but there is admittedly a certain cool factor with the indexed view. It can also double as a quick lookup for finding all paths in a directed notation.

Basic Graph Queries: Who Am I Connected To?

Before traversing the graph to answer questions, it's again important to discuss the differences between directed and undirected edges and the way in which they are modeled. Figure 11-4 shows two graphs: **I** is undirected, and **J** is directed.

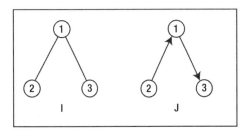

Figure 11-4. *Directed and undirected graphs have different connection qualities.*

The following node pairs can be used to represent the edges whether or not the edges table is considered to be directed or undirected:

```
INSERT Edges VALUES (2, 1)
INSERT Edges VALUES (1, 3)
```

Now we can answer a simple question: starting at a specific node, what nodes can we traverse to?

In the case of a directed graph, any node Y is accessible from another node X if an edge exists that starts at X and ends at Y. This is easy enough to represent as a query (in this case, starting at node 1):

```
SELECT Y
FROM Edges e
WHERE X = 1
```

For an undirected graph, things get a bit more complex. In that case, any node Y is accessible from another node X if an edge is represented as either starting at X and ending at Y, or the other way around. If both start and end points are not checked, the graph has effectively become directed. Answering the same question as before now requires a bit more code:

```
SELECT
    CASE
        WHEN X = 1 THEN Y
        ELSE X
    END
FROM Edges e
WHERE
    X = 1 OR Y = 1
```

Aside from the increased complexity of this code, there's another much more important issue: performance on larger sets will start to suffer due to the fact that the search argument cannot be satisfied based on an index seek because it relies on two columns with an OR condition. The problem can be fixed to some degree by creating multiple indexes (one in which each column is the first key) and using a UNION ALL query, as follows:

```
SELECT Y
FROM Edges e
WHERE X = 1

UNION ALL

SELECT X
FROM Edges e
WHERE Y = 1
```

This code is somewhat unintuitive and, because the two indexes must be maintained and the query must do two index operations to be satisfied, performance will still suffer compared with querying the directed graph. For that reason, I recommend generally modeling graphs as directed and dealing with inserting both pairs of edges, unless there is a compelling reason not to, such as an extremely large undirected graph where the extra edge combinations would challenge the server's available disk space. The remainder of the examples in this chapter will assume that the graph is directed.

Traversing the Graph

Finding out which nodes a given node is directly connected to is a good start, but in order to truly answer questions, the graph must be traversed. For this section, a more rigorous example data set is necessary. Figure 11-5 shows an initial sample graph, representing an abbreviated portion of a street map for an unnamed city.

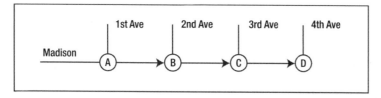

Figure 11-5. *An abbreviated street map*

A few tables are required to represent this map. To begin with, a table of streets:

```
CREATE TABLE Streets
(
    StreetId INT NOT NULL PRIMARY KEY,
    StreetName VARCHAR(75)
)
GO

INSERT Streets VALUES (1, '1st Ave')
INSERT Streets VALUES (2, '2nd Ave')
INSERT Streets VALUES (3, '3rd Ave')
INSERT Streets VALUES (4, '4th Ave')
INSERT Streets VALUES (5, 'Madison')
GO
```

Each street is assigned a surrogate key so that it can be referenced easily in other tables.

The next requirement is a table of intersections, the nodes in the graph. This table creates a key for each intersection, which is defined in this set of data as a collection of one or more streets:

```
CREATE TABLE Intersections
(
    IntersectionId INT NOT NULL PRIMARY KEY,
    IntersectionName VARCHAR(10)
)
GO

INSERT Intersections VALUES (1, 'A')
INSERT Intersections VALUES (2, 'B')
INSERT Intersections VALUES (3, 'C')
INSERT Intersections VALUES (4, 'D')
GO
```

Next is a table called IntersectionStreets, which maps streets to their respective intersections. Note that I haven't included any constraints on this table, as they can get quite complex. One constraint that might be ideal would specify that any given combination of streets should not intersect more than once. However, it's difficult to say whether this would apply to all cities, given that many older cities have twisting roads that may intersect with each other at numerous points. Dealing with this issue is left as an exercise for you to try on your own.

```
CREATE TABLE IntersectionStreets
(
    IntersectionId INT NOT NULL
        REFERENCES Intersections (IntersectionId),
    StreetId INT NOT NULL
        REFERENCES Streets (StreetId),
    PRIMARY KEY (IntersectionId, StreetId)
)
```

```
INSERT IntersectionStreets VALUES (1, 1)
INSERT IntersectionStreets VALUES (1, 5)
INSERT IntersectionStreets VALUES (2, 2)
INSERT IntersectionStreets VALUES (2, 5)
INSERT IntersectionStreets VALUES (3, 3)
INSERT IntersectionStreets VALUES (3, 5)
INSERT IntersectionStreets VALUES (4, 4)
INSERT IntersectionStreets VALUES (4, 5)
GO
```

The final table describes the edges of the graph, which in this case are segments of street between each intersection. I've added a few constraints that might not be so obvious at first glance. Rather than using foreign keys to the Intersections table, the StreetSegments table references the IntersectionStreets table for both the starting point and ending point. In both cases, the street is also included in the key. The purpose of this is so that you can't start on one street and magically end up on another street or at an intersection that's not even on the street you started on. The CK_Intersections constraint ensures that the two intersections are actually different—so you can't start at one intersection and end up at the same place after only one move.

```
CREATE TABLE StreetSegments
(
    IntersectionId_Start INT NOT NULL,
    IntersectionId_End INT NOT NULL,
    StreetId INT NOT NULL,
    CONSTRAINT FK_Start
        FOREIGN KEY (IntersectionId_Start, StreetId)
        REFERENCES IntersectionStreets (IntersectionId, StreetId),
    CONSTRAINT FK_End
        FOREIGN KEY (IntersectionId_End, StreetId)
        REFERENCES IntersectionStreets (IntersectionId, StreetId),
    CONSTRAINT CK_Intersections
        CHECK (IntersectionId_Start <> IntersectionId_End),
    CONSTRAINT PK_StreetSegments
        PRIMARY KEY (IntersectionId_Start, IntersectionId_End)
)

INSERT StreetSegments VALUES (1, 2, 5)
INSERT StreetSegments VALUES (2, 3, 5)
INSERT StreetSegments VALUES (3, 4, 5)
GO
```

In addition to these tables, a helper function is useful, in order to make navigation easier. The GetIntersectionId function returns the intersection at which the two input streets intersect. As mentioned before, this schema assumes that each street intersects only once with any other street, and the function makes the same assumption. It works by searching for all intersections that the input streets participate in, and then finding the one that had exactly two matches, meaning that both input streets intersect. Following is the T-SQL for the function:

```
CREATE FUNCTION GetIntersectionId
(
    @Street1 VARCHAR(75),
    @Street2 VARCHAR(75)
)
RETURNS INT
WITH SCHEMABINDING
AS
BEGIN
    RETURN
    (
        SELECT
            i.IntersectionId
        FROM dbo.IntersectionStreets i
        WHERE
            StreetId IN
            (
                SELECT StreetId
                FROM dbo.Streets
                WHERE StreetName IN (@Street1, @Street2)
            )
        GROUP BY i.IntersectionId
        HAVING COUNT(*) = 2
    )
END
GO
```

Using the schema and the function, we can start traversing the nodes. The basic technique of traversing the graph is quite simple: find the starting intersection and all nodes that it connects to, and iteratively or recursively move outward, using the previous node's ending point as the starting point for the next. This is easily accomplished using a recursive **Common Table Expression** (CTE). The following is a simple initial example of a CTE that can be used to traverse the nodes from Madison and 1st Avenue to Madison and 4th Avenue:

```
SELECT
    @Start = dbo.GetIntersectionId('Madison', '1st Ave'),
    @End = dbo.GetIntersectionId('Madison', '4th Ave')

;WITH Paths
AS
(
    SELECT
        @Start AS theStart,
        IntersectionId_End AS theEnd
    FROM dbo.StreetSegments
    WHERE
        IntersectionId_Start = @Start

    UNION ALL
```

```
    SELECT
        p.theEnd,
        ss.IntersectionId_End
    FROM Paths p
    JOIN dbo.StreetSegments ss ON ss.IntersectionId_Start = p.theEnd
    WHERE p.theEnd <> @End
)
SELECT *
FROM Paths
GO
```

The anchor part of the CTE finds all nodes to which the starting intersection is connected—in this case, given the data we've already input, there is only one. The recursive part uses the anchor's output as its input, finding all connected nodes from there, and continuing only if the end point of the next intersection is not equal to the end intersection. The output for this query is shown in Figure 11-6.

	theStart	theEnd
1	1	2
2	2	3
3	3	4

Figure 11-6. *Result of traversing from Madison and 1st Avenue to Madison and 4th Avenue*

While this output is fine and perfectly descriptive with only one path between the two points, it has some problems. First of all, the ordering of the output of a CTE—just like any other query—is not guaranteed without an ORDER BY clause. In this case, the order happens to coincide with the order of the path, but this is a very small data set, and the server on which I ran the query has only one processor. On a bigger set of data and/or with multiple processors, SQL Server could choose to process the data in a different order, thereby destroying the implicit output order.

The second issue is that in this case there is exactly one path between the start and end points. What if there were more than one path? Figure 11-7 shows the street map with a new street, a few new intersections, and more street segments added. The following T-SQL can be used to add the new data to the tables:

```
--New street
INSERT Streets VALUES (6, 'Lexington')
--New intersections
INSERT Intersections VALUES (5, 'E')
INSERT Intersections VALUES (6, 'F')
INSERT Intersections VALUES (7, 'G')
INSERT Intersections VALUES (8, 'H')
--New intersection/street mappings
INSERT IntersectionStreets VALUES (5, 1)
INSERT IntersectionStreets VALUES (5, 6)
INSERT IntersectionStreets VALUES (6, 2)
```

```
INSERT IntersectionStreets VALUES (6, 6)
INSERT IntersectionStreets VALUES (7, 3)
INSERT IntersectionStreets VALUES (7, 6)
INSERT IntersectionStreets VALUES (8, 4)
INSERT IntersectionStreets VALUES (8, 6)
--North/South segments
INSERT StreetSegments VALUES (2, 2, 6, 2)
INSERT StreetSegments VALUES (4, 4, 8, 4)
--East/West segments
INSERT StreetSegments VALUES (8, 6, 7, 6)
INSERT StreetSegments VALUES (7, 6, 6, 6)
INSERT StreetSegments VALUES (6, 6, 5, 6)
GO
```

Note that although intersections E and G have been created, their corresponding north/south segments have not yet been inserted. This is on purpose, as I'm going to use those segments to illustrate yet another complication.

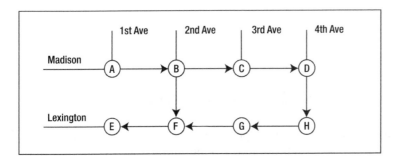

Figure 11-7. *A slightly more complete version of the street map*

Once the new data is inserted, we can try the same CTE as before, this time traveling from Madison and 1st Avenue to Lexington and 1st Avenue. To change the destination, modify the SELECT statement that assigns the @Start and @End variables, as follows:

```
SELECT
    @Start = dbo.GetIntersectionId('Madison', '1st Ave'),
    @End = dbo.GetIntersectionId('Lexington', '1st Ave')
```

The output of this run of the CTE is shown in Figure 11-8. There are now two paths from the starting point to the ending point, but it's impossible to tell what they are; the intersections involved in each path are mixed up in the output.

	theStart	theEnd
1	1	2
2	2	3
3	2	6
4	6	5
5	3	4
6	4	8
7	8	7
8	7	6
9	6	5

Figure 11-8. *Result of traversing from Madison and 1st Avenue to Lexington and 1st Avenue*

To solve this problem, the CTE will have to "remember" on each iteration where it's been on previous iterations. Since each iteration of a CTE can only access the data from the previous iteration—and not all data from all previous iterations—each row will have to keep its own records inline. This can be done using a **materialized path** notation, where each previously visited node will be appended to a running list. This will require adding a new column to the CTE. To do this, first add the following to the anchor member's SELECT list:

```
CONVERT(VARCHAR(900),
    CONVERT(VARCHAR, @Start) + '.' +
    CONVERT(VARCHAR, IntersectionId_End) + '.'
) AS ThePath
```

This code will start to form a list of visited nodes. If node A (IntersectionId 1) is specified as the start point, the output for this column for the anchor member will be 1.2., since node B (IntersectionId 2) is the only node that participates in a street segment starting at node A.

The recursive member will need a similar modification. Add the following to its SELECT list:

```
CONVERT(VARCHAR(900),
    p.ThePath +
    CONVERT(VARCHAR, IntersectionId_End) + '.'
)
```

As new nodes are visited, their IDs will be appended to the list, producing a "breadcrumb" trail of all visited nodes. Note that the columns in both the anchor and recursive members use the CONVERT function to make sure their data types are identical. This is required because the VARCHAR size changes due to concatenation, and all columns exposed by the anchor and recursive members must have identical types. The output of the CTE after making these modifications is shown in Figure 11-9.

	theStart	theEnd	ThePath
1	1	2	1.2.
2	2	3	1.2.3.
3	2	6	1.2.6.
4	6	5	1.2.6.5.
5	3	4	1.2.3.4.
6	4	8	1.2.3.4.8.
7	8	7	1.2.3.4.8.7.
8	7	6	1.2.3.4.8.7.6.
9	6	5	1.2.3.4.8.7.6.5.

Figure 11-9. *The paths (and subpaths) from Madison and 1st Avenue to Lexington and 1st Avenue*

The output now includes the complete paths to the end points, but it still includes all subpaths visited along the way. To finish, add the following to the outermost query:

```
WHERE theEnd = @End
```

This will limit the results to only paths that actually end at the specified end point—in this case, node E (IntersectionId 5). After making that addition, only the two paths that actually visit both the start and end nodes are shown.

The CTE still has one major problem as-is. Figure 11-10 shows a completed version of the map, with the final two street segments filled in. The following T-SQL can be used to populate the StreetSegments table with the new data:

```
INSERT StreetSegments VALUES (5, 1, 1, 1)
INSERT StreetSegments VALUES (7, 3, 3, 3)
GO
```

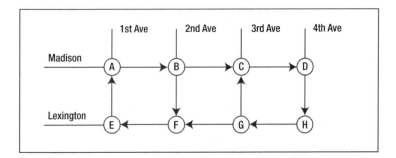

Figure 11-10. *A version of the map with all segments filled in*

Rerunning the CTE after introducing the new segments results in the output shown in Figure 11-11 (abbreviated for brevity), along with the following error:

```
Msg 530, Level 16, State 1, Line 9
The statement terminated.
The maximum recursion 100 has been exhausted before statement completion.
```

Results | Messages

	theStart	theEnd	ThePath
1	6	5	1.2.6.5.
2	6	5	1.2.3.4.8.7.6.5.
3	6	5	1.2.3.4.8.7.3.4.8.7.6.5.
4	6	5	1.2.3.4.8.7.3.4.8.7.3.4.8.7.6.5.
5	6	5	1.2.3.4.8.7.3.4.8.7.3.4.8.7.3.4.8.7.6.5.
6	6	5	1.2.3.4.8.7.3.4.8.7.3.4.8.7.3.4.8.7.3.4.8.7.6.5.
7	6	5	1.2.3.4.8.7.3.4.8.7.3.4.8.7.3.4.8.7.3.4.8.7.3.4.8.7.6.5.
8	6	5	1.2.3.4.8.7.3.4.8.7.3.4.8.7.3.4.8.7.3.4.8.7.3.4.8.7.3.4.8.7.6.5.

Figure 11-11. *Recursively visiting the same paths over and over again*

The issue is that these new intersections create cycles in the graph. The problem can be seen to start at the fourth line of the output, when the recursion visits node `G` (`IntersectionId 7`). There are two possible options for travel from there: west to node `F` (`IntersectionId 6`) or north to node `C` (`IntersectionId 3`). Following the first route, the recursion eventually completes. But following the second route, the recursion will keep coming back to node `G` again and again, following the same two branches. Eventually, the default recursive limit of 100 is reached and execution ends with an error. Note that this default limit can be overridden using the `OPTION (MAXRECURSION N)` query hint, where `N` is the maximum recursive depth you'd like to use. In this case, `100` is a good limit because it quickly tells us that there is a major problem!

Fixing this issue, luckily, is quite simple: check the path to find out whether the next node has already been visited, and if so, do not visit it again. Since the path is a string, this can be accomplished using a `LIKE` predicate. First, modify the `ThePath` column in the anchor member so that each `IntersectionId` in the list, including the first, is delimited on both the left and right sides (this will make it easier to write the search argument):

```
CONVERT(VARCHAR(900),
    '.' +
    CONVERT(VARCHAR, @Start) + '.' +
    CONVERT(VARCHAR, IntersectionId_End) + '.'
) AS ThePath
```

Next, add the following argument to the recursive member's `WHERE` clause:

```
AND p.thePath NOT LIKE '%.' + CONVERT(VARCHAR, ss.IntersectionId_End) + '.%'
```

This predicate checks to make sure that the ending `IntersectionId`, delimited by `.` on both sides, does not yet appear in the path—in other words, has not yet been visited. This will make it impossible for the recursion to fall into a cycle.

Running the CTE after adding this fix eliminates the cycle issue. The full code for the fixed CTE follows:

```
DECLARE
    @Start INT,
    @End INT

SELECT
    @Start = dbo.GetIntersectionId('Madison', '1st Ave'),
    @End = dbo.GetIntersectionId('Lexington', '1st Ave')

;WITH Paths
AS
(
    SELECT
        @Start AS theStart,
        IntersectionId_End AS theEnd,
        CONVERT(VARCHAR(900),
            '.' +
            CONVERT(VARCHAR, @Start) + '.' +
            CONVERT(VARCHAR, IntersectionId_End) + '.'
        ) AS ThePath
    FROM dbo.StreetSegments
    WHERE
        IntersectionId_Start = @Start

    UNION ALL

    SELECT
        p.theEnd,
        ss.IntersectionId_End,
        CONVERT(VARCHAR(900),
            p.ThePath +
            CONVERT(VARCHAR, IntersectionId_End) + '.'
        )
    FROM Paths p
    JOIN dbo.StreetSegments ss ON ss.IntersectionId_Start = p.theEnd
    WHERE
        p.theEnd <> @End
        AND p.thePath NOT LIKE '%.' + CONVERT(VARCHAR, ss.IntersectionId_End) + '.%'
)
SELECT *
FROM Paths
WHERE theEnd = @End
GO
```

This concludes this chapter's coverage on general graphs. The remainder of the chapter deals with modeling and querying of hierarchies. Although hierarchies are much more specialized than graphs, they tend to be more typically seen in software projects than general graphs, and developers must consider slightly different issues when modeling them.

ADVANCED ROUTING

The example shown in this section is highly simplified, and it is designed to teach the basics of querying graphs rather than serving as a complete routing solution. I have had the pleasure of working fairly extensively with a production system designed to traverse actual street routes and will briefly share some of the insights I gained in case you are interested in these kinds of problems.

The first issue with the solution shown here is that of scalability. A big city has tens of thousands of street segments, and determining a route from one end of the city to another using this method will create a combinatorial explosion of possibilities. In order to reduce the number of combinations, a few things can be done.

First of all, each segment can be **weighted**, and a score tallied along the way as you recurse over the possible paths. If the score gets too high, you can terminate the recursion. For example, in the system I worked on, weighting was done based on distance traveled. The algorithm used was fairly complex, but essentially, if a destination was two miles away (based on latitude and longitude—see Chapter 9 for more information) and the route went over three miles, recursion would be terminated for that branch. This scoring also lets the system determine the shortest possible routes.

Another method used to greatly decrease the number of combinations was an analysis of the input set of streets, and a determination made of major routes between certain locations. For instance, traveling from one end of the city to another is usually most direct on a freeway. If the system determines that a freeway route is appropriate, it breaks the routing problem down into two sections: first, find the shortest route from the starting point to a freeway onramp, and then find the shortest route from the end point to a freeway exit. Put these routes together, including the freeway travel, and you have an optimized path from the starting point to the ending point. Major routes—like freeways—can be underweighted in order to make them appear higher in the scoring rank.

If you'd like to try working with real street data, you can download US geographical shape files (including streets as well as various natural formations) for free from the US Census Bureau. The data, called TIGER/Line, is available from `http://www.census.gov/geo/www/tiger/index.html`. Be warned: this data is not easy to work with and requires a lot of cleanup to get it to the point where it can be easily queried.

Adjacency List Hierarchies

As mentioned previously, any kind of graph can be modeled using an adjacency list. This of course includes hierarchies, which again are nothing more than rooted, directed, acyclic graphs with exactly one path between any two nodes (irrespective of direction). Adjacency list hierarchies are very easy to model, visualize, and understand, but can be tricky or inefficient to query in some cases since they require iteration or recursion. However, adjacency lists are not the only hierarchical model available to developers. This chapter also discusses the materialized paths and nested sets models, which can help in a variety of scenarios.

The most commonly recognizable example of an adjacency list hierarchy is a self-referential personnel table that models employees and their managers. Since it's such a common and easily understood example, the AdventureWorks.HumanResources.Employee table—which is modeled as an adjacency list—will be used as the primary example for this section and the rest of this chapter (I will show you how to convert the adjacency list into the other models in their respective sections).

The `HumanResources.Employee` table includes three columns that will be used:

- `EmployeeId` is the primary key for each row of the table.

- `ManagerId` is the key for the employee that each row reports to in the same table. If `ManagerId` is `NULL`, that employee is the root node in the tree (i.e., the head of the company). It's common when modeling adjacency list hierarchies to use either `NULL` or an identical key to the row's primary key to represent root nodes.

- Finally, the `Title` column, representing employees' job titles, will be used to make the output easier to read.

The types of questions generally posed against a hierarchy are somewhat different from the example graph traversal questions examined in the previous section. For adjacency lists as well as the other hierarchical models discussed in this chapter, the following questions will be used:

- What are the direct descendants of a given node? In other words, who are the people who directly report to a given manager?

- What are all of the descendants of a given node? Which is to say, how many people all the way down the organizational hierarchy report up to a given manager? The challenge here is how to sort the output so that it makes sense with regard to the hierarchy.

- What is the path from a given child node back to the root node? In other words, following the management path up instead of down, who reports to whom?

I will also discuss the following data modification challenges:

- Inserting a new node into the hierarchy, as when a new employee is hired

- Relocating a subtree, such as might be necessary if a division gets moved under a new manager

- Deleting a node from the hierarchy, which might, for example, need to happen in an organizational hierarchy due to attrition

Each of the techniques discussed in this chapter have slightly different levels of difficulty with regard to the complexity of solving these problems, and I will make general suggestions on when to use each model.

Querying Adjacency List Hierarchies: The Basics

Traversing an adjacency list hierarchy is virtually identical to traversing an adjacency list graph, with one key difference: since hierarchies don't have cycles, you don't need to worry about them in your code. This is a nice feature, since it makes your code shorter, easier to understand, and more efficient. However, being able to make the assumption that your hierarchy is actually a hierarchy—and not a general graph—takes a bit of work up front. See "Constraining the Hierarchy" later in this section for information on how to make sure that your hierarchies don't end up with cycles, multiple roots, or disconnected subtrees.

Most of the time, adjacency list hierarchies are modeled in a node-centric rather than edge-centric way; that is, the primary key of the hierarchy is the key for the given node, rather than a key representing an edge. This makes sense, because each node in a hierarchy can only have one direct ancestor.

Before getting started with some examples, you should create a new table from the `AdventureWorks.HumanResources.Employee` table, using the following T-SQL:

```
USE AdventureWorks
GO

CREATE TABLE Employee_Temp
(
    EmployeeId INT NOT NULL
        CONSTRAINT PK_Employee PRIMARY KEY,
    ManagerId INT NULL
        CONSTRAINT FK_Manager REFERENCES Employee_Temp (EmployeeId),
    Title NVARCHAR(100)
)
GO

INSERT Employee_Temp
(
    EmployeeId,
    ManagerId,
    Title
)
SELECT
    EmployeeId,
    ManagerId,
    Title
FROM HumanResources.Employee
GO
```

I like to keep the sample databases as stable as possible so that I can use them again and again for experimental queries. Throughout the rest of this chapter, this table will be modified several times, and by creating a new table, the data can be modified without the chance of forgetting to clean it up afterward and having to go back and restore the sample database.

Finding Direct Descendants

I will cover each of the standard set of example questions in order. To begin with, finding the direct descendants of a given node is quite straightforward in an adjacency list hierarchy; it's the same as finding the available nodes to which you can traverse in a graph. Start with the parent node for which you're interested in descendants, and find all nodes that it is a parent of. To find all employees that report directly to the CEO (the root node, with a `NULL` `ManagerId`), use the following T-SQL:

```
DECLARE @ManagerId INT

SELECT
    @ManagerId = EmployeeId
FROM Employee_Temp
WHERE ManagerId IS NULL
```

```
SELECT *
FROM Employee_Temp
WHERE ManagerId = @ManagerId
```

■ **Tip** Instead of using a variable and two SELECTs, you might instead merge this into a single SELECT with a subquery. This will have the benefit of making the code independent of the data type used for the key. In this case, I've used two SELECTs in order to help make both the code and its execution plan slightly clearer to read.

This query returns the results shown in Figure 11-12, showing the six branches of AdventureWorks, represented by its upper management team—exactly the results that we expected. However, this query has a hidden problem: traversing from node to node in a hierarchy involves finding a top-level node to begin from, finding its subordinates, then their subordinates, and so on, all the way down to the leaf nodes. In the case of the Employee_Temp table, finding subordinates means searching based on the ManagerId column. Considering that and the fact that the column is not indexed, it should come as no surprise that the query plan for this query involves a table scan, as shown in Figure 11-13—actually, the complete query involves two scans, one to find the CEO and one to find the subordinates. I've only shown the second scan for brevity (the query plans are identical).

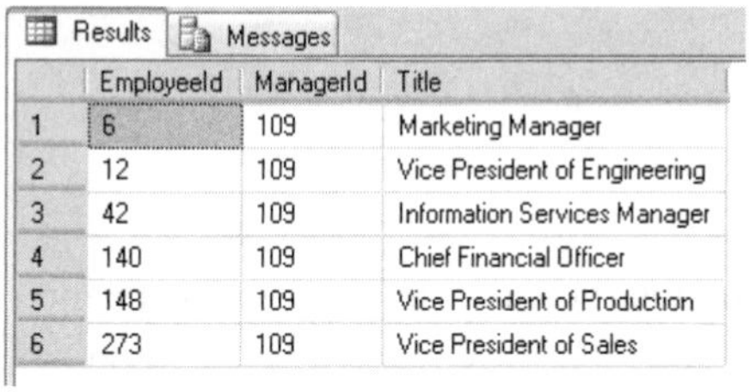

	EmployeeId	ManagerId	Title
1	6	109	Marketing Manager
2	12	109	Vice President of Engineering
3	42	109	Information Services Manager
4	140	109	Chief Financial Officer
5	148	109	Vice President of Production
6	273	109	Vice President of Sales

Figure 11-12. *Direct reports to the CEO*

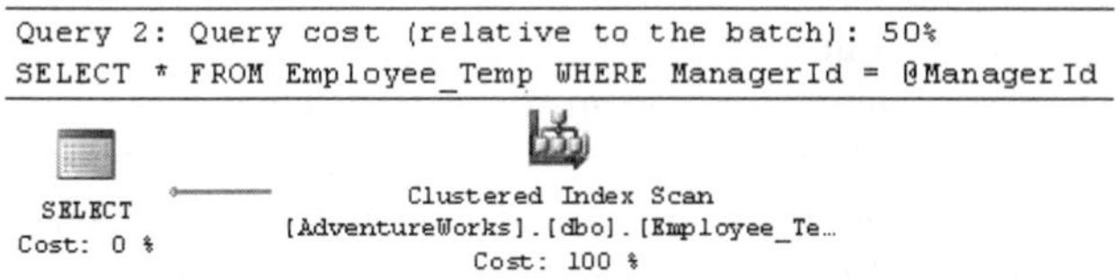

Figure 11-13. *Querying on the ManagerId causes a table scan.*

To eliminate this issue, an index on the ManagerId column must be created. However, choosing exactly how best to index a table such as this one can be difficult. In the case of this small example, a clustered index on ManagerId would yield the best overall mix of performance for both querying and data updates, by covering all queries that involve traversing the table.

However, in an actual production system, there might be a much higher percentage of queries based on the EmployeeId—for instance, queries to get a single employee's data—and there would probably be a lot more columns in the table than the three used here for example purposes, meaning that clustering key lookups could be expensive. In such a case, it is important to test carefully in order to determine which combination of indexes delivers the best balance of query and data modification performance for your particular workload.

In order to show the best possible performance in this case, change the primary key to use a nonclustered index and create a clustered index on ManagerId, as shown in the following T-SQL:

```
BEGIN TRAN

ALTER TABLE Employee_Temp
DROP CONSTRAINT FK_Manager

ALTER TABLE Employee_Temp
DROP CONSTRAINT PK_Employee

CREATE CLUSTERED INDEX IX_Manager
ON Employee_Temp (ManagerId)

ALTER TABLE Employee_Temp
ADD CONSTRAINT PK_Employee
PRIMARY KEY NONCLUSTERED (EmployeeId)

COMMIT
GO
```

Once this change has been made, rerunning the T-SQL to find the CEO's direct reports produces a clustered index seek instead of a scan—a small improvement that will be magnified when doing larger queries against the table.

Traversing down the Hierarchy

Shifting from finding direct descendants of one node to traversing down the entire hierarchy all the way to the leaf nodes is extremely simple, just as in the case of general graphs. A recursive CTE is one tool that can be used for this purpose. The following CTE, modified from the section on graphs, traverses the Employee_Temp hierarchy starting from the CEO, returning all employees in the company:

```
WITH n AS
(
    SELECT
        EmployeeId,
        ManagerId,
        Title
    FROM Employee_Temp
    WHERE ManagerId IS NULL
```

```
    UNION ALL

    SELECT
        e.EmployeeId,
        e.ManagerId,
        e.Title
    FROM Employee_Temp e
    JOIN n ON n.EmployeeId = e.ManagerId
)
SELECT
    n.EmployeeId,
    n.ManagerId,
    n.Title
FROM n
GO
```

Note that this CTE returns all columns to be used by the outer query—but this is not the only way to write this query. The query could also be written such that the CTE uses and returns only the EmployeeId column, necessitating an additional JOIN in the outer query to get the other columns:

```
WITH n AS
(
    SELECT
        EmployeeId
    FROM Employee_Temp
    WHERE ManagerId IS NULL

    UNION ALL

    SELECT
        e.EmployeeId
    FROM Employee_Temp e
    JOIN n ON n.EmployeeId = e.ManagerId
)
SELECT
    e.EmployeeId,
    e.ManagerId,
    e.Title
FROM n
JOIN Employee_Temp e ON e.EmployeeId = n.EmployeeId
GO
```

I thought that this latter form might result in less I/O activity, and after testing several combinations of indexes against both query forms, using this table as well as tables with many more columns, I decided that there is no straightforward answer. The latter query tends to perform better as the output row size increases, but in the case of the small test table, the former query is much more efficient. Again, this is something you should test against your actual workload before deploying a solution.

Regardless of the performance of these queries, the fact is that we haven't really done much here. The output of either of these queries as they currently stand is logically equivalent to the output of SELECT * FROM Employee_Temp. In order to add value, the output should be sorted such that it conforms to the hierarchy represented in the table. To do this, we can use the same path technique described in the section "Traversing the Graph," but without the need to be concerned with cycles. By ordering by the path, the output will follow the same nested order as the hierarchy itself. The following T-SQL shows how to accomplish this:

```
WITH n AS
(
    SELECT
        EmployeeId,
        ManagerId,
        Title,
        CONVERT(VARCHAR(900),
            RIGHT(REPLICATE('0', 10) + CONVERT(VARCHAR, EmployeeId), 10) + '.'
        ) AS thePath
    FROM Employee_Temp
    WHERE ManagerId IS NULL

    UNION ALL

    SELECT
        e.EmployeeId,
        e.ManagerId,
        e.Title,
        CONVERT(VARCHAR(900),
            n.thePath +
            RIGHT(REPLICATE('0', 10) + CONVERT(VARCHAR, e.EmployeeId), 10) + '.'
        ) AS thePath
    FROM Employee_Temp e
    JOIN n ON n.EmployeeId = e.ManagerId
)
SELECT
    n.EmployeeId,
    n.ManagerId,
    n.Title,
    n.thePath
FROM n
ORDER BY n.thePath
GO
```

Running this query produces the output shown in Figure 11-14 (truncated for brevity). In order to support proper numerical ordering on the nodes, I've left-padded them with zeroes. This ensures that, for instance, the path 1.2. does not sort higher than the path 1.10.. The numbers are padded to 10 digits to support the full range of positive integer values supported by SQL Server's INT data type. Note that siblings in this case are ordered based on their EmployeeId. Changing the ordering of siblings—for instance, to alphabetical order based on Title—requires a bit of manipulation to the path. Instead of materializing the EmployeeId, materialize a row number that represents the current ordered sibling. This can be done using SQL Server's ROW_NUMBER function, and is sometimes referred to as **enumerating** the path. The following modified version of the CTE (output shown in Figure 11-15) enumerates the path:

```
WITH n AS
(
    SELECT
        EmployeeId,
        ManagerId,
        Title,
        CONVERT(VARCHAR(900),
            '0000000001.'
        ) AS thePath
    FROM Employee_Temp
    WHERE ManagerId IS NULL

    UNION ALL

    SELECT
        e.EmployeeId,
        e.ManagerId,
        e.Title,
        CONVERT(VARCHAR(900),
            n.thePath +
            RIGHT(
                REPLICATE('0', 10) +
                    CONVERT(VARCHAR, ROW_NUMBER() OVER (ORDER BY e.Title)),
                10
            ) + '.'
        ) AS thePath
    FROM Employee_Temp e
    JOIN n ON n.EmployeeId = e.ManagerId
)
SELECT
    n.EmployeeId,
    n.ManagerId,
    n.Title,
    n.thePath
FROM n
ORDER BY n.thePath
GO
```

	EmployeeId	ManagerId	Title	thePath
1	109	NULL	Chief Executive Officer	0000000109.
2	6	109	Marketing Manager	0000000109.0000000006.
3	2	6	Marketing Assistant	0000000109.0000000006.0000000002.
4	46	6	Marketing Specialist	0000000109.0000000006.0000000046.
5	106	6	Marketing Specialist	0000000109.0000000006.0000000106.
6	119	6	Marketing Specialist	0000000109.0000000006.0000000119.
7	203	6	Marketing Specialist	0000000109.0000000006.0000000203.
8	269	6	Marketing Assistant	0000000109.0000000006.0000000269.
9	271	6	Marketing Specialist	0000000109.0000000006.0000000271.
10	272	6	Marketing Assistant	0000000109.0000000006.0000000272.
11	12	109	Vice President of Engineering	0000000109.0000000012.
12	3	12	Engineering Manager	0000000109.0000000012.0000000003.

Figure 11-14. *Traversing down the employee hierarchy, including a path based on EmployeeId*

	EmployeeId	ManagerId	Title	thePath
1	109	NULL	Chief Executive Officer	0000000001.
2	140	109	Chief Financial Officer	0000000001.0000000001.
3	139	140	Accounts Manager	0000000001.0000000001.0000000001.
4	216	139	Accountant	0000000001.0000000001.0000000001.0000000001.
5	178	139	Accountant	0000000001.0000000001.0000000001.0000000002.
6	166	139	Accounts Payable Specialist	0000000001.0000000001.0000000001.0000000003.
7	201	139	Accounts Payable Specialist	0000000001.0000000001.0000000001.0000000004.
8	130	139	Accounts Receivable Specialist	0000000001.0000000001.0000000001.0000000005.
9	94	139	Accounts Receivable Specialist	0000000001.0000000001.0000000001.0000000006.
10	59	139	Accounts Receivable Specialist	0000000001.0000000001.0000000001.0000000007.
11	103	140	Assistant to the Chief Financial Officer	0000000001.0000000001.0000000002.
12	71	140	Finance Manager	0000000001.0000000001.0000000003.

Figure 11-15. *Traversing down the employee hierarchy, enumerating the path based on the order of employees' titles*

■**Tip** Instead of left-padding the node IDs with zeroes, you could expose the thePath column typed as VARBINARY and convert the IDs to BINARY(4). This would have the same net effect for the purpose of sorting and at the same time take up less space—so you will see an efficiency benefit, and in addition you'll be able to hold more node IDs in each row's path. The downside is that this makes the IDs more difficult to visualize, so for the purposes of this chapter—where visual queues are important—I use the left-padding method instead.

The downside of including an enumerated path instead of a materialized path is that the enumerated version cannot be easily deconstructed in order to determine the keys that were followed. For instance, simply looking at the thePath column in Figure 11-14, we can see that the path to the Engineering Manager (EmployeeId 3) starts with EmployeeId 109, and then EmployeeId 12, before getting to the Engineering Manager. Looking at the same column in Figure 11-15, it is not possible to discover the actual IDs that make up a given path without following it back up the hierarchy in the output.

Are CTEs the Best Choice?

CTEs are certainly the most convenient way to traverse adjacency list hierarchies in SQL Server 2005, but they do not necessarily deliver the best possible performance. I was alerted to the performance issue by SQL Server MVP Paul Nielsen, who mentioned during a conversation that he had had much better success using iterative methods involving temp tables or table variables than using recursive CTEs. I ran several tests, and my results concur with Paul's findings—CTEs, especially as the hierarchy grows, simply do not deliver the best possible performance.

To highlight the performance difference between CTEs and iterative methods, a larger hierarchy is necessary. To begin with, we can add **width** to the Employee_Temp hierarchy. This means that the hierarchy will maintain the same depth, but each level will have more siblings. To accomplish this, for each row below a given subtree, both the employee IDs and manager IDs can be incremented by the same known amount, thereby producing a duplicate subtree in place. The following T-SQL accomplishes this, running in a loop five times and doubling the width of the hierarchy on each iteration:

```
DECLARE @CEO INT
SELECT
    @CEO = EmployeeId
FROM Employee_Temp
WHERE ManagerId IS NULL

DECLARE @width INT
SET @width = 1

WHILE @width <= 16
BEGIN
    INSERT Employee_Temp
    (
        EmployeeId,
        ManagerId,
        Title
    )
    SELECT
        e.EmployeeId + (1000 * @width),
        CASE e.ManagerId
            WHEN @CEO THEN e.ManagerId
            ELSE e.ManagerId + (1000 * @width)
        END,
        e.Title
    FROM Employee_Temp e
    WHERE
        e.ManagerId IS NOT NULL

    SET @width = @width * 2
END
GO
```

There are two key factors you should pay attention to in this example. First is the `@width` variable, which is doubled on each iteration in order to avoid key collisions as the keys are incremented. Second, look at the `CASE` expression in the `SELECT` list, which increments all IDs except that of the CEO. This ensures that the duplicate subtrees will be appended to the tree as a whole, by virtue of the roots of those subtrees being subordinates of the CEO's node.

Once this code has been run, the `Employee_Temp` hierarchy will have 9,249 nodes, rather than the 290 that we started with. However, the hierarchy still has only five levels. To increase the **depth**, a slightly different algorithm is required. To add levels, find all managers except the CEO, and insert new duplicate nodes, incrementing their employee IDs similar to before. Next, update the preexisting managers in the table to report to the new managers. The following T-SQL does this in a loop four times, producing a hierarchy with a depth of 50 levels and 31,329 nodes:

```
DECLARE @CEO INT
SELECT
    @CEO = EmployeeId
FROM Employee_Temp
WHERE ManagerId IS NULL

DECLARE @depth INT
SET @depth = 32

WHILE @depth <= 256
BEGIN
    DECLARE @OldManagers TABLE
    (
        EmployeeId INT
    )


    --Insert intermediate managers
    --Find all managers, except the CEO, and increment their EmployeeId by 1000
    INSERT Employee_Temp
    (
        EmployeeId,
        ManagerId,
        Title
    )
    OUTPUT inserted.EmployeeId - (1000 * @depth) INTO @OldManagers
    SELECT
        e.EmployeeId + (1000 * @depth) as newemp,
        e.ManagerId,
        'Intermediate Manager'
    FROM Employee_Temp e
    WHERE
        e.EmployeeId <> @CEO
        AND EXISTS
```

```
        (
            SELECT *
            FROM Employee_Temp e1
            WHERE e1.ManagerId = e.EmployeeId
        )

    --Update existing managers to report to intermediates
    UPDATE Employee_Temp
    SET ManagerId = EmployeeId + (1000 * @depth)
    WHERE
        EmployeeId IN
        (
            SELECT EmployeeId
            FROM @OldManagers
        )

    SET @depth = @depth * 2
END
GO
```

Be careful when adding additional depth to an experimental hierarchy. I've found that depth has a much greater performance impact than width, and extremely deep hierarchies are not especially common—for instance, even the largest companies do not have many more than 20 or 30 levels of management.

To iteratively traverse the hierarchy using a table variable, think about what recursion does: at each level, the employees for the previous level's managers are found, and then that level becomes the current level. Applying this logic iteratively requires the following table variable:

```
DECLARE @n TABLE
(
    EmployeeId INT,
    ManagerId INT,
    Title NVARCHAR(100),
    Depth INT,
    thePath VARCHAR(900),
    PRIMARY KEY (Depth, EmployeeId)
)
```

The Depth column maintains the level for nodes as they are inserted. The table is clustered on the combination of Depth and EmployeeId; at each level, the depth will be queried first, and we know that EmployeeId will be unique and so can exploit it as a "uniquifier" for the key.

To start things off, prime the table variable with the node you wish to use as the root for traversal. In this case, the CEO's node will be used, and the path is started with 1., as I'll be implementing the enumerated path output shown in the previous example:

```
DECLARE @depth INT
SET @depth = 1
```

```
INSERT @n
SELECT
    EmployeeId,
    ManagerId,
    Title,
    @depth,
    '0000000001.'
FROM Employee_Temp
WHERE ManagerId IS NULL
```

After the first row is in place, the logic is identical to the recursive logic used in the CTE. For each level of depth, find the subordinates. The only difference is that this is done using a WHILE loop instead of a recursive CTE:

```
WHILE 1=1
BEGIN
    INSERT @n
    SELECT
        e.EmployeeId,
        e.ManagerId,
        e.Title,
        @depth + 1,
        n.thePath +
            RIGHT(
                    REPLICATE('0', 10) +
                        CONVERT(VARCHAR, ROW_NUMBER() OVER
                            (PARTITION BY e.ManagerId ORDER BY e.Title)),
                    10
                ) + '.'
    FROM Employee_Temp e
    JOIN @n n on n.EmployeeId = e.ManagerId
    WHERE n.Depth = @depth

    IF @@ROWCOUNT = 0
        BREAK

    SET @depth = @depth + 1
END
```

Finally, the output can be queried from the table variable. Like before, an ORDER BY clause is necessary:

```
SELECT
    EmployeeId,
    ManagerId,
    Title,
    thePath
FROM @n
ORDER BY
    thePath
```

This method uses over 50% more code than the CTE, is quite a bit less intuitive, and has many more potential areas in which you might introduce logic bugs. However, its performance is quite a bit better than the CTE. The enumerated path CTE does 347,282 reads and runs in 27.6 seconds on my laptop, against the enhanced `Employee_Temp` table. The iterative method, on the other hand, does only 173,536 reads and runs in 13.2 seconds.

Despite the clear performance improvement in this case, I do not recommend this method for the majority of situations. I feel that the maintainability issues overshadow the performance benefits in all but the most extreme cases (such as that highlighted here). For that reason, the remaining examples in this chapter will use CTEs. However, you should be able to easily convert any of the examples so that they use iterative logic. Should you decide to use this technique on a project, you might find it beneficial to encapsulate the code in a multistatement table-valued UDF for greater potential for reuse.

■**Note** If you're following along with the examples in this chapter and grew the table, you should drop and re-create it before continuing with the rest of the chapter.

Traversing up the Hierarchy

For an adjacency list, traversing "up" the hierarchy—in other words, finding any given node's ancestry path back to the root node—is essentially the same as traversing down the hierarchy in reverse. Instead of using `ManagerId` as a key at each level of recursion, use `EmployeeId`. The following CTE shows how to get the path from the Research and Development Manager, `EmployeeId` 217, to the CEO:

```
;WITH n AS
(
    SELECT
        ManagerId,
        CONVERT(VARCHAR(900),
            RIGHT(
                REPLICATE('0', 10) +
                    CONVERT(VARCHAR, EmployeeId) + '.', 10)
        ) AS thePath
    FROM Employee_Temp
    WHERE EmployeeId = 217

    UNION ALL

    SELECT
        e.ManagerId,
        CONVERT(VARCHAR(900),
            n.thePath +
                RIGHT(
                    REPLICATE('0', 10) +
                        CONVERT(VARCHAR, e.EmployeeId),
```

```
                10) + '.'
        ) AS thePath
    FROM Employee_Temp e
    JOIN n ON n.ManagerId = e.EmployeeId
)
SELECT *
FROM n
WHERE ManagerId IS NULL
```

This query returns the path from the selected node to the CEO as a materialized path of employee IDs. However, you might instead want to get the results back as a table of employee IDs. In order to do that, change the outer query to the following:

```
SELECT
    COALESCE(ManagerId, 217) AS EmployeeId
FROM n
ORDER BY
    CASE
        WHEN ManagerId IS NULL THEN 0
        ELSE 1
    END,
    thePath
```

In this case, the COALESCE function used in the SELECT list replaces the CEO's ManagerId—which is NULL—with the target EmployeeId. The CASE expression in the ORDER BY clause forces the NULL row to sort at the top, so that the target EmployeeId is returned first. All other sorting is based on the materialized path, which naturally returns the CEO's row last.

Inserting New Nodes and Relocating Subtrees

In an adjacency list hierarchy, inserting new nodes is generally quite straightforward. Inserting a leaf node (i.e., a node with no subordinates) requires simply inserting a new node into the table. To insert a nonleaf node, you must also update any direct subordinates of the node you're inserting under, so that they point to their new manager. This is effectively the same as inserting a new node and then relocating the old node's subtree under the new node, which is why I've merged these two topics into one section.

As an example, suppose that AdventureWorks has decided to hire a new CTO, to whom the current Vice President of Engineering (EmployeeId 12) will be reporting. To do this, first insert the new CTO node, and then update the VP's node to report to the new CTO:

```
INSERT Employee_Temp
(
    EmployeeId,
    ManagerId,
    Title
)
```

```
VALUES
(
    999,
    109,
    'CTO'
)
GO

UPDATE Employee_Temp
SET ManagerId = 999
WHERE EmployeeId = 12
GO
```

This same logic can be applied for any subtree relocation—one of the advantages of adjacency lists over the other hierarchical techniques discussed in this chapter is the ease with which data modifications like this can be handled.

Deleting Existing Nodes

Removing nodes in an adjacency list is only slightly trickier than inserting a new nonleaf node. This time, the first step is to relocate any subordinates that report to the node to be deleted—the key is that subordinates is plural this time, as there may be more than one. Once those subtrees are relocated to their new manager, the leaf node can simply be removed.

Suppose that on her first day at the office, the new CTO won the lottery and decided that she would rather race her yacht than work at AdventureWorks. Backing out her addition to the organizational hierarchy requires relocating her reports back to the CEO, and then deleting her node, which will be a leaf. Due to the self-referencing foreign key on the table, nonleaf nodes cannot be deleted—this is another nice fringe benefit of adjacency lists.

The following T-SQL can be used to remove the CTO's node:

```
UPDATE Employee_Temp
SET ManagerId =
    (
        SELECT ManagerId
        FROM Employee_Temp
        WHERE EmployeeId = 999
    )
WHERE ManagerId = 999

DELETE FROM Employee_Temp
WHERE EmployeeId = 999
```

This code works by finding the manager for the node to be removed, and updating all of its direct subordinates to point to that manager (in other words, the "grandfather" node for each of the subordinates becomes their "father" node). Once the update is complete, the node is a leaf, and so can be removed.

Constraining the Hierarchy

Each of the hierarchical traversal examples shown in this chapter makes a very important assumption about the data: it is taken for granted that there are no cycles or other data issues that would make the hierarchies invalid. The main implication of this is that the resultant code is a lot simpler; the problem is that the simpler code is prone to various problems should bad data creep in—and as most readers are no doubt aware, bad data can and *will* creep in if given the opportunity.

Simple code is a good thing, so instead of making the code more complex, we have a choice: either cross our fingers for luck and hope that the system never has occasion to melt down at run time, or better, actually constrain the data to ensure that it remains valid. Personally, I highly recommend the second approach.

There are two possible issues that can make life difficult for hierarchical queries: forests and cycles. Forests usually occur when there are multiple root nodes in the hierarchy. And although they may make sense for some types of data, for organizational charts they do not. Cycles occur when, somewhere downstream from a given node, that node is suddenly referenced again. For example, if George manages Ed, Ed manages Steve, and Steve manages George, a cycle has been formed—this is not only unrealistic, but also cause for a runtime exception due to an endless loop!

The `Employee_Temp` table we've been working with already has a couple of constraints that help guard against certain issues: a primary key and a self-referencing foreign key. The primary key, which is on the `EmployeeId` column, guards against most cycles by making it impossible for a given employee to have more than one manager. And the self-referencing foreign key guards against most forest issues, because the every node must be connected to another node that already exists—unless it's a root node.

The first thing that must be constrained against is multiple root nodes. The first way that comes to mind to handle this is probably a trigger, but I find it slightly more interesting to employ an indexed view:

```
ALTER VIEW OnlyOneRoot
WITH SCHEMABINDING
AS
    SELECT
        ManagerId
    FROM dbo.Employee_Temp
    WHERE
        ManagerId IS NULL
GO


CREATE UNIQUE CLUSTERED INDEX IX_OnlyOneRoot
ON OnlyOneRoot (ManagerId)
GO
```

The view returns all rows in the table with a `NULL` manager ID, and the index, because it is `UNIQUE`, only allows one such row to be inserted.

While this works great for keeping newly inserted root nodes at bay, it doesn't stop someone from updating the root node and assigning a manager (the unique constraint can only enforce rows that exist, and by updating the table the `NULL` manager ID would no longer exist at all). To solve this problem, a trigger can be used, to make sure that there is always at least one `NULL` manager ID in the table:

```
CREATE TRIGGER tg_AtLeastOneRoot
ON Employee_Temp
FOR UPDATE
AS
BEGIN
    SET NOCOUNT ON

    IF NOT EXISTS
    (
        SELECT *
        FROM Employee_Temp
        WHERE ManagerId IS NULL
    )
    BEGIN
        RAISERROR('A root node is required', 16, 1)
        ROLLBACK
    END
END
GO
```

To root out cycles, we need to think about what kinds of cycles can exist in the table. To begin with, the simplest cycle—and one that's not constrained against by either the primary key or the foreign key—is an employee managing herself. This is easily solved with a check constraint:

```
ALTER TABLE Employee_Temp
ADD CONSTRAINT ck_ManagerIsNotEmployee
    CHECK (EmployeeId <> ManagerId)
GO
```

This constraint does nothing for deeper cycles, where an employee manages himself or herself one or more levels below. For instance, if George manages Ed and Ed manages Steve, someone could issue an update to the table so that Ed manages George. This would create a deeper cycle that the constraint would not be able to catch. In order to solve this problem, a trigger must be employed. The trigger should start with the updated row, traversing up the tree towards the root node. Should it encounter the same employee that was updated a second time before hitting the root, it is apparent that there is a cycle. Following is the code for such a trigger:

```
CREATE TRIGGER tg_NoCycles
ON Employee_Temp
FOR UPDATE
AS
BEGIN
    SET NOCOUNT ON

    --Only check if the ManagerId column was updated
    IF NOT UPDATE(ManagerId)
        RETURN
```

```
--Avoid cycles
DECLARE @CycleExists BIT
SET @CycleExists = 0

--Traverse up the hierarchy toward the
--leaf node
;WITH e AS
(
    SELECT EmployeeId, ManagerId
    FROM inserted

    UNION ALL

    SELECT e.EmployeeId, et.ManagerId
    FROM Employee_Temp et
    JOIN e ON e.ManagerId = et.EmployeeId
    WHERE
        et.ManagerId IS NOT NULL
        AND e.ManagerId <> e.EmployeeId
)
SELECT @CycleExists = 1
FROM e
WHERE e.ManagerId = e.EmployeeId

IF @CycleExists = 1
BEGIN
    RAISERROR('The update introduced a cycle', 16, 1)
    ROLLBACK
END
END
GO
```

This type of cycle can only be caused by either updates or multirow inserts, and in virtually all of the hierarchies I've seen in production environments, there were no multirow inserts. Therefore, this trigger is set to only fire on updates. Remember to change the trigger definition if you need to work with multirow inserts in your environment.

Persisting Materialized Paths

The adjacency list model, while both a de facto standard for modeling hierarchies and extremely easy to work with from a data manipulation point of view, suffers from inefficiencies due to the fact that the hierarchy must be traversed using either recursion or iteration. In the following two sections I will present two techniques that have been created to help with this problem: persisted materialized paths and the nested sets model. Both of these techniques can act as stand-alone replacements for adjacency lists, but I recommend using them in conjunction with existing adjacency list hierarchies. In the following sections, I will show you how to maintain either hierarchy type alongside an adjacency list hierarchy, using a series of triggers.

In the previous section's examples, a materialized path was used in order to provide an ordered representation of the hierarchy for output purposes. This same path can be persisted in the table in order to allow you to answer all of the same hierarchical questions as with an adjacency list, but without the necessity for recursion or iteration.

To add and populate a materialized path column to the `Employee_Temp` table, add the column as type `VARCHAR(900)` and then update the table using a recursive CTE used to get the path for each node:

```
ALTER TABLE Employee_Temp
ADD thePath VARCHAR(900)
GO

WITH n AS
(
    SELECT
        EmployeeId,
        CONVERT(VARCHAR(900),
            RIGHT(REPLICATE('0', 10) + CONVERT(VARCHAR, EmployeeId), 10) + '.'
        ) AS thePath
    FROM Employee_Temp
    WHERE ManagerId IS NULL

    UNION ALL

    SELECT
        e.EmployeeId,
        CONVERT(VARCHAR(900),
            n.thePath +
            RIGHT(REPLICATE('0', 10) + CONVERT(VARCHAR, e.EmployeeId), 10) + '.'
        ) AS thePath
    FROM Employee_Temp e
    JOIN n ON n.EmployeeId = e.ManagerId
)
UPDATE Employee_Temp
    SET Employee_Temp.thePath = n.thePath
FROM Employee_Temp
JOIN n ON n.EmployeeId = Employee_Temp.EmployeeId
GO
```

`VARCHAR(900)` is important in this case because the materialized path will be used as an index key in order to allow it to be efficiently used to traverse the hierarchy. Index keys in SQL Server are limited to 900 bytes. This is also a bit of a limitation for persisted materialized paths; a path to navigate an especially deep hierarchy will not be indexable and therefore will not be usable for this technique. In the section "Optimizing the Materialized Path Solution," I'll present a method for increasing the range by encoding the IDs using a different scheme.

As with a pure adjacency list hierarchy, the best indexing scheme for a persisted materialized path should be determined through careful testing of your particular workload. That said, I can all but guarantee that a clustered index will never be the right choice. Since the paths can grow quite large, and every nonclustered index inherits the clustered index's keys, clustering on the path will grow the page sizes of every index created on the table. The path doesn't bring any value in its nonindexed form, so I don't recommend trying that technique. Instead, create a nonclustered index, and use the INCLUDE clause to bring along any columns that are commonly used in conjunction with hierarchical searches of the data. In the case of the Employee_Temp table, the index will include the Title and EmployeeId columns, so that the same output shown before can be most efficiently produced via the materialized path (the table is clustered on ManagerId, so that does not have to be explicitly included):

```
CREATE NONCLUSTERED INDEX IX_Employee_Temp_Path
ON Employee_Temp (thePath)
INCLUDE (EmployeeId, Title)
```

Finding Subordinates

Since the materialized path is a string, we can take advantage of SQL Server's LIKE predicate to traverse down the hierarchy. The path for every given node N that is a subordinate of some node M starts with node M's path. Looking back at Figure 11-14, notice that since all nodes are descendants of EmployeeId 109 (the CEO), every path starts with the string 109.. Likewise, moving down the hierarchy, every subordinate node inherits its parent's path and adds its own ID to the end.

Therefore, searching for all subordinates of a given employee is as simple as using the LIKE predicate and adding the wildcard character, %. The following query finds all subordinates of the Vice President of Engineering (EmployeeId 12), using the materialized path:

```
DECLARE @Path VARCHAR(900)
SELECT @Path = thePath
FROM Employee_Temp
WHERE EmployeeId = 12

SELECT *
FROM Employee_Temp
WHERE
    thePath LIKE @Path + '%'
ORDER BY thePath
```

Performance of this query compared to the CTE solution, even against the small table, is fairly impressive. To find all subordinates of the Vice President using the CTE, the query engine must do 187 logical reads. To do the same thing using the materialized path requires only 6.

Finding only the direct reports for a given node is just a bit trickier. This time, a naked wildcard does not do the trick, as it will return the input node, its children as well as children of its children. To eliminate the input node, the predicate can be changed to thePath LIKE @Path + '%.'. This will return false for the input node, since the additional period is not present in its path. However, this still includes all children nodes, as each have a path suffixed by a period. To eliminate children of children, the following NOT LIKE predicate must be added: AND thePath NOT LIKE @Path + '%.%.'. Essentially, this predicate says that the target path can only have one more period than the input path—and therefore, that path is one level of depth below. The following T-SQL finds the direct reports for the Vice President of Engineering:

```
DECLARE @Path VARCHAR(900)
SELECT @Path = thePath
FROM Employee_Temp
WHERE EmployeeId = 12

SELECT *
FROM Employee_Temp
WHERE
    thePath LIKE @Path + '%.'
    AND thePath NOT LIKE @Path + '%.%.'
```

Navigating up the Hierarchy

One of the limitations of persisted materialized paths is that there is no especially efficient way to use them to navigate up the hierarchy in order to produce the "how do we get to the CEO from the current node" report. However, the materialized path itself already contains all of the information necessary—it's just that the data needs to be manipulated a bit to get it into a usable format.

The path for each employee is a period-delimited ordered list of the nodes that lead from the root node to the given employee. In order to generate a table from the list, it must be split up based on its delimiters. This can be done by recursively using the SUBSTRING function. To find the first node in a list, you can take advantage of the knowledge that each node occupies 10 characters for the actual node ID and use the following expression: SUBSTRING(thePath, 1, 10). This expression takes the substring from the first character to the tenth character—leaving the delimiter, which appears at character 11 in the path.

By putting this logic in a recursive CTE, we can take the substring of each node in the path on each iteration. Simultaneously, we can remember the order of the nodes in the list so that the output can be ordered properly. The following CTE, the output of which is shown in Figure 11-16, finds the path to the CEO starting at the Research and Development Manager:

```
;WITH n AS
(
    SELECT
        CONVERT(INT,
            SUBSTRING(thePath, 1, 10)
        ) AS EmployeeId,
        SUBSTRING(thePath, 12, LEN(thePath)) AS thePath,
        1 AS theLevel
    FROM Employee_Temp
    WHERE EmployeeId = 217

    UNION ALL

    SELECT
        CONVERT(INT,
            SUBSTRING(thePath, 1, 10)),
        SUBSTRING(thePath, 12, LEN(thePath)),
        theLevel + 1
```

```
    FROM n
    WHERE thePath <> ''
)
SELECT *
FROM n
ORDER BY theLevel
OPTION(MAXRECURSION 81)
```

	EmployeeId	thePath	theLevel
1	109	0000000012.0000000003.0000000158.0000000217.	1
2	12	0000000003.0000000158.0000000217.	2
3	3	0000000158.0000000217.	3
4	158	0000000217.	4
5	217		5

Figure 11-16. *Traversing up the employee hierarchy, using substring logic*

Aside from the expression used to pull out the current first node, another expression I used in both the anchor and recursive members cuts the first node out of the path, so that the path progressively shrinks as the CTE recurses at each level. This time, the cut starts at character 12—just after the first delimiter—and takes the entire remainder of the path.

The MAXRECURSION option is also used, in case of especially large hierarchies (although, of course, in this case that's not an issue). 81 is the maximum depth of hierarchies modeled using this scheme, due to the fact that the maximum length of a path is 900 and each node occupies 11 characters in the path. Although the EmployeeId column is probably the only one necessary in the output, I've left the other columns in Figure 11-16 so that you can see how the path is affected by the CTE's logic at each level.

Optimizing the Materialized Path Solution

Many times when working to find the "best" database solutions, there are tradeoffs that can be made in favor of performance. Those tradeoffs usually involve simplicity and/or maintainability. The persisted materialized path solution is no different—we can both extend its usable range beyond hierarchies that are 81 levels deep and make it more efficient by manipulating the way the strings are encoded. However, keep in mind as you read this section that doing so will make the solution somewhat more difficult to use. This might not be an issue, if you as a database developer are writing all of the queries that will access the table, but it will be a problem should another user need to quickly get up to speed.

As mentioned previously in this chapter, one solution for holding a larger number of nodes in a path is to use binary encoding rather than string encoding. However, the hierarchy navigation logic (using the LIKE predicate) does not work with binary, so that's not an option. Instead of modifying the data type, I looked at changing the way the numbers were encoded in the string.

■**Note** A binary-encoded path *can* actually be used to answer many of the questions illustrated in this chapter. For instance, to find all subordinates of a node based on binary ordering, look for all nodes where the path is between the parent node's path and the parent node's path with a high byte (0xFF) appended. However, binary encoding cannot be efficiently used for other questions. For instance, finding only direct subordinates using materialized paths relies on both the paths' sort order and the knowledge that exactly two delimiters appear between a parent and its direct descendants. This kind of logic is extremely difficult to efficiently apply to a binary-encoded path.

By default, integers converted to strings are converted using base-10 encoding—which is to say that there are 10 characters (0–9) used to represent the digits in each number. By increasing the base, you boost the number of characters that can be used, meaning that you can store a larger integer in a smaller number of characters.

I tried to find the biggest base I could represent in SQL Server, and still be able to use all of the string functions (most importantly, the LIKE predicate) so as to manipulate a materialized path encoded in that base. I decided to avoid CHAR(0), as strings become nonprintable when appended to it. I also decided to avoid all characters usable in string matching patterns: %, [,], and _. This leaves 251 out of the total 256 non-Unicode characters to work with.

The following function takes an integer as input and returns the integer encoded as a 4-byte base-251 string:

```
CREATE FUNCTION EncodeBase251(@i INT)
RETURNS CHAR(4)
AS
BEGIN
    DECLARE @byte TINYINT

    DECLARE @base_to_char CHAR(4)
    SET @base_to_char = ''

    DECLARE @j INT
    SET @j = 1

    WHILE @j <= 4
    BEGIN
        --Get each byte of the input, carrying over values > 251
        SET @byte = @i / power(251, (4 - @j))
        SET @i = @i % power(251, (4 - @j))

        SET @byte =
            CASE
                --Avoid CHAR(0)
                WHEN @byte <= 35 THEN @byte + 1
                --Avoid CHAR(37)
                WHEN @byte BETWEEN 36 AND 88 THEN @byte + 2
                --Avoid CHAR(91), CHAR(93), and CHAR(95)
```

```
                    WHEN @byte = 89 THEN 92
                    WHEN @byte = 90 THEN 94
                    WHEN @byte >= 91 THEN @byte + 5
                END

        SET @base_to_char = STUFF(@base_to_char, @j, 1, CHAR(@byte))
        SET @j = @j + 1
    END

    RETURN(@base_to_char)
END
GO
```

This function works by looping over each of the 4 bytes in the input integer, carrying bits up when the byte has a value greater than 251. Once the value of the byte is ascertained, it is manipulated to avoid any of the five characters that we do not want in the output. Finally, it is converted to a character and added to the output array of four characters. Note that the benefit of this encoding is that you can represent any positive integer in exactly four characters. However, the sacrifice made is that it cannot encode negative numbers. I do not believe this to be an issue when this is used for materialized paths.

I also created a partner function to decode base-251 strings back into integers. That function follows:

```
CREATE FUNCTION DecodeBase251(@base_to_char CHAR(4))
RETURNS INT
AS
BEGIN
    DECLARE @byte TINYINT

    DECLARE @i INT
    SET @i = 0

    DECLARE @j INT
    SET @j = 1

    WHILE @j <= 4
    BEGIN
        SET
            @byte = ASCII(SUBSTRING(@base_to_char, @j, 1))

        SET
            @byte =
            CASE
                WHEN @byte >= 96 THEN @byte - 5
                WHEN @byte = 94 THEN 90
                WHEN @byte = 92 THEN 89
                WHEN @byte BETWEEN 38 AND 90 THEN @byte - 2
                ELSE @byte - 1
            END
```

```
        SET @i = @i +
            @byte * POWER(251, (4 - @j))

        SET @j = @j + 1
    END

    RETURN(@i)
END
GO
```

This function uses the opposite logic of the encoding function, to get back the integer.
The functions can be tested by encoding and decoding an integer; if the input is the same as
the output, the functions worked for that integer:

```
DECLARE @i INT
SET @i = 1234567

SELECT @i, dbo.DecodeBase251(dbo.EncodeBase251(@i))
GO
```

■**Note** As a general note on this and other testing, keep in mind that just because this code works for one
number does not necessarily mean that it works for all others. There could be a bug, and whenever testing
code it is important to maintain the attitude that there *are* bugs—we just haven't found them yet! That said,
I tested these heavily and was not able to find any problem cases, so I'm fairly certain that these functions
work as advertised.

Using the EncodeBase251 function, we can re-create the materialized path for the
EmployeeTemp table. This time no delimiter is necessary, since every node will use exactly
4 bytes:

```
WITH n AS
(
    SELECT
        EmployeeId,
        CONVERT(VARCHAR(900),
            dbo.EncodeBase251(EmployeeId)
        ) AS thePath
    FROM Employee_Temp
    WHERE ManagerId IS NULL

    UNION ALL

    SELECT
        e.EmployeeId,
        CONVERT(VARCHAR(900),
            n.thePath + dbo.EncodeBase251(e.EmployeeId)
```

```
        ) AS thePath
    FROM Employee_Temp e
    JOIN n ON n.EmployeeId = e.ManagerId
)
UPDATE Employee_Temp
    SET Employee_Temp.thePath = n.thePath
FROM Employee_Temp
JOIN n ON n.EmployeeId = Employee_Temp.EmployeeId
GO
```

The benefits of this encoding will not be especially apparent if you use the Employee_Temp table as-is, since the table is fairly small. However, after growing the table using the code found in the "Are CTEs the Best Choice?" section found earlier in this chapter, the benefits become obvious: the index size for the table drops from 25,880KB to 11,184KB (as reported by sp_spaceused), and the average length of the paths drops from 398 characters to 144 characters.

Querying the data using this encoding is just a bit different than before. Since there are no delimiters to work with, we must instead take advantage of the fact that each node uses exactly four characters. So while the query to find all subordinates is exactly the same, the query to find only direct reports changes to the following:

```
SELECT *
FROM Employee_Temp
WHERE
    thePath LIKE @Path + '____'
```

Likewise, the code to move up the hierarchy changes a bit:

```
;WITH n AS
(
    SELECT
        CONVERT(INT,
            dbo.DecodeBase251(SUBSTRING(thePath, 1, 4))
        ) AS EmployeeId,
        SUBSTRING(thePath, 5, LEN(thePath)) AS thePath,
        1 AS theLevel
    FROM Employee_Temp
    WHERE EmployeeId = 217

    UNION ALL

    SELECT
        CONVERT(INT,
            dbo.DecodeBase251(SUBSTRING(thePath, 1, 4))),
        SUBSTRING(thePath, 5, LEN(thePath)),
        theLevel + 1
    FROM n
    WHERE thePath <> ''
)
SELECT *
```

```
FROM n
ORDER BY theLevel
OPTION(MAXRECURSION 225)
GO
```

The fact that the nodes occupy exactly 4 bytes eliminates the need for use of the `CHARINDEX` function, and the fact that the strings are encoded differently means that the `DecodeBase251` function must be used to get back the actual employee IDs. As shown in Figure 11-17, the path is not human readable, so debugging might be more difficult when using this method.

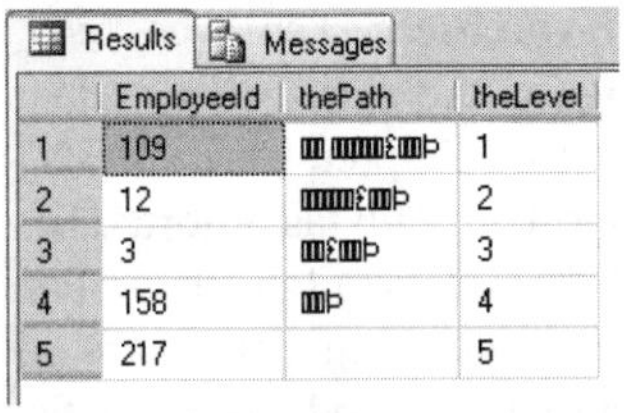

Figure 11-17. *Traversing up the base-251-encoded employee hierarchy*

As I stressed before, this technique may not be for everyone. I recommend limiting its use to situations in which performance is paramount and only a team of database developers will be directly working with the data. In my experience, end users—even those savvy enough to write basic queries—do not play well with nonprintable characters! For simplicity, the examples in the remainder of this chapter will not use this technique, but it should be a simple exercise for the reader to convert them if necessary.

Inserting Nodes

Whenever a new leaf node is added to the hierarchy, its parent's path must be determined, and the new node appended to the path. This logic can be encapsulated in a trigger such that whenever new nodes are inserted into the adjacency list, their paths will automatically be updated. The following trigger handles this logic:

```
CREATE TRIGGER tg_Insert
ON Employee_Temp
FOR INSERT
AS
BEGIN
    SET NOCOUNT ON

    IF @@ROWCOUNT > 1
    BEGIN
        RAISERROR('Only one node can be inserted at a time', 16, 1)
        ROLLBACK
    END
```

```
    UPDATE e
    SET
        e.thePath =
            Managers.thePath +
                RIGHT(
                    REPLICATE('0', 10) + CONVERT(VARCHAR, i.EmployeeId),
                    10
                ) + '.'
    FROM Employee_Temp e
    JOIN inserted i ON i.EmployeeId = e.EmployeeId
    JOIN Employee_Temp Managers ON Managers.EmployeeId = e.ManagerId
END
GO
```

The logic of this trigger is relatively simple: find the updated row in the Employee_Temp table by joining on the EmployeeId columns of both it and the inserted virtual table, and then join back to Employee_Temp to get the manager's path. Finally, concatenate the employee's ID onto the end of the path.

The most important thing to mention about this trigger is its limitation when it comes to multirow inserts. Due to the fact that SQL Server does not have any guarantees when it comes to update order, it is possible to create invalid paths by inserting two nodes at the same time. For instance, try disabling the row count check and inserting a subordinate first, followed by a manager, in the same statement:

```
INSERT Employee_Temp
(
    EmployeeId,
    ManagerId,
    Title
)
SELECT 1000, 999, 'Subordinate'
UNION ALL
SELECT 999, 109, 'Manager'
```

Since the order in which the UPDATE processes rows is not guaranteed, the result of this operation is nondeterministic. However, at least as of SQL Server 2005 SP1, the subordinate will end up with a NULL path, since at the moment its row is updated the manager's path will not yet have been processed. It may be possible to solve this problem by traversing any hierarchy present in the inserted table using a cursor, but I decided not to attempt this as I have never seen a situation in a real-world project in which this limitation would be a barrier.

Relocating Subtrees

Data modification is the real downside of the persisted materialized paths technique. Any time you affect a node's path, you must cascade the new path to all of its subordinates. This can mean that some updates are extremely expensive—should one of the vice presidents replace the CEO, every node in the hierarchy must be updated! Luckily, the average cost is not huge; the following T-SQL finds the average number of subordinates—four, as it turns out—for all nodes in the Employee_Temp hierarchy:

```
SELECT AVG(NumberOfSubordinates)
FROM
(
    SELECT COUNT(*) AS NumberOfSubordinates
    FROM Employee_Temp e
    JOIN Employee_Temp e2 ON e2.thePath LIKE e.thePath + '%'
    GROUP BY e.EmployeeId
) x
```

Relocating a materialized path's subtree involves finding the new manager's path and replacing it in the updated node as well as all of its child nodes. This becomes clearer through example, so consider the five paths shown in Figure 11-18. If the Engineering Manager (EmployeeId 3) gets a promotion and will now report directly to the CEO, her path will change to the CEO's path with her employee ID concatenated to the end: 0000000109.0000000003.. This operation will also invalidate the paths of the Design Engineer and the Senior Tool Designer, both of whose paths depend on that of the Engineering Manager. So the same operation—replacement of the beginning of the path—has to happen for all three nodes. It also has to happen for any of their subordinates, all the way down the tree, since every subordinate inherits its manager's path.

EmployeeId	ManagerId	Title	thePath
109	NULL	Chief Executive Officer	0000000109.
12	109	Vice President of Engineering	0000000109.0000000012.
3	12	Engineering Manager	0000000109.0000000012.0000000003.
4	3	Senior Tool Designer	0000000109.0000000012.0000000003.0000000004.
9	3	Design Engineer	0000000109.0000000012.0000000003.0000000009.

Figure 11-18. *Five paths in the Employee_Temp hierarchy*

Once again, a trigger can be employed to automatically do this update when a subtree is located based on the adjacency list. The following trigger handles the logic:

```
CREATE TRIGGER tg_Update
ON Employee_Temp
FOR UPDATE
AS
BEGIN
    DECLARE @n INT
    SET @n = @@ROWCOUNT

    IF UPDATE(thePath)
    BEGIN
        RAISERROR('Direct updates to the path are not allowed', 16, 1)
        ROLLBACK
    END

    IF UPDATE(ManagerId)
    BEGIN
        IF @n > 1
        BEGIN
```

```
                RAISERROR('Only update one node''s manager at a time', 16, 1)
                ROLLBACK
        END


        --Update all nodes using the new manager's path
        UPDATE e
        SET
            e.thePath =
                REPLACE(e.thePath, i.thePath,
                    Managers.thePath +
                        RIGHT(
                            REPLICATE('0', 10) + CONVERT(VARCHAR, i.EmployeeId),
                            10
                        ) + '.'
                    )
        FROM Employee_Temp e
        JOIN inserted i ON e.thePath LIKE i.thePath + '%'
        JOIN Employee_Temp Managers ON Managers.EmployeeId = i.ManagerId
    END
END
GO
```

There are a few things to discuss in this trigger. Starting at the top, the trigger first obtains the number of rows affected by the update operation. Just like when dealing with inserting new nodes, relocation of subtrees must be serialized to one node at a time in order to avoid logical ambiguities. However, an error is not thrown right away in this case; it is possible that someone might be updating a different column in the table, such as changing all of the "Production Technicians" to "Production Specialists". As long as the update is not to the hierarchy, multi-row updates are certainly allowed.

The first error check done is for direct updates to the path—this is not allowed, since it's the job of the trigger. Next, the trigger checks to see whether the ManagerId column is being updated. If not, it has nothing to do. If so, it then throws an error if multiple rows have been affected. Finally, if there are no issues, the paths of the affected node and all subordinates are updated based on the new manager's path. The logic used is to find the previous path of the updated node—using the inserted virtual table, which will still have that original path because direct updates to the path are not allowed—and replace it in all nodes with the new path.

As before, this trigger could probably be made to handle multirow updates by using a cursor, but I do not feel that the effort required to implement such a solution would be worthwhile.

■Note If you're using the tg_AtLeastOneRoot trigger in conjunction with the tg_Update trigger, you'll have a problem if you need to swap the root node, because to satisfy the tg_AtLeastOneRoot trigger's logic, the update must end with a root note in place, and this will require a multirow update. Luckily, that's not generally something that has to happen very often, but if you do need to do it, remember to disable one of the triggers before making the change, and reenable it immediately afterward to make sure that other callers don't introduce data inconsistencies in the interim.

Deleting Nodes

Thanks to the fact that the adjacency list is being used in conjunction with the materialized path, deleting nodes requires no additional logic. Due to the self-referential constraint on the adjacency list, only leaf nodes can be deleted. Leaf nodes have no subordinates and therefore there is nothing to cascade—the row will be deleted, and no further logic is necessary. This is one of the main benefits of keeping both hierarchical models in the same table—each inherits the other's constraints, helping to ensure greater data integrity.

Constraining the Hierarchy

All of the logic mentioned in the previous "Constraining the Hierarchy" section (which dealt with adjacency lists) still applies to materialized paths. However, with a materialized path, it's much easier to detect cycles, so there is no need to use the tg_NoCycles trigger. Instead, a simple check constraint should be used that makes sure the given employee only appears once, at the end of the path:

```
ALTER TABLE Employee_Temp
ADD CONSTRAINT ck_NoCycles
    CHECK
    (
        thePath NOT LIKE
        '%' +
        RIGHT(REPLICATE('0', 10) +
            CONVERT(VARCHAR, EmployeeId), 10) +
        '.%' +
        RIGHT(REPLICATE('0', 10) +
            CONVERT(VARCHAR, EmployeeId), 10) +
        '.'
    )
GO
```

■**Note** There is a subtle difference between the logic expressed here and the same logic used to prevent endless loops in the section "Traversing the Graph." In that section, the nodes in the path were not left-padded with zeroes, so the first node had to be delimited in order to make sure to detect a cycle involving it. This was done to prevent a false alarm in case of a path like 123.456.3. In this case, the left-padding means that there is no way to misinterpret a section of one ID as another, so we do not have to modify the basic path logic already established.

Nested Sets Model

The final hierarchical technique I will discuss in this chapter is the nested sets model. This technique was popularized by Joe Celko in *SQL for Smarties: Advanced SQL Programming* (Morgan Kaufmann, 2005) and *Trees and Hierarchies in SQL for Smarties* (Morgan Kaufmann, 2004)—both of which I highly recommend. This technique is, admittedly, somewhat difficult to work with, and implementation may not yield a great return on investment compared with the persisted materialized paths technique discussed in the previous section.

The strength of the nested sets model comes in scenarios in which you need to read an entire subtree at once. As I'll show in the following sections, it can be difficult to do simpler queries against nested sets hierarchies. That said, it is an incredibly clever technique, and studying and understanding it will enhance your overall grasp of how hierarchies work. So while I can recommend this technique for only very few real-world projects, I do think that it is worthwhile to cover it here.

The nested sets model works by defining two columns representing a counter as would be incremented on both left and right visits when doing a **preorder** (depth-first) traversal of the hierarchy starting at the root node. This is best described in conjunction with an image, so please refer to Figure 11-19, which depicts a four-node hierarchy on the left, and the same hierarchy marked up as if for nested sets on the right. The traversal starts at the left of the root node, where we mark a 1. That node's leftmost subtree is traversed next—starting with a visit to the left side of node B, where we mark a 2. Next, node D is visited, first on the left, then on the right, because it's a leaf node and has no subtrees. We then revisit node B before visiting node C on both the left and right sides, before finally getting back to node A.

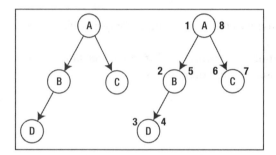

Figure 11-19. *Doing a preorder traversal of the hierarchy*

Marking up the nodes in this fashion brings some interesting mathematical properties into play. To begin with, at each node we can determine the total number of subordinates based on the formula floor((right-left)/2). This formula will return 0 for leaf nodes, but another mathematical property is that if right-left = 1, the node is a leaf. This model also makes it easy to navigate between siblings: the next sibling (to the right) has a left counter equal to the current sibling's right counter incremented by 1.

The name "nested sets" is not accidental; the major mathematical quality of a hierarchy marked up in this way is that for every node, all of its subordinates' left or right counters will be between the parent node's left and right counters. This is illustrated in Figure 11-19: the root node has the values 1 and 8 as left and right, respectively. Its direct descendants' values are all between 1 and 8, as are their descendants. Looking at the subtree rooted at node B, we see that its descendant is also nested, with values falling between 2 and 5. This property is what makes the nested sets model very powerful when you need to look at an entire subtree.

Building a nested sets hierarchy from an adjacency list is a bit tricky until you realize that the basic ordering provided by the left and right counters is exactly the same as a path ordering. For the hierarchy shown in Figure 11-19, the materialized and enumerated paths (with minimal padding, to make things easier to read) for each of the four nodes are as follows:

```
A:    A.        01.
B:    A.B.      01.01.
D:    A.B.D.    01.01.01.
C:    A.C.      01.02.
```

This is the same order that would be obtained by ordering the nodes by the left counter. The only difference is that these paths represent only a single visit to each node, but the nested sets counters represent two visits: one visit for the parent node itself, and a second visit after visiting all subordinate subtrees. To represent both visits to the CTE in the correct nested order, we can add fake paths for each node, which are forced to sort high:

```
A:    A.        01.
B:    A.B.      01.01.
D:    A.B.D.    01.01.01.
D:    A.B.D.Z.  01.01.01.99.
B:    A.B.Z.    01.01.99.
C:    A.C.      01.02.
C:    A.C.Z.    01.02.99.
A:    A.Z.      01.99.
```

Walking this new list in the same order produces the desired output for two visits to each node.

Now that we have a methodology for creating the ordering, the Employee_Temp table should be modified to accept the new columns necessary to support nested sets:

```
ALTER TABLE Employee_Temp
ADD
    lft INT,
    rgt INT
GO
```

Note that the column names are abbreviated as lft and rgt, so as to not collide with T-SQL's LEFT and RIGHT keywords.

The logic necessary to create the ordering can be easily and efficiently expressed in a recursive CTE, as I learned during a conversation on nested sets with SQL Server MVP Itzik Ben-Gan. I've made slight modifications to the CTE that Itzik originally showed me. My final version, designed to update the Employee_Temp table, follows:

```
WITH SortPathCTE
AS
(
    SELECT
        EmployeeId,
        nums.n,
        CONVERT(VARBINARY(900),
            CASE nums.n
                WHEN 1 THEN 0x00000001
                ELSE 0x00000001FFFFFFFF
            END
        ) AS SortPath
```

```
    FROM Employee_Temp
    CROSS JOIN
    (
        SELECT 1
        UNION ALL
        SELECT 2
    ) nums (n)
    WHERE ManagerId IS NULL

    UNION ALL

    SELECT
        e.EmployeeId,
        nums.n,
        CONVERT(VARBINARY(900),
            sp.SortPath +
                CONVERT(BINARY(4),
                    ROW_NUMBER() OVER(ORDER BY e.EmployeeId)
                ) +
                    CASE nums.n
                        WHEN 1 THEN 0x
                        ELSE 0xFFFFFFFF
                    END
        )
    FROM SortPathCTE sp
    JOIN Employee_Temp AS e ON e.ManagerId = sp.EmployeeId
    CROSS JOIN
    (
        SELECT 1
        UNION ALL
        SELECT 2
    ) nums (n)
    WHERE sp.n = 1
),
SortCTE
AS
(
    SELECT
        EmployeeId,
        ROW_NUMBER() OVER(ORDER BY SortPath) AS SortVal
    FROM SortPathCTE
),
FinalCTE
AS
(
    SELECT
        EmployeeId,
```

```
            MIN(SortVal) AS Lft,
            MAX(SortVal) AS Rgt
    FROM SortCTE
    GROUP BY EmployeeId
)
UPDATE e
SET
    e.lft = f.lft,
    e.rgt = f.rgt
FROM Employee_Temp e
JOIN FinalCTE f ON e.EmployeeId = f.EmployeeId
GO
```

Walking through the stages of this query one by one, here's how it works:

1. The SortPathCTE is evaluated first. The anchor part finds the root node and begins a binary-encoded enumerated path. The query is cross-joined to a table with two rows, in order to turn the single root node into two rows, adding the fake high-sort row to the output. The recursive part of the CTE takes only rows where the high-sort bytes were not appended (identified by n = 1), finding their subordinates just like the previous hierarchical traversal CTEs shown in this chapter. It also enumerates the path, using the ROW_NUMBER function—to change the subordering of siblings, you can change the order specified for the row numbering. Just like the anchor part, the recursive member cross-joins to a table with two rows, in order to facilitate adding high-sort rows for each node.

2. Next, the SortCTE is evaluated. This CTE produces a row number for the output from the SortPathCTE, based on the enumerated path produced therein. It outputs each node's ID as well as the row number.

3. The FinalCTE gets the minimum and maximum row number for each node's ID. These are the left and right values necessary for using the nested sets model.

4. Finally, the Employee_Temp table is updated via a JOIN in the outer query.

Once again, as with the other techniques discussed in this chapter, we arrive at the question of indexing. And once again, the answer is that it depends on your situation. However, much like the materialized path technique, I feel that the optimal index in this choice is a nonclustered index on the columns that make up the hierarchy, with other commonly used columns included, in order to cover most queries:

```
CREATE UNIQUE NONCLUSTERED INDEX IX_rgt_lft
ON Employee_Temp (rgt, lft)
INCLUDE (EmployeeId, ManagerId, Title)
```

Finding Subordinates

As mentioned in the previous section, the true strength of the nested sets model is the simplicity with which complete subtrees can be queried. To find the complete subtree for a specific node, find that node's lft and rgt values, and then find all nodes whose lft value is between them. It's important to use lft for this latter seek, as it is the first key in the index.

The following T-SQL finds all children of `EmployeeId 12`:

```
SELECT
    children.EmployeeId,
    children.ManagerId,
    children.Title
FROM Employee_Temp parent
JOIN Employee_Temp children ON
    children.lft BETWEEN parent.lft AND parent.rgt
WHERE
    parent.EmployeeId = 12
ORDER BY
    children.lft
```

Note that by virtue of the fact that the `lft` column follows the same ordering as the materialized path, the `ORDER BY` clause used here sorts the output rows the same as a path would, providing the rows ordered based on the management hierarchy.

Finding only direct subordinates using nested sets is quite a bit trickier. To accomplish this, you must find all subordinates, and then filter down the set to those subordinates that have no additional subordinates between them and the parent node. Looking at nodes A, B, and D in Figure 11-19, we can make the following determination about what properties a node—B, in this case—has when it falls between two other nodes:

- The middle node's `left` value is greater than the parent node's `left` value.

- The middle node's `left` value is less than the child node's `left` value.

- The middle node's `right` value is less than the parent node's `right` value.

- The middle node's `right` value is greater than the child node's `right` value.

Putting this all together, we can add a `NOT EXISTS` predicate to the previous query, such that it returns all rows that qualify as child nodes, but no rows for which there exists another row between them and the parent—in other words, only direct subordinates. The following T-SQL embodies this query:

```
SELECT
    children.EmployeeId,
    children.ManagerId,
    children.Title
FROM Employee_Temp parent
JOIN Employee_Temp children ON
    children.lft > parent.lft
    AND children.lft < parent.rgt
WHERE
    parent.EmployeeId = 109
    AND NOT EXISTS (
        SELECT *
        FROM Employee_Temp middle
        WHERE
            middle.lft > parent.lft
```

```
            AND middle.lft < children.lft
            AND middle.rgt < parent.rgt
            AND middle.rgt > children.rgt
    )
ORDER BY
    children.lft
```

Navigating up the Hierarchy

Finding the path back to the root for a given node in a nested sets hierarchy is the opposite of finding all children. Based on the mathematical properties, it can be shown that the parent nodes have a lower `left` value than their children, and a higher `right` value. The following T-SQL finds the path from `EmployeeId` 11 up to the root node:

```
SELECT
    parent.EmployeeId,
    parent.Title
FROM Employee_Temp parent
JOIN Employee_Temp child ON
    parent.lft < child.lft
    AND parent.rgt > child.rgt
WHERE child.EmployeeId = 11
```

This query can also be modified similarly to the subordinate's query, in order to find the node's immediate supervisor. I'll leave that as an exercise for you to try, but here's a hint: there are actually a couple of different ways to accomplish this—following the same pattern as the preceding subordinates query is one, but there is a much more efficient way to go if you think about the ordering of the nodes.

Inserting Nodes

As with the persisted materialized path technique, when working with nested sets, I recommend keeping the adjacency list around and using triggers to maintain the alternate hierarchy. The biggest issue with the nested sets model—aside from the somewhat left-brained thinking required to successfully query it—is that any kind of data modification operation will affect, on average, 50% of the hierarchy. Figure 11-20 shows the effects of inserting a node; all of the bold values on the right are new or updated.

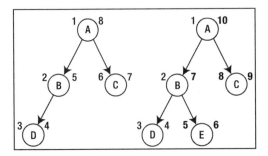

Figure 11-20. *Inserting a new node into a nested sets hierarchy*

The algorithm to do the update uses the following steps:

1. Find the `right` value of the sibling to the left, if one exists. If not, find the `left` value of the parent node.

2. Increment the value obtained in the previous step by 1—that's the new node's `left` value.

3. Increment the new node's `left` value by 1 for its `right` value.

4. Update every node in the hierarchy where the `right` value is greater than or equal to the new node's `left` value. For each of the nodes, increment the `left` value by 2 if the `left` value is greater than or equal to the new node's `left` value. In all cases, increment the `right` value by 2.

Just as with the materialized path approach, data modifications that affect the hierarchy will be limited to a single node at a time in order to avoid logical ambiguity. The following trigger handles the case of inserting new nodes:

```
CREATE TRIGGER tg_INSERT
ON Employee_Temp
FOR INSERT
AS
BEGIN
    SET NOCOUNT ON

    IF @@ROWCOUNT > 1
    BEGIN
        RAISERROR('Only one row can be inserted at a time.', 16, 1)
        ROLLBACK
    END

    --Get the inserted employee and manager IDs
    DECLARE
        @employeeId INT,
        @managerId INT

    SELECT
        @employeeId = EmployeeId,
        @managerId = ManagerId
    FROM inserted

    --Find the left value
    DECLARE @left INT

    --First try the right value of the sibling to the left
    --Sibling ordering based on EmployeeId order
    SELECT TOP(1)
        @left = rgt + 1
    FROM Employee_Temp
```

```
    WHERE
        ManagerId = @managerId
        AND EmployeeId < @employeeId
    ORDER BY EmployeeId DESC

    --If there is no left sibling, get the parent node's value
    IF @left IS NULL
    BEGIN
        SELECT
            @left = lft + 1
        FROM Employee_Temp
        WHERE EmployeeId = @managerId
    END

    --Update the new node's left and right values
    UPDATE Employee_Temp
    SET
        lft = @left,
        rgt = @left + 1
    WHERE EmployeeId = @EmployeeId

    --Update the rest of the nodes in the hierarchy
    UPDATE Employee_Temp
    SET
        lft = lft +
            CASE
                WHEN lft > @left THEN 2
                ELSE 0
            END,
        rgt = rgt + 2
    WHERE
        rgt >= @left
        AND EmployeeId <> @employeeId
END
GO
```

Relocating Subtrees

The action taken when a subtree is relocated is shown in Figure 11-21. This involves the following steps:

1. Find the left value of the relocated node's sibling to the right, or if that does not exist, find the right value of the node's new parent. If the found value is greater than the relocated node's previous right value, decrement it by 1 to find the node's new right value. Subtract the relocated node's previous right value from its new right value to find the difference. Add the difference to the relocated node's previous left value to find its new left value. Follow the remaining step for a move to the right.

2. If the value found in the last step was less than the relocated node's previous `right` value, this is a move to the left and the found value is not correct. Discard it and find the `right` value of the sibling to the left, if one exists. If not, find the `left` value of the parent node. Increment the value by 1. That is the new `left` value for the relocated node. Subtract the new `left` value from the node's previous `left` value to find the difference. Subtract this difference from the node's previous `right` value to find its new `right` value. Follow the remaining step for a move to the left.

3. If this is a move to the right, update every node with a `right` or `left` value that falls between the relocated node's previous `left` value and its new `right` value. If the left value falls between the node's previous `left` and `right` values, we know that node is part of the relocated node's subtree. Increment its `left` and `right` values by the difference found in the first step. Otherwise, find the number of nodes in the subtree rooted by the relocated node and add 1. Subtract this value from the `left` if the `left` value is greater the node's previous `left` value, and from the `right` if the `right` value is less than or equal to the node's new `right` value.

4. If this is a move to the left, update every node with a `right` or `left` value that falls between the relocated node's new `left` value and its previous `right` value. If the `left` value falls between the nodes previous `left` and `right` values, decrement its `left` and `right` values by the difference found in the first step. Otherwise, find the number of nodes in the subtree rooted by the relocated node and add 1. Add this value to the `left` if the `left` value is greater than or equal to the relocated node's new `left` value and to the right if the `right` value is less than the node's previous `right` value.

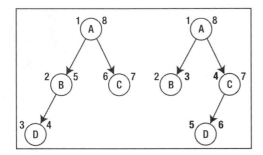

Figure 11-21. *Relocating a subtree in a nested sets hierarchy*

The following trigger contains the update logic:

```
CREATE TRIGGER tg_UPDATE
ON Employee_Temp
FOR UPDATE
AS
BEGIN
    SET NOCOUNT ON

    DECLARE @rowCount INT
    SET @rowCount = @@ROWCOUNT
```

```
--Do nothing if this trigger was fired from another
IF TRIGGER_NESTLEVEL() > 1
    RETURN


IF @rowCount > 1 AND UPDATE(ManagerId)
BEGIN
    RAISERROR('Only one row can be updated at a time.', 16, 1)
    ROLLBACK
END


IF UPDATE(lft) OR UPDATE(rgt)
BEGIN
    RAISERROR('The hierarchy cannot be directly updated.', 16, 1)
    ROLLBACK
END


--Get the employee ID, new manager ID, and previous lft and rgt values
DECLARE
    @employeeId INT,
    @managerId INT,
    @previousLeft INT,
    @previousRight INT,
    @numNodes INT

SELECT
    @employeeId = EmployeeId,
    @managerId = ManagerId,
    @previousLeft = lft,
    @previousRight = rgt,
    @numNodes = rgt - lft
FROM inserted

DECLARE
    @left INT,
    @right INT

--First try the left value of the sibling to the right
--Sibling ordering based on EmployeeId order
SELECT TOP(1)
    @right = lft - 1
FROM Employee_Temp
WHERE
    ManagerId = @managerId
    AND EmployeeId > @employeeId
ORDER BY EmployeeId ASC
```

```
--If there is no right sibling, get the parent node's value
IF @right IS NULL
BEGIN
    SELECT
        @right = rgt - 1
    FROM Employee_Temp
    WHERE EmployeeId = @managerId
END

DECLARE @difference INT

--This is a move to the right
IF @right > @previousRight
BEGIN
    SET @difference = @right - @previousRight
    SET @left = @previousLeft + @difference

    UPDATE Employee_Temp
    SET
        lft =
            CASE
                WHEN lft BETWEEN @previousLeft AND @previousRight THEN
                    lft + @difference
                WHEN lft > @previousLeft THEN lft - (@numNodes + 1)
                ELSE lft
            END,
        rgt =
            CASE
                WHEN lft BETWEEN @previousLeft AND @previousRight THEN
                    rgt + @difference
                WHEN rgt <= @right THEN rgt - (@numNodes + 1)
                ELSE rgt
            END
    WHERE
        lft BETWEEN @previousLeft AND @right
        OR rgt BETWEEN @previousLeft AND @right
END
--This is a move to the left
ELSE
BEGIN
    --First try the right value of the sibling to the left
    --Sibling ordering based on EmployeeId order
    SELECT TOP(1)
        @left = rgt + 1
    FROM Employee_Temp
    WHERE
        ManagerId = @managerId
```

```
            AND EmployeeId < @employeeId
        ORDER BY EmployeeId DESC

        --If there is no left sibling, get the parent node's value
        IF @left IS NULL
        BEGIN
            SELECT
                @left = lft + 1
            FROM Employee_Temp
            WHERE EmployeeId = @managerId
        END

        SET @difference = @previousLeft - @Left
        SET @right = @previousRight - @difference

        UPDATE Employee_Temp
        SET
            lft =
                CASE
                    WHEN lft BETWEEN @previousLeft AND @previousRight THEN
                        lft - @difference
                    WHEN lft >= @left THEN lft + (@numNodes + 1)
                    ELSE lft
                END,
            rgt =
                CASE
                    WHEN lft BETWEEN @previousLeft AND @previousRight THEN
                        rgt - @difference
                    WHEN rgt < @previousRight THEN rgt + (@numNodes + 1)
                    ELSE rgt
                END
        WHERE
            lft BETWEEN @Left AND @previousRight
            OR rgt BETWEEN @Left AND @previousRight
    END
END
GO
```

The only thing to note about this trigger aside from the logic described previously is the first few lines. The number of rows affected is placed into a variable so that it will not be lost when checking for error conditions. After that, the trigger nesting level is checked. Because the insert trigger updates the table, it will cause the update trigger to fire (assuming that SQL Server's default setting to allow nested triggers is still enabled). The update trigger will then throw an error, due to the fact that the insert trigger updates the hierarchy directly. To get around this, the update trigger returns control without doing anything, if it was fired due to another trigger. Finally, the row count variable is used to make sure that only one row was updated.

■**Note** The maximum trigger nesting level in SQL Server is 32. If your triggers nest deeper than that, an exception will be thrown and your transaction will be rolled back. On a related note, you should be aware that in SQL Server 2000, the recursive triggers database option was disabled by default. In SQL Server 2005, on the other hand, the option is turned on by default. Make sure to check during upgrade projects to ensure that this change will not cause unintended side effects when your triggers fire.

Deleting Nodes

As shown in Figure 11-22, deleting a node from a nested sets hierarchy is quite simple—much more straightforward than either inserting new nodes or relocating a subtree. The only logic required is to update all rows with right values greater than the deleted node's right value, decrementing the nodes' right values by 2, and the nodes' left values by 2 if their left values are greater than the deleted node's right value.

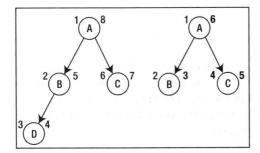

Figure 11-22. *Deleting a node in a nested sets hierarchy*

The following trigger contains the logic required to handle node deletions in a nested sets hierarchy:

```
CREATE TRIGGER tg_DELETE
ON Employee_Temp
FOR DELETE
AS
BEGIN
    SET NOCOUNT ON

    IF @@ROWCOUNT > 1
    BEGIN
        RAISERROR('Only one row can be deleted at a time.', 16, 1)
        ROLLBACK
    END

    --Get the deleted right value
    DECLARE
        @right int
```

```
SELECT
    @right = rgt
FROM deleted

--Update the rest of the nodes in the hierarchy
UPDATE Employee_Temp
SET
    lft = lft -
        CASE
            WHEN lft > @right THEN 2
            ELSE 0
        END,
    rgt = rgt - 2
WHERE
    rgt >= @right
END
GO
```

Constraining the Hierarchy

In nested sets hierarchies, because no recursion is used for querying, cycles cannot cause runtime problems—although they can cause strange results. It is therefore recommended that if you use the nested sets model, you should keep all of the same constraints on the table that were defined in the section on constraining adjacency list hierarchies. That way, you can be certain that your hierarchy does not contain any invalid data.

EXTENDING YOUR HIERARCHIES: MAINTAINING A NODE'S LEVEL

A common reporting requirement with hierarchies is to show which nodes appear at which level of the hierarchy, often in relation to another node. For instance, someone might want to ask how many levels away a certain employee is from the CEO.

When working with adjacency lists, the hierarchy must be traversed level by level via recursion or iteration, so calculation of the level at run time is easy. However, you might want to maintain the level for each node when working with materialized path or nested sets hierarchies, in order to make these kinds of queries simpler.

Adding a level column to a materialized path hierarchy is quite easy: simply add a computed column that counts the number of delimiters in the path. If you'll be using the level column in a lot of queries, I recommend using the `PERSISTED` option in order to ensure that SQL Server only needs to count the delimiters once:

```
ALTER TABLE Employee_Temp
ADD theLevel AS
    (
        LEN(thePath) -
        LEN(REPLACE(thePath, '.', ''))
    ) PERSISTED
```

The expression works by finding the length of the path, and then subtracting it from the length of the path after converting all of the delimiters to empty strings.

Adding a level column to a nested sets table isn't quite as simple. Although there are a variety of ways to find the level using the nested sets hierarchy itself, in my opinion it's much simpler to traverse up the hierarchy via the adjacency list and count the number of recursions. This logic can be added to the nested sets update trigger so that the updated node is counted first, and then the new level cascaded down the subtree. I'll leave implementation of that enhancement as an exercise for the reader.

Summary

Graphs and hierarchies are extremely common throughout our world, and it is often necessary to represent them in databases. By utilizing adjacency lists, you can describe virtually any graph's form, and recursive CTEs allow you to navigate graphs with relative ease. Hierarchies—special types of graphs—can also be modeled using adjacency lists, but other techniques can be employed to make querying them much more efficient, without the need for recursion or iteration.

There are a lot of ways to solve hierarchical problems, but in the end it comes down to the best choice for the given scenario you're faced with. As always, the most important thing you can do as a developer is to carefully consider your options, testing whenever possible to find the optimal solution.

Index

Symbols

% Processor Time counter, 36
@@ERROR, 61–62

A

access control, 74–75, 79–81, 138
Access Control Lists (ACLs), 74
acyclic graphs, 375–376
ad hoc SQL, 169–171
Adabas database management system, 8
ADD SIGNATURE command, 86
adjacency list model (hierarchies). *See also*
        nested sets model; persistent
        materialized paths
   constraining, 392, 407–409, 422
   deleting nodes, 406, 422
   described, 377, 391–392
   edges, constraining, 378–380
   finding ancestors, 412–413
   finding descendants, 393–395, 404–405,
      411
   inserting new nodes, 405–406, 418–419
   modeling connections, 392
   relocating subtrees, 405–406, 419–421
   traversing, 392, 395–397, 399–404, 422
ADO.NET for unit testing, 27
Advanced SQL Programming (Celko), 422
age, calculating, 328
aggregates, user-defined, 162–167
Agile Development for regression testing, 30
AllowPartiallyTrustedCallersAttribute
   (APTCA), 150
ALTER AUTHORIZATION command, 78
ALTER DATABASE command, 82, 148
ALTER SCHEMA command, 78
altitude, 312
anarchic concurrency control, 210–211, 216
ancestor relationships, 377
anti-patterns, 19
APIs (application programming interfaces),
   18–19
application logic, 12
application-level parameterization, 175–177
applications. *See also* performance; testing,
   application
   architecture, 2–5, 8–9, 10, 12–13, 20
   database role in, 19
   development, 19–21, 23

   hierarchy, 9–10
   interfaces, 18–19
   maintainability, 19–20
   size, 33
   types, 1
APTCA (AllowPartiallyTrustedCallersAttribute),
   150
AS keyword for creating column aliases, 7
Aschenbrenner, Klaus, 225
as-of data component, 316
assemblies, 137–143, 145–147, 148–150
Assert method (IStalkWalk interface),
   146–147
assertions, debug, 26–27
astronomical spatial data, 312
asymmetric encryption. *See also* asymmetric
   keys
   advantages, 101
   controlling data by column, 106
   defined, 94
   described, 98–99
   drawbacks, 101
   key management, 95
   performance, 108, 111, 117
   service master keys in, 95
   uses, 101
asymmetric keys, 96, 98–100, 101
authentication, 31, 73, 75. *See also* message
   authentication code
authorization. *See also* certificates; privileges,
   resource
   access control, 74–75, 79–81, 138
   defined, 73
   developer's concerns, 73
   in dynamic SQL, 204–205
   ownership chaining, 77, 81–85
   testing, 31
auto-parameterization, query,
   174–175
Average Wait Time (ms) counter, 37
Avg. Disk Queue Length counter, 36

B

baseline performance tests, 34
"Batch Compilation, Recompilation, and
   Plan Caching Issues in SQL Server
   2005" (Marathe), 173
benchmarking, 280. *See also* performance

You Need the Companion eBook

Your purchase of this book entitles you to buy the companion PDF-version eBook for only $10. Take the weightless companion with you anywhere.

We believe this Apress title will prove so indispensable that you'll want to carry it with you everywhere, which is why we are offering the companion eBook (in PDF format) for $10 to customers who purchase this book now. Convenient and fully searchable, the PDF version of any content-rich, page-heavy Apress book makes a valuable addition to your programming library. You can easily find and copy code—or perform examples by quickly toggling between instructions and the application. Even simultaneously tackling a donut, diet soda, and complex code becomes simplified with hands-free eBooks!

Once you purchase your book, getting the $10 companion eBook is simple:

❶ Visit **www.apress.com/promo/tendollars/**.

❷ Complete a basic registration form to receive a randomly generated question about this title.

❸ Answer the question correctly in 60 seconds, and you will receive a promotional code to redeem for the $10.00 eBook.

2560 Ninth Street • Suite 219 • Berkeley, CA 94710

eBookshop

THE EXPERT'S VOICE™